343

DECENTRALISED DEMOCRATIC GOVERNANCE IN NEW MILLENNIUM

About the Editor

U.B. Singh, M.P.A. formerly Reader and Head of the Department of Public Administration at the Mizoram (Central) University, Aizawl, is presently working as Joint Director with Regional Centre for Urban and Environmental Studies, Lucknow University, Lucknow. He was awarded fellowship under Colombo Plan at the University College, London, U.K. and certificate course from Asian Institute of Technology, Bangkok.

Dr. Singh has to his credit many books including *Administrative System in India*, *Fiscal Federalism in Indian Union*, *Urban Local Government*, and *Urban Governance in Southern India*. His edited works include *Revitalised Urban Governance*, *Urban Development in India*, *Empowerment of Women*, and *Leaders in Making*. Also, he has published more than 50 papers.

Decentralized Democratic Governance in New Millennium

Local Government in the USA, UK, France, Japan, Russia and India

U.B. Singh
Regional Centre for Urban and Environmental Studies, Lucknow University, Lucknow

CONCEPT PUBLISHING COMPANY, NEW DELHI-110059

Cataloging in Publication Data—DK
Courtesy: D.K. Agencies (P) Ltd. <docinfo@dkagencies.com>

Singh, U. B. (Udai Bhan), 1953-
Decentralized democratic governance in new millennium : local government in the USA, UK, France, Japan, Russia and India / U.B. Singh.
p. cm.
Includes bibliographical references (p.
Includes index.
ISBN 10: 8180695409

1. Local government—Western countries. 2. Local government—Japan. 3. Local government—Russia (Federation) 4. Local government—India. 5. Decentralization in government. 6. Democracy. I. Title.

DDC 320.8 22

ISBN-13: 978-81-8069-540-7
ISBN-81: 8069-540-9

First Published 2009

Published and Printed by
Ashok Kumar Mittal
Concept Publishing Company
A/15-16, Commercial Block, Mohan Garden
New Delhi-110059 (INDIA)

Phones : 25351460, 25351794
Fax : 091-11-25357103
Email : publishing@conceptpub.com

Preface

Decentralized governance at the grassroots level is the most suitable mechanism for realizing the cherished goals of a parliamentary democracy. Effective decentralization and empowerment of people through elected local government has been one of the fundamental essentials of a democratic country. The 21st century is the era of decentralized democratic governance. Local government is such a system of governance which can empower the community to play its destined role in governance of a country.

This book is in the response of the felt need of students. During my short tenure at Mizoram University in the Department of Public Administration I realized the difficulties faced by my students in getting the latest books in the library of the infant Central University. The inquisitive students would surf internet in search of appropriate reading materials on local government in different countries. There were large number of books on Indian local government (especially on Panchayati Raj), a few books were available on local governance systems in France, Japan, Russia, the United States of America and United Kingdom. The present volume is the outcome of my realization. I humbly dedicate this book as a mark of respect, affection and gratitude to the whole fraternity of the Mizoram University, Aizawl, and the 'praiseworthy' people of the beautiful state of Mizoram, who have a long history of traditional local governance and have fascination for adopting the new system of local governance as envisaged in the supreme law of the land.

At the outset, therefore, I owe my sincere gratitude to my students at the Mizoram University whose requirement became main inspiring force for me. I am confident this modest effort will necessarily provide an academic base to the students at large.

I am thankful to embassies of France, Japan, Russia, the U.S.A. and the U.K. for providing relevant references, literature etc. on the subject.

My sincere thanks are due to my younger colleague Dr. Alka Singh for her help in developing the draft framework. Initially, she showed great interest but probably due to other assignments she could not continue the association. Her contribution deserves recognition.

I have very special words of appreciation to my family members for encouraging me to accomplish the job expeditiously and especially to my daughter Nivedita, who guided many a time as 'computer guru' in this endeavour.

I am thankful to my friend Dr. R.K. Trivedi for arranging books, journals and other relevant materials. I am indebted to all the authors whom I have consulted and quoted extensively.

Last but not the least, I am thankful to M/s Concept Publishing Company, New Delhi for their untiring efforts in bringing out the book in this beautiful shape in a record time.

Lucknow **U.B. Singh**
Budha Purnima, 2007

Contents

Chapter 1

Understanding Local Government

Meaning

Local government implies the management of local affairs. It is a system under which people of a locality possess a certain responsibility of local political affairs and the raising of money to meet the expenses[1]. Local government is local in the sense that it has to deal with an aggregate of people having common interests, living in close vicinity in a locality. It is a government in the sense that instead of depending on more delegated powers, local government is vested with statutory authority to deal with local problems and affairs. Local government is that part of the State Government in our federal structure dealing mainly with local affairs, administered by authorities, subordinate to the State Government. The local authorities may be elected independently of the state authorities by residents or they may consist of partly elected and partly nominated members. Thus, the local authority derives its powers from a portion of the same electorate from which the state authority derives its powers. But the local authorities are the creation of the state legislature. They cannot do many things without the explicit sanction of the state government.[2]

Local government forms a subsystem of the political system at the state and national level. Considering the point of jurisdiction, a local government can be viewed as a small political system, which exists and functions in interaction with its environment. Like any other political system, local government is subjected to the input-output process by which it receives demands from the environment and responds through its output transactions. However, local governments articulate aggregate demands and provide services in the areas of their activities as set by the statute.[3]

Definitions

Local government has been defined from various angles. Local government may be loosely defined as a public organization authorized to decide and administer a limited range of public policies within a relatively small territory which is a sub-division of a regional or national government. Local government is at the bottom of the pyramid of governmental institutions with the national government at the top and intermediate governments (states, regions, provinces) occupying the middle range.[4] The term 'local government', as defined by W.E. Jackson indicates the management of local affairs and services by popularly elected councils even within the area administered by a council.[5] It has been defined as "an authority to determine and execute measures within restricted area inside and smaller than the whole state. The variant local self-government is important for its emphasis on the freedom to decide and act".[6] Jennings defines local government as governmental organs "having jurisdiction not over the whole of the country but over specific portions of it".[7] G.M. Harris opines that local government is "government by local bodies, freely elected while subject to supremacy of the national government is endowed in some respect power, discretion and responsibilities, which they can exercise without control over their decisions by the higher authority. The extent of power and discretion and responsibilities the local bodies possess is a matter of degree which varies considerably in the various countries".[8]

According to John J. Clarke, "local government appears to be that part of the government of a nation or state which deals mainly with such matters as concerns the inhabitants of particular district or place".[9] In words of Humes and Martin "local government possesses most of the following attributes: a population, a clearly defined area, the capacity to sue and be sued, the ability to make contracts, a continuing organization, the authority to undertake and the power to conduct public activities and the right to collect revenue and determine a budget".[10] P. Stones defines local government as "that part of the government of a country which deals with those matters which concern the people in a particular locality".[11] As per Golding, "local government is the management of their own affairs by the people of a locality".[12] According to Byrne, "local government is marked out as a distinctive form of public administration by five features. It is elected, multi-purpose, operates on a local scale, has a clearly defined structure and is subordinate to parliament".[13]

The examination of various definitions of local government reveals that local government is combination of various elements and no single definition includes all of them. These elements include a local statutory body, local inhabitants, electing and controlling that body, limited autonomy, in the sense that state governments in a federation and Central Government in unitary system give them a limited freedom to perform their functions prescribed by law, a recognition of distinction between local and non-local services, and power to levy taxes.[14] Nevertheless, bodies which possess all of the following characteristics can be thought of as pure local government: jurisdiction as a substantially smaller area than the national government, election by popular vote, powers of taxation and genuine discretion over service provision.[15] Thus the essential attributes of a local government are, firstly, its statutory status; secondly, its power to raise finance by taxation in the area under its jurisdiction; thirdly, participation of the local community in decision-making in specific subjects and their administration; fourthly, the freedom to act independently of central control; and lastly, its general purpose in contrast to single purpose character.[16]

Dimensions

Local government has got several dimensions such as social, economic, geographic, legal and political. As regards social dimensions, it is found that it concentrates on the fact of a feeling of oneness among the people residing within a particular geographical bound. These people possess certain distinctive socio-economic characteristics and they constitute a distinct social entity.[17]

From an economic point of view, local government reflects the economic conditions of a locality.[18] Local government has got an important role in the socio-economic development of the country. Local finance is that part of the public finance which is concerned with the economic activity of the small government (local bodies) in a specific locality.[19] The grass root government works on the sound economic principles of decentralization, division of labour and specialization. Planning at local level is more appreciated, as it is more pragmatic being based on local knowledge, local decision, local action and local conditions.[20]

Geographically, local government is produced by amalgamation of subordinate territories created within larger units.[21] The physical, demographic, ecological and environmental conditions have their impact on the policies of local administration.[22] The administrative zone for the implementation of local laws is confined only to that particular geographical territory. Collection of taxes for local government is also confined only to that geographical local unit.

Legally, local government is a miniature form of body politics and a body corporate having legal personality. In the eyes of law, it has life, will and power of action of its own. [23] It is agent of State and as such represents public interest. In that capacity local government exercises a part of sovereignty of the state delegated to it. As self governing institution, it enjoys minimum powers of autonomy relating to raising of revenue, preparation of budget and management of local human, fiscal and natural resources. It has governmental character as a public agency and it is chosen by the people to whom it is accountable. Local government has right to enter into contracts and to own and dispose of property.

The most important dimension of the local government pertains to its political character. Irrespective of the different political philosophy and form of government, local government exists in every nation as a part of governmental or constitutional structure.[24] In a unitary state like U.K. and France, it is a decentralized unit of administration and it receives delegated power from the Central Government.[25] But in the federations like the United States of America and India, power has been distributed by the Constitution between centre and state. The local government receives powers from state government.[26] In both types of political set up however, the local government is constituted by popular mandate. The responsibility of a local government is both upward and downward. It is upward in the sense that it exercises power delegated by the state government. Its responsibility is downward in the sense that it receives mandate from the local people.[27] The institutions and politics of local governance are even more personalized than one finds in state governments. In part this is because officials (including elected ones) are friends, neighbours and acquaintances living in the community they serve. Most elected officials fulfil their responsibilities on a part time basis. In part, the personal nature of local governance is due to the immediacy of the issues.[28]

Essential Elements

William A. Robson writes: "In general local government may be said to involve the conception of a territorial, non-sovereign community possessing the legal right and the necessary organization to regulate its own affairs. This in turn presupposes the existence of a local authority with power to act independently of external control as well as the participation of the local community in the administration of its own affairs. The extent to which these elements are present must in all cases be a question of degree".[29]

B.B. Gupta has discussed five elements of local government[30], namely:

(i) Existence of authorities at various levels—each closer to the ultimate sovereign i.e. the people,
(ii) Allocation of sphere of activities to these authorities,
(iii) Democratic composition of these authorities,
(iv) Democratic working of these authorities, and
(v) Autonomy to these authorities in their allocated sphere limited only by the supervision of democratic authorities at higher level.

Thus, the essential elements of local government are: its statutory status, i.e. a legal body; fiscal autonomy; democratic and representative in character; autonomy; and specified functional domain, i.e. areas of operations.

Rationale and Necessity

The importance of local government has been depicted by many scholars, prominent among them are J.S. Mill, De Tocque Ville and Lord Bryce. They called local government a school for democracy where citizens are imparted political and popular education regarding issues of local and national importance. It develops qualities of initiative, tolerance and compromise, so essential for the working of a democracy. It not only relieves congestion at centre, but it also checks the increasing power of bureaucracy. It stands positively for distribution and diffusion of powers leading to administrative deconcentration and political decentralization. It opens an outlet for the articulation of lesser groups in a large society. It exercises a kind of self-economy, a financial measures to reduce expenses of the government. It is a reservoir of talents for local and national leadership.[31]

Local government is necessary precisely because some public requirements are local in their intensity, character and scope. It provides an extensive range of services to the people and performs functions of great variety and magnitude. Mere pragmatic reasons speak well for the continuance and even strengthening of local government.

The local government relieves the state government of a sizeable volume of routine work, which is its responsibility to carry out. It ensures two-way communication between the state government and itself. Desires and aspirations of the state government and plans and programmes of the central and state governments flow in the reverse direction.[32]

Local government has a number of values—both positive and educative. Positively, it plays a vital role in the social and cultural life of a nation. Health, happiness and progress towards ideals depend on the efficiency of the local administration. Apart from this, local government has also an important educative value. It functions as an instrument of self-education. It is observed that the countries, in which the democratic government has most attracted the interest of the people and drawn from their ranks, have been most developed. It justifies that the best school of democracy and the best guarantee for its success is the practice of local government.[33] The educative value of a democracy depends very largely upon the nature and spirit of its local institution. Another value is the concept of individual local units of governments as laboratories in which social, economic, political and administrative devices may be tested before being widely applied. Also the elections in a local government unit reflect the mood of the voters. It indicates the programmes and policies of the political party, which is most acceptable to the people.[34] Jenks points out that a country of strong local government may be slow to move and blundering in its methods, but it will be a country of steady progress and of political ability and honesty.[35]

However, as a secondary (quasi autonomous), not a primary form of government, it is erroneous to regard local government as the basis of democracy.[36] Critics observe that neither democracy comes into being due to local government nor it ceases with the disappearance of the latter. Local government breeds parochialism against the national unity and also inimical to national democracy. Further, some scholars hold the view that local government is not an exclusive arena whereby the citizen's political awareness may be sharpened into.[37] To J.S. Mill, local government may degenerate with a narrow minded, selfish and ignorant institution. Because of its small size it may not attract competent and public-spirited person and so, it becomes sluggish and inefficient. The greatest imperfection of popular local institutions, and the chief cause of the failure which has often attended them, is the low caliber of the men by whom they are almost always carried on.[38]

The most essential attribute of local government is its representative and responsible nature. The execution of local administrative powers must be controlled by elected or otherwise selected representatives, who are responsible to the local community. The government in its geographical jurisdiction is restricted to a local area, a well-defined territorial portion of the state. Its operations are confined to a locality. The guiding principle is that the residents of a place have a community of social and civic problems, which are peculiar to their own area and which warrant a solution not necessarily suitable to their counterparts in other areas.[39]

Thus it can be said that local government contributes to resilience, strength and richness of democracy by promoting diversification of political experience and by setting itself up as yet another center of creative activity through democratic action.

In countries where the organs of local government are under the thumb of the central authority, the efficiency of administration may be great, but the political character of the people will be unsatisfactory; it will be apathetic for long periods and then get dangerously excited with the result of instability and corruption in the Central Government.

The 'centralists' however criticize the case of local government on many grounds. These include:[40]

(i) Local government allows a variation in the standard of provision of local services which may be regarded as inequitable or unfair in an age of equality or at least equality of opportunity;

(ii) Local government is seen either too bureaucratic or too party political to be efficient or sufficiently responsive to public opinion;

(iii) Local authorities are closed to new ideas and change, encourage narrow attitudes and policies; and

(iv) The local government acts as a bastion against excessive state power and as catalyst to the release of stimmering community participation is too ambitious claim.

In practice, higher level government exercises considerable control over the policies of local government, and the general public shows a considerable lack of enthusiasm for local government matters.[41]

Importance of Local Government

In a democracy people have to work with great patience and perseverance. People should have faith in democracy to become capable of achieving progress. If democracy has to function properly, as many citizens as possible should be encouraged and provided with opportunity to take a continuing interest in its activities and problems. The first Prime Minister of India, Pt. Nehru, while inaugurating the first Local Self-Government Ministers' Conference, in 1948, had said that "local self-government is and must be the basis of any true system of democracy. We have got rather into the habit of thinking democracy at the top and not so much below. Democracy at the top may not be a success unless you build on its foundation from below".[42] The importance of local government may be discussed under following heads:

School (Nursery) of Democracy

Local government can be said to encourage citizenship or democracy and to promote political education in its widest sense. It does this by involving large number of people in the political decision making process.[43] Robson opined that "democracy on the national scale can function in a healthy manner only if it was supported and nourished by democratic local government".[44] It has been recognized that "Local government has a value as an education for democracy. It is education for the electors, who are called upon to do their voting in relation to issues that are readily comprehensible to them and for councillors who can gain experience in the art of responsible leadership". [45] Thus local government proves to be a reservoir for the growth of national leadership. John Stuart Mill argued convincingly that participation in "the process of government was a valuable education in public affairs which helped to produce a sense of responsibility in the community and stimulated the creation of local leadership".[46]

Forum for Political Education and Training

Local government trains people to work for and with others and teaches them the need for compromise, tolerance and respect for others. Lord Ripon also emphasized that "It is not primarily with a view to improvement in administration that this measure is put forward and supported. It is chiefly designed as an instrument of political and popular education".[47]

Elections to local government units provide opportunities for participation through voting which provides lot of political education. Local government serves as training ground for emerging leaders who after getting experience in the art of government and politics in these institutions go up to the state level or national level. Prof. Laski says that "the institution of local self-government is educative in perhaps a higher degree at least contingently than any other part of government. And it must be remembered that there is no other way of bringing the mass of citizens into intimate contact with persons responsible for decisions".[48] Local government cultivates a sense of civic duties and responsibilities and develops among the citizens a corporate spirit of common interest.

Promotes Spirit of Liberty and Equality

Democratic decentralisation, functional and fiscal autonomy, to some extent, may invoke equality and liberty to masses. Equity may enhance equality by providing access to political office and political activity for wider groups of people than are accommodated through national politics.[49] Jocqueville says that a nation may establish a free government but without municipal institutions it cannot have the spirit of liberty.[50] Hampton justifies local government because it promotes liberty by the dispersal of power from the centre to the localities.

Effective Solution of Local Problems

The problems that are local in nature need to be solved locally as per the needs, environment and wishes of the people. The local bodies, on account of their nearness to the people and familiarity with their needs and wants, are better placed to meet them.

Provides Civic Services

Local government institutions perform numerous functions to provide civic amenities to the inhabitants. These services include garbage collection, cleaning of roads/streets, drainage, sewerage, water supply, fire services, electricity, transport, and health services etc., which are very important for good civic life.

Reduces the Burden of Work of State/Central Government

Local government performs a number of functions which in the absence of local government would have been performed by the state or Central Government. The division of functions lightens the burden of functions to be performed by state/Central Government. If the state/ Central Government are over-loaded with works it becomes incompetent, incapable and indifferent to perform its duties. Thus local government is necessary for the development of initiative and interest of local masses in government.

Laboratory for Experiments and Testing Government Policies

Local authorities are almost bound to enhance the learning capacity of government. They develop their own solutions and initiatives, some of which may prove unsuccessful or applicable only to their specific locality, but some of which may be adaptable either by other local authorities or even by state/Central Government. Thus local government is an invaluable socio-political laboratory for trying and testing, on a small scale, various new proposals for government organizations and socio-economic policies.[51]

Control and Check against Bureaucracy

One of the goals of any democratic country is to prevent concentration of executive powers in few hands. The existence of local government makes way for the decentralization of powers and lead to reduction in the powers of bureaucrats. Besides providing the services, a strong local government system prevents unnecessary increase in the powers of bureaucracy over the community.

Local Government is Economical

The local people manage the local affairs at the lowest cost because they know that it is their money which is spent on the local services. Therefore they remain conscious to make services more economical and avoid wastage.

Thus local government is necessary in form of a government. In one way it reduces the work loads of upper tier governments, in another, it nourishes the leadership and educates the people. But in all forms local government makes provisions for services.

REFERENCES

1. Jha, C., (1953). *Indian Local Self-Government*, Patna: Novelty.
2. Rao, V. and Hazarika, N., (1980). *Local Self-Government in India*, New Delhi: S. Chand & Co., 10.
3. Bhargava, B.S. and Ramarao, S., (1978). *Indian Local Government—A Study*, New Delhi: Minerva, 143.
4. Mohanty, B., (1999). *Glimpses of Local Government*, Bhubaneshwar: Gyanajuga, 1.
5. Jackson, W.E., (1965). Local Government in England, *Civic Affairs*, 12 (11), June, 3.
6. *Encyclopedia Britannica*, London, Vol. 14.
7. Jennings, I., (1947). *Principles of Local Government Law*, London.
8. Harris, G.M., (1948). *Comparative Local Government*, London.
9. Clarke, John, J., (1948). *Local Government of the United Kingdom*, London.
10. Humes, S., and Martin, E., (1961). *The Structure of Local Government*, The Hague.
11. Stones, P., (1963). *Local Government for Students*, London: Mac Donald and Evons Ltd.
12. Golding, L., (1975). *Local Government*, London: Cox Wayman Ltd.
13. Byrne, Tony, (1990). *Local Government in Britain*, London: Penguin Books.
14. Singh, Hoshiar, (1997). *Local Government*, Allahabad: Kitab Mahal.
15. Cole, M. and Boyne, G., (1995). So You Think You Know What Local Government is?, *Local Government Studies*, 21(2), 197-200.
16. Maheshwari, S. R., (1994). *Local Government in India*, Agra: L.N. Aggrawal.
17. Muttalib, M.A., and Khan, M.A.A., (1993). *Theory of Local Government*, New Delhi: Sterling Publishers.
18. Lampard, E.E., (1954). History of Cities in the Economically Advanced Areas, *Economic Development and Cultural Change*, Vol. II, 81-136.
19. Venkatraman, K., (1964). *Local Finance in Perspective*, Mumbai: Asia Publishing House, 1.

20. Mohanty, B., (1999). *op cit.*, 5.
21. Johnson, R.J., (1979). *Political, Electorate and Spatial Systems—An Essay in Political Geography*, Oxford: Calendon Press, 28.
22. Venkatarangiya, M.J., and Pattabhiram, M. (eds.), (1969). *Local Government in India* (Selected Readings), Mumbai: Allied, 1.
23. Venkat Rao, V., (1960). *A Hundred Years of Local Self-Government in the Andhra and Madras States* (1850-1950), Mumbai: AIILSG, 2.
24. Srivastava, O.P., (1980). *Municipal Government and Administration in India*, Allahabad: Chugh, 1.
25. Ashford, D.E., (1982). *British Dogmatism and French Pragmatism*, London: George Allen and Unwin, 1.
26. Nigam, S.R., (1982). *Local Government (England, France, U.S.A, U.S.S.R, and India),* New Delhi: S. Chand & Co. 4.
27. Muttalib and Khan, (1982). *op cit.*, 10-11.
28. Connor, Karen O' and Sabato, Larry, J., (1997). *American Government: Continuity and Change,* Boston: Allyn and Becon.
29. *Encyclopedia of Social Sciences,* Vols. IX-X 1967, New York: Macmillan, 130.
30. Gupta, B.B., (1968). *Local Government in India,* Allahabad: Central Book Depot, 3.
31. Singh, Hoshiar (ed.), (2000). *Local Governance: Concepts and Networks*: Jaipur: RBSA.
32. Singh, U.B., (1997). *Urban Local Government*, Delhi: Rawat, 9.
33. Bryce, J., (1991). *Modern Democracies*, New York: Macmillan, 130.
34. Mohanty, B., (1999). *op cit.*, 3.
35. Jenks, E., (1925). *An Outline of English Local Government*, London: Methen & Co., 8-9.
36. Mackenjie, W.J.H., (1961). Theories of Local Government, Greater London Paper, London: London School of Economics, 5.
37. Hill, D.M., (1974). *Democratic Theory and Local Government*, London: George Allen and Unwin, 174.
38. Mill, J.S., (1954). *Representative Government,* London: Every Man's Library Edition, 351.
39. Mohanty, (1999). *op cit.*, 2.
40. Jones, G. and Stewart, J., (1985). *The Case for Local Government,* London: Allen and Unwin.
41. Byrne, Tony, (1998). *Local Government in Britain*, London: Penguin Books, 9.
42. Singh, (1997). *op cit.*
43. Byrne, (1990). *op cit.*
44. Robson, W.A., (1949). *Encyclopedia of Social Sciences,* Vol. IX.
45. Hicks, U.K., (1961). *Development from Below*, Oxford.
46. As quoted in Peter, G. Richards, (1970). *The New Government System*, London: George Allen Unwin.
47. Lord Ripon's *Resolution of 1882 on Local Self-Government.*

48. Laski, H.J., (1960). *Grammar of Politics*, Reprint, London.
49. Hampton, W., (1991). *Local Government and Urban Politics*, London: Longman.
50. Jocqueville, Alexis de, (1997). *Democracy in America*, New York; Alfred A. Knoft.
51. Ranney, Austin, (1958). *Governing the Man*, New York.

Chapter 2

American Local Government

Introduction

The United States' Constitution established the Federal Government of the United States. At the time of writing of that document, the separate colonies, that became states, had their own governments, which had grown out of smaller units. The many strata of Government were preserved by the Constitution even as it allocated supreme power, such as the power to declare war, to Congress. In fact, it gave practically all powers to the states except those that could, conceivably, work against the good of the whole.[1]

The American political framework has three dominant features, which are different in sense that they are not commonly found, at least in combination, in the developed democracies. These features are constitutional (a written constitutional document conferring and limiting governmental powers), federalism (a division of functions constitutionally between a Central Government and a number of constituent units in the federal system) and, presidential (a popularly elected chief executive heading the executive branch within a constitutional tripartite separation of powers which also includes legislative and judicial branches).

Each of these features has administrative consequences. These basic characteristics of the central level of government are found also at the state and local government levels. All the states have written constitutions incorporating the 'separation of powers' doctrine and all have chief executive governors, who are counterparts of the president. Local units are legally considered to be creatures of the several states, so they do not have separate constitutions but operate under state constitutional or legislative mandates. They also show more variations in how the executive branch is organized; the most common pattern historically in cities has been to have a Mayor directly elected at large as chief executive but many cities now have an appointed professional city manager or administrative officer and some divide administrative supervisory responsibilities among the elected members of the city council, which is primarily a legislative body. Similar variations occur in counties and other local units.[2]

Unlike state governments that are recognized by the U.S. constitution as full-fledged partners in the federal system, local governments have traditionally been creatures of their state with only the structures and powers their state chooses to allow them. States, as architects of local government organization either specify the type of structure local governments may use or give their local governments a choice of structures. Greater choice either through state constitutional provisions, statute, or grant of home rule powers to local governments, has been the past recent trend.[3]

Emergence

Romanic notions of democracy in America regard local governments as the building block of governance by the people. Jocqueville described government in the new country as a series of social contracts starting at the grassroots. He said, "*The Township was organized before the union*".[4] A more accurate description was included in a ruling issued by judge Dillon in 1868 and known as Dillon's Rule: "*The true view is this: Municipal Corporations owe their origins to and derive their power and rights wholly from the state legislature. It breathes into them the breath without which they cannot exist. As it creates, so it may destroy. If it may destroy, it may abridge and control.*"[5]

Under prevailing judicial decisions local governments are the legal creatures of their states. Cities, villages and in some states, boroughs and towns are known in law as municipal corporations or governments. The states create them, define their authority, determine the possible form of government they may adopt and may even abolish municipal governments, state control over units of government such as counties is, if anything, more complete.

Cities at one time were almost completely under the domination of state legislature. Prior to the early decades of the twentieth century, cities were generally created and governed by special acts of the state legislature. Local communities wishing to achieve the status of municipal corporations would petition the legislature for a charter conferring governmental powers on them. The charters were commonly so narrow that the municipalities had to return to the legislature to secure authority to do such things as, have a street paved, install a fire hydrant, or increase the salaries of their officials. At other times, legislation affecting only a particular municipality would be passed without regard to or in spite of local sentiments.

Special legislation was condemned by municipal reforms in the early decades of the twentieth century on the grounds that the powers and status of individual municipal governments were varied according to the wishes of the legislature. This criticism led to state constitutional prohibitions on special constitutional provisions.

In general, American local governments are modelled on the British system (going back to 'shires') of elected councils. The difference is that in the American system there is also a strong executive level. Local governments in the United States are either territorial or corporate. Examples of the territorial units are some county governments and local school districts. A corporate government is based on a charter, such as the state may grant to a city, town or village. These city charters are similar to constitutions, only (of course) on a smaller scale. Such charters are approved and authorized by the state, and they must not contradict state law.[6]

Laws in most states now require that state legislatures deal with municipalities through general rather than special legislation. Depending on various factors like population or the value of property municipalities are classified and these classifications condition the form of government and powers of the municipality. Thus state legislatures commonly pass laws for all classes of cities or towns as a group rather than for specific municipalities.[7]

There are a variety of types of local governments—some of these are created in a somewhat arbitrary way by state governments. Counties and local districts are good examples. State statutes establish the authority for their jurisdiction, set the boundaries and determine what these governments may and may not do and how they can generate funds.[8]

Some local governments emerge as people and industries locate together and form a community. These governments must have a charter that is acceptable to the state legislature. Charter describes the institutions of government, the processes used to make legally binding decisions, and the scope of issues and services that fall within the jurisdiction of the governmental bodies. There are five basic types of charter:[9]

- *Special charters*: Historically, as urban areas emerged, each one developed and sought approval for its own charter. In order to avoid inconsistencies, most state constitutions now prohibit granting special charters for a particular community.
- *General charters*: Some states use a standard charter for all jurisdictions, regardless of size or circumstances.
- *Classified charters*: This approach classifies cities according to population and then has a standard charter for each classification.
- *Optional charters*: A recent development is for the state to provide several acceptable charters and then let voters in a community choose from among them.
- *Home Rule charters*: Increasingly, states are specifying the major requirements that a charter must meet and allow communities to draft and amend their own charters. Every state allows this process except Alabama, Indiana, Illinois, Kentucky, North Carolina and Virginia.

An important feature of home rule is that the local government is authorized to legislate on any issue that does not conflict with existing state or federal laws. Other approaches list the subjects that a town or city may address.

Types of Local Government

Diversity in size, political climate, and administrative functions make it difficult to classify local governments. But the generally accepted classification is:

- Counties,
- Municipalities,
- Townships,
- School Districts, and
- Special Districts.

School Districts and other special (water, sanitation, housing, fire protection etc.) districts still comprise the majority of local governments, even though the number of school districts has declined significantly. Yet the number of counties, municipalities and townships has remained fairly stable.

Data collected in the 1982 Census of Governments reveal that more than 80,000 units of local government exist in the United States. This figure included some 19,000 municipalities, 3,000 counties, 17,000 townships, 15,000 school districts and 28,000 special districts. Over the years, the most dramatic drop has been in the number of school districts and the most dramatic increase has been in the number of special districts. The number of local governments per state ranges from 6464 in Illinois to only 19 in Hawaii. On the average, there are 1,654 units of local government per state.[10]

COUNTY GOVERNMENT ORAGANISATION

Counties have been derived from the English 'shires' of Anglo-Saxon government. Counties are among the oldest and widest form of local government in the United States. Counties are found in every state except Connecticut, Rhode Island, Alaska, Montana and South Dakota.[11] With few exceptions, counties have very broad responsibilities and are used by state governments as basic administrative units for welfare and environmental programmes, courts and the registration of land, births and deaths. County and city boundaries may and do overlap, although state actions have merged city and county in New York, San Francisco, Denver, St. Lousis, Nashville, Jacksonville, Miami and Honolulu.[12] Despite wide spread use, patterns of county government vary widely among states and even within states. The major forms of county governments include:

- Commission Plan ⇒ plural executive
- Council Administrator } single executive
- Council elected Executive } single executive

Commission Form

The most traditional and widely used form of county government is the commission form. Under this form, an elected board of 2 to 100 has legislative powers, such as passing ordinances, adopting budgets; and also administrative powers such as supervising some or all departments and appointing some administrative employees. A hallmark of this form is that "county commissioners share administrative responsibility with a number of independently elected 'row' officers who include: a county clerk, auditor and recorder, assessor, treasurer, prosecuting attorney, sheriff and coroner".[13] In practice many variations of this form exist. The most common and important variations are:

(i) *Strong Chairman*: In many counties the chairman of the board, because of seniority, expertise or willingness, makes daily administrative decisions. Other commissioners rubber stamp those decisions or delegate decisions to the chairman who functions in some ways like a county administrator.

(ii) *Co-equal Commissioners*: Where no strong chairman exists, commissioners share leadership and duties, reaching decisions by consensus or vote. Commissioners have many administrative and legislative duties.

(iii) *Supervisor Form*: It is special case of the commission form characterized by larger county boards. Traditionally these boards had form of township supervisors sitting *ex-officio* on the board. Now the supervisor is selected.

(iv) *Strong Supporting Official*: Another variation of the commission plan features a strong elected administrative official, typically a county clerk, who performs much of the administrative functions in addition to supervising elections, keeping records and carrying the other duties of his office. This may particularly be the case when the clerk is full time and the commissioners part time and when there is heritage of leadership for the clerk's office.

(v) *Strong Appointed Officer or Assistant*: Under this scheme the strong administrative official assisting the commission is appointed rather than elected. An appointed county clerk, administrative assistant or other official assists the council in preparing the budget and advises commissioners on managerial matters.[14]

(vi) *Elected Judge as Commission Chairman*: In some states, an elected county judge serves as chairman of the county commission. These judges perform administrative duties in addition to their judicial responsibilities and, in some cases, have the power of an elected executive.

Council-Administrator Form

This form has a number of variations but two primary types are—the council manager and council administrator.[15]

(i) *Council-Manager Plan*: This form features a professional manager appointed by the commission or board and serves at the board's pleasure. The county board performs the legislative role-adopting ordinances, approving taxes and overseeing administrative operations. County manager typically prepares the county budget, appoints most or all department heads, advises the board on administrative matters and makes daily decisions on programmes and policies.

(ii) *Counçil-Administrator Plan*: The council-administrator closely resembles the council manager form, differing primarily in the powers held by the administrator. County administrators typically hold most of the budget and advisory powers. County managers employ but usually lack the power to appoint and supervise department directors.

Council Elected Executive Form

Under this form, the board or commission carries out the legislative functions, and the county executive is elected to preside over the administrative branch. County executives have power to prepare the budget, recommend legislation and appoint, supervise and dismiss all or most department heads. Elected county executives usually have power to veto bills passed by the county boards, although this veto can be overridden by a two-third majority. Another distinction is the number of independently elected county administrative officials. Council-executive-counties have fewer elected administrative officers besides the county executives than do commission plan counties.[16]

The trend in county reorganization is towards executive leadership-centralizing more control in the hands of an elected or appointed executive. Another trend has been towards expanding the services counties provide.

MUNICIPAL GOVERNMENT ORGANISATION

Villages, towns and cities are established and authorized by state governments as individuals congregate and form communities. Some of the most intense struggles among governments within the United States are over the boundaries, scope of authority and sources of revenue for municipalities.[17]

The 1982 Census of Governments defines a municipality, as a political sub-division that meets several criteria: (a) municipal incorporation has been established to provide (b) general local governments for (c) a specific population concentration in a (d) defined area. A municipality can be called a city, village, borough or town. For most citizens, a municipality is the government that most closely affects them.

Types

Municipal governments take three basic forms: Mayor-Council, Commission and Council Manager. These forms parallel their counterparts at the county level and also have varieties.

Major forms of municipal government in different population size cities are depicted as under:[18]

Major Forms of Municipal Government

Population Group	All Cities	Forms of Government			
		Mayor-Council	Council-Manager	Commis-sion	Town Meeting
Over 10 lacs	8	6 (75)	2 (25)	—	—
5-10 lacs	16	13 (81)	3 (19)	—	—
2.5-5 lacs	39	16 (41)	22 (56)	1 (3)	
25,000-2.5 lacs	1137	407 (36)	681 (60)	22 (2)	27 (2)
10,000-25,000	1602	676 (42)	751 (47)	52 (3)	123 (8)
2500-10,000	3792	2192 (58)	1240 (33)	73 (2)	287 (8)
Total	6594	3310 (50)	2699 (41)	148 (2)	437 (7)

It is clear that the mayor-council form of government is most popular in very large and very small cities. The council-manager form on the other hand is most popular in medium-size cities. The commission form continues to lose popularity.

Mayor-Council Form

The mayor-council form is used by half of the municipalities, majority of them over 2.50 lakhs population. Three major variations of this form exist: Weak Mayor- Council, Strong Mayor-Council and Strong Mayor-Council with chief administrative officer.

(i) *Weak Mayor-Council*: This form predominated in the early and mid-nineteenth century when cities were primarily small, rural and suspicious of strong executive control. Mayors were supplemented with many other elected administrative officials-auditors, assessors, clerks, treasurers and administrative boards and committees. Some weak mayors had veto powers over council actions but little or no powers to develop a budget or co-ordinate the work of administrative agencies. Weak Mayor-Council system exists today primarily in smaller cities and villages but some large cities also have weak mayor form. The system today is likely to have smaller councils, use non-partisan elections and allow the mayor to develop the budget as well as initiate and veto legislation.

(ii) *Strong Mayor-Council*: This form is an attempt to overcome the centripetal force of numerous elected officials, boards and agencies pulling in different directions. The strong mayor form embodies executive leadership value-centralization of authority and responsibility in one office.

Today, this form shows variations among municipalities. Typically, it features the veto and budget preparation powers of the weak mayor form but gives the mayor few or no other elected administrative officials with whom to compete, fewer boards and commissions, and strong mayoral appointive and budget administrative powers.

(iii) *Strong Mayor-Council with Chief Administrative Officer*: Emphasis on strengthening mayors to cure the ills of over representativeness and independent bureaucratic fiefdom left some problems unresolved. As with elected county executives, mayors sometimes have greater interest and ability in campaigning, dealing with councils, and relating to community and interest groups than in overseeing administrative and service delivery operations. One remedy used by cities adds a chief administrative officer to relieve the mayor of many managerial functions. Variously called City Administrator, Deputy Mayor of Operations, these chief administrative officers typically serve at the mayor's pleasure and oversee city administration. In some cities chief administrative officers appoint major department heads subject to the mayor's approval.[19]

Commission Plan

Like the county commission form of government, the municipal commission plan combines legislative and administrative powers within one body. Collectively, city commissioners serve as the legislative, and individually, they administer city departments or functions. The mayor is usually one of the commissioners and serves largely ceremonial role. But unlike county commission form which predominates city or village commissions are used by a few municipal governments and only a few big municipalities, primarily smaller cities use it. In large commission plan cities, a chief administrative officer is often used to manage the city and this reduces the problem of diffused authority and lack of co-ordination almost inherent with the commission form.[20]

Council-Manager Plan

This form was born as a result of severe flood situation in one city. The council manager plan, like the strong mayor-council system spread widely through municipal reforms. Under the plan, voters (stakeholders) elect council members (directors) who appoint a manager (chief executive) to oversee administrative operations. In theory, city councils concentrate on making policy by preparing and executing the budget and appointing and supervising department heads. In practice, councils often delve into administrative details and city managers frequently initiate policy.[21]

Variations are also found in the plan. Some plans include an elected mayor to serve with the council appointed manager. The manager's role in such hybrid forms varies from ceremonial figurehead to political leader, depending upon the charter, the local political culture, and the mayor's relationship with the manager. Methods for selecting the council members also vary. Some elections are partisan, most non-partisan. Some council members are elected at large, some represent wards. Some cities have both wards and at large representatives on the council.

Use of council-manager system is greater in suburbs than in central cities, stronger in white-collar communities than in blue collar ones, and higher in smaller and medium size cities than in larger ones. But some large cities also use this form. All cities above one million population have manager-council system, but some of these cities also have appointed administrators.[22]

MUNICIPAL GOVERNMENT REORGANISATION

The overall trend has been towards the strong executive structure-the strong mayor form and council- manager plan. At the same time centralization has been the overall trend in the municipal reorganization, some decentralization to community districts or service delivery districts within cities has also been undertaken.[23]

Township Organisation

In few small states and in the Midwest, "town" refers to a form of government in which everyone in a community is invited to an annual meeting to elect officers, adopt ordinances, and pass a budget. Another use of this term is simply to refer to a medium sized city.[24]

Townships, according to the Census of Governments, refer to organized governments in 20 states. This category includes governmental units officially designated as towns, plantations and locations as well as governments called townships in other areas. Townships differ from municipalities as townships serve inhabitants of areas defined without regard to population concentration. This reflects their roots as geographic sub-division of counties. Another difference is that townships unlike the other types of local government, are found in only 20 north eastern and north central states, rather than in all states.[25]

Townships differ widely in role and powers. Towns and township governments administer a wide variety of services including fire and police protection, rescue services, roads and bridges, repairs and maintenance, social services for the poor and parks and recreation facilities.

Township structures vary, as do their powers. The three principal township forms of governance are the town meeting, the representative town meeting, and the council-administrator form.[26]

(i) *Town Meeting Form*: The town meeting is the closest American form to pure democracy. An annual or semi-annual meeting where citizens directly discuss their concerns and vote on local policy is characteristic of this form. Budgets are prepared, ordinances passed, contracts approved and other major business transacted in open meetings where eligible voters participate. Special meetings can be called by voter petition but most governing takes place, in general, at scheduled meetings.

(ii) *Representative Town Meeting*: The direct town meeting comes from an earlier simpler era. Today, larger urban townships and even rural townships are too populous and too complex to be governed directly by citizens. In this form voters elect representatives called selectmen or councilmen, who serve on town boards or councils and act on the voter's behalf. Non-elected citizens may attend meetings but cannot vote. In some states resident citizens are permitted to vote on a limited number of issues, some vestiges of the direct democratic form remain. Between meetings township government is delegated to the board of usually three to seven members.

(iii) *Council-Administrator Form*: This form parallels the municipal council-manager plan and county council-administrator form. Part-time townships councils unable to handle day-to-day administrative routine increasingly hire a professional administrator who serves at the council's pleasure. Township administrator functions like city mayor or county administrator although typically without such broad responsibility.

Reorganising Townships

A trend towards council-administrator exists. About half the township states are Administrators. This trend is consistent with executive leadership value, and to a lesser extent, neutral competency's emphasis on professional, apolitical administration. Despite this trend, township structures, especially in rural township states, tend to reflect the continued dominance of representativeness. Township, like other forms of local government, reflects tremendous diversity. No single level of powers, services or structures holds for all township. They vary because of geography, custom, law, politics and the particular needs of the areas and people they serve.[27]

Special District Organisation

Special districts are the most numerous form of government. A special district is restricted to a particular policy or service area. Special districts are limited purpose units created to perform one or at least several functions. Special districts comprise the most numerous and fastest growing form of local government. Their narrowness of purpose distinguishes special districts from general-purpose local governments—counties, municipalities and townships. Most, but not all public authorities, are considered special districts. Majority of special districts perform a single function. However, multiple function districts, which usually perform several services are increasing faster than those performing single functions. [28]

Special district boundaries typically do not coincide with those of general-purpose government. Only one-fourth of all special districts have boundaries that conform to those of counties, townships or municipalities and even though most special districts fall entirely within one county.

Critics claim the proliferation of special districts and their failure to coincide with general governments causes fragmentation and competition among governments. Another common criticism is that special districts, because they have their own revenue sources and often investors to satisfy, are less accountable to voters.[29]

For all the criticism surrounding special districts, many reasons exist for their widespread usage.[30] First, despite complaints about special districts infringement, general-purpose governments' managerial inability or political unwillingness to assume new functions, has, sometimes, created need for special districts. Second, fee-for-service financing, the cornerstone of most special districts tends to be more flexible and more politically expedient than levying taxes. Special districts are also a means for circumventing spending restrictions on general-purpose governments. Third, federal government mandates and incentives have triggered some special districts.

Most special districts have a part-time board of directors or commissioners charged with making policy. As with business, these directors usually take their policy cues from the full time staff. But, unlike business, special district directors are typically appointed by officials of those governments sponsoring the district or authority rather than bond holders. Directors or commissioners normally reach internal consensus on policy, presenting consensus decisions at open meetings. Operating control is typically centralized in the hands of a general manager or executive director, who holds most budget, appointment and supervisory powers of city managers with greater autonomy than most city or county managers enjoy. Executive directors oversee central staff and operating units.

Special districts are governed through a variety of structures. Some have elected heads and others appointed. Some of this levy a fee to generate their revenues, while others depend on appropriations from a state or city or county.[31]

School Districts

School districts have traditionally been included in a separate category, although they really constitute a particular case of special district. School districts are the most common form of special districts.

Special District Re-organisation

One form of special district organization involves changing the method for selecting directors. Most directors are now appointed because they represent special economic or special interests in the district's service area. Another method is to appoint public officials who serve, by virtue of their office, as transportation commissioner or housing administrator. Most districts have the directors of the first type. To help make special districts more responsive to the public interest, constitutions or laws increasingly specify the inclusion of public representatives on the boards. Another trend is to select directors via direct election by voters.[32]

The general trend for state, county, township, municipal and special district organization has been towards executive leadership-greater centralization of power and consolidation of functions under a chief executive. The greater complexity and faster pace technocratic society have emphasized single executive forms and de-emphasized slower plural executive forms. [33]

URBAN REFORM

In response to wide spread corruption around the turn of the 19th century, a municipal reform movement sprang up a movement that resulted in a host of innovations, now common features of city governments. The reform movement was to contribute to the decline of the machine by (i) using the ballot to elect reform candidates to enforce laws against graft and corruption, election frauds and the misappropriation of public funds; (ii) adopting civil service regulations to cut-off the supply of patronage; (iii) replacing party nominating conventions with direct primaries to reduce the influence of the boss within the party and make it easier to nominate reform candidates; (iv) promoting the adoption of the initiative, referendum and recall to ensure greater popular control over the operation of city government; and (v) instituting non-partisan elections to be held at different times from state and national elections. The latter innovations represented efforts to insulate city politics from state and national politics and further reduce the power of the boss.

The basic ideology of the reformers was that there was no need for politics and conflict in the operation of city government. Local governments, according to the reformers, must be insulated from partisan politics and be free to operate on a sound business like basis under the leadership of those concerned with the common good of the community rather than their party's interest or personal self-interest. To further this insulation, reformers often championed the goal of more local home rule.[34] Thus the urban reform movement started in the latter years of the 20th century as a protest against living and political conditions in larger cities. It seemed clear that patronage had become so insidious that basic functions of urban governments themselves were faltering. To get at the problems of management and patronage, the reforms had to concentrate on organization of the urban executive office. The main purpose aimed to remove politics from administration and patronage from the executive operations.

The municipal movement started in late 19th century left a deep and lasting imprint on the structure and politics of municipal governments. Several cities adopted all or most of the reform package. That is they have a city manager, a small city council, a merit system for hiring personnel, devices for direct democracy and elections that were non-partisan at large, and at different times from state and national elections. These reformed cities tend to have relatively wealthy, well educated and predominantly white Anglo-Saxon Protestant populations.[35]

The main result was the emergence of the city manager's position. It began to take form in 1912 in small towns, within a decade it had become the predominant form of executive in the United States. In the reform, backwash mayors lost status and recognition. In many cities, the city manager charters included a mayor in a ceremonial capacity only. City managers, on their part, quickly emerged as the competent, professional city executives, working closely with the governing bodies to install merit personnel systems and modern engineering. The objectives of these reformed city governments were heavily biased in favour of physical infrastructure.[36]

In addition to its effects on local structure and ideology, the reform movement gave birth to a number of influential organizations that continue to influence the course and direction of city government. Local civic associations not only expounded the tenets of the reform movement, acting as watch dogs against boss rule, but also often played the role of political parties themselves by recruiting local candidates, nominating them and campaigning for their election. On the national level, the principal representative of the reform movement is the National Municipal League, founded in 1894. The reform movement also contributed mightily to the creation of organizations like International City Management Association, designed to upgrade public employees professionalism by disseminating information through conferences and publications.

On the positive side, municipal reform has undoubtedly increased the professionalism of various aspects of municipal administration. On the other hand, it has been charged that the reform movement by suppressing the political function and making many decisions out of the recognized political process into a more complex and technical administrative process has made it more difficult for both citizens and their elected officials to influence public policy. To some observers, the end result has been the creation of new machines, in the form of large and powerful city bureaucracies with their own special system of rewards and clientele relationships. [37]

Some cities that have not been able to discard their mayor's position as chief executive nevertheless have attempted to upgrade management simple patronage or mayoral politics. In the process they have created a little known position entitled the chief administrative officer. All three of these officers (mayor, city manager and chief administrative officer) need to be assessed in light of their different origins and perspectives.[38]

The City Manager

The city manager is the recognized professional chief executive in council-manager governments. The institution's strength has been the removal of administration from politics and the embodiment of the reform movement's chief principle of professionalism in the city's executive agency.

The most significant facet of the chief manager's position is its relation with the council. Those councils that elect a mayor as ceremonial head seldom infringe on the real control by the city manager over the executive functions of the city. The councillors usually consider themselves all equals. They are the board of directors to the city corporation and the city manager is the president and chief executive officer. As chief executive, city manager exercises substantial control over the administration. Only the limited personal influence of the mayor as ceremonial figure or prominent politician sometimes intrudes on the city manager's domination of policy. A city manager could even defy a mayor in the council-manager form of government as long as he retains the support of the council majority.[39]

The council theoretically dominates in policy making, but Nolting (1969) points out that very early in the evolution of the city manager as an executive institution, it became clear that the council needed initiative and suggestion from the city manager.[40] Bromage (1970) described the city manager-council relation as one of partnership, which varies considerably from city to city. The city-manager institution achieved maturity during a period of nearly seventy years.[41] Nolting (1969) itemizes the usual requirements of the council-manager system as follows:[42]

(i) The city manager is appointed by the council and given full authority over the administrative affairs of the city.
(ii) The city manager has full authority to appoint and remove department heads and other key personnel and to make recommendations regarding appointments to other municipal positions such as boards and task forces.
(iii) The city manager also has the responsibility of preparing

and presenting the budget, advising the council on all matters, preparing reports and enforcing the law and ordinances of the city.

(iv) The council deals with administrative officials only through the city manager.

In the typical city, the city manager position is non-partisan, professional and encompasses the functions of chief executive. A delicate balance is managed with the council in policy-making. The city manager traditionally concentrates on implementation and avoids active politics. He generally initiates new policies carefully and with full awareness of the risks involved if he should lose the support of the council majority.

The urban scene today, especially in large cities tests the council-manager form of government to the maximum. Major issues of recent times create conditions often incompatible with the best features of the city manager institution. The main issue is whether professional managers can continue to determine the lifestyle and nature of city government for millions of increasingly sophisticated urban dwellers. A few cities such as Kansas City, Dallas and San Diego have retained the council-manager form of government, but it seems likely that the mayor in much large cities has considerably more influence over the performance of the city manager than in smaller cities.[43] The large majority of cities of more than 2,50,000 population have adopted the mayor-council form, but in an increasing number of them, the position of the chief administrative officer (CAO) appears.

Table 2.1: Professional and Non-Professional Attributes of City Managers[44]

Attributes Favouring Professional Status	*Attributes Favouring Non-professional or Political Status*
• *General influence on American life:* Significant and growing in terms of numbers of managers/CAO with increasing job responsibilities	Dispersing authority due to increased participation of federal/state action in local government and new minority/union participation
• *Ethos and outlook:* Outlook characteristically of an administrative generalist	Exercise of administrative/leadership skills highly dependent upon and subject to shifting political nature of community life, causing the bulk of managers to be 'in -and -outers'

(*Contd.*)

Table 2.1 (*Contd.*)

Attributes Favouring Professional Status	*Attributes Favouring Non-professional or Political Status*
• *Informal social background of managers:* Homogeneous/middle class occupation with professional-level salary	Social make of city management, especially influenced by parochial small town, suburban political pressures
• *General educational preparation:* Survey shows increasing college/graduate educational preparation	No required degree or certification to obtain employment
Core skills necessary for the job Informally favours administrative generalist background with preference for skills of budgeting, personnel and management, as well as newer specialities like energy conservation or federal grantsmanship (which depends on needs of individual communities)	No skills specified by law for employment
• *Career patterns:* An informal route of career advancement developing for many managers through assistant managership, consulting work, business or related government careers	None legally or formally specified
• *Lifetime occupation:* Possibility for all managers	The bulk of managers are 'in-and-outers' moving across a broad range of comparable administrative-type jobs
• *Self perception of occupation:* Most managers see themselves akin to public professional groups like diplomats or school superintendents	Less than one quarter of managers believe that they are "an established profession" like law or medicine
• *Peer-group influence of professional association—the ICMA:* The ICMA informally promotes professional and ethical codes of conduct through training programmes, meetings and publications	No formal control by the professional elite or professional association relative to entrance, work standards, promotion in profession, nor does ICMA attempts to enforce an ethical code of behaviour on the practitioner, employment of manager remains subject to local council decision
• *Degree of professional autonomy in relation to politics and community affairs:* Classic theory of manager plan as well as most manager charters view managers as neutral experts in municipal affairs	Reality of management role deeply affected by the nature and distribution of community politics, extent and scope of manager involvement in policy leadership is influenced by (i) community size, (ii) degree of political conflict, and (iii) self definition of leadership styles
• *Conflict or political competition with other professional groups:* In theory, managers are viewed as the chief professional administration in charge of various professional services	In reality, possibilities exist for wide array of conflict with community professional as well as minority and minor groups

The Chief Administrative Officer (CAO)

Recognition of the Chief Administrative Officer system came very gradually in second half of the twentieth century. Bollens (1952) described such system among California city in the early 1950s.[45] Sayre (1954) wrote the initial description and defence of the Chief Administrative Officer system in larger cities in 1954. Many authors have discussed the Chief Administrative Officer in different context—when appointed by the council, when appointed by the mayor alone and, when appointed by the mayor with the council's consent. An alternative term applied to CAO system has been mayor-manager system.[46]

Hogan (1976) suggests that the Chief Administrative Officer is unlike a city-manager, to aid the mayor in the performance of his administrative and policy responsibilities and only indirectly is he to be responsible to the council. Based on the Hogan's survey, the position of the Chief Administrative Officer can be summarized as:[47]

(i) The Chief Administrative Officer is not the chief executive but is a professional administrator in charge of the city's daily operations and accountable to the mayor.
(ii) Most Chief Administrative Officers have personnel and budget powers nearly equal to the city managers, however, they are subject to the final authority of the mayor.
(iii) Chief Administrative Officers are recognized as having policy making potential, but are reluctant participants in public policy debates and policies. They see administration as their main concern and administrative achievements as their main rewards.
(iv) The Chief Administrative Officer system is a flexible, powerful adaptation of the reform model to large city strong-mayor system.
(v) The mayor has the ability to adjust the Chief Administrative Officer position to suit his political and personal needs, without abandoning the attributes of a professional administrator role in urban management.

The Chief Administrative Officer and the City Manager—A Comparison

Comparison of the Chief Administrative Officer and the City Manager positions reveals several important differences. The Chief Administrative Officer from the beginning is an integral component in an elective executive agency concerned with executive leadership as well as professional administration. The City Manager is an appointed executive trying to carry out professional administration with a collective political body. The Chief Administrative Officer has appointive powers over the city departments and power to develop a budget, but the policy decisions involved with those activities are predominantly in the hands of the mayor. The City Manager makes appointments and prepares budget subject to the potentially shifting council majority. Although in some states procedural safeguards exist, the Chief Administrative Officer can usually be removed by the mayor. On the other hand, the City Manager can be removed by the majority of the council.

Reed (1985) compares both as under:[48]

	Chief Administrative Officer	*City Manager*
Method of selection	Appointed by mayor with consent of council	Appointed by council
Method of removal	Removal by mayor, sometimes with consent of council	Removal by majority of council
Appointment power	• Appoints most department heads and other key personnel • Oversights of merit system • Competes with mayor's assistants • Seldom recommends board appointees	• Appoints all key personnel and department heads • Oversights of merit system • Recommends boards' appointees
Removal power	• May take initiative in removing key personnel, requires mayor's approval • Competes with mayor's assistants	May remove key personnel, although subject to override and political influence of department heads
Budget power	Top budget official of city, usually prepares and defends budget, in unity with mayor	• Prepares and presents budget • Responsible for all aspects of financial management
Policy role	Considerable ability to set priorities for mayor, initiates discussions of policy, defends policies to council and public	• Theoretical limits on policy initiative, not always followed in practice • Often major policy initiator

Thus the Chief Administrative Officer's position in urban administration is increasingly accepted as a legitimate reform professional position when the city manager does not seem adequate. In American cities of more than 2,50,000 population, a definite trend is towards strong-mayor system. When professional administration is desired as an adjunct to the mayor's political and policy making roles, the Chief Administrative Officer can meet this need.

If one assumes that growing cities and changing public perceptions require clear forceful executive leadership by an elected chief executive, the strong-mayor system presents itself as the best model. If large cities seem to require different executive-administrative strengths than those offered by the city-manager system, the Chief Administrative Officer's position appears to offer an attractive alternative. The election of the mayor resolves political cleavages temporarily and the appointment of a Chief Administrative Officer brings promise of administrative competence and the reform influence against the spoils system. [49]

The Office of the Mayor

Mayor is one of the central executive officials in municipal politics. On paper at least, it is only in the strong-mayor form that a chief executive whose official powers and duties resembles those of the President of the United States. The mayor under this system has the authority to appoint and remove a large number of officials, prepare and execute an executive budget, veto legislation, and prepares a legislative programme. The mayor is the only executive official directly elected by the voters, and department heads look to his or her leadership rather than to that of the city council.

Mayors, in large mayor-council cities, may have a large number of immediate staff advisors concerned with the development and implementation of policy and with the establishing of working relations with the bureaucracy, the media, community groups, the city council and officials representing other governments. In most council-manager cities and in small cities with a mayor-council form of government, the immediate staff resources of the mayor are minimal. The mayor's job in these types of municipalities is considered to be part-time and is rewarded with only a nominal salary. [50]

Manager and Mayor

Just as the actual function of the manager differs from the model so does that of the mayor especially in large cities. The council-manager form gives the mayor only a limited role of presiding over council meetings and performing ceremonial functions. The mayors directly elected by the voters have considerably increased position's political base.

The basic relationship between the mayor and manager more often involves teamwork. In the cooperative endeavours, the mayor dominates the political role, though, he is often involved in administration and, the manager dominates the administrative matters though he also becomes involved in the mayor's political programme. The team relationship is frankly political and tenure of the manager is clearly linked to that of the mayor and the stability of community political leadership. [51]

Grassroots Politics

While there is always a distinction between formal and informal power, the face-to-face character of governance at the grassroot level provides increased visibility to this dimension of politics. Most of the positions in local governments are only part-time. Mayors, school board presidents are also teachers, business owners, accountants and farmers. [52]

Political participation in local politics is both more personal and more issue oriented than at the national level. Elections for some local government offices, in-fact, are non-partisan elections, which means parties do not nominate candidates and ballots do not include any party identification. The concerns that are communicated tend to be specific and neither partisan nor ideological. [53]

Urban political parties not only are fragmented but also have to share what influence they have with a multitude of institutions and groups active in city politics. Perhaps the most notable of these represent the many-faceted business community and local newspapers.

Commonly identified, as influential economic notables in city politics are bankers, builders, public utility officials and the owners of large departmental stores. The influence and importance of the business community is also felt through general organisations like the Lions and Rotarians, and other specialized groups. Business people obviously are often in a position to better their own interests by serving the city.[54]

Local news media invariably play a key role. The major newspaper in a community can shape the agendas of local government bodies and the images of government officials.[55]

Besides ad hoc, issue specific organizations are prevalent in local governments. The groups active in local politics include candidates' appraisal committees, citizen leagues, residential or neighbourhood improvement associations, tax payers groups, labour unions, churches, low income groups, racial, religious and nationality groups.[56]

Executives and Legislatures

Except for the traditional New England Town Meeting, local governments have some or all of the following offices:[57]

(i) Elected executive, such as a mayor, village president, or county executive.
(ii) Elected council or commission, such as a city council, school board or county board.
(iii) Appointed manager, such as a city manager or school superintendent.

Local government institutions in America are not necessarily bound to the principles of separation of powers or checks and balances, like the U.S. Constitution requires the federal government. School boards commonly have both legislative and executive authority. They make policies regarding instruction and facilities and they do the hiring and contracting to implement those policies. With few exceptions, school board members are part-time officials, so they hire superintendents and rely heavily on them for day-to-day management and for ideas for new policies. The legislative and executive authority and responsibility, netherless remains with the school boards.[58]

As part of their efforts to destroy the political machines, progressives sought reforms that would minimize the politics in local government institutions. They favoured local governments headed by professional managers instead of elected executives. Managers would be appointed by councils, the members of which were elected on a non-partisan ballot, thus removing the role of parties. Another way of making the ethnic block voting of the machines irrelevant, progressive reformers advocated that council members be elected from the city at large rather than from neighbourhood districts.

Progressives argued that the commission form of government was an accepted alternative to mayors and boss politics. The commission evolved as a response to a tidal wave in 1900 in Galveston, Texas. After the disaster a group of prominent business leaders in Galveston formed a task force assuming responsibility for a specific area, such as housing, public safety and finance. Task force members essentially assumed the roles of both legislators making policy and managers implementing policy. The citizens of Galveston were so impressed that they amended their charter to replace the mayor and city council with a commission, elected at large and on a non-partisan basis. Presently a few cities have the commission form of government. Julsa, Oklahoma and Portland, Oregon are the largest cities run by commissions. Galveston is one of the cities that has abandoned this structure. [59]

Many of the county governments are run by boards or councils that are elected from geographic districts and without any executive. Committees of the county boards manage personnel, finance, roads, parks, social services and the like. Many of the committees elect an executive as well as a board and thus follow the mayor-council model. Many more hire a professional manager. [60]

School districts follow the council-manager model. Other special districts have boards that are elected or appointed by elected officials. If the district is responsible for service like water or sewerage or mass transit, the board is likely to hire and then supervise a manager.[61]

Finances

The budgeting process involves making projections of expenses and revenues. Local officials face some special uncertainties when they make these guesses. One important factor is the health of the economy. Another important factor affecting local government budgets is the level of funding that governments give to one another. Local governments do not receive much, but water and sewerage districts have been getting about 15 per cent of their funds from the federal government. Local governments depend heavily on aid from state governments. The pattern varies from one state to another but on an average school districts get slightly over half of their funds from state governments, counties get almost one third and cities get about one fifth.

Local governments rely primarily on property taxes; have little from levies on sales and virtually nothing from income. Schools in particular, depend on property taxes. Local governments levy user fees such as admission to parks, licenses for hunting and fishing, tuition for public universities and charges based on the amount of water used.[62] The diminishing of the tax base and finances of cities through the movement of the middle class to the suburbs have led to the inability of property taxes to maintain inner cities and has resulted in turn to greater alliance on other kinds of taxation, including sales and commuting taxes.[63]

The Transportation Equity Act for the 21st Century of 1999 is the biggest infrastructure programme in the United States. It is about finding new ways for the private sector to access federal resources through innovative legislation, such as state infrastructure banks and revolving funds. The grant programmes of prior decades have given way to private funding and greater local government control.[64]

Personnel Systems

Generally, there are two personnel practices—the continuum model and the competing system model. The professional continuum model is the older conception of the two. It represents a liner process by which a successive addition of new professional personnel principles slowly replaces patronage and other deficient practices. The process began in the late 19th century with the concept of merit system or civil service reform.[65] Originally, four primary principles were involved: meritorious hiring, based on competence, political neutrality, tenure in office and administration of the personnel function by a relatively independent civil service commission. Later on, after the emergence of the scientific management school, job classifications and standardized pay scales were added.[66] One might call this model the optimistic one, in that, its representatives believed in steady progress and the power of cooperation in overcoming possible incompatibilities.[67]

Mosher is perhaps the outstanding proponent of the competing personnel systems argument. He distinguishes among five competing claims: demand for management discretion, goals of the profession, civil service or merit principles, collective bargaining requirements and affirmative action goals. A good summary of the competing personnel systems model is presented by Klingerer and Nalbandian. The authors distinguish four clusters, most of which correspond with the typologies offered by Mosher and others.[68] These are political systems, where personnel decisions are primarily based on patronage and party loyalty; civil service systems, where neutral competence is supposed to determine personnel decisions; collective bargaining systems, where many employment conditions are set by contract negotiations; and affirmative action systems, where affirmative action regulations are supposed to ensure non-discriminatory personnel actions.[69]

A grassroots movement to reform government began at the local level, and then spread upward. [70] The goal of the reformers was to create a non-partisan career civil service that was staffed on the basis of ability. These civil servants were to operate the government in the public interest using sound business principles and allocating resources based on objective criteria. The major manifestation of the reforms is the merit system of personnel management. Merit is characterized by non-partisan system of recruitment, watchdog oversight system to preclude political interference in the recruiting process and to preclude employees' participation in partisan politics. The system also guarantees that employees will only be removed for cause.

The determination of how much time and how many resources to dedicate to human resource management vary according to the size of the city and the level of personnel specialization. State-of-the art public personnel systems view the merit rules as the method of preventing corruption in government for protecting the rights of public employees. Only line managers can adequately lead, select, motivate and, discipline public employees. Personnel are treated as a management support system rather than an obstacle to be surmounted or circumvented. A cooperative approach can secure union help in the identification of functions that can be combined, eliminated or contracted out. Unions may also be entrusted to co-sponsor diversity training.[71]

In conclusion, cities are labour intensive organizations that cannot ignore the personnel function or treat it as nuisance-causing auxiliary function. Merit equal employment opportunity and unionized workers in one configuration or another will continue to be the distinguishing features of public personnel systems for the foreseeable future.

REFERENCES

1. Swift, Nick, (2003). Mayors Play the Central Role in US Municipal Government, City Mayors Government, http://city mayors.com/government/us-locgov.html.
2. Heady, F, (1988). The United States, in Donald C. Rowat (ed), *Public Administration in Developed Democracies: A Comparative Study*, Marcel Dekker Inc., New York and Basel.
3. Mohanty, Bijoyini, (1999). *Glimpses of Local Government*, Bhubaneshwar: Gyanajuga Publications.
4. Tocqville, Alexiș de, as quoted in Connors, Karen O., (1997). *American Government: Continuity and Change*, Boston: Allyn and Bacon.
5. Dillon, J.F., (1911). *Commentaries on the Law of Municipaql Corporation*, Boston: Little Brown & Co.
6. Swift, *op cit.*; Bose, C., Searching for the Best Structure for American Local Government, *International Journal of Public Administration,* 18(4).
7. Berman, David R., (1984). *State and Local Politics*, Allyn and Bacon, Inc., Boston.
8. Burns, N.E., (1994). *The formation of American Local Governments: Private Values in Public Institutions*, New York: OCIP.
9. Berman, *op cit.*; Snyder, Clyde F., (1965). *American State and Local Government,* New York: Appleton-Century-Crofts.
10. Connor, Karen O, (1997). *American Government: Continuity and Change*, Boston: Allyn and Bacon.
11. Mohanty, (1999). *op cit.*; Volkomer, W.E., (2003). *American Government*, Pearson Education.
12. Connor, (1997). *op cit.*; Vincent Ostrom, Robert Bish, Elinor Ostrom, 1988, Local Government in the United States, Sanfransisco, California ICS Press:
13. Duncon, 1998, as quoted in Rowat, *op cit.*
14. *Ibid*; Geller, W.A., Stephens, D.W., (ed.), (2003). *Local Government police Management*, ICMA University of the International City/County Management Assọciation.
15. Dye, Thomas R., (1990). *American Federation: Competition among Government,* Lexington: M.A: D C Health.
16. Jewell, N.E. and Marcia Lynn Whicker, (1994). *Legislature Leadership in the American States*, Ann Arbor: University of Michigan Press.
17. Connor, (1997). *op cit.*
18. Calculate from International City/County Management Association, the Municipal Year Book, 1993, ICMA, Washington, D.C. as adapted from Conner & Sabato, *op cit.*
19. Dahl, R.A., (1996). *Who Governs? Democracy and Power in an American City*, New Haven: Yale University Press.
20. Fiorina, M.P. and Paul E. Peterson, (1997). *The New American Democracy*, Boston: Allyn and Bacon.

21. Banfield, E.C., (1970). *The Unheavenly City*, Boston: Little Brown.
22. Crenson, M.A., (1993). *A Neighbourhood Politics*, Cambridge: Harvard University Press.
23. Shalala, as quoted in Connor, *op cit.*; Zimmerman, J.F., (1970). *State and Local Government*, London: Berns &Noble Books.
24. Connor, (1997). *op cit.*; ICMA, (1991). *Emergency Management Principles and Practice for Local Government.*
25. Mohanty, *op cit.*; Margnerite, J. Fisher and Donald G. Bishop, (1950). Municipal and Other Local Governments, New York: Prentice Hall.
26. Fiorina, M.P. and Paul E. Peterson, (1997). *op cit.*
27. Peterson, Paul E., (1995). *The Price of Federalism*, Washington, D.C: Bookings.
28. Fiorina, Morris, (1992). *Divided Government*, New York: Macmillan.
29. Walsh, as quoted in Rowat, *op cit.*; Euchner, C.E., McGovern, S.J., (2003). Urban Policy Reconsidered: Dialogues on the Problems and Prospects of American Cities, Routledge.
30. Riker, W.H., (1964). *Federalism: Origin, Operation*, Significance, Boston: Little Brown.
31. Connor, *op cit.*; Sayre, W.S., (1962). *American Government*, College Outline Series, New York: Barnes & Noble, Inc.
32. Mohanty, *op cit.*; Wilson, J.Q., (2003). American Government, Houghton Mifflin.
33. Jewell and Marica, *op cit.*; Judd, D., Swanstrom, T., (2005). *City Politics: Private Power and Public Policy*, Addison-Wesley.
34. Alford, R.R. and Scoble, M., (1965). *Political and Socio-economic Characteristics of American Cities*, Municipal Year Book.
35. *Ibid.*; Wager, P. W. (ed), (1950). *Council Manager Government Across the Nation*, Chapel Hill: University of North Carolina Press.
36. Benjamin, G and Michael, J.M. (eds.), (1992). *Limiting Legislative Terms*, Washington, D.C: Congressional Quarterly Press.
37. Loi, Theodore J., (1969). *The End of Liberalism*, W.W. Norton Co., New York.
38. Erie, S.P., (1998). Rainbow's End: Irish American and the Dilemmas of Urban Machine Politics, Berkeley: University of California Press.
39. Bromage, A.W., (1970). *Urban Policy Making: The Council Manager Partnership*, Public Administration Service, Chicago.
40. Nolting, O.F., (1969). Progress and Impact of the Council-Manager Plan, Public Administration Service, Chicago.
41. Bromage, *op. cit*; East, John P., (1965). *Council Manager Government: The Political Thought of Its Founder*, Chapel Hill: University of North Carolina Press.
42. Nolting, *op cit.*; Sellers, J.M., *Governing from Below: Urban Regions and the Global Economy*, Cambridge University Press.
43. Reed, Alan, (1995). Chief Executives and Administrative Officers, in J.

Robin and D. Dodd (eds.), *State and Local Government Administration,* Marcel Dekker Inc., New York and Basel.

44. Stillman, R.C. II, (2003). The City Manager, in Douglas J. Watson and Wendy L. Hassett (eds.), *Local Government Management: Current Issues and Best Practices*, New York: M.E. Sharpe, Armonk.
45. Bollens, J.C., (1952). *Appointed Executive Local Government: The California Experience*, The Haynes Foundation, Los Angles.
46. Sayre, W.S, (1954). The General Manager Idea For Larger Cities, *Public Administration Review*, 14.
47. Hogan, J.B., (1976). *The Chief Administrative Officers: An Alternative to Council-Manager Government*, The University of Arizona, The Institute of Government Research, Tueson.
48. Reed, (1995). *op cit.*; Welch, S., Rigdon, S.M., Gruhl, J., Comer, J., (2005). *Understanding American Government*, Thomson Learning
49. Stillman, *op.cit*; Kammerer, G. M. *et.al*., (1962). *City Managers in Politics: An Analysis of Manager Tenure and Termination*, Gainesville, Fla: University of Florida Press.
50. Berman, (1984). *op cit.*
51. Boynton, R.P. and Wright, D.S, (1971). Mayor-Manager Relations in large Council-Manager Cities: A Reinterpretation, *Public Administration Review*, 31.
52. Crenson, *op cit.*Morgan, D.R., England, R.E., Pelissero, J.P., (2003). *Managing Urban America*, Stylus Pub.Mc.
53. Dahl, *op cit.*; Mills, W., Davis, H. R., (1962). *Small City Government*, New York: Random House.
54. Berman, (1984). *op cit.*; Bowman, Ann'O, Kearney, R.C, State and Local Government, Houghton Mifflin College Div.
55. Connor, *op cit.*; Bingham, R.D. (ed.), (1991). *Managing Local Government: Public Administration in Practice*, Sage.
56. Berman, (1984). *op cit.*; Foster, W.S., (1978). *Handbook of Municipal Administration and Engineering*, Mc Graw Hill.
57. Conlan, Timothy, (1980). *New Federalism: Intergovernmental reform from Nixon to Reagan*, Washington, D.C: Bookings.
58. Elkins, S. and Eric, Mc Kionick, (1993). *The Age of Federalism*, New York: Oxford.
59. Connor, *op cit.*; Maddox, R.W. and Fuquay, R.F., (1975). New York: D. Van Nostrand Co.
60. Alford, R. and Eugene, C. Lee (1968). Voting Turnout in American Cities, *American Political Science Review*, 62, September.
61. Bryce, J., (1991). *Modern Democracies*, New York, Macmillan, Vol. I.
62. Connor, *op cit.*; Zimmerman, J.F., *State and Local Government*, Barnes and Noble Books, New York.
63. Swift, *op cit.*; Chandler, J. A. (ed), (1993). *Local government in Liberal Democracies*, London: Routledge.

64. *Ibid*; George, S. Blair (1964). *American Local Government*, New York: Harper & Row.
65. Bebey, G.L., (1938). Personnel Administration, *The Municipal Year Book*, 1938, ICMA, Chicago.
66. Riper, Van, (1958). *History of the United States Civil Service*, Row Peterson, Evanston, IL.
67. Freyss, S.F., Municipal Government Personnel Systems: A Tale of Two Archetypical Models, in D.C. Waston and W.L. Hassett (eds.), *2003, Local Government Management*: Current issues and best practices, New York: M.E. Sharpe.
68. Mosher, F.C., (1982). Democracy and Public Service, OUP, New York; Municipal Personnel Administration, 1960, Chicago: ICMA; ICMA, 2004, Human Resource Management in Local Government: An Essential Guide.
69. Lingner, D.E and Nalbandian, J., (1993). *Public Personnel Management: Context and Strategies,* Prentice Hall, Englewood Cliffs, NJ.
70. Hoogenboom, A., (1961). *Outlawing the Spoils: A History of the Civil Service Reform Movement, 1865-1883*, University of Illinois Press, Urbana, IL
71. Sylvia, R.D., (1997). Managing Human Resource: Personnel Administration in Local Government, in John J. Gargan (ed.) *Handbook of Local Government Administration*, Marcel Dekker, Inc., New York.

Chapter 3

British Local Government

The United Kingdom is a unitary state. In contrast to federal government, there is no division of powers between the centre and the local government units. The Central Government is in the enjoyment of all governmental powers. The unwritten British constitution has blurred the history and hence the Local Government institutions in England are the product of evolution that has taken place over hundreds of years. Before proceeding further, it is pertinent to clarify certain terminology. The United Kingdom consists of four countries: England, Scotland, Wales and Northern Ireland. The constituent units of Great Britain are England, Scotland and Wales. Britain consists of England and Wales. British Isles consists of England, Wales, Scotland, Northern Ireland, and Eire. All these constituents, for our purpose, have been given a common term English/British.

Evolution and Historical Development

Although United Kingdom is a unitary state, local government is a key element in the constitutional arrangements. Among the modern states, Britain offers a mode of the Local Government which has kept up its strong traditions of decentralized pattern in spite of the steady invasion by the Central Government of the sphere formerly left entirely to local authorities.[1] Thus, among the leading countries, Britain is one in which local history and spontaneous local growth have determined the shape and size of the local areas and the local political process.[2] Accordingly, the Local Government in Britain is not a direct projection of the Central Government.

John Stuart Mill admitted that local authorities and their members would almost certainly have limited capacity and are accountable to limited segment of public opinion. Nevertheless, Local Self-Government has an admirable arena for carrying out local detailed administration and a training school for political education and for discharging political responsibility. The Fabianists favoured the concept of Local Government on a different count. The Webbs suggested that it strengthens the concept of municipal socialism which would replace private profit with public service with a minimum of central supervision.[3]

In Britain, the actual origins of Local Government are not known. Townships and shires go back to the days before King Alfred at least five hundred years before the emergence of the Central administration in the twelfth century. Most of the local authorities were not entirely or only political in character. The county was a feudal or pre-feudal unit, and the parish an ecclesiastical unit. The ancient boroughs managed from an early date to establish some kinds of local council and obtained political recognition embodied in a character from the local lord or king. In the counties, however, the only regular form of government, until the end of the 19th century, consisted of centrally appointed officers. Practically, all the county officers were subject to appointment by the Crown, although since the times of Tudors justices of peace have been selected from the local gentry to perform judicial, legislative and administrative functions.[4]

The origin of local government was in a fog of detail. The difficulty was the lack of system. Every municipal corporation had a separate and different character; various ad hoc bodies; each had their own Acts of Parliament; parish councils arose from the operation of the common law without benefit of statute.[5] In Scotland, local government services were provided by parishes, county commissioners of supply, and burghs which were governed according to their own different constitution. In contrast with England, the magistrates played only a relatively minor role in local government.[6]

Traditional local government arrangements came under increasing pressure from the continuing industrialization that gathered momentums from the middle of the 18th century. People began to move from rural areas into the new industrial towns. The immediate response was to create ad hoc bodies by local or private Acts of Parliament.[7] Before 1835, the boroughs were privately organized bodies. Growing cities were governed for some local government purposes by the county magistrates. The manufacturers found themselves excluded alike from the County Commission of the Peace and the Municipal Corporation.[8] Thus one of the first decisions of the reformed Parliament, elected in 1833, was to appoint a Royal Commission staffed by eager young intellectuals to inquire into the municipal corporation. The consequent Municipal Corporations Act, 1835, gave the existing boroughs a new constitution based upon an elected council.[9] Although the county areas remained unreformed until the end of the 19th century, the modern system of local government really begins with the creation of the municipal corporations in 1835. Local Government is thus clearly intertwined with the growth of the towns.[10]

Local government, in the United Kingdom, as local elected councils, thus, can be dated from the 1835 Municipal Corporations Act which created a model that was later applied throughout the country with elected county councils being created by the 1888 Local Government Act and elected district councils by the 1894 Local Government Act. These new authorities replaced old and often corrupt corporations in the towns and cities.[11] In the remainder of the country, many of the powers of local government were exercised up to the creation of county councils by justice of peace (the local magistrates) with a system of parishes, often controlled by a small oligarchy.[12]

Edward Jenks remarked that England was a 'localised state' before it witnessed the trend from decentralization to integration. The integration process adopted dual direction. Firstly, the local bodies sought shelter under the umbrella of a common Central Government—leading to national integration. Secondly, until the reforming efforts were made by the Government, there existed two types of local bodies: Local Government and ad hoc, statutory, elective and appointive local bodies till all the ad hoc boards emerged with the Local Governments—thus integration also took place at this level.[13]

Yet another development was the adoption of a uniform principle of democratization of the Local Government. The Parliament played a significant role in the democratization process. As long as the functions of the Local Governments were confined to traditional civic functions, they were allowed to bask in the sun of full local autonomy. But with the assignment of new duties, the Government's involvement in the regulation and management of Local Government increased with the Municipal Corporations Acts of 1835 and 1882 and the Local Government Acts of 1899 and 1958.[14]

Even after legislative efforts to remove some of the anomalies, the complexity of the system was apparent in the number of authorities existing at local level. Lipman (1949)[15] gives figures for each of the main classes of local government existing in England and Wales in 1870. They included some 3,000 authorities at town, district or county level, and nearly 25,000 smaller authorities such as parishes and school boards. The confusion of local authorities provided the need for a reorganization of the structure of local government. The extensions of the franchise in 1867 and 1884 were accompanied by further discussions of local government reform. The 1884 Act, which brought a wider suffrage to the countryside, was particularly significant as it was in the counties that local government retained its unreformed structure. The structure of local government existing immediately before the changes in the 1960s and 1970s was largely settled by the end of the 19th century.[16]

England and Wales were divided in two counties each of which contained a number of districts known as municipal or non-county, boroughs, urban districts or rural districts. The rural districts were further divided into parishes. The main services provided by local government were divided between the counties and the districts with the parish councils. Completely outside this county structure were the county boroughs in cities and larger towns. The county boroughs were responsible for all local government services within their boundaries.

In London, the 1888 Act had created London County Council as an administrative county. In 1899 twenty-eight London boroughs were created within the area. The City of London retained its ancient privileges and independence.

Developments in Scotland followed a rather different pattern from that of England and Wales. The Royal Burghs (Scotland) Act, 1833, established elected burgh councils.[17] In 1889, the counties were given additional responsibilities and subsequently, the four largest cities became counties of cities. The Local Government (Scotland) Act, 1929 created a local government system that persisted until reorganization until 1975. There were five kinds of local authority, each with its elected council: counties of cities (4), large burghs (21), small burghs (176), counties (33), and districts (196)[18]. The parishes for local government purposes were abolished in 1929.[19]

Municipal reform came later in Ireland than in England or Scotland. The Act of 1840 gave more restricted powers to new councils.[20] The Local Government (Ireland) Act, 1898 introduced county councils, county boroughs and county districts on the English pattern. Parish councils were not created.[21]

The importance of the 19th century in the history of local government is that established the basis of the elected multi-purpose local authority that on that basis led to a concept of the role of local government in the government of towns and cities.[22] The second main contribution of the century was the development of a concept of city or town government. The local authority was seen as a means by which a town overcame its problems and realized its potential for development.[23] Through local government the aspiration was to the creation of the conditions of prosperity in urban areas. Local authorities however had no power of general competence. They were restricted to the powers given to them by parliament, which were limited in relation to the scale of the problems of the newly industrialized towns and cities.[24]

In the 19th century much of the focus of the local authority was on the infrastructure and on local action to create the physical conditions for healthy urban living, the emphasis in the succeeding century was upon the delivery of services as part of the welfare state. Local authorities were still concerned with the physical conditions of the city, in post-war reconstruction in slum clearance and in town center development. Even in these activities local action came to be seen as part of a national performance.[25] A local authority thus had a specific set of duties and powers laid down in legislation and had to act within those powers. This limitation on powers encouraged the concept of local government as an agency for the delivery of a specified range of services and limited the concept of local authorities as local government with a wide ranging concern for its area.[26]

In nutshell, Local Government in Britain is found structured in two contrasting ways. In Scotland, Wales and parts of England, a single tier "all-purpose council" is responsible for all local authority functions (Unitary, Metropolitan or London Borough). The remainder of England has a two-tier system, in which two separate councils divide responsibilities between district and county councils.

Counties and Unitary Authorities of England

The pattern in England is more complex. England has no separate governing body for the whole of it other than that of the *Government of the United Kingdom*. It is subdivided into 9 *regions*. One of these,

Greater London, has an elected *Assembly* and *Mayor*, but the others have a relatively minor role, with *un-elected regional assemblies* and *Regional Development Agencies*.[27]

Excluding Greater London, England has two different patterns of local government in use. In some areas there is a *county council* responsible for some services within a *county*, with several *district* councils responsible for other services. These councils are elected in separate elections. Some areas have only one level of local government, and these are dubbed *unitary authorities*. Overall responsibility for issues, such as transport in Greater London, is vested in the *Greater London Authority*. London is then divided into 32 *London boroughs* and the *City of London*, which have powers between a normal district and a unitary authority.[28]

Councils of counties are called 'X County Council', whereas district councils can be 'District Council', 'Borough Council', or 'City Council' depending upon the status of the district. Unitary authorities may be called County Councils, Metropolitan Borough Councils, Borough Councils, City Councils, District Councils, or sometimes-just Councils. These names do not change the role or authority of the couneil.[29]

Counties, Non-Metropolitan Districts and Unitary Authorities

In 1974, a two-tier administrative structure of (shire) counties and non-metropolitan districts was set up across the whole of England and Wales, except for the Isles of Scilly, Greater London and the six metropolitan counties. Council functions were divided according to the level at which they could be practised most efficiently. In consequence, counties took on functions including education, transport, strategic planning, fire services, consumer protection, refuse disposal, small holdings, social services and libraries, whereas the districts had responsibility for local planning, housing, local highways, building, environmental health, refuse collection and cemeteries. Responsibility for recreation and cultural matters was divided between both the tiers.[30]

Northern Ireland is sub-divided into 26 district council areas [although within Northern Ireland they are also known as 'Local Government Districts' (LGDs)]. These, in turn, are divided into electoral wards. Scotland is sub-divided into 32 council areas, which, in turn, are divided into electoral wards and communities. Wales is sub-divided into 22 unitary authorities, which, in turn, are divided into electoral divisions and communities[31].

Local Government Reorganisation

The Local Government Act, 1972 provides for a two-tier structure throughout England with the addition in some places of a third tier of parish councils. The two-tiers are not intended to exist in a hierarchical relationship to each other. Each tier has its separate responsibilities. There is no provision for a regional or provincial level of government.[32]

A landmark in the evolution of Local Governments in Britain may be traced to the reforming efforts made in the early seventies. In 1974, the six different classes of local bodies (Administrative Counties, County Boroughs, Municipal or Non-county Boroughs, Urban Districts, Rural Districts and Parishes) were substituted by Metropolitan and Non-Metropolitan Counties and Metropolitan and Non-Metropolitan Districts. The traditional units of local administration, the Borough, the District and the Parish, however, survived.[33]

The concept of Local Government, as an agency for delivery of services, was one of the dominant elements in the 1974 local government reorganization. The reorganization led to the universal adoption of a two-tier system, even though the Radcliff Maud Commission had recommended the creation of unitary authorities for most of England. The reorganization reduced the number of local authorities from over 1500 to 522. The division of functions varied in different parts of the country. The size of local authority was determined on the assumption that the role of local authorities was delivery of a series of services, efficiency of administration and self-sufficiency. Leach *et al.* (1992) identify the principal organizational assumptions underlying the formal structure of the authority as under:[34]

(a) *Self sufficiency*—If local authorities have been seen largely as agencies for the delivery of services required by the welfare state then it has been seen as inevitable that they should provide them directly. Not merely that local authorities should provide services directly, but they should themselves normally employ all the staff and other resources required for the delivery of the services.

(b) *Uniformity*—Local authorities should provide a uniform standard of services throughout their area.

(c) *Direct Control*—The problem of organizational control is to ensure that activities are carried out, in accordance with the purposes prescribed by the organization, while reorganizing the activities are carried out by individuals with their own potential. The assumption of direct control is that control has to be exercised as it happens. The aim of direct control is that control will be as a continuous process as the activities themselves.

(d) *The dominance of professionalism*—The dominance of the key profession in the workings of departments means that in departments the chief officer and the majority of the senior management will be drawn from the dominant profession.

(e) *The formalities of accountability*—Accountability in local authorities has been seen as being expressed through the electoral process and through the observance of proper procedures. The representative system therefore has been the first condition of accountability. Formal accountability supports detailed control by ensuring authority for action taken.

These assumptions underlay the workings of committees as much as the workings of departments. The committee system was and is, by element, in the political structure of the council. It is through the committee system that councils have traditionally made their decisions although those decisions might have to be confirmed by the full council. The dominance of the committee system is grounded in the role of council as the effective authority for all that happens in the authority. The main distinguishing feature of the current local government model is that decisions are taken corporately by or on behalf of the whole council. There is no source of executive authority other than the council itself.

The Local Government Act, 1972 and the Local Government (Scotland) Act, 1973 provide that local authorities are corporate bodies and vest all functions in the council of each authority.[35] The council can and does delegate its authority. The traditional model was based on a series of separate executive committees. There was not merely no separate political executive, but no effective overall committee within the local authority with an overall responsibility for determining the policies of the authority.[36]

The influential Bains and Peterson reports did not challenge the basic organizational assumptions or alter the basic building blocks of committees. The number of departments and committees was however reduced, merging the responsibility of different services. Committees continued to operate largely on the undifferentiated cycle, exercising control as it happens. Departments maintained the hierarchy of control and reflected professional dominance. One change did take place. An attempt was made to strengthen the corporate working of local authorities.[37] It also recommended the appointment of a chief executive who would work through a management team. However, over-ambitious attempts to develop a corporate approach had limited impact because generally the role and method of working remained relatively unchanged.[38]

The distinction between the metropolitan and non-metropolitan areas lies in the distribution of services between the counties and their districts. In metropolitan areas, the districts are responsible for education, social services and libraries. In non-metropolitan areas these responsibilities are retained by the county.[39]

Metropolitan Counties

In the present set up of local government, Metropolitan County, which is the top tier, is wholly a new comer without any tradition. While the greater part of metropolitan areas has a two- tier system, the remainder has a third level. Six metropolitan counties were created—four were based almost exclusively on continuous urban areas (conurbation), but the two stretched to rural countryside. Each metropolitan county has a population of one million.

Non-Metropolitan Counties

The non-metropolitan counties or shire counties are substantial local authorities in terms of both area and population. Non-metropolitan counties average more than half a million.

Metropolitan Districts

The metropolitan counties were divided into metropolitan districts. The number varied according to the population size and nature of the area. They were formed out of amalgamation of County to Boroughs to Rural Districts. Only three of 36 metropolitan districts do not include a former county borough within their boundaries.

Non-Metropolitan (Shire) Districts

The detailed arrangements for the non-metropolitan districts were not included in the 1972 Act but determined subsequently. Of the 296 districts, 111 had a population below 75,000 and 14 were below 40,000.[40] The new districts were very largely based on amalgamations of existing district authorities, which, in turn, derived from the sanitary districts created in the mid-19th century.

Parishes

For local government purposes, the parish had only existed within the boundaries of the former rural district councils. The 1972 Act enabled these parishes to continue into the new system and also made provision for some former boroughs or urban districts to continue with parish status. There is new parish or town councils within London or the major urban centres of other large cities, though some exist within the more rural parts of metropolitan districts.[41]

Local Government: Changes During the 1990s

From 1974 (1975 in Scotland) to 1986, the whole of England, Scotland and Wales had a two-tier system, with district councils and county (or in Scotland, regional) councils.

The 1980 saw another twist in the controversy surrounding the structure of local government. The Conservatives, who introduced the country wide two-tier system, came to believe that in the case of Greater London and the six metropolitan counties, the hopes of the last reorganization had been disappointed.[42] They abolished both the metropolitan counties and the Greater London County. In the further reorganization in the 1980s some former Greater London Council and metropolitan county services were allocated to the London boroughs and metropolitan districts which became single tier authorities.[43]

This was changed in 1986 by the abolition of metropolitan county councils. A local government reform took place in the 1990s. Scotland and Wales moved to a fully unitary system, whilst expansion of unitary government in England happened haphazardly, leaving parts of the country unitary, and other parts two-tier—a system similar to that which prevailed before 1974 in the whole of *Great Britain.*[44]

In the early 1990s, the structure of local government in Britain once again became a subject of public debate. The Government created the independent Local Government Commission (LGC) to look at the case for replacing the existing two-tier structure of county and district councils with a structure based on all-purpose unitary authorities. However, it was made clear that there was to be no national blueprint for reorganization and decisions were to be made according to the needs of each local area. The Local Government Commission concluded that a mixed system should be created. It recommended the creation of unitary authorities in some parts of the country and the retention of the existing two-tier system elsewhere. The Government accepted most of the Commission's recommendations. However, it was conceived that some large towns and cities with a cohesive civic identity would be better governed by a unitary authority. Many of these had been county boroughs until 1974 and had a significant need for economic and social regeneration.[45]

As a result of these further reviews, the Commission recommended the creation of additional eight unitary authorities. The main changes resulting from the review process therefore were as follows:[46]

- The abolition of the three 'new' counties (Avon, Cleveland and Humberside) created in 1974, and their replacement with four unitary authorities in each case. Following the abolition of these county councils, revised arrangements were made for ceremonial functions (for example Lord Lieutenancy arrangements).
- The abolition of the Royal County of Berkshire, and its replacement with six unitary authorities.
- The creation of 46 new unitary authorities in 22 counties, mostly with large towns and cities such as Bournemouth, Milton Keynes and Derby becoming all-purpose authorities.
- The retention of the *status quo* in the remaining 12 counties. This was generally without change.

The last changes were made between 1995 and 1998 and until then there were two models for providing services for the public. In

England, outside the larger towns, services were rendered by 'two-tier' councils. One tier was made up of the county councils, each of which serviced populations of around 5-15 lacs. The other tier comprised the district councils. There were between four and 14 of them within each county council area, covering local populations of about one lakh. [47]

Following the Local Government Re-organisation in the 1990s, major changes were implemented to create administration most appropriate to the needs of the area concerned. The key feature of this change was the introduction of unitary authorities, single-tier administration with responsibility for all areas of local government. Between 1995 and 1998, these were established in a number of areas across the country, especially in medium-sized urban areas, whilst other areas retained a two-tier structure.

There are currently 46 unitary authorities in England, and 34 shire counties split into 239 (non-metropolitan) districts. This district total includes the Isles of Scilly, which has a unitary council but is considered as a district of the county of 'Cornwall and the Isles of Scilly' for coding purposes. London and the metropolitan counties retain their own structure. Counties, districts and unitary authorities are subdivided into Electoral Wards/Divisions.[48]

Council Areas

The Local Government (Scotland) Act, 1973 created nine regional councils—53 district councils and three islands councils. The Act also provided for the introduction of community councils as a vehicle for the expression of local opinion.[49] The nine regions have widely differing populations and areas. The Wheatley Commission was concerned to establish regions that would conform to four criteria: they should be large enough to carry out their functions effectively; they should correspond with genuine communities; they should form distractive parts of Scotland, and finally, there should be a certain balance between the various regions.[50] The districts were even more varied in size than the regions. Parish councils for local government purposes were abolished in Scotland in 1929. The 1973 Act provided for community councils to operate at a similar grassroots level, and introduced a new concept into British local government a statutory body without statutory functions.

The 1994 Local Government (Scotland) Act led to the abolition of the existing structure of 9 regions and 53 districts, although the 3 island councils remained. Since April 1996 therefore Scotland has been divided into 32 units, known as council areas, whose councils are unitary administrations with responsibility for all areas of local government.[51] Council areas are built from *electoral wards* and are also divided into *communities*.

Sizes of council areas vary wildly from 977,087 people (2001 census) in Birmingham to 34,563 in Rutland. However, these are outliers, and most unitary authorities have a population in the range 150,000 to 300,000. The non-unitary districts vary from 24,457 people in Teasdale to 194,458 in Northampton. All but 9 non-unitary districts have less than 150,000, though.[52]

District Council Areas

In a formal sense, local government in Northern Ireland consists of 26 unitary district councils. Each of these is centred on a town and includes the adjacent rural areas. At the reorganization in October 1973 Northern Ireland's two-tier administrative structure was replaced by one of 26 districts known as 'district council areas' (although within Northern Ireland they are also known as 'local government districts'). The district councils are unitary administrations responsible for all areas of local government, but their remit is more limited than that of local authorities in the rest of the UK. The six historic counties (Antrim, Armagh, Down, Fermanagh, Londonderry and Tyrone) are still referred to in common parlance but do not constitute a level of administration.[53] District council areas are built from *electoral wards*.

The *boroughs* are in many cases descendents of boroughs set up hundreds of years ago, and so have accreted a number of traditions and ceremonial functions. In borough, councils not to have adopted a directly elected mayor, the chair of the council is the *mayor*. In certain cities the mayor is known as the *Lord Mayor*. Councils may make people honorary *freemen* or honorary *aldermen*.[54]

The system in *Northern Ireland* dates from 1973, before then a system was used identical to that used on the mainland before 1974. Elected regional assemblies are planned in the future, and in any region, which has one, the existing local government structure will be made unitary. Voters will choose between a unitary council on the current county boundaries, or based on smaller districts formed by merging current districts.[55]

Electoral Wards/Divisions

Electoral wards/divisions are the key building block of UK administrative geography, being the spatial units used to elect local government councillors in metropolitan and non-metropolitan districts, unitary authorities and the London boroughs in England; unitary authorities in Wales; council areas in Scotland; and district council areas in Northern Ireland. Electoral wards are found in Scotland, Northern Ireland and most of England. In Wales and the Isle of Wight, the equivalent areas are legally termed 'electoral divisions', although they are frequently also referred to as wards. The only part of the UK without electoral wards/divisions is the Isles of Scilly, which has its own council but no electoral zoning. For statistical purposes however, ONS treats the islands' five parishes as electoral wards. Electoral wards/divisions (and the Scilly parishes) cover the whole of the UK; in addition, all higher administrative units are necessarily built up of whole electoral wards/divisions.[56] They are also used to constitute many other geographies such as NUTS areas, health geographies and Westminster parliamentary constituencies.

English districts (metropolitan and non-metropolitan), London boroughs and unitary authorities average around 23 electoral wards/divisions each, Northern Irish districts around 22 and Scottish council areas and Welsh unitary authorities about 39. Population counts can vary substantially, even within a single local authority, but the national average is about 5500. More populous electoral wards/divisions tend to occur in large urban areas.[57]

County Electoral Divisions

Apart from the special cases of the Isles of Scilly and the Greater London Authority (GLA), the English county councils are the only type of local authority in the UK, which does not use standard electoral wards/divisions for electing councillors. Instead they use their own larger units, which are confusingly also termed electoral divisions. These county electoral divisions must be confined within district boundaries, but need not be based on whole electoral wards. Like electoral wards/divisions, county electoral divisions are defined by the Boundary Committee for England (BCFE).[58]

Government Office Regions (GORs)[59]

Government Offices for the Regions were established across England in 1994. Reflecting a number of government departments, they aim to work in partnership with local people and organizations in order to maximize prosperity and the quality of life within their area. In 1996 the regions covered, known as Government Office Regions, became the primary classification for the presentation of regional statistics.

At creation, there were 10 GORs, but, in 1998, Merseyside was merged with the rest of the North West. These Government Office Regions are built up of complete counties/unitary authorities so although they are subject to change. They always reflect administrative boundaries as at the end of the previous year. Scotland, Wales and Northern Ireland are not subdivided into Regions but are listed with them as regions in UK-wide statistical comparisons.

Metropolitan Counties and Districts

In 1974, a new two-tier system of counties and districts was established across England and Wales. Six of the upper-tier units, all in England and representing heavily built-up areas (other than Greater London), were designated 'metropolitan counties' and were sub-divided into 'metropolitan districts'. As with non-metropolitan areas the respective authorities covered all areas of local government, but the distribution of responsibilities was different to that of the county/ district structure.[60]

In 1986, however, the metropolitan county councils were abolished although the county areas are still recognized, especially for statistical purposes. The 36 metropolitan district councils were left as single-tier authorities; a status retained to date, and accordingly, has more powers than their non-metropolitan district equivalents. Metropolitan districts are subdivided into electoral wards.[61]

Parishes/Communities

The smallest type of administrative area in England is the parish (also known as 'civil parish'); the equivalent units in Wales are 'communities'. Scotland also has 'communities', but their councils are generally a channel of opinion to other authorities rather than an administration in their own right. Northern Ireland does not have any similar units.[62]

Parishes and Communities

Below the district level, a district may be divided into several civil parishes (with all or no land left unparished). In Wales and Scotland parishes are instead known as 'communities'. Collectively, these are known as 'local councils'. Local councils have various local responsibilities. Typical activities undertaken by a parish council include allotments, parks, public clocks, and entering Britain in Bloom. They also have a consultative role in planning. The absence or presence of local councils does not count towards whether a district is unitary or not. Local councils tend not to exist in metropolitan areas such as Greater London, but there is nothing to stop their establishment.[63]

English Parishes

English Parishes are a very old form of spatial unit, which originally represented areas of both civil and ecclesiastical administration. They used to be significant local government areas but now have very limited functions. Modern parish councils (which may choose to call themselves a town council) can provide facilities such as village halls, war memorials, cemeteries, leisure facilities and playgrounds. They have duties concerning maintenance of public footpaths and may also spend money on cultural projects, community transport initiatives and crime prevention equipment. In addition they must be notified of all planning applications and consulted on the making of certain bye-laws.[64] However, not all parishes have a council—if there are fewer than 200 parishioners, or if the parishioners do not want one, decisions can instead be taken at parish meetings. The geography is further complicated by the fact that several smaller parishes may come together to elect a joint council. Parishes are confined within local authority boundaries but are not contiguous with electoral wards. In some smaller urban areas, successor parishes were then created, but this was not universal.[65] In consequence some areas of the country have parishes and others not, making them an unsatisfactory unit for national statistical production.

Although parishes are affected by the boundary changes of the county districts or unitary authorities in which they fall, they are not contiguous with electoral wards. Many parishes are a similar size to wards, but some can contain several wards, and ward boundaries need not be followed. As at 1 April 2003 there were 10,397 parishes in England.[66]

Welsh Communities

Communities, which fit into and charge with unitary authorities, are the Welsh equivalent of parishes. Their councils have similar powers to English parish councils and may also choose to call themselves town councils. Unlike parishes in England, communities cover the whole of Wales, and this gives them greater potential as a statistical unit. There are 868 communities in Wales, 735 of which currently have a council.[67] Prior to 1974, Wales also had parishes but these were technically abolished when communities were introduced, despite the new communities initially being delineated to the old parish boundaries.

Scottish Communities

All of Scotland has had communities delineated, which fit into and change with council areas. However, community councils (CCs) are not statutory and only exist, if volunteers are willing to run them. In consequence, there are approximately 1,150 such councils, which can represent either single delineated communities or groups of them. There are also nearly 200 communities, mostly in the larger cities, which have no council.

The principal role of community councils is to act as a channel for the views of local communities. They have a legal right to be notified of and respond to planning applications and can be involved in a range of activities, mostly related to local infrastructure and community events (e.g. playgrounds, bus shelters, village halls, footpaths, flower beds, Christmas celebrations). Not all community councils participate, however, and those that do have to rely on voluntary work and fund-raising; many receive local authority funding for running costs only.[68] These councils can however obtain grants for specific schemes.

In fact, although some are supportive, many local authorities tend to disregard their community councils and do not consider them to be a tier of government, even though they legally can have that role. It is only in Eilean Siar (formerly known as 'Western Isles'), Orkney and especially in Shetland that community councils are viewed as an important tier in the administrative structure and have a correspondingly larger budget. Scotland's network of parishes was abolished for administrative purposes in 1973, when community councils were initiated. Unlike in Wales, these new community councils were not necessarily based on old parish areas.[69] As indicated, community councils fit inside council area boundaries, whereas the old parish geography no longer corresponds with any modern administrative pattern.

Local Revenue

Local councils are funded by a combination of central grants and Council Tax, a locally set tax based on house value, along with business rates. The proportion of revenue that comes from Council Tax is low, meaning that if a council wishes to increase its funding modestly, it has to put up Council Tax by a large amount. Central government retains the right to 'cap' Council Tax, if it deems it to be too much.[70]

Council Tax is collected by the district-level council. Authorities such as the Greater Landon Authority, parish councils, county councils, passenger transport authorities, fire authorities, police authorities, and national parks authorities can make a precept. This shows up as an independent element on council tax bills, but is collected by the district and funneled to the precepting authority. Some joint ventures are instead funded by levy.[71]

Local authorities raise their income in a number of different ways, with the council tax in 1999/2000 only raising 25 per cent of total local authority revenue. The rest is made up of central government grants, which at around 48 per cent forms the majority of local government revenue. The Non-Domestic Rate is a charge to businesses, which is set by Central Government and this raises about 25 per cent of local authority revenue with the remainder being made up by charges for services and reserves.[72]

Current expenditure of local authorities is supported by income from three broad sources: grants from Central Government, rates and a residual mixture referred to as other income.

Grant may be paid to local authorities in either a specific or general form. Specific grants provide a set proportion of approved expenditure on particular services. A specific grant allows Central Government to encourage local authorities to pursue particular policies by making money available only for programmes which they approve. Specific grants have increased in importance since 1974 and now account for approximately one-fifth of current grants from Central Government to local authorities. General grants, on the other hand, provide a lump sum in support of local authority expenditure: the amount is not allocated to specific services.[73]

The proportion of local authority income deriving from central government grants grew steadily from the middle of the 19th century. At that time grant was minimal but by the 1930s it matched the rates as a source of current income.[74] The declining importance of grants after the mid-1970s put greater burden on the rates which could only be met either by cuts in services or increases in rate demands. The reduction in the proportional importance of government grants to local authorities accompanied a general attempt by governments in the 1970s and 1980s to reduce public expenditure.[75]

Any local tax should meet several criteria, if it is to be introduced. The Layfield Committee (1976) suggested two principal considerations,[76] first, any new source of revenue should be capable of producing a yield large enough to provide for the possibility of a substantial reduction in both grant and domestic rates. Second, in order to enhance accountability, local taxation should be clearly perceptible. Thus, the level and most importantly, the change in the level, of any source of revenue should be set locally. In addition to these considerations of Layfield, the collection of the tax should not be excessively costly or present substantial new administrative problems. Finally, a local tax should interfere, as little as possible, with the ability of central government to pursue its economic policies.[77] After a careful examination of all these factors, the Layfield Committee concluded "a local income tax on personal incomes, lined according to where people live, is the only serious candidate for a new source of local revenue that could give a substantial yield and at the same time maintain or enhance accountability".[78] Despite the advantages, British governments have not considered it either desirable or possible to introduce local income tax. The reasons are political, economic and practical. The government accepted that rates should remain for the foreseeable future the main source of local revenue for local government.[79]

Councils and Councillors

Local authorities in Britain are part of a wider democratic system of government. They possess in the full council meeting a 'centre of decision-making', but they do not control all public policy decisions within the geographical area in which they operate. Many decisions are taken by local and regional offices of national government departments and other agencies. These provide a network of public services complementing those provided by local authorities.

Despite these possible obstacles, local government has traditionally shown two characteristics of autonomous behaviour. These two characteristics are: control over an independent source of taxation, and the legitimacy conveyed by popular election of the local council. Local government is based on the system of representative democracy. Councillors are elected to make policy on behalf of the general population.[80] Councillors are elected in a similar manner to Members of Parliament.

The incursion of party politics into local government is, some times, deplored, but it is not a new development. The vestries that pre-dated the modern system of local government were sometimes centres of party political activity at the beginning of the 19th century, and this activity was carried forward into the town councils and other local bodies in Victorian England.[81] The role of political parties in local government is similar to their role in national affairs. They recruit and support candidates for election and by preparing local manifestos present a choice between several coherent approaches to policy. Political party groups on local authorities organize themselves with a greater or lesser degree of formality. Increasingly, they are all adopting the full procedures accepted in major cities for many years.[82] The group appoints a leader who becomes leader of the council when in majority.[83]

All the functions are vested in the council itself, and then exercised usually by committees or sub-committees of the council. The chair of the council itself is an honorary position, with no real power. [84]

Under the Local Government and Housing Act, 1989, committees must roughly reflect the political party makeup of the council; before it was permitted for a party with control of the council to 'pack' committees with their own members. This pattern was based on that established for municipal boroughs by the Municipal Corporations Act, and then later adopted for county councils and rural districts.[85]

In 2000, Parliament passed the Local Government Act, 2000, to force councils to move to an executive-based system, either with the council leader and a cabinet acting as an executive authority, or with a directly-elected mayor, either with a mayor and cabinet drawn from the councillors; or a mayor and council manager. There is a small exception to this, whereby smaller district councils (population of less than 80,000) can adopt a modified committee system.[86]

Most councils are using the council leader and cabinet option, whilst 52 smaller councils have been allowed to propose alternative arrangements based on the older system, and Brighton and Hove invoked a similar provision when a referendum to move to a directly elected mayor was defeated.[87]

There are now eleven directly elected mayors, in districts where a referendum was in favour of them. Many of the mayors are independents (notably in Hartlepool and Middlesbrough), and the government is no longer actively advocating the creation of new mayors. Since May 2002 only three referendums have been held, and they have all been negative.[88] Of the mayors, all but Stoke-on-Trent's are mayor and cabinet-based.

The Executive, in whichever form it is, is held to account by the remainder of the councillors acting as the 'scrutiny function'—calling the Executive to account for their actions and to justify their future plans. As a new concept within local government, this is currently an under-developed part of local municipal administration.[89]

In Great Britain, the area, which the council covers, is divided into electoral divisions—known in district councils, as 'wards'. Each ward can return one or more members—multi-member wards are quite common. There is no requirement for the size of wards to be the same within a district, so one ward can return one member and another ward can return two. In the election, the candidates to receive the most votes win—the multi-member plurality system.[90] There is no element of proportional representation. This has been criticised as undemocratic, but third, minor and local single-issue parties do tend to do much better at local elections than general elections, and it is unlikely to be reformed in England and Wales.

In Scotland, however, the Labour-Liberal Democrat coalition agreed to introduce the single transferable vote for local government elections. This is a long-standing objective of the Liberal Democrats, and despite its unpopularity in the Labour Party, no coalition was possible without it. Wards will elect three or four members each. It is expected that the next Scottish local government elections in 2007 will be conducted using single transferable vote.[91]

The term of a councillor is usually four years. Councils may be elected wholly, every four years, or 'by thirds', where a third of the councillors get elected each year, with one year with no elections. Recently, the 'by halves' system, where half of the council is elected every two years, has been allowed. All Scottish and Welsh councils are elected all at once on a four-year cycle. Scottish authorities are chosen at the same time as elections to the Scottish Parliament; Welsh authorities are elected the year after the Welsh Assembly elections.[92]

Sometimes wholesale boundary revisions will mean the entire council will be re-elected; and then return to the previous elections by thirds or by halves over the coming years.

In Northern Ireland, local elections are run instead on the basis of the single transferable vote, with several multi-member electoral areas in each district. Elections take place for the whole council every four years.[93]

Officers

Councillors cannot do the work of the council themselves, and so are responsible mainly for appointment and oversight of officers, who are delegated to perform most tasks. Local authorities nowadays have to appoint a 'Chief Executive Officer', with overall responsibility for council employees, and who operates in conjunction with department heads. The Chief Executive Officer's position is weak compared to the council manager system seen in other countries (and in Stoke).[94]

Much work undertaken directly by council employees has now been privatized.

Functions and Powers

The services provided by local government are related to the social conditions associated with the growth of urbanization; the need to regulate health and sanitary conditions, and to maintain public order. At first these services were administered by ad hoc bodies but legislation covering England and Wales in 1888 and 1894 began to draw them together into modern units of local government. Scotland followed the same pace.[95] In Ireland a similar but slower growth reflected both the political circumstances of the country and the slower rate of economic growth and urbanization.[96]

The Acts of 1888 and 1894 did not bring all local services under the control of the new local authorities. Some ad hoc bodies remained. The responsibilities of local authorities are not limited to those conveyed in general legislation. The promotion of private Acts of Parliament continued throughout the 19th century, and indeed beyond, bringing a bewildering and surprising range of services within the power of local authorities.[97] After 1900 there was a dual development with regard to the services provided by local government. First, there was the accretion of new powers and the growth in scale of those that continued to rest with local authorities. Second, there was the loss of certain responsibilities either to central government departments or to the regional structure of nationalized industries or services.[98]

Districts are responsible for leisure, environmental health, housing, rubbish collection, and local roads. Counties are responsible for more strategic services, such as education, libraries, main roads, social services, trading standards and transport. Unitary authorities exercise all these functions. Approximately, half the total current expenditure on goods and services provided by local authorities goes on education. Housing is another local authority function that grew rapidly after the First World War.[99] Housing represents most of the capital assets of local government.

The Royal Commission on Local Government in England preferred a unitary approach but distinguished between an environmental group of services—planning, transportation and development—and a personal group of services—education, personal social services and housing. Where two tiers of local government were necessary, the services should be divided in this manner and related services kept together.[100]

All sorts of councils also have a general power to 'promote economic, social and environmental well-being' of their area. However, like all public bodies, they are limited by the doctrine of ultra vires, and may only do things that common law or an Act of Parliament, specifically or generally, allows for—in contrast to the earlier incorporated municipal corporations, which were treated as natural persons and could undertake whatever activities they wished to.

Following the reorganization of local government in the early 1970s, the police became the responsibility of the counties in England and Wales and of the regions in Scotland. Local authorities have the right to appoint members of Police Authorities and Fire Authority. These services are often run on a joint basis with other authorities, usually in areas where unitary authorities have been created, to avoid splitting up police forces or fire brigades. However, in some areas, they really do represent a pooling of resources.[101] For example, Herefordshire, Worcestershire and Shropshire share the West Mercia Constabulary. However, local authority control of the police is complicated by many organizational factors.[102]

The current distribution of responsibilities goes against the principle endorsed by the Herbert Commission of giving each local authority functions and powers which are separate and distinct.[103] The present system is no more comprehensible to the public in this respect that was its predecessor. Moreover, the recommendations of the Radcliff Maud and Wheatley Commissions that the personal services of education, social services and housing should be allocated to the same local authority were not followed outside London and the English metropolitan areas. In non-metropolitan England and Wales and in Scotland, housing is allocated to the districts, thus separating it from the personal social services. This separation has caused considerable difficulties and again fresh legislation was needed in 1977 to provide adequate procedures for housing the houseless.[104]

The complexity of the British local government system is increased by two further features: first, the possibility of cooperation between different local authorities, and second, the more formal agency arrangements.[105] Councils may promote Local Acts in Parliament to grant them special powers. For example, Kingston upon Hull, had for many years a municipally-owned telephone company, Kingston Communications.[106]

Internal Organisation

Local authorities are public bodies having a duty of accountability, both to central government and to the electorate in their area. Most significantly, the responsibility for providing local services is shared between appointed officials and elected councilors in a way that corresponds neither to the practices found in private organizations, nor to those obtaining in other branches of public administration.[107]

Greenwood and Stewart refer to the traditional conception which emphasizes the provision of limited, statutorily defined services. Each of these services had a separate department with its own officer. The departmental structure was paralleled by a committee system for councillors. The chief officer and the chairperson of the committee would often work closely together for years to run their particular service. The clerk to the local authority was the principal legal adviser. He was regarded as first among equals by the other chief officers, but the coordination of services was at a minimum and some times non-existent.[108]

In addition to the traditional approach, Greenword and Stewart identify two other possible conceptions of the role of the local authority in relation to its environment that have implications for internal management structure. The 'federal' approach recognizes the advantages to be gained, if the separate local authority services are provided within a framework that allows for economies in the use of resources and recognizes departmental interdependencies. The 'governmental' approach moves away from a preoccupation with individual services altogether to a concern for the well-being of the entire local area.[109] These two approaches correspond to the main movements for organizational change that dominated the1960's and 1970's: the pressure for improvements in administrative efficiency and the encouragement of corporate planning.[110]

Development of Committee System

The committee, as a feature of local government, is generally accepted in many countries. But mostly, committees are created to enquire and to advise, and not to administer. But in English Local Government, committees perform a dual role of advising and administering.[111]

The evolution of the committee system is interlinked with the development of local government itself. During the 13th and 14th centuries, a Parish institution set up to serve the requirements of the church got involved in the business of providing the civic services. The expenditure incurred by the church was a contribution made by the landowners of the Parish. During the 16th and 17th centuries, the Parish, apart from the statutory duties took up the management of services which the inhabitants demanded. The industrial revolution witnessed the emergence of new services thus expanding further the functions of Parish meetings. In larger Parishes, the impossibility of dealing with increasing business by Government of Public Meetings led to the establishment of a Parish Committee. All these various developments of Parish government gave energetic vestries the opportunity of establishing a representative executive. In 1731, in the Woolwich Vestry, after the construction of the workhouse, its administration was entrusted to a standing committee of Governors of the Poor. This was initiated by adjourning Parishes and eventually embodied in various local acts. Another representative committee was the audit committee, which was composed of the literate inhabitants.[112]

Since the Parish Committee did not have the statutory basis, the officials refused to carry out its decisions and, in some cases, committee decisions were successfully challenged by the rate payers in the court of law. The Struge-Bourne Acts passed in 1818-1819 enabled any Parish to appoint annually a Parish Committee empowered to carryout some of the functions of the Parish and reporting to the Parish meeting. Since the acts required local adoption, their permissive nature contributed to their total ineffectiveness.[113] The latter part of the 18th century and the early part of the 19th century witnessed the establishment of various special authorities to deal with matters as drainage, paving and street lighting. Thus in these 'Statutory Authorities for Special Purposes', first developed the essentially English system of administration by committees consisting of representatives of the electorate directing and controlling the staff of the professional officers. When these bodies of Improvement Commissioners became large, local councils began to entrust the executive work to the Standing Committees.[114]

By the time the Municipal Corporations Act was passed in 1835, the committee system was already in vogue and was considered a practical necessity for conducting business, where executive authority was entrusted to a large body. The Act permitted boroughs to appoint whatever committees they considered fit. Subsequently, statutory requirement and the increasing functions of the town councils led to the universal adoption of the committee system by the Municipal Corporations.[115]

Certain committees administer a single service, like education or health, on the basis of vertical division of labour. These are known as vertical committees. Others are entrusted with such an aspect of council work that affects several services. The Finance Committee and the Establishment Committee are examples of this kind. These are known as horizontal committees.[116]

Local authorities were, in certain cases, required to have a committee to administer particular services or discharge particular functions. These are known as statutory committees. This system originated from a desire to ensure that local authorities devote sufficient attention to the services concerned and to promote the development of new services. The general rule is that a council enjoys power to set up whatever committees it may need. This power was given, for the first time, under the Local Government Act, 1933.[117]

The provision of establishment of statutory committees for certain services came in for vehement criticism. The Committee on the Management of Local Government considered it to be an unnecessary interference with local authorities. It recommended that they should be left free to develop and experiment with their own schemes of organization and called for the repeal of the statutory provisions.[118] The interim report of the Study Group on Local Authority Management Structures observed that statutory committees were likely to hinder the new local authorities from being good managers.[119]

The council has both permissive and obligatory power to include persons who are not councillors as members of committees, for other than a Finance Committee. Normally, they should form one-third of any committee. They are known as co-opted members. The principle of co-option enables experts to make valuable objective and impartial contribution to local government work.[120] It also provides a link with other bodies and organizations.

The role of the chairman is very important for the efficient functioning of the committees. Under the old system, a Chairman was elected annually and often the choice was unanimous. Apart from presiding over the meetings he has few formal functions. The Bains report held that though the chairman has no legal powers, chairmanship of a major committee is of considerable influence.[121]

Maud Committee Report

The Committee on the Management of Local Government with Sir John Maud as chairman was appointed in March 1964, "to consider in the light of modern conditions how local government might best continue to attract and retain people (both elected representatives and principal officers) of the caliber necessary to ensure its maximum effectiveness".[122]

A parallel Committee on the Staffing of Local Government was established at the same time "to consider the existing methods of recruiting local government officers and of using them; and what changes might help local authorities to get the best possible service and help their officers to give it".[123]

Both committees therefore were concerned with similar questions and they were serviced by the same secretariat. The Wallaby Committee concentrated on the problems presented for local government recruitment in a time of full employment and a declining number entering the labour market. They also made recommendations concerning training, including the establishment of a Local Government Training Board.[124]

The Maud Committee identified the internal management of local authorities as an important factor in attracting and retaining councillors and officers of sufficient caliber and went on to be very critical of the existing system. Its report was submitted in June 1967. The Committee emphasized that a distinction must be drawn between the undoubted value of deliberation and the shortcomings of detailed administration by committees.[125]

The inadequacies pointed out by the Maud Committee were:[126]

1. The number of committees had grown with the addition of new services for which local authorities had been made responsible.
2. Scientific and technical developments had made the work of local government departments more complex and complicated. Hence, it was increasingly becoming difficult for committees to supervise their working.
3. The system wasted time, resulted in delays and caused frustration by involving committees in matters of administrative details.
4. The system did not encourage discrimination between the major objectives and the means to attain them and the chain of consequential decisions and the action required.
5. The agenda of the committee meetings was too long resulting in inadequate time and attention being given to the major issues. The committee members were misled into a belief that they are controlling and directing the departments, while in practice, they were only deliberating on issues which did not deserve their consideration.

6. The system involved production of an increasing volume of paper work which demanded staff, was often waste of officers' time and was expensive to produce. It also discouraged delegation of responsibility to members.
7. The committee made heavy demands on members' time and hence discouraged persons whose services were really useful to the local authority from participating in the local affairs.
8. Association of each service with a committee and of a department and a principal officer produced a loose confederation of disparate activities, dispersed responsibility and diffused decision-making centres. It was often unintelligible to the public.
9. Leadership and responsibility in the local authority cannot easily be identified and coordination of thought and work was made more difficult.
10. The work of local authorities was fragmented between too many separate departments, and these were seldom coherently organized or led by the Clerk. The result was often both inefficient and undemocratic.

Recommendations

To streamline the internal organization of local authorities, the Maud Committee made the following recommendations:[127]

(i) *Management Board*: All but the smallest local authorities should appoint a Management Board of five to nine members. The board would receive wide delegated powers and be the sole channel through which business done in committees reached the full council. Hence its task will be to lead and coordinate the work of the local authority, whose departments will be accountable to the council through it.

The functions of the Management Board would be to formulate the principal objectives of the authority and to present them together with plans before the council for its consideration and decision, to review progress and assess results of the council, to maintain an overall supervision of the organization of the authority and of its coordination and integration, to take decisions on behalf of the councils which exceed the authority of the principal officers and to recommend decisions to the council where authority has not been delegated to the Management Board and to be responsible for the presentation of the business to the council.

(ii) *New Role of Committees*: While favouring the retention of the committees in local government, the Maud Committee envisaged a different role for them. It recommended that committees should cease to be executive or administrative bodies and should concentrate on policy determination. They should not be directing or controlling bodies, nor should they be concerned with routine administration.

The committees should be deliberative and representative bodies in the sense that they make recommendations to the Management Board on the major objectives, the means to attain them and examine new ideas and review progress on plans and programmes and on the operation of individual services. They had an important role in conveying the public reactions and criticisms to the officers and the Management Board. The committees' task to take executive decisions should be limited to exceptional circumstances. They are to do so only when the Management Board so requires.

The Maud Committee further recommended the reduction of the number of committees drastically. No committee should have more than 15 members including co-opted members.

(iii) The Maud Committee recommended that there should be a clear division between council members and officers.

(iv) There should be an increase in the amount of delegation from committees to both their chairmen and officers.

(v) There should be a reduction in the number of committees appointed by a local authority. It proposed that related services should be grouped and allocated to one committee. It thought that half a dozen should be enough and it followed that each committee would be concerned with a wide range of matters than the existing committee.

(vi) A chief executive officer should be appointed as the undisputed head of the paid officers of the local authority.

Thus the Maud Committee came out with a well laid out plan to ensure coordination of both administration and policy in local authorities by radically altering the type of committees' work and the overall structure of local administration.[128]

Reactions to Maud Committee's Report

The response to the Maud Report was mixed. Jeffrey Stanyer (1970) concluded "that the Maud Committee must be regarded as one of the most disastrous uses of an advisory committee that can be envisaged...."[129] According to Richards (1973), "Inevitably this Report aroused much criticism, a lot of which was defensive and came from those who wished to retain established positions. Because the Maud Report raised fundamental issues about our local government institutions and illuminated serious shortcomings in their practical operation, it stimulated a great debate".[130]

The response from practitioners was scarcely more enthusiastic. Councillors rejected completely the proposal for a management board with its implied differentiation of councillors into board members and the rest. Some local authorities pointed to the debasing effect which the Board could be expected to have on the attraction of local councils for councillors who were reduced to serving on advisory and deliberative bodies only.[131] Almost all local authorities referred to the undemocratic nature of a scheme which involved the focusing of all executive responsibility upon five to nine members of the Management Board.[132]

There was general agreement, however, on the recommendations relating to the committee structure. Many local authorities were already re-examining their management structures. The members of full committees were being reduced from two-three dozen, common in early 1960s, to a more manageable fifteen or sixteen and chief executive officers were being appointed in many parts of the country. There were even some moves towards a central coordinating committee, though none of these shared the characteristics of Maud's Management Board.[133]

Because of the controversial nature of the recommendation relating to the Management Board and its functions, Lord Redcliffe Maud addressing the Conference of the Royal Institute of Public ...istration, declared that the establishment of the Management ... was not intended to be mandatory, and that most authorities ... had some such body whether of party groups or an official ...ommittee. The board was not intended to be an executive ...ich was the function of officers. He observed that other ...s would continue to have a crucial role, their members would be neither "lobby fodder nor rubber stamps". The committee would draw up ideas, formulate policy and assess progress, but would be freed from schedules and sub-committee reports which now cluttered up their procedure.[134]

The Bains Committee Report

Following the decision to reorganize the structure of local government in the 1970s, further consideration was given to matters of internal organization. The Royal Commission on Local Government (Radcliff Maud Commission) touched upon Local Government Management and reiterated the criticism made by Maud Committee on committee system. It pleaded for the creation of a central committee at the core of administration and asserted that the proliferation of committees must be ended.[135] It urged that internal organization of the reorganized local authorities should be studied well in advance before the new local government system becomes operative. So in 1971, a study group was appointed jointly by the Secretary of State for the Environment and the local authority associations under the chairmanship of M.A. Bains, Clerk of the Kent County Council, to examine management principles and structures in local government at both, elected member and official, levels. A similar working groups were appointed in Scotland under the chairmanship of I.V. Peterson.[136] The Bains Report was submitted in August 1972.

The Bains Report, in order to provide a framework for its working, identified nine areas of management as particularly important. The central theme of the Bains Report is reflected in the following quotation: "...the traditional departmental attitude within much of local government must give way to a wide-ranging corporate outlook".[137] The report has been, therefore, as essentially practical though it was heavily influenced by the corporate planning theories.[138]

The main recommendations of the Bains Report are as follows:[139]

1. *Policy and Resource Committee*: In order to tender comprehensive and coordinated advice to the council to take policy decisions deciding the overall plan for the community, the Report underlined the need to create a Policy and Resource Committee. Apart from advising the council, this committee is to coordinate and control the implementation of the programmes.[140]

The Policy and Resource Committee will have four Resources sub-committees on Finance, Personnel, Land and Performance Review. These sub-committees are responsible for routine matters. A substantial proportion of members of the sub-committees should not be members of the parent committee. The Performance Review sub-committee was suggested as a "watchdog body" with the standing and formal authority to make detailed investigation into any project, department or area of activity. This committee will be chaired by a member of the parent committee and would include representatives of appropriate committees. It is to submit its report to the Policy and Resource Committee.

The main functions of Policy and Resource Committee, as suggested, [141] were:

(i) to guide the council in the formulation of the corporate plan of objectives and priorities,

(ii) without prejudice to the duties and responsibilities of the programme committees to review the effectiveness of the council's works and standards and levels of service provided to identify the need for new services and to keep under review the necessity for existing ones,

(iii) to submit to the council concurrent reports with the programme committees upon new policies or changes in policy formulated by such committees, particularly those which may have significant impact upon the corporate plan or the resources of the council,

(iv) to be responsible for allocating and controlling the financial, manpower and land resources of the council,

(v) to ensure that the organisation and management processes of the council are designed to make the most effective contribution to the achievement of the council's objectives, to keep them under review in the light of changing circumstances, making recommendations as necessary for change in either the committee of departmental structure or the distribution of functions and responsibilities,

(vi) to be concerned together with the appropriate programme committee in the appointment of Head of Departments and any deputies.

2. The Bains Committee centred on the respective responsibilities of members and officers. While members must make the major policy decisions, officers contribute to the stimulation and formulation of

policy. On the other hand, members must have an interest in matters of day-to-day administration when these affect their constituents. At the policy-making level, decisions should be taken within an administrative context that allowed policy objectives to be examined against the financial constraints imposed by resources.[142]

3. The Committee also believed that while corporate management had implications for councillors and officers, the identification of one committee with one department should be ended. They therefore recommended that the committee structure should be linked to the objectives of the local authority rather than to the provisions of particular services.

4. The report suggested the adoption of a community approach that would include joint committees of county and district members for each district within the county to coordinate the interaction of all county and district functions and policies for the locality.[143]

The majority of local authorities have adopted Bains recommendations without much change, though their recommendations were intended to be only an advice to new local authorities.

Central-Local Government Relations

The statutory relationship between Central and Local Government is always subject to the power of the courts to interpret legislation in the light of previous cases and general legal principles. The courts are more effective at preventing unlawful action than at enforcing the performance of statutory duties.[144]

The presence of powers to take direct responsibility for a service enables the government to place greater pressure on local authorities that are considering a refusal to carryout certain duties. Griffith quotes the appointment of commissions to provide civil defence services where local authorities refused to comply for political reasons as occasional examples of the use of default powers. He concludes: "Such powers are, in practice, rarely or never used".[145] The relationship between central and local government has on occasion become so strained that the installation of a commissioner has been a more significant responsibility.[146]

Administrative Relations

Central Government departments constantly communicate with local authorities with respect to specific services. The nature of the relationship varies, however, both between departments and within departments when they are responsible for several services. The variations in the character of the service obviously have a major effect on these differences in attitude. Three separate attitudes are broadly distinguishable:[147] one is basically laissez faire, one is basically regulatory, and one is basically promotional. By *laissez faire*, Griffith implies a positive philosophy of as little interference as is possible within the necessary fulfillment of department duties. By contrast, the regulatory attitude is adopted by appointing inspectorate to advise local authorities and to see that the statutory regulations are kept. The promotional attitude is to appoint inspectors to advise, supervise and inspect the service with a view to maintaining and improving standards.[148] The difference between the regulatory and promotional attitudes is one of degree, but the latter is more positive in its approach.[149]

Financial Relations

There may be three aspects of financial relationship. First, local authorities must obtain permission before they can borrow to finance any capital project and are subject to an overall limit on capital expenditure. The control afforded by the system of loan sanctions obviously enables the government to control the capital expenditure of local authorities and to direct it into policies consistent with its existing priorities.[150] The control may be exercised more subtly to influence decisions about policy values. Second, Central Government may influence the current expenditure of local authorities by providing specific grants in support of particular services.[151] A local authority is thus encouraged to that service to the requisite standard as the grant provided cannot be transferred elsewhere.[152] Third, central government may use its general grant to local authorities both as a legitimation for a general influence on local policies and, as a method of influencing overall local authority expenditure.[153]

REFERENCES

1. Muttalib, M.A. and Khan, M.A.A., (1982). *Theory of Local Government*, Sterling, New Delhi.
2. Robson, W.A., (1963). *Encyclopedia of the Social Sciences*, Vol. IX-X, Macmillan & Co.

3. *Ibid*; Chandler, J. A. (ed.), (1993). *Local Government in Liberal Democracies: an Introductory Survey*, Routledge, London.
4. Muttalib, and Khan, *op cit.*; Allen, G., (1993). *Independent Local Government*, European Policy Forum, London.
5. Keith-Lucas, B., (1980). *The Unreformed Local Government System*, Croom Helm. 1.
6. Page, E., (1983). Local Government in Scotland, in Bowman, M., and Hampton, W. (eds.) *Local Democracies: A Study in Comparative Local Government*, Longman, Cheshire, Melbourne.
7. Hampton, W. (1987). *Local Government and Urban Politics*, Longman, London.
8. Webb, S., and Webb, B. (1963). *The Development of English Local Government 1689-1835*, Oxford University Press.
9. Redlich, J., Hirst, F.W. (1958). The History of Local Government in England, in Keith Lucas B., (ed), *The History of Local Government in England*, Macmillan.
10. Hampton, *op cit.*; Byrne, T. (1994). *Local Government in Britain*, Penguin, Harmondsworth.
11. Smellie, K.B. (1963). *A History of Local Government*, Allen and Unwin, London.
12. Singh, Hoshiar (1997). *Local Government*, Kitab Mahal, Allahabad.
13. Jenks, W., as quoted in Muttalib, *op cit.*; Layfield, F. (1976). *Local Government Finance*, HMSO, London.
14. Muttalib, and Khan, *op cit.*; Bentwich, H. (1962). *Our Councils: The Story of Local Government*, Routledge & Kegan Paul.
15. Lipman, V.D. (1949). *Local Government Areas, 1834-1945*, Basil Blackwell.
16. Hampton, *op cit.*; Gardiner, Vince, and Matthews, Hugh (eds.) (2000). *The Changing Geography of the United Kingdom*, Routledge, London.
17. Keating, M., Midwinter, A. (1983). *The Government of Scotland*, Mainstream Publishing.
18. Wheatley, Lord (1969). *Report of the Royal Commission on Local Government in Scotland, 1966-69*.
19. Page, *op cit.*; Loughlin, M. (1986). *Local Government in the Modern State*, Sweet and Maxwell, London.
20. Roche, D. (1982). *Local Government in Ireland*, Institute of Public Administration, Dublin.
21. Rowat, D.C. (ed.) (1980). *International Handbook on Local Government Reorganization*, Aldwych Press.
22. Radcliff Maud, Lord (Chairman) (1969). *Royal Commission on Local Government in England 1966-1969*, Report, HMSO, London.
23. Mill, J.S. (1984). *Consideration on Representative Government*, George Rautledge and Sons, London.
24. Upton, C. (1993). *A History of Birmingham*, Phillimore.

25. Dunleavy, P. (1981). *The Politics of Mass Housing in Britain, 1945-75*, Clarendon Press, London.
26. Singh, *op cit.*; Clarke, J.J. (1969). *Outlines of Local Government of the United Kingdom*, Pitman.
27. www.keele.ac.uk; Keith-Lucas, B. (1977). *English Local Government in the Nineteenth and Twentieth Centuries*, Historical Association, London.
28. Hampton, *op cit.*; Stewart, J., and Stoker, G. (1995). *Local Government in the 1990s,* Macmillan, Basingstoke.
29. Muttalib and Khan, *op cit.*
30. Hampton, *op cit.*
31. en.wikipedia.org; Stanyer, Jeffrey (1967). *County Government in England and Wales*, Routledge, London.
32. Hampton, *op cit.*; Cole, Alistair and Peter, John (2001). *Local Governance in England and France*, Routledge, London.
33. Muttalib, *op cit.*; Local Government Commission (1993). *Renewing Local Government in the English Shires*, HMSO, London.
34. Leach, S. David, H., Gave, C. and Skelcher, C. (1992). *After Abolition: The Operation of the Post-1986 Metropolitan Government System in Britain*, INLOGON, Birmingham.
35. Widdicombe, D. (1996). *The Conduct of Local Authority Business Report*, HMSO, London.
36. www.british-history.ac.uk; Commonwealth Secretariat (2003). *The U. K. Experience of Public Administration Reform,* Stylus Publications, LIC.
37. Greenwood, R., Walsh, K., Hinngs, C.R. and Ranson, S. (1980). *Patterns of Management in Local Government,* Martin Robertson, Oxford.
38. Stewart, John (1997). Local Government in United Kingdom, in Hoshiar Singh (ed.) *Local Government*, Kitab Mahal, Allahbad.
39. Hampton, *op cit.*; Commonwealth Secretariat (2003). *The U.K. Experience of Public Administration Reform*, Stylus Pub. LIC.
40. LGBC (1972). Local Government Boundary Commission for England, Report No.1, Cmnd 5148, HMSO, London.
41. pa.oxfordjournals.org; Keith Lucas, B. (1977). *English Local Government in the Nineteenth and Twentieth Centuries*, Historical Association, London.
42. Department of the Environment (1983). *Streamlining the Cities*, Cmnd 9063, HMSO.
43. www.palgrave-usa.com; Gardiner, V. and Matthews, H. (eds.) (2000). *The Changing Geography of the United Kingdom,* Routledge, London.
44. Hampton, *op cit.*; Leach, S., Davis, H. Game, C. and Sketcher, C. (1992). *After Abolition: The Operation of the Post—1986 Metropolitan Government System in Britain*, INLOGOV, Birmingham.
45. www.westminsterbookshop.co.uk; Stanyer, J. (1967). *County Government in England and Wales,* Routledge, London.
46. *Ibid*; Department of Environment (1992). Policy Guidance to the Local Government Commission for England, London; Travers, T., 1995, *Local Government in the 1990s,* Basingstoke, London.

47. Moore, Brian, Changes to U.K. Local Government Aim to Streamline Decision Making, http://citymayors.com/government/uk_locgov.html
48. *Ibid*; Drummond, J.M. (1962). *The Finance of Local Government*, Allen & Unwin.
49. Hampton, *op cit*; Cole, A., Peter, John (2001). *Local Governance in England and France*, Routledge.
50. Wheatley, Lord (Chairman) (1969). *Report of the Royal Commission on Local Government in Scotland, 1966-69.*
51. www.uk-governmentdirectory.co.uk;Elocock, H. (1991). *Local Government*, Methuen, London.
52. *Ibid*; Jones, G.W. and Traqvers, T. (1994). *Attitudes to Local Government in Westminster and Whitehall*, Commission for Local Democracy, London.
53. *Ibid*; Wiseman, H.V. (1967). *Local Government at Work*, Routledge & Kegan Paul.
54. Hampton, *op cit.*
55. Wilson, D., and Game, C. (1994). *Local Government in the United Kingdom*, Macmillan, Basingstoke.
56. www.british-towns.net;Welsh office (1991). *Local Government Structure in Wales,* HMSO, London.
57. Hampton, *opcit*; Bentwitch, H. (1962). *Our Councils: The Story of Local Government*, Routledge and Kegan Paul, London.
58. www.udbs.dur.ac.uk;Nigam, S.R. (1975). *Local Government (England, France*, USA, USSR and India), S.Chand & Co., New Delhi.
59. *Ibid*; Wiseman, H.V. (1970). *Local Government in England (1958-69)*, Routledge & Kegan Paul.
60. Stewart, J. (2003). *Modernising British Local Government,* Palgrave Macmillan.
61. Politics of the United Kingdom, Wikipedia article "Local Government in England", Dictionary LabourLawTalk.com
62. Hampton, *op cit.*
63. Commonwealth Secretariat (2003). *The U. K. Experience of Public Administration Reform,* Stylus Pub., LIC.
64. Administrative Geography of U.K, National Statistics; Clarke, J.J. (1955). *A History of Local Governmentof the United Kingdom,* Jenkins.
65. Labour Law Talk.com; Association of Municipal Corporations, Reorganisation of Local Government, Report of AMC, 1954-58.
66. Administrative Geography, *op cit.*
67. *Ibid*; Clarke, J.J. (1956). *Local Government of the United Kingdom,* Pitman
68. Hampton, *op cit.*; Stewart, *op cit.*
69. www.algebra.com;Clarke, J.J., *Outlines of Local Government of the United Kingdom*, Pitman.
70. Stewart (2003). *op cit.*
71. Hampton, *op cit.*
72. *Ibid*; Drain, G. (1966). *The Organisation and Practice of Local Government*, Heinemann.

73. *Ibid.*
74. Bennett, R.J. (1982). *Central Grants to Local Governments*, Cambridge University Press, London.
75. www.odpm.gov.uk; Amies, F.A., *et al.* (1965). *Law of Rating*, Rating Publishers.
76. Layfield, F. (Chairman) (1976). Local Government Finance, Report of the Committee of Inquiry, Cmnd 6453, HMSO, London.
77. Foster, C.D., Jackman, R. and Perlman, M. (1980). *Local Government Finance in a Unitary State*, Allen and Unwin, London.
78. Layfield, *op cit.*; Department of Environment (1996). *The Financing of Local Government in Ireland: A Report*, KPMG Management Consulting, Ireland.
79. Department of the Environment (1983). Rates, Cmnd 9008, HMSO, London
80. Hampton, *op cit.*; Thomas, D., 1964, *Local Government: An Introduction to the British System*, Pergamon Press.
81. Fraser, D. (1976). *Urban Politics in Victorian England: The Structure of Politics in Victorian Cities*, Leicester University Press.
82. Green, D.G. (1981). *Power and Party in an English City*, Allen and Unwin, London.
83. Jones, G.W. and Norton, A. (1978). *Political Leadership in Local Authorities*, Institute of Local Government Studies, London.
84. Wikipedia, *op cit.*; Welsh, L. (1967). *Royal Commission on Local Government*, Knight.
85. Ministry of Housing and Local Government, Committee on the Management of Local Government: Management of Local Government, Report of the Committee (1967). HMSO, London.
86. Stewart, John (2000). *Nature of British Local Government*, Palgrave Macmillon.
87. Hampton, *op cit.*
88. Somanathan, E. (2001). Empowering Local Government, Lessons from Europe, *Economic and Political Weekly*, October 13.
89. Wikipedia, *op cit.*; Wiseman, H.V. (1967). *Local Government at Work*, Routledge and Kegan Paul.
90. Hampton, *op cit.*; Wiseman, H.V. (ed.) (1970). *Local Government in England (1958-69)*, Routledge and Kegan Paul, London.
91. www.sylviamlne.btinternet.co.uk; Bains, M.(Chairman) (1972). *The New Local Authorities*, Management and Structure, HMSO, London.
92. Hampton, *op cit.*
93. *Ibid*; Department of Environment (1986). *Paying for Local Government*, HMSO, London.
94. www.citymayors.com; Loughlin, *op cit.*
95. Page, *op cit.*
96. Roche, *op cit.*
97. Keith Lucas, B. and Richards, P.G. (1978). *A History of Local Government in the Twentieth Century*, Allen and Unwin, London.

98. Hampton, *op cit.*
99. Cullingworth, J.B. (1966). *Housing and Local Government*, Allen and Unwin, London.
100. Radcliff Maud, Lord (Chairman) (1969). *Royal Commission on Local Government in England, Report*, Cmnd 4040, HMSO, London.
101. Hampton, *op cit.*
102. www.abcounties.co.uk;Leach, Davis,Sketcher, *op cit.*
103. Herbert, *op cit.*
104. Alexander, A. (1982). *Local Government in Britain Since Reorganisation,* Allen and Unwin, London.
105. Hampton, W. (1970). *Democracy and Community,* Oxford University Press, London.
106. www.direct.gov.uk
107. Hampton (1987). *op cit.*
108. Greenwood, R., Stewart, J.P. (1974). *Corporate Planning in English Local Government,* Charles Knight & Co. Ltd.
109. *Ibid.*
110. Stewart, J.D. (1974). *The Responsive Local Authority,* Charles Knight & Co. Ltd.
111. Sreeram, K. (1979). *Committee System in English Local Government,* RCRTMA, Lucknow.
112. Webb, S. and Beatrice (1960). *English Local Government from the Revolution to the Municipal Corporation: The Parish and the County*, Longmans Greene & Co., London.
113. Sreeram, *op cit.*; Bains, *op cit.*
114. Hampton (1987). *op cit.*
115. Sreeram, *op cit.*
116. *Ibid.*
117. Jones and Travers, *op cit.*
118. Ministry of Housing, *op cit.*
119. Royal Commission on Local Government in England 1966-1969, Vol. I, Report, HMSO, London.
120. Sreeram, *op cit.*
121. Royal Commission on Local Government in England, 1966-69, HMSO, London.
122. Radcliff, Maud Report, *op cit.*
123. Mallaby, G. (Chairman) (1967). *Staffing of Local Government, Report of the Committee on the Staffing of Local Government*, HMSO, London.
124. Hampton, *op cit.*
125. Sreeram, *op cit.*
126. Redcliffe Maud, *op cit.*
127. *Ibid.*
128. Sreeram, *op cit.*

129. Stanyer, J. (1970). The Maud Committee Report, in Wiseman H.V., (ed.), *Local Government in England 1959-69*, Routledge and Kegan Paul, London
130. Richards, P.G. (1973). *The Reformed Local Government System*, George Allen & Unwin Ltd., London.
131. Sreeram, *op cit.*
132. Local Government Chronicle, 1967.
133. Hampton (1970). *op cit.*
134. Royal Commission on Local Government in England, 1966-69, Report, Vol. I.
135. *Ibid.*
136. Keating, M., Midwinter, A. (1983). *The Government of Scotland*, Mainstream Publishing.
137. Bains Report, *op cit.*
138. Stewart (2000). *op cit.*
139. Bains Report, *op cit.*
140. Sreeram, *op cit.*
141. Department of Environment (1972). *The New Local Authorities: Management and Structure*, HMSO, London.
142. Stewart (2003). *op cit.*
143. Bains Report, *op cit.*
144. Hampton (1987). *op cit.*; Elocock, *op cit.*
145. Griffith, J.A.G. (1966). *Central Departments and Local Authorities*, Allen and Unwin, London.
146. Hampton (1987). *op cit.*; Department of Environment, 1986, *op cit.*
147. Griffith, *op cit.*
148. *Ibid*; Allen, *op cit.*
149. Stewart (2000). *op cit.*
150. Wikipedia, *op cit.*; Department of Environment, 1992, *op cit.*
151. Stewart (2003). *op cit.*
152. Bennett, *op cit.*
153. Hampton (1987). *op cit.*; Byrne, *op cit.*

Chapter 4

French Local Government

Introduction

France is a country governed by unitary system of government. The Central Government is responsible for establishing, co-ordinating, directing and controlling the local government authorities. The French Revolution (1789-1799) had a significant impact on the growth of the French Constitutional system. Since the revolution, France has changed its constitution on an average after every 12 years. It adopted three monarchic, two dictatorial, three imperial and four republican constitutions. The present French Constitution, which established the Fifth Republic, came into force in 1958. It was prepared under the instructions of General de Gaulle to give France a strong and stable government.[1]

The French administrative system is reputed to be the archetype of the centralized Nation-State, and it has often served as a model for the construction of hierarchical administrations, centralized under government control and organized according to a rational and uniform conception of the state. Under the nominal authority of the central administration, the field services of the state, the local administration and the many *ad hoc* administrative institutions enjoy a large margin of manoeuvre and a considerable capacity of independent action.[2]

The Field Services

The French Constitution provides for a unitary state. Hence, all the powers of the government are vested in the supreme central government. It can create or abolish the units of local government for administrative convenience. The units of local government derive their authority from the central government.

While the central services are few in number but highly influential in decision-making, the field services account for three million state servants in France and play a considerable role in the implementation of government policies. The field services of the ministries are generally organized at the level of the French 'department' (district) which, since the French Revolution, has been the strongest of the local administrative units.[3]

The field services can be divided into two major categories:[4] those specialized services connected to the central services of each ministry; and those with general responsibilities under the direct authority of prefect in the region or department, or of the mayor at the level of local government. In certain cases, specialized services, at the level of the department, play a role not only in implementing state policy but also in conceiving and executing the policies of decentralized local authorities. Quite often there is an intermingling of state and local services[5] either, because state and local authority personnel work on behalf of the local authorities. Thus the district health authority includes civil servants, both from the state and from the local authorities. Similarly, the district planning authority is responsible for the investment programmes and town planning of most of the 36,000 communes with the exception of the large towns.

In fact, France professes that it does not possess any system of local government. In the Constitution of Fourth Republic of France, the Local Government Institutions were referred as Local Administration units. The constitution had also designated these institutions as the entities.[6] Nevertheless, the organizational structures and rules for governing these bodies were framed in the beginning of the Third Republic, when the great laws in 1971 were enacted for the municipal departments. The law for the communes was enacted in 1884.[7]

History of Local Government

France reveals a swinging history of local government. Considerable municipal autonomy was sanctioned by General de Gaulle administration under Roman Empire, though the autonomy corrupted to bureaucratic centralization. When feudalism reigned in France, the local government obtained new type of freedom by agreement with the feudal lords. The fourteenth century event of centralization in France witnessed a strong tendency for centralization for local government with encroachment of the pre-existing autonomy. During the rule of Louise XIV and Richelieu, Intendants were posted outside the provincial Governors to look after local government as agents of the Crown. The towns of France passed through a chaotic period thereafter until seventeenth century, when an elective pattern emerged. Even then, the hereditary and purchasable elements had prevailed for sometime in local government during this period. The French Constituent Assembly abolished the intendants in 1709 and replaced the provinces by Departments, each presided over by a prefect.[8]

Thus the basic pattern of local government in France was laid down in the French Revolution. The revolutionary lawmakers of the Constituent Assembly turned the parishes of the Ancient Regime into municipalities and divided France into Departments.[9] During the period of revolution, municipalities were recognized as basic administrative units and each unit enjoyed a wide range of independence with regard to the Central Government.

Although Napolean put the seal to the break down of France into municipalities and departments, supreme power was kept under central custody and local institutions kept under the centre. As an intermediary the power was vested in the Prefect at department level. The Prefect as a dynamic and departmental leader, was supposed to represent the national authority and leadership at the locality.[10]

Various attempts were made under Directory and Napolean. Most significant reform was the popularly elected municipal council. The 19th century witnessed universal suffrage and subsequently the election of the town councillor (Municipal Councillor) and the county councillor (Department Assembly) took a sharp change. The Municipal Charter, adopted in 1884, worked stably until Second World War was an attempt of decentralisation.[11] The years 1954 and 1958 saw combined efforts of social and economic change for devolution.[12] Rapid industrialization and urban growth altered demography and put fourth an adaptive challenge to local government. The Central Government has been over-burdened with ever increasing span of activity. The gap between Paris and the Provinces was so distant that many described it as the 'French Desert'.[13] The issue of decentralization was initiated in 1960s and series of reforms were brought out and decentralization of some government services and regional economy could be achieved. The government staged a Referendum in 1969 for regional devolution. The people were asked whether they wanted the regional scheme incorporated into the institutional organization. The reply was a negative vote. General de Gaulle's attempts of emphasizing participation as a right, unfortunately, failed.[14]

Features of Local Government

The most important feature of the local government is its high degree of centralization. In France, everything is centralized and local government units are controlled by the Central Government through the Minister of Interior. Thus the local government is neither autonomous nor self-governing. In fact, it is only local administration, not local self-government. The units of local government are the agencies of central government for the purpose of local administration.[15]

Another feature of the local government is its rigid uniformity in two aspects-organizational pattern, and powers and functions. Throughout France are the same elective councils, the same Perfects, Sub-Prefects and Mayors, the same laws and police, the same school system and education.[16]

The decentralization law of 2nd March 1982 and the legislation completing it marked the Paris government's desire to alter the balance of power between the state and local authorities (regions, departments and communes). It gave far greater autonomy in decision-making by sharing administrative and budgetary tasks between central and local authorities.

A set of reforms instituted between 1981 and 1983 gave more powers to the authorities of local government and changed the relationship between them and the State's field services. The principal measures were:[17] the transfer of the powers of the regional and department executives from the prefects to the chairmen of the regional and department councils; the prefect has become simply a representative of the state responsible for coordinating the field services; prefectoral supervision of the Communes and Departments has been removed and replaced by the jurisdictional control of the regional administrative tribunals and the financial control of the new chambers *regionales des computes*; local authority personnel have been awarded a new stature, analogous to that of civil servant; the regional assemblies will be elected by universal suffrage; the responsibilities of local authorities have been redefined and extended, assigning local management to the communes, social services to the departments, and responsibility for economic development to the regions.

Types of Local Government

For the purpose of governance, the whole area of France is divided into Departments (96). Each Department is further sub-divided into Arrondisements (324). Each Arrondisement is again divided into Cantons (325). Each Canton is divided into Communes (36,000). The other unit is Region (26).[18] At present, France has following types of local units: Department, Region, Arrondisement, Canton and Commune. The Arrondisements and Cantons are created only for administrative conveniences and hence, are not the real unit of local government. Therefore, only Departments, Regions and Communes are the real units of local government.[19]

The Arrondisement does not enjoy a legal status. It is purely administrative sub-division and has neither a corporate personality, nor an elected council. Its primary duty is to reduce and ease the administrative burden of the Department. It is headed by a sub-prefect, who acts as an agent of the Prefect of a Department.[20]

Each Arrondisement is sub-divided into nine cantons. It is also a purely administrative sub-division and not a real unit of local government. It does not enjoy legal status and has no elected council. It is a territorial unit mainly for the administration of Army and Judiciary. It does serve as a ward for the election of the General Council of Department. One Councillor is thus elected from each Canton to the Department Council.[21]

In France, thus, there are three main tiers of local administration: the commune, department and region. There are both districts in which administrative decisions made at national level are carried out by local authorities with powers of their own. Legally speaking, a local authority is a public-law corporation with its own name, territory, budget, employees, etc. and has specific powers and a certain degree of autonomy vis-à-vis central government. In addition, there are France's overseas territories and regional bodies (collectivités territoriales) with special status (Paris, Marseille, Lyon, Corsica, Mayotte and Saint-Pierre-et-Miquelon).[22]

The Communes

A Commune is the smallest but basic unit of local government—urban or rural. The term 'Commune' indicates not only a sub-division of a Canton but also the government of a city, town, village or township. The French language is termed as 'mairies office'.[23] The Commune, as a unit of local government, has a historical background and existed even before the French Revolution of 1789-1799. All the Communes are governed by the same municipal code and have the same system of government. Unlike other local authorities, communes play a dual role and perform diverse responsibilities. On one hand, they function as the units of central administration and on the other, commune is the lowest unit of three tier system of local government. John Loughling and Daniel L. Seiler write, "Communes have two aspects, firstly, as unit of state administration, it is obliged to carry out task assigned to it by the state and, secondly, also to function as the institution of representative government entitled to exercise competencies, not specifically forbidden by law".[24]

The commune is the lowest tier of the French administrative hierarchy. There are nearly 36,000 communes, many more than are found in the other countries of the European Union. The term commune is applied to all municipalities whatever their size—80 per cent of them have fewer than 1,000 residents.[25]

This fragmentation of the commune's structure guaranteed the existence of a direct contact between the administrators and the administered, but did not permit the solution of the demographic, economic and social problems. To achieve this, Government had favoured inter-commune cooperation in different forms and the creation of a two-tier administration. The fusion of the communes was a much more radical step. The merger of the adjacent communes was a radical solution to the problem of reconstruction of the communes, as it abolished many smaller communes to create one formidable commune. The communes had a choice between the simple fusion leading to an abolition of old communes, which decided to become associate communes, maintaining a number of individual institutions inside the communes, such as denigrated Mayor, Mayor's annexes, consulting bodies, decision of constituencies for elections, the creation of local office for social welfare etc.[26]

As regards the two-tier administrative organization, a law was passed on 22nd March 1890, which provided for the formation of commune syndicates. These public inter-communal establishments allowed small and medium size communes to rationalize the creation of a certain number of equipments (la creation d'um certain nombre d'equipments). This situation has led the government to encourage smaller communes to merge to form urban communities (communautés urbaines) or group together in associations of several communes (syndicats intercommunaux).[27]

Nevertheless, since 1945, this type of regroupment revealed itself to be insufficient to deal with the inconveniences of community decisions. As their activities were limited to only one purpose, these syndicates went on multiplying in numbers. It was from 1959 that the formulas proposed to the communities for their regroupment had been diversified. Two ordinances of 5 January1959 created multipurpose syndicates and district communes.[28]

In addition, the law of 6 February 1992 suggested new forms of co-operation to rationalize municipal administration by taking common interests into consideration.[29] In reality, the closer links often go no further than pooling a few services and mergers are extremely rare, as both residents and local councillors often retain a strong sense of identity with their communes.

Like the department and region, the commune has a deliberative or decision-making body (the municipal council) and an executive (the Mayor), elected by the municipal council. The number of municipal councillors is proportional to the population and ranges between eleven and thirty seven.[30] Elected for six years by direct universal suffrage, municipal councillors lay down guidelines for municipal policy, adopt the budget, manage municipal assets, notably primary school buildings and equipments, and decide how the municipal administration is to operate.

The Mayor has two hats, since he or she is both the commune's elected authority and the state's representative in it. As the commune's chief executive, the Mayor carries out the decisions of the municipal council. As the municipality's legal representative, the Mayor proposes and implements the budget, ensures the conservation and management of the commune's natural environment and built heritage and issues building permits. Mayors also have powers in their own right, being responsible for security and public health and having at their disposal the municipal administration, which they head.[31]

As the state's representative, the Mayor is the registrar of births, marriages (at which he/she officiates) and deaths and, is an officer of the police 'judiciaire' and so entitled to exercise special powers in connection with the repression of crime under the authority of the public prosecutor. He/she is also responsible for various administrative tasks, including publicizing laws and regulations and drawing up the electoral register.[32] Mayoral acts are unilateral administrative acts, generally orders, whose legality is subject to a control by the courts, when they are issued by the Mayor, as the commune's chief executive and to the approval of the Prefect, to whom the Mayor is subordinate, when acting in the capacity of the state's representative. In addition to their role in the partnerships, local communes shape the policies through the informal influence of the leading mayors. [33]

So the commune's own powers cover activities, which affect its inhabitants' daily lives. Its economic and social brief, long limited to granting aid for job creation and helping needy families, has been broadened to enable it to play an important role in combating unemployment and social exclusion and engage actively in economic restructuring and development of new activities.

The Departments

The Department, as an intermediate layer of local government, is the level on which social and infrastructure programmes operate. Although, expenditure on social services today account for over half of the budget of the Departments, the role they play in education, rural infrastructure, housing, economic development, highway maintenance and public transport is no less important. [34]

There are 100 Departments in France-96 in metropolitan France and four overseas (Martinique, Guadeloupe, Réunion and French Guiana). The Department was introduced during the Revolution period by the Act of January 1790 and became a local authority in the Act of August 1871.[35] Established in 1789, the Department has developed from a partially decentralized local authority to one with full powers of its own (since 1982). It has played a prominent role in the country's administrative and geographical organization. The department essentially has competence in health and social services, rural capital works, departmental roads, and the capital expenditure and running costs of colleges.[36]

Garrish (1968) writes " It is at the level of the Department—often described, with more or less irony, as the big winner from decentralization—that its effects are most obvious. It is to the

Department that the biggest blocks of function—social aid, school, transport, colleges, many ports—have been transferred. Above all, the general council has been turned from essentially a debating chamber, with the prefect preparing, introducing and executing the budget, to a place of real decision. It has also become a place of hard choices, as the general council finds themselves progressively squeezed between rising revenue costs, over most of which they have relatively little control, and financial compensation from the state which is unlikely to keep pace with them but can scarcely be replaced by local taxes, which are themselves narrowly based and difficult to raise."[37]

Since 1970, the districts (communes) were also be created in rural as well as urban areas. However, most of them were created around small or medium size towns. They were also constituted by the qualified majority but their status differed from that of the syndicates on two points:[38]

(a) They had certain compulsory roles (Housing Service, Fire Fighting Bodies, Attribution of the syndicates existing before creation of the district).
(b) They had like communes, individual tax structure.

The Department is the largest and topmost unit of local government. The French Departments broadly correspond to the counties of England. On the basis of population, wealth and political importance, Departments are classified into four classes:[39]

(i) Horse Class or Special Class Departments (15),
(ii) First Class Departments (19),
(iii) Second Class Departments (22),
(iv) Third Class Departments (34).

Each Department has a General Council as its legislative branch. It consists of councillors, elected directly for a period of six years, in a two ballot uninominal majority poll. Cantons serve as the constituencies for the election. The number of councillors differs from minimum seventeen to maximum sixty-seven. The council elects its own president every year. He acts as the presiding officer of the council. The council has a standing committee, called Departmental Commission.[40]

The Department has a Prefect appointed by the Central Government. He is the Chief Executive Officer of the Department and is the agent of the Central Government. As such, he occupies a dual position. As an executive head, he carries out resolutions and policies of the General Council. As representative of the Central Government, he has to implement its laws, instructions and orders within its Department.[41]

Two consultative assemblies assisted the Prefects. The general council, whose administrative role consisted in advising him and the Prefectural Councils, were transformed into administrative courts completely independent of Prefects. Although, general council began as purely consultative bodies, by the first half of the 19th century, they had acquired the power to vote the budget. Their power continued to increase up to 1982, till law authorized them to make and implement policies.[42]

For almost 200 years (1800 to 1982), regional department Prefects held the executive power in the Departments, but the law of March 1982 modified their powers. Appointed by the government, the Prefect is still the sole person empowered to act on the state's behalf in the Department. A Prefect represents the Prime Minister and all the members of the government, has authority over the state's external services in the Department and ensures the administrative supervision of the Department's local authorities.[43]

However, the law of 2 March 1982 conferred executive authority for the Department on the chairman of the general council. Elected by the councillors for a six-year term, the chairman prepares the council's debates and implements its decisions, including decisions on budgetary matters. He/she represents the Department at the legal level, heads the Department's staff and services and, finally, as the person in charge of running the Department, exercises certain police powers in the areas of conservation and Departmental highways, without prejudice to the powers of the Mayor and Prefect in these areas. [44] Since 1982, the President of the General Council, who is head of the departmental administration, is responsible for drawing up and implementing the budget passed by the council.

The field services with general responsibilities were earlier placed under the authority of the Prefect of the region or the department or under that of the sub-prefect at the level of the sub-department (arrondisement).[45] Since the 1982 reform, Prefects have become Commissioners of the Republic and are no longer both government representatives and executives of the regional and department assemblies. Henceforth, they have become simply state representatives responsible for coordinating the field services of all ministries. Although, he no longer exercises any control over the assemblies of the department and communes, he remains the *de facto* adviser, consulted by mayors, in particular those from the smallest communes.[46]

The Regions

France has 26 regions, 22 in metropolitan France and four overseas. The latter have a special status, being at the same time departments and regions. Regions are the newest administrative units in France. Although the foundations were laid in 1955, they were not formally created until 1986. It was only in 1982 that regions were "first allowed to create their own services rather than use the name of the state. The first direct election to them, at least, has been announced, for 1986 at the same time as the national elections".[47] Created in 1955 to provide a framework for regional town and country planning, the region became a local authority in 1982. Its main spheres of competence are planning, regional town and country planning, economic development, vocational training, and the building, equipment and running costs of schools (lycées). The decentralization reforms reinforced the role of the regions in considering, encouraging and initiating action in the field of planning and infrastructure development as well as generally, stimulating economic development.[48]

The decision-making organ is the regional council, whose members are elected for six years. They are assisted by an economic and social committee, which is a consultative assembly made up of representatives of businesses, the professions, trade unions and other employees' organizations, regional voluntary organizations, etc. This committee must be consulted on the preparation and implementation of national plans, the establishment of the regional development plan and the major guidelines for the regional budget. The committee is also free to comment on any regional matter or, at the initiative of the regional council's chairman, any economic, social or cultural proposal. The regional council chairmen, elected by the councillors, are the region's executive authority. Their responsibilities are identical to those of the general council chairman in the areas within the region's sphere of competence.[49]

The creation of twenty-two elected regions has been an important reform, as they have powers in economic development and land use planning, control aspects of secondary education, higher education, training and transport. Though they do not challenge the unitary character of the state and have few powers and functions, their creation marked a change of direction of the French state.[50] The critics comment that they have a low level of political legitimacy, since important local politicians do not wish to serve as regional councillors. Powerful mayors have retained local communal leadership and their national offices, dropping regional representation. Moreover, the regions do not have vast budgets, they have reduced expenditure development and face competition from other units of governments.[51]

Post-1982 (Decentralisation) Local Government

In the French Jacobin tradition, even though, in principle, the local level implements government policy, in reality, the central government tolerates pressure from local authorities—hence the term 'tamed Jacobinism'. Because of the political and administrative domination of the central, state, local power has for a long time been a residual power. In no other democratic system have politics and administration been so profoundly integrated: firstly, there is an un-elected vertical administrative axis centered on the Prefect; secondly, there is an elected horizontal axis shared between Mayors and general councillors.[52] The two axes are integrated by the local public services of the state (Equipment, Agriculture, Health, etc.).

Despite this, in France, local government is still seen as important in the eyes of the public. For instance, participation levels for local government elections are appreciably higher than for others, averaging 75 per cent since Second World War. Even in these days of political disenchantment, public opinion polls show that, of all political mandates, that of the Mayor is most highly regarded; all agree that elected local representatives perform the most useful roles.[53]

The 'commune'—the smallest unit of local government—remains to this day the traditional preserve of local community cooperation and the main prize after the presidential elections. The minimal reduction in the number of communes since their creation is witness to the permanence of this typically French institution.[54] There were 44,000 communes in 1793 during the Revolution, often retaining the boundaries of the old parishes; which reduced to 38,000 in 1799; and further to 36,000 in 2001. All attempts to amalgamate communes have failed. Thus, for 200 years, the communes and the state have been the two fundamental decision-making polès on the political map.[55]

So while basic principles and structures have not changed and there is a clear distinction between the spheres of competence of the different tiers, the decentralization legislation (March 1982) did bring in some innovations, especially regarding supervision. Some degree of *ex-post facto* monitoring of local government action is necessary, in order to reconcile the fact that the authorities are self-governing with the need for coordinated action within a unitary state and ensure that the principle of equality of all citizens does not override the general interests of the nation, as a whole.[56]

The March 1982 law also made several changes concerning financing. Any transfer of state competence to a local authority must be accompanied by transfer of resources (chiefly fiscal). In practice, local taxes have tended to rise. The reform also extended the responsibilities of the communal, departmental and regional accountants, giving them the status of chief accountant directly responsible to the treasury. Lastly, the 1982 law assigned to a new court, the regional audit chamber, and responsibility for a posterior auditing of local authority accounts.[57]

The process of decentralization has profoundly altered local government in France. The new system is indisputably more costly than the old for the public purse and has led to some fragmentation of tasks and objectives, as local authorities act primarily in their own rather than the national interest. However, decentralization is helping to ensure that tasks are carried out at the most appropriate level of responsibility in all sectors of public life, so bringing greater democracy to the country's administration and management.[58]

The 1982 laws on decentralization, with increased autonomy of other levels, such as the department and the region, have muddied this bi-polar model. Nevertheless, decentralization is today an incomplete process, which is proceeding with some confusion. The question is: is France moving towards the emergence of real local powers, such as exist in several European countries (Spain, Germany, Belgium, and Great Britain), whose political structures are more or less federal? This movement of decentralization (in 1982) was the result of several factors. These factors are:[59]

- Firstly, the increased autonomy of the decision-making process of local government units may have originated in the three post-war decades (1945-75) of sustained and exceptional growth. In effect, this period legitimized the provision of some public services by these units on behalf of the state. In the context of growing consumption, the state felt compelled to use them to distribute goods and services. This provision of services has allowed local institutions to mediate between civil and political society, whilst ensuring the protection of local economic and social interests.

- Secondly, this development would not have come about without the ideological evolution of the central elites. The senior public servants, who were the most innovative and most concerned with efficiency, became aware of the need to adapt the multi-levelled political system to the need to manage the national system, whilst preserving at the same time, a most traditional administrative and political control.
- Thirdly, the new middle classes achieved increased power in municipal representation. This group, made up essentially of private or public sector executives, increased local government pressures on the state in order to acquire financial resources to meet the growing demand for public goods, especially since the 1960s.
- Fourthly, other factors have contributed to this transformation, in particular the difficulties, which emerged in 1975 following the OPEC oil crisis. As these developed, elected local representatives found themselves under the direct pressure of local populations demanding the creation of jobs, necessitating proactive economic policies, and policies of social security to meet unemployment and marginalization.
- Finally, the European context itself favoured this evolution. Several countries (Benelux countries, Spain, Sweden, Germany, Italy) came to adopt institutional reforms, which in different ways, gave local representatives increasingly bigger responsibilities, not only in urban management, but also in economic development, social security, culture and education.

This complex evolution culminated in 1982 and 1983 in the passing of decentralization laws by the newly elected left-wing government. Such a redistribution of power by the state strengthened the resolve of local forces to take their destiny into their own hands. They could thus present themselves as increasingly autonomous actors, capable of mobilizing resources and formulating strategies to implement urban, economic, cultural and other projects.[60]

Local political systems were thus in a position to contribute to the regulation of the general and national political system. As a consequence, a series of institutions were created and a series of reforms were launched which completed the 1982 decentralization laws:[61]

- The new amalgamated communes (agglomerations), in 1983;
- The inter-communal charters, in 1983;
- The communities of communes and towns, in 1992;
- The law for the management and sustainable development of the nation, in 1999; and
- The law to simplify and reinforce inter-communal cooperation (elimination of districts, introduction of 'communities of agglomerations'), in 1999.

The law of 6 February 1992, completed and amended by the law of 12 July 1999, has put in place two possible forms of amalgamation: communities of agglomerations in urban areas, and communities of communes in rural areas. For the latter, the state allows autonomy in the choice of amalgamations[62], whilst remaining mindful of the coherence of boundaries. It also encourages the process through specific grants to the amalgamated communes. Some functions are compulsorily transferred to both forms of communities, for example, economic development and management of space. Others are optional, for example, culture, and sport and social affairs.

The administrative structures of these groupings, in so far as they respect community identity, whilst at the same time assisting the common focus of their energies and resources on precise goals, have seemingly been an undeniable success. There are, however, some pockets of resistance. In 2000, there were 1,493 communities of communes, 51 communities of agglomerations, 12 urban communities and 281 districts—a total of 1,837 structures, which had amalgamated 21,000 communes and 37 million inhabitants. The average size of each grouping was 11 communes, with a total of 22,000 inhabitants. This corresponded to the average local government unit in the main European countries.[63]

However, despite these new developments, many of the old structures have been retained. This has led to a characteristically French pattern: the blurring of the links between the old and the new, confusing both the citizens and their elected representatives.[64]

Since 1993, the Constitution authorizes state government to constitute and design the local authorities in a general framework to suit their individual provisional requirements. Local government in France has "become involved in regional and local development."[65]

The law of 4 February 1995 attempted to return to a management policy, which had been somewhat, abandoned since 1970, reclaiming the notion of the 'country' (*le pays*) as a further grouping of communes. This law was completed by the law of 25 June 1999. By 2000, there were 160 counties, covering more than 30 per cent of France and amalgamating 11,566 communes, or 16 per cent of the population. They are not full-fledged levels of government, but have an associate status, in order to develop common projects or to achieve economies of scale.[66]

The decentralization led amalgamation is creating a curiosity, whether is it possible to speak of local government in the Anglo-Saxon meaning of the term? It would be more correct to speak of an evolution towards real local governments on a mono-communal or inter-communal scale. Today, it is even said that what we have is an evolution towards a 'governance', wherein the actors of civil society (associations, businesses, local committees etc.) are no longer content with a representative democracy, but seek a more participatory democracy based on contractual relationships.[67]

Nevertheless, in contrast with European and American federal states, the autonomy of local institutions remains limited; the central government controls their institutional roles. However, the *a priori* control of the Prefect is replaced by an *a posteriori* process of legal protections (Administrative Tribunal, Regional Chamber of Accounts). At the same time, other technical controls don't disappear, particularly in urban planning, with the possible intervention of local public servants. Furthermore, other indirect controls, such as the planning state-region contracts, ensure maximum compliance with the goal of the national plan.[68]

Undoubtedly the decentralization laws of 1982 have released new energies, and local initiatives have multiplied. The increased number of levels and their growing powers are the source of projects financed from different levels, which, in turn, initiate constant negotiations between representatives in local, national and European spheres. In a way, problems tend to be addressed more at the local than at the national level.[69] The exercise of local government powers in France is becoming more complex, with increased variations and multiple overlays. The growth of zones of uncertainties, in encouraging strategic power plays at the local levels, may be contributing to the formation of local alliances and to the overall opacity of the effective focus of power. The state is no longer the absolute centralized regulator. It tends to become one player amongst many, insinuating itself into the complex network of play and counter-play at all levels.[70] Thus, it becomes apparent that, more than any other factor, it is the process of amalgamation of communes, which is leading towards an increasingly autonomous local government administration, and a new delineation of local government power.[71]

The Mayor

French Mayor is an executive elected by the municipal council. The Mayor has two hats, since he is both the commune's elected authority and the state's representative in it. As the commune's chief executive, the Mayor carries out the decisions of the municipal council. As the municipality's legal representative, the Mayor proposes and implements the budgets, ensures the conservation and management of the commune's natural environment and built heritage and issues building permits. Mayors also have powers in their own right, being responsible for security and public health and having at their disposal the municipal administration which they head. As the state's representative, the Mayor is the registrar of births, marriages and deaths and is an officer of the police 'judiciaries' and so entitled to exercise special powers in connection with the repression of crime under the authority of the public prosecutor. He is also responsible for various administrative tasks including publicizing laws and regulations and drawing up the electoral register. Mayoral acts unrelated administrative acts, generally orders, where legality is subject to a control by the courts, when they are issued by the Mayor as the commune's chief executive to the approval of the perfect to which the Mayor is subordinate when acting in the capacity of the state's representative.[72]

Functional Responsibilities

Local jurisdictions are distributed among rural and urban employment centers. In 1999, metropolitan France contained 354 urban employment centers where employment is at least 5,000. The rest of the country is classified into different levels of peri-urban (remote urban) and rural areas. Rural employment centers are all rural municipalities or urban units, where employment is 2,000 to 4,999 and where the number of jobs available is greater than or equal to the number of residents. In 1999, there were about 330 rural employment centers.[73]

As discussed earlier, the French local institutional context is characterized by three tiers of overlapping local governments. The lowest tier is made up of 36,000 local jurisdictions or localities. The middle tier consists of 96 departments. Finally, 22 regions are at the highest level of local government. Municipalities are responsible for local urban services, building, and maintaining nursery and primary schools and sport facilities, municipal roads and urban public transport. Departments are in-charge of administering social assistance, departmental roads and maintaining middle schools. Regions are responsible for vocational training, economic development and building and maintaining high schools.[73]

In March 2003, the French Parliament amended the Constitution of the Fifth Republic. This reform comprises of the granting of responsibilities and jurisdiction to the local authorities and with this the concerning laws also focussed the Departments and Regions as their main areas for implementing the concept of the reform. The government's idea is to base policy in two pairs, with the Departments and the Communes taking responsibility for management of public services and the Central, State and the Regions addressing the strategic issues.

According to the whole decentralization process, the Regions will now take overall the matters of economic development, vocational training and also the responsibility for the large scale infrastructures. The role of the Department would be of a provider of social assistance and the welfare subsidies would be going to be assisted. Broadly, the management of certain technical staff in the national education system will also be the Department's responsibility. The Communes now have to take over local housing policy and various pilot projects in the field of education, health and the management of colleges and secondary schools and also of legal protection to local people.[74]

Public Service Personnel

On the personnel plan, the policy of the Government for the local collectivities aims to find the equilibrium between two principles that may be considered as fundamental:[75]

(i) The interest of leaving the maximum amount of autonomy in this matter to the local collectivities. Hence, these bodies have their own personnel departments that they manage freely.
(ii) The necessity of controlling the decision of the local authorities for avoiding the risk of straining the relations between the Government and its employees. Hence, the rules imposed by law put a restriction on the local collectivities not to give salaries to their agents higher than those given by the Government to their officers exercising equivalent services.

Since the Second World War, each important political rupture has been accompanied by reforms of significance for the development of the civil service. The civil service in France is highly heterogeneous despite the general rules, which govern it.[76] There are three broad categories of personnel outside the civil service as much who work for the central or local authorities.

The local authority officials include mainly from the departments and communes and their establishments publics, the regions having been allowed their own public officials only since 1982. Before 1982, this local civil service was inferior in both numerical and statutory terms, communal officials being the only ones benefiting from a legislative statute, while departmental officials were governed by a statute decided by each departmental council. But about one-third of communal officials, and more than half of departmental officials and those attached to local housing offices were not governed by any public statute.[77] To the local authority personnel, are added hospital staff, housing staff and officials of the city of Paris, who have their own statutes.

The law itself fixes the general status of the commune personnel. The nomenclatures of the commune employment, their recruiting conditions, salaries etc. are fixed by the Central Government. The commune authorities may decide the creation of a certain number of special posts but these decisions are to be submitted to the government for approval. It remains that the commune authorities define freely their personnel need and take all their decisions concerning the individual.[78]

Until 1983, local civil servants did not enjoy guarantees regarding either recruitment or career. The discretionary powers of the Mayor were very large. Their incomes were well below those of state officials at familiar professional levels. In 1983, a new statute, creating a territorial public service aligned the statute for local authority officials with that for state officials, and allowed for the professional mobility between the two groups.[79]

The continuous improvement of status of recruitment and training of commune officers has helped rapid development of the modern methods for the management of towns and cities.

The Finances

The income of operational section is generally composed of Income from Taxes (43%), Allotment concerning income tax on salaries (25%) and Subventions receipts from other collectivities.[80] Income from Taxes comes mainly from four local taxes, amount of which is fixed by the local collectivity and the assemblies (municipal council of the comminute, general council for the department) without any control exercised from the Government.

These four local taxes are:[81]

(i) Property Tax on Vacant Land, which concerns mainly the owners of the vacant land;
(ii) Property Tax on built up area, which concerns the owners of the buildings;
(iii) Living Tax, which concerns the occupants of buildings, whether they are owner-occupiers or the tenants; and
(v) Professional Tax, which concerns the people exercising activity dealing with various professions.

Allotment representing Income Tax on Salaries deals, in reality, with the resources taken from Government budget and divided between the different local collectivities following certain objective criterion representing their needs. This allotment tries to guarantee to local collectivities the same structure as an old abolished tax, the tax on salaries. Its average contribution is slightly higher than the general tax structure. Local collectivities are entirely free to do what they like with this allotment.[82]

The total expenditure of the communes, departments (districts) and Paris represent, as an average, 40 per cent of the Government's civil budget. Within this total expenditure, the amount of investment expenses (defenses disinvestment) is higher (*est superieur*) by 15 per cent than the amount of civil expenditure of the capital.[83]

The creation of new local resource is characteristic of fundamental aims of reform being carried out, place the public responsibility at the level where they are best felt by the citizens, give the local collectivities the financial means corresponding to their expenses, in order to achieve a more efficient functioning of the French Democracy at local level.

Every local collectivity evokes an annual budget which may be revised within the financial year, if required. The annual budget details the totality of its incomes and the totality of its expenditures for the term. This budget is traditionally sub-divided into two sections.[84] The section details the income and expenditure, which are general and recurring. The section dealing with investment, describes operations of capital formation or the re-imbursement of the borrowed capital.

The decentralization reforms implemented since 1982 "have given local government in France a larger influence in regional development. There has been, however, for many years an underlying tendency of local governments to become more active in improving the French economy. Communes and Departments have increased public investments for serviced land, authorized to grant tax exemptions in depressed areas".[85]

A critical assessment by Prof. Marcon is also important. He writes "Local finance is still the back spot of decentralization reform. Despite the reform of the state grants, the transfer of new tax sources to Departments and Regions to offset the financial burden of new taxes, local finance still suffers permanent drawbacks."[86]

State-Local Relationship

The Fifth Republic has given the executive and the administration a considerable role. Even in domains falling under its jurisdiction, the parliament has in practice lost the initiative. Most of the laws passed come from the government and all legislation proposed by the government must be reviewed by the council of state, whose advice is generally followed.

The role of the state administration is equally determinant at the local level. Throughout the 19th century and until the 1950s neither those elected to the local councils nor the central government has wanted to create a local civil service capable of challenging role of the state administration. It has only been with the urban and economic development of the post-war period that the most dynamic local elites have sought to provide themselves with an independent means of formulating and implementing their policies. Despite these attempts, local administrative personnel are inferior, in terms of both of numbers and expertise. Above all, local authorities lack the expertise of senior personnel and most of the French communes will never have the technical and financial resources for obtaining it.[87]

However, there has been a growing determination of the most dynamic local politicians to free themselves from the supervision of the technical services of the state. Larger towns have created a local public service with more and more of the resources required for elaborating and implementing their policies and certain departments have created technical agencies, independently to the state, to assist the familiar communes.

The organizational provisions of the 1988 reforms were implemented by the contractual rules that the French state introduced to govern the relationships between central and local public authorities. European funding enhances the role of the central state, which takes on the gatekeeper role and, creates more complex networks, whilst learning the elected regions weak.[88] The *cumul de mandates* have allowed local politicians to be both local and national politicians at the same time and to exercise power at both levels.[89]

REFERENCES

1. Laxmikant, M. (2001). *Public Administration*, New Delhi: Tata Mc Graw Hill.
2. Gremion, Pierre (1976). Le Pouvior Peripherique, Paris, (ed.) Du Secuil; Nigam, S. R. (1982). *Local Government (England, France, USA, USSR, and India)*, New Delhi, S. Chand & Co.
3. Muttalib, M. A., and Khan, M. A. A. (1982). *Theory of Local Government*, New Delhi, Sterling.

4. Laxmikant, *op cit.*
5. Raymond, G. G. (ed.) (1999). *Structure of Power in Modern France*, St. Martin's Press.
6. Constitution of Republic of France, 1958.
7. Marmolejo, N. (2004). Leader Values, Leadership Development—Results Focused Leadership Thinking and Practice from Around, www.ComadreCoaching.com.
8. Mohanty, Bijoyini (1999). *Glimpses of Local Government*, Bhubaneshwar: Gyanjuga Publication.
9. Gremion, P. (1976). Le Pouvior Peripherique, Paris: (ed.) Du Secuil; Birubaum, Pierre (2001). *The Idea of France*, Hill and Wang.
10. Chapman, B. (1953). *Introduction to French Local Government*, London, George Allen and Unwin.
11. *Ibid*; Bache, Ian and Flinders, M. (eds.) (2005). *Multi-Level Governance*, OUP.
12. Laxmikant, *op cit.*
13. Ashford, Douglas E. (1982). *British Dogmatism and French Pragmatism*, London, George Allen and Unwin.
14. Nigam, S. R. (1982). *Local Government (England, France, USA, USSR, and India)*, New Delhi, S. Chand & Co.
15. Humes, S. and Martin, E. M. (1961). *The Structure of Local Government Throughout the World*, IULA, The Hague, Martinus Nijhoff.
16. Mintricher, Nicolede (2000). The Prefect and State Reform, *Public Administration*, 78 (3).
17. Laxmikant, M. (2001). *Public Administration*, New Delhi: Tata Mc Graw Hill.
18. Swift, N. and Karvella, G. (2003). A complex system aims to bring French local government to the people, European Editor, Paris: Association of French Mayors.
19. Laxmikant, *op cit.*; Raymond, *op cit.*
20. Marmolejo, *op cit.*; Macffin, Howard (1977). *The Prefect in French Public Administration*, Croom Helm.
21. Mohanty, *op cit.*; Ridley, F.F. (1973). *The French Prefectoral System: An Example of Administrative Decentralisation*, H.M. Stationery Off.
22. Ashford, *op cit.*; Magleby, David B., Paul Light, P. C. Light, J.W. Peltason, *et al.* (2006). *Government by the People*, Pearson Edu çation.
23. Sharma, A. (2005). Local Government in France: Recent Reforms, *Nagarlok*, XXXVII(2).
24. Loughlin, J., Seigler, D.L., France: Between Centralization and Fragmentation, as quoted in Sharma, *op cit.*
25. Laxmikant, *op cit.*; Bennett, R.J. (1993). sons la direction de, *Local Government in the New Europe*, Londres, Bethaven Press.
26. Jean, Mari Bect (2001). The Role of the Commune, in Mary and A. Stevens (ed.), *Local Government in France, Paris, Institut International d' Administration Publique.*

27. *Ibid*; Macffin, *op cit.*; Ridley, *op cit.*
28. Swift, *op cit.*; Arouson, J. Richard (ed.) (2004). *Management Policies in Local Government France*, ICMA.
29. Mintricher, *op cit.*
30. Laxmikant, *op cit.*
31. Jean, Marie, *The Role of Commune*, in Mary and Stevens, *op cit.*
32. Rowat, D. C. (ed.), *Public Administration in Developed Democracies (A Comparative Study)*, New York and Basel: Marcel Dekker Inc.
33. Gremion, *op cit.*; Cochrane, A. (1993). Whatever happened to local government?, OUP, Buckingham.
34. Sharma, A. (2005). Local Government in France: Recent Reforms, *Nagarlok*, XXXVII (2).
35. *Ibid*; Gales, P., Mawson, J. (1994). *Management Innovations in Urban Policy, Local Government Training Board,* Luton.
36. Goldsmith, M. (1992). Local Government, *Urban Studies*, 29(3/4).
37. Garrish, S. (1968). *Decentralization: The Reforms, in An Introduction to French Administration,* as quoted in Sharma, *op cit.*
38. *Ibid*; Stoker, G. (1991). *The Politics of Local Government,* Macmillan, Londres
39. Laxmikant, *op cit.*
40. *Ibid*; Lorrain, D. (1992). The French Model for Urban Services, *West European Politics*, No. 2.
41. Goldsmith, M. (1993). The Europeanisation of Local Government, *Urban Studies*, 30(4/5).
42. Sharma, *op cit.*
43. Wolman, H., Goldsmith, M. (1992). *Urban Policy and Politics, A Comparative Approach*, Blackwell, Oxford.
44. *Ibid*; Jain, L.C. (2005). *Decentralisation and Local Governance*, Orient Longman.
45. Machin, Howard (1977). *The Prefect in French Public Administration*, London: Crown.
46. Rowat, Donald C. (ed) (1988). *Public Administration in Developed Democracies (A Comparative Study)*, New York and Basel: Marcel Dekker Inc.
47. Garrish, *op cit.*
48. Berthon, C. (2001). *The Role of the Region*, in Mary and Stevens, *op cit.*
49. Rowat (1988). *op cit.*
50. Loughlin and Seigler, *op cit*; deSouza, Peter, R. (2002). Decentralisation and Local Government: The Second Wind of Democracy in India, in Hasan, Z., Sridharan, E., and Sudarshan, R.(eds.), *India's Constitution: Ideas, Practices, Controversies*, Permanent Black, New Delhi.
51. Negrier (1999). as quoted in John, Peter (2001). *Local Governance in Western Europe*, London, Sage.

52. Gales, P.L., John, Peter, Is the Grass Greener on the Other Side? What went Wrong with the French Regions and the Implications for England, *Journal of Policy and Politics*, 25 (1), 55
53. Rowat, *op cit.*
54. Laxmikant, *op cit.*
55. Swift and Carvella, *op cit.*
56. Negrier, *op cit.*
57 Rowat, *op cit.*
58. Mintricher, *op cit.*;
59. Woleman and Goldsmith, *op cit.*
60. Laxmikant, *op cit.*
61. Lorrain, *op cit.*
62. Negrier, *op cit.*
63. Sharma, *op cit.*
64. Rowat, *op cit.*
65. Marcon, G. (1990). Regional Development, Local Intervention and National Policies in France: New Tendencies, in Robert J. Bennet (ed.), *Decentralization, Local Governments and Markets—Towards a Post-Welfare agenda*, Oxford, Clarendon Press.
66. Stoker, *op cit.*
67. Bennett, *op cit.*
68. Cochrane, *op cit.*
69. Rowat, *op cit.*
70. Goldsmith (1993). *op cit.*
71. Laxmikant, *op cit.*
72. Marcon, *op cit.*
73. INTRA-INSEE (1998). *Les campagnes et leuss villes, serie Contours et Caracteres*, INSEE, Paris.
74. Charlot, S. and Paty, S. (2005). The French Local Tax Setting: Do Interactions and Agglomeration Forces Matter?, INTRA-ENESAD, UMR CESAER, Bd Dr Petitjean, DIJON Cedex.
75. Sharma, *op cit.*
76. Peter, *op cit.*
77. Rowat, *op cit.*
78. Machin, *op cit.*
79. Rowat, *op cit.*
80. Mohanty, *op cit.*
81. Laxmikant, *op cit.*
82. Meny, *op cit.*
83. Cole, A., Peter John (2001). *Local Governance in England and France*, Routledge.
84. Poniatowski, Monsieur Michel (1977). The Municipal Organisations in France, Golden Jubilee Commemoration Volume, AIILSG, Mumbai.
85. Marcon, *op cit.*; Nigam, *op cit.*

86. Marcon, G. (1994). Governance and Development in Paris and lie de Paris, in R. J. Bennett (ed.), *Local Government and Market Decentralisation,* NU Press, Paris.
87. Rowat, *op cit.*
88. Balme (1995). as quoted in John Peter (2001). *Local Governance in Western Europe*, Sage, London.
89. Gremion (1976). as quoted in John Peter, *op cit.*

Chapter 5

Local Government in Japan

Introduction

Japan is a constitutional monarchy, in which the Emperor is designated as the symbol of the State and sovereignty resides with the people. Democracy is ensured through a distribution of power between executive, legislative and judicial branches of government. It is a unitary state with three levels of government: the national government, the prefectural government and, the municipal government. Both the prefectural government and municipal government are classified as local government. The Constitution of Japan, which came into effect on May 3, 1947, included four articles on local self-government, in Chapter 8. Article 92 of the Constitution states that "regulations concerning organization and operations of local public entities shall be fixed by law in accordance with the principle of local autonomy."[1] Pursuant to this provision, the Local Autonomy Law of 1947 was adopted as a fundamental law for the local government. Thus, from the view of a constitutional system, the Constitution guarantees local autonomy and that local autonomy represents the principle of political system in Japan, which is as important as the principle of separation of powers in the executive, legislative and judicial branches.[2]

There were no provisions concerning local autonomy in the pre-war Imperial Constitution of Japan (the Meiji Constitution). However, terms, such as local autonomy or, local authorities had been frequently used in various quarters. The general trend in local government since the Meiji Restoration (1868) has been for the expansion of local decision-making authority in areas of local concern and the fuller participation of citizens in the local process except for an interlude during the Second World War years.[3]

Legal Status of Local Government

Local government in Japan has its basis in the nation's Constitution, adopted in 1946, which recognizes local government as essential to democracy and establishes it as part of the nation's system of governance. Under the heading "Local Autonomy," Chapter 8 of the Constitution contains:[4]

- Opens with a declaration of respect for local autonomy and its basic principles;
- Provides that members of the Legislative and Executive branches be elected by direct public elections;
- States clearly that local authorities should have a broad range of authority over a broad range of administrative functions, and grants local legislative authority; and
- Imposes restrictions on the enactment of special legislation applicable only to a given local authority.

Accordingly, a number of laws were enacted concerning local government, but the core legislation for dealing with its organisation and management is the Local Autonomy Law.[5] The provisions of the Local Autonomy Law deal mainly with residents' affairs, elected councils, and their executive bodies—all that which forms the core of local government. The law also defines the status of local authorities, including their relationship with central government as well as with other local authorities, and has legal provisions for their financial affairs and other important administrative matters.

Basis of Local Government

Local government in Japan is based on a system introduced by the national government as part of its drive to modernise the country at the end of the 19th century. At that time, the system reflected stronger central governmental control than that of today. Local government's authority has increased substantially since the early post-war period, despite little structural change.[6] Accordingly, Japan has had no experience of any group in a given geographical area taking the initiative to establish a self-governing body through a set of legal procedures, and no such mechanism exists to date.[7]

The Local Autonomy Law specifies that the basic units of local government shall be two-tiered, i.e. the prefectures and the municipalities: prefectures serving wider areas, and municipalities providing local services.

The number of municipalities has steadily decreased since the end of Second World War, mainly to improve their local economy by widening their fiscal base. Many towns and villages merged between 1953 and 1961, following the Central Government's introduction of legislation promoting municipal mergers, in accordance with the Law of Promotion of Merger of Towns and Villages, and the number of municipalities fell to one-third of the previous high of some 10,000.[8] This led to improvements in their administrative and financial capabilities, and helped to promote the growth of local autonomy and the urbanisation that followed. From then on, mergers took place according to the realities and requirements of municipalities, and also following the enactment of the Law Concerning Special Measures for the Merger of Municipalities, in 1965.[9]

The 1965 Law for Exceptional Measures on Municipal Mergers provides for exceptional measures to be applied to associated laws to facilitate the voluntary merger of municipalities. It has a provision for declaring the intent to promote voluntary municipal mergers. Moreover, a residents' initiative system was created. With the signatures of at least 1/5th of the local electorate, residents can demand the organisation of merger conference, allowing them direct participation in the merger process.[10] The merger conference is based on the Local Autonomy Law and organized by municipalities intending to merge.

Features of Local Government[11]

A comparison of local government in Japan and in the United States of America reveals some important features of the Japanese system. First, despite decentralization efforts, government in Japan is still highly centralized. This is evidenced by both the absence of municipal courts, as well as, by the adherence of the prefectures to the national constitution, rather than to their own individual constitutions, as is the case in the United States.

A second key feature of local government in Japan is the high degree of uniformity, with administration based exclusively on the strong mayor system. The Local Autonomy Law grants local authorities basically identical organizational forms and functions, with the exception of Tokyo's central districts and the 12 large metropolitan cities, despite the differences, which exist between the authorities in terms of area and population. This emphasis on uniformity and central guidance is rooted in the belief that the quality and level of services should be on the same plain throughout the country. To achieve this goal, authorities are committed to the principle of applying nationally devised solutions and plans to all problems and solutions, rather than establishing ad hoc organizations to deal with circumstances as they arise. The central government retains primary responsibility for the formulation of policies guiding local government administration in such areas, as finance, social welfare, education, and planning.

Japanese local government has a two-tier system: one tier is concerned with the regional government, the other with municipalities. It enjoys constitutional recognition. The Constitution guarantees local autonomy, with election of governors, mayors and assembly members. The National Parliament cannot abolish local government, without amending the Constitution, which is very hard.

In Japan, local governments have general competence powers. These powers are provided in the Japanese Local Government Act. Through this Act, local government can do anything as long as it benefits the local residents. While Japanese Local Government has a wide range of ability or powers, in reality, these powers are controlled by the National Government, through other act of parliament.

The governors and mayors of the local assembly are elected by residential votes. This system is called a presidential system.

Local Authority Population and Area[12]

The classification of local government units based on population and area is depicted as under:

(a) Population

Population	Prefectures	Population	Cities	Special Wards	Population	Towns and Villages
10 million and above	1	1 million and above	10	—	40,000 and above	30
5 million and above	8	500,000 and above	13	7	30,000 and above	83
3 million and above	1	300,000 and above	41	4	20,000 and above	195
2 million and above	10	200,000 and above	39	5	10,000 and above	633
1 million and above	20	100,000 and above	120	5	5,000 and above	779
Less than 1 million	7	50,000 and above	230	1	1,000 and above	635
—	—	30,000 and above	166	1	Less than 1,000	50
—	—	Less than 30,000	76	—	—	—
Total	47		695	23		2405

(b) Area

Area	Prefectures	Area	Cities	Special Wards	Towns and Villages
10,000 km^2 and above	7	1000 km^2 and above	4	—	5
5,000 km^2 and above	21	500 km^2 and above	33	—	57
3,000 km^2 and above	13	300 km^2 and above	59	—	96
2,000 km^2 and above	4	200 km^2 and above	101	—	163
1,000 km^2 and above	2	100 km^2 and above	188	—	466
Less than 1,000 km^2	—	50 km^2 and above	154	3	632
		25 km^2 and above	83	6	554
		Less than 25 km^2	73	14	432
Total	47		695	23	2405

Mechanism of Local Government

It is said that the local autonomy system of Japan was established in the 1890s after trials and errors, since the Meiji Restoration. The then Meiji Government established the four Local Authority Laws in late 1880s: Shi-Sei (city system) and Cho-Son-Sei (town and village system), in 1888, and Fu-Ken-Sei (prefectural system) and Gun-Sei (county system), in 1890. The Gun-Sei was abolished in 1921, but other laws remained until reform measures were implemented after Second World War.[13]

Japan is divided into 47 prefectural areas, which are further sub-divided into municipalities. There are no over-lapping areas or any gaps between prefectures and between municipalities. In other words, every resident in Japan lives in both, a prefecture and a municipality.

Following the Meiji Restoration, the government began replacing the approximately 260 domains (Han) and local administrative organs of the 'bakuhan' system with a centralized administrative structure consisting primarily of prefectures (ken) and urban prefectures (fu). In 1871, the government instituted a nationwide administrative system, consisting of 72 prefectures, with prefectural governors appointed by the Central Government. Local administration within prefectures was provided by large and small census districts. The Home Ministry, created in 1873, had the authority to sanction or disapprove of the actions of prefectural governors and became the central administrative element in state control by local government.[14]

In 1878, the Three New Laws was promulgated to unify local administrative organization and governance. The first law called for the institution of districts (gun), in rural areas, and wards (ku), in populous urban areas, as units of local administration. Prefectural governors appointed and supervised the chief officers of 'gun' and 'ku', while citizens selected the ruling chiefs on a more local basis, such as town and village. The second law established representative assemblies in all prefectures, but reserved for the governors the power to originate bills. This marked the establishment of elective representative institutions in Japanese government. The third law established rules for the collection of taxes at the prefectural and sub-prefectural levels. Amalgamations reduced the number of prefectures to 47 (3 fu, 43 ken and 1 do) by 1888, further promoting uniformity in sub- national governance.[15]

In 1888, the Local Autonomy System superseded the first of the Three New Laws and established a Municipal Code and Town and Village Code declaring that these units of local government should administer their own affairs subject to the supreme control of the Central Government. The codes provided for the establishment of Mayorship and elected assemblies and specified that male citizens, who met certain criteria of age, family and tax paying status could vote or hold elective office.[16]

In 1890, the Prefectural Code and District Code made further revision to the structure of local government. Prefectural councils were created to handle business, delegated to them by the prefectural assemblies. The District Code made the district (gun) a unit of local government with a chief, an elected district assembly, and a district council.[17]

Districts were abolished as local government entities in 1923, and as state administrative units, in 1926. Universal male suffrage adopted in 1925, expanded citizen's participation in local government. In 1929, local self-government powers were strengthened and local and prefectural assemblies were given more legislative authority.[18]

Following the outbreak of conflict with China in 1937, community councils (Chonaikai) were organized in cities, towns and villages, in 1940. Neighbourhood associations (tonarigumi) were made responsible for the policing and welfare of their areas. In 1943, the government created nine Regional Administrative Councils to coordinate the action of local bodies and further strengthen central authority.[19]

The new Constitution (1947) guaranteed the decentralisation of political authority by confirming the principle of local autonomy. It established the separation of local from the national administration and the direct popular election of prefectural governors and mayors, as well as local assemblies. The new system of local government was intended to break up concentrated bureaucratic power revolving around governors, increase citizens' participation and control, assure fairness in the conduct of local affairs and expand the scope of the autonomous local jurisdiction. In December 1947, educational and police affairs were placed largely in local hands. The introduction of popular election gave voters the potential for controlling the executive authority, thereby providing incentives for the governors and mayors to address the concerns of the local electorate. However, there was strong bureaucratic resistance to administrative and financial decentralization.[20]

Beginning in the mid-1950s, local governments became participants in national drive for economic growth. New national laws for regional development were established in the early 1960s. In response, local authorities competed with each other to receive national government designation as target areas for development, thereby furthering the nationwide spread of the industries. By the late 1960s and early 1970s, many local government began recording their priorities. Economic growth encouraged a rapid urbanization of the population and urban land prices spiraled.[21] At the same time, new urban problems, such as pollution related diseases, traffic congestion and uncontrolled urban sprawl, proliferated.

The intensity of such problems resulted in substantial grassroots protest and efforts by citizens to seek ameliorative policies from local government. Under these circumstances, local authorities began to pioneer new forms of communication with residents, pollution control measures, and social welfare programmes. As a result, local priorities diverged significantly from national ones and contribution to the eventual shift in national priorities from unrestricted economic growth to establishing a higher quality of life. Moreover, government reform efforts of the late 1970s and early 1980s led to an increased reliance on local authorities for the implementation of national, social and environmental programmes.[22] There emerged a broad recognition that local governments had matured in their administrative competence, had a unique role in setting local priorities and coordinating public programmes and were necessary partners of the national government in creating livable communities.

Since the Constitution guarantees the system of local government, no national law can abolish all local authorities or create a single centralized state without a constitutional amendment.

Local Authority Classification

Local authorities are legally classified as, ordinary or special. Prefectures and municipalities are ordinary local authorities, whereas, special authorities include special wards, unions of local public entities, property wards and local development corporations.[23]

Ordinary Local Authorities

Ordinary local authorities share a common organization, area of responsibility and power, and are present throughout Japan.

Prefectures

A prefecture is a local government public entity, covering a wide area, encompassing multiple municipalities.

The country is divided into 47 prefectures (collectively known as todofuken). Of these one is the Tokyo Metropolitan Government, which is a metropolis (to), rather than a prefecture; two (Osaka and Kyoto) are metropolitan areas (fu); and one (Hokkaido) is a region (do). Responsibility for the development of Hokkaido rests with the Hokkaido Development Agency under a Minister of State. The other 43 are ordinary prefectures (ken). The development of Okinawa also comes under the Okinawa Development Agency.[24]

Each prefecture has a legislature called the prefectural assembly. Members of the prefectural assemblies are elected for four year term. The Tokyo Metropolitan Assembly has 130 members. Other prefectural assemblies have between 40 and 120 members depending on the population.[25] Assembly members receive salaries for their services. Although, there are some independent members in prefectural assemblies, these tend to be dominated by the political parties operating at the national level.[26]

Each prefecture is headed by a Governor (Chiji), who is elected by direct popular vote for a four-year term. Candidates must be at least thirty years of age. The Governor, who is the chief executive of the prefecture, has one or more deputies, who are appointed officials. The Governor convenes the Assembly (Kengikai) four times a year. He also retains the right to dissolve the Assembly and call for new elections. His powers include the right to submit legislation, draft the local budget for approval by the assembly to levy and collect local taxes as approved by the assembly.[27] He is also responsible for the local government officials and for prefectural public enterprises.

The Governor also appoints an independent Election Commission, an Audit and Inspection Commission, a Treasurer and a Chief Accountant, but these operate independently and cannot be dismissed by him.[28]

The Governor can veto measures approved by the Assembly but his veto can be overridden by two-thirds majority in the assembly. The Assembly may pass a vote of no-confidence in the Governor by two-thirds majority. Demands for the dissolution of local Assemblies or the recall of Assembly members and chief executive can be submitted to the local Election Administration Commission, if they bear the signatures of at least one-third of the eligible voters in the area.[29]

Prefectures normally consist of a number of geographical districts, known as gun. These have no government status. This is accorded to the cities (shi), municipalities (cho or machi) and villages (son or mura). The designation of city, municipality or village is largely made on the basis of population, and the terms are not synonymous with the terms used in England. These differences in nomenclature are purely historical. There are, in effect, no systematic differences between do, fu and ken.[30]

Each shi, cho and son has its own assembly, its directly elected chief executive and its own local officials. The chief executives are known as Mayors and called as shicho, chocho or soucho. Tokyo has in addition to a number of cities and municipalities, twenty-three special wards, which have their own assemblies and chief executives. Some other large cities are also divided into wards (ku).[31]

Prefectural responsibilities are:[32]

1. functions over a wide area, drafting comprehensive local development plans, forest conservancy and river improvements;
2. functions, involving communication between the central government and municipalities, or entailing advice and guidance for municipalities, for example, making recommendations on streamlining organization and management; and
3. functions, whose scale of operation is deemed inappropriate for municipalities, for example, the establishment and management of upper secondary schools and hospitals.

Municipalities

At the lower tier of local government, municipalities provide the basic services most familiar to the public.

Municipalities provide the following services: [33]

1. functions, related to day-to-day matters, e.g. resident and family registration, residence designation and various certificates;
2. functions, concerned with public health and safety and

environmental conservation e.g. fire services, refuse and sewage disposal, water supply and public parks;
3. functions, connected with urban development, e.g. city planning, construction and maintenance of roads, rivers and other public facilities; and
4. functions, concerning the establishment and management of various municipal facilities, including public halls, nurseries, primary and lower secondary schools and libraries.

Municipalities are further broken down into cities, towns, and villages. As of April 2004, there were 3,100 municipalities. A municipality must satisfy certain conditions to be considered a city, including a population requirement of at least 50,000. Towns and villages are usually found in so called counties (gun), but the title is purely geographical and has no administrative significance.[34] Towns are more urbanized with more persons engaged in commerce and industry, but of administrative functions and authority.

Special Local Authorities[35]

These have special nature and circumstances. There are following types of special local authorities:

- *Special Wards*: These are found only in Tokyo, and there are 23, in all. Their functions are similar to municipalities, with exceptions of fire services. Mayors and councillors of wards are directly elected.
- *Municipal Cooperatives*: Municipal cooperatives are usually formed by two or more municipalities to carry out functions, that would be more effective and efficient, if provided alone. The following types of cooperatives are possible:

  (i) Partial cooperatives, formed to provide specific services such as the establishment and management of schools and hospitals;
  (ii) Wide-area unions, formed to plan and provide services over a wide area in a comprehensive and systematic manner;
  (iii) Administrative cooperatives, formed to carry out all the administrative duties of a number of towns and villages;
  (iv) Full cooperatives formed to carry out all the services of a number of towns and villages.

- *Property Wards*: These are special authorities formed by certain property-owning areas or districts within a municipality for the purposes of property management. Property wards are fairly common in farming in mountain villages, but less so in urban areas. The most common properties involved are mountain forests, while others include irrigation channels, marshland, cemeteries, housing land, farms, and hot springs.
- *Local Development Corporations*: Formed by two or more ordinary local authorities, local development corporations are set up specifically to acquire and prepare sites for the construction of public facilities in areas subject to comprehensive development plans.

Prefectural-Municipal Relationship

Prefectures and municipalities are mutually independent entities. The legal relationships between them are not one of superior and subordinate. The scope of their functions differs because of the difference in their basic nature. While a prefecture is a regional public entity covering a wide area that includes multiple municipalities within that area, a municipality is a basic unit of local government closely related to people's daily lives. Prefectures may give local municipalities various guidance and advice from a wider regional perspective. Some prefectural business involves granting approvals to municipalities.[36]

Ternds in Local Autonomy: Decentralization

There have been many proposals to promote decentralisation since the Shoup Recommendation of 1949. Particularly in recent years, there have been strong demands to cope with the changing international community and the ageing society, and to correct the uni-polar concentration in Tokyo, while building local communities with individual character.[37]

In face of the need to develop dynamic, unique regional societies, where citizens are able to live comfortable and affluent lives, the role of the local government continues to grow, as the comprehensive administrative entity in the region. At the same time, however, it must respond to the socio-economic changes of globalization, demographic changes of a declining population and birthrate and the ageing of society, and advances in the Information Technology revolution, as well as, the diverse needs of the people.[38]

To respond to the needs of the people, administrative decentralisation, founded on the conviction that local government services should be handled closer to the people in their local communities, has become an important issue. For this purpose, the Decentralisation Promotion Law, aimed at promoting systematic and general advances in government decentralisation, was legislated in May 1995.[39] The Decentralisation Promotion Committee, formed under the Law, examined specific guidelines in developing a decentralisation plan and submitted five recommendations over a period of time, including the abolition of the delegated administrative service system. On the national government level, the Decentralisation Promotion Plan was adopted with cabinet approval, and the Omnibus Decentralisation Act was adopted in July, 1999. The Act marked the transition from the centralised government administration system, that was developed in the Meiji Period, to a decentralised scheme and holds great significance in promoting the transfer of power to local governments. The Act was enacted in April 2000, and the promotion of decentralisation is entering full-scale implementation.[40]

Major points of the decentralisation reform under enforcement of the Omnibus Decentralisation Act are the following:[41]

(i) *Clarification of the respective roles of central and local governments*—The central government should assume responsibility primarily for international affairs and matters in which nation-wide unified decision-making is desirable, while the administration of affairs close to the people should, to the extent possible, be entrusted to local government.

(ii) *Abolition of the system of delegated functions*—In order to build a new equal and cooperative relationship between central and local government, the system of delegated functions will be abolished and the functions of local government will be restructured into self-governing functions and statutory entrusted functions. Accordingly, the local administrative official system shall be abolished.

(iii) *Re-examination of central government participation*—The Local Autonomy Law establishes the basic principles for participation, the basic types of participation for new administrative categories, the procedures for participation, and the procedures for handling disputes concerning such participation. Participation, pertaining to Individual Laws, is kept to a bare minimum, in line with the basic types.

(iv) *Promotion of the delegation of authority*—Central government authority is transferred to prefectures, and prefectural authority is transferred to cities, towns, and villages in accordance with the amendment of the Individual Laws. In conjunction with this, the special case city system was established, in accordance with the amendment of the Local Autonomy Law.

(v) *Curbing regulatory obligations*—Out of respect for the self-organising rights of local governments and to promote more rational and effective administration, the system, wherein central government regulations impose obligations on local government to establish organisations or employment, shall be abolished or relaxed in accordance with the amendment of the Individual Laws.

(vi) *Establish local government administrative systems*—Promote voluntary mergers of municipalities, revitalize local assemblies, and ease the requirements for core cities, in order to improve the administrative and financial capabilities of local government and establish local administrative systems.

Improvement of the Local Administrative Structure

As the trend towards decentralisation continues, the public has become aware of the need to address the task of improving the structure of local government, the driving force behind decentralisation. A series of changes in the system have been made towards strengthening the administrative and financial capabilities of local authorities. On their part, the local authorities are stepping up their own efforts to improve their administrative structures.

Designated Cities

Cities, that have population of 5 lakhs or more and are approved by cabinet order, are defined by the Local Autonomy Law as designated cities. In practice, however, cities, with population of one million or more or with population of 800,000 or more but expected to reach one million in the future, are being designated as such. Presently, there are 13 designated cities. Designated cities are authorised to administer the same level of governmental jurisdiction as prefectures in 19 policy areas including social welfare, public health, and urban planning. Some laws also delegate to the designated cities authority in such areas, as national road management and compulsory education.[42]

Core Cities

The Core City System was introduced by a partial amendment to the Local Autonomy Law, in June 1994. The system was designed to give stronger authority to larger cities, which are functioning as the core of their respective regions. Cities, that have a population of at least 3 lakhs but less than 5 lakhs and land area of over 100 sq km, are designated as core cities. There were 35 core cities as of April 2004. In addition to establishing public health centres, the core cities may undertake all the functions delegated to the designated cities, with the exception of those, which may be more efficient, if handled in an integrated manner by prefectures.[43]

Special Case Cities

The Special Case City system was introduced on April 1, 2000. It is intended to promote the conveyance of authority to cities, towns, and villages. Cities, that have a population over 2 lakhs and are designated by cabinet order, are known as special case cities. There were 40 such cities as of April 2004. Special case cities are delegated the same functions, as delegated to core cities, with the exception of those, that may be more efficiently handled in an integrated manner by prefectures.[44]

Local Authority Organisation

An ordinary local authority consists of an executive branch and a legislature. The legislature determines budgets, enacts local legislation and makes decisions on its policies. It includes the prefectural or municipal assembly.[45]

The executive branch implements the policies decided by the legislature. It includes governors, mayors and their executive committees.

Local government in Japan is based on the presidential system, where governors, mayors, and councillors are directly elected, and functions on the principle of separation of powers and internal checks and balances to ensure democratic local administration.[46]

The Elected Council [47]

The Council, consisting of directly elected councillors, is responsible for deciding the policies of the local government. Councillors are elected for a term of four years. They cannot concurrently be members of the Diet, serve as councillors in another area, nor serve as governors, mayors or regular officials, or hold any other jobs, that could interfere with their official responsibilities.

The system of determining the number of councillors was changed in January 2003. In the previous system, the number of councillors was fixed by law according to population, but may be reduced by local bylaws. The system was changed in accordance with the amendment of the Local Autonomy Law, by the Omnibus Decentralization Act, to the current system, wherein local authorities determine the number of councilors by enacting bylaws, and the maximum number is fixed by law and based on the population of the each area.

The council has the right to vote on all matters within its jurisdiction, most importantly the right to approve, amend or abolish bylaws, and the right to determine budgets.

The council elects its chairman and members to the election committee.

It has rights to inspect documents on the local authority's affairs, to demand the governor, mayor or any other executive body to submit reports, to examine the management of the authority's work and the execution of their resolutions, and to audit the receipts and disbursements of the authority. It can similarly conduct its own investigation and inspect written records, as well as requires the testimony of electors and others concerned.

Governors and Mayors are empowered to call council meetings, though a quorum of one-quarter of the council members can demand that an extraordinary meeting be called. Regular meetings are held, at most, four times a year, and any matter can be discussed there. Extraordinary meetings are held, as necessary, on the basis of an advance agenda.

Councillors, as well as Governors and Mayors, have the right to introduce bills, although specific kinds of bills are the prerogative of one side, e.g., budget bills are exclusively the responsibility of governors and mayors.

Administrative Committees

To prevent the over concentration of power in one place, the executive branch also includes a number of administrative committees, independent of the Governor or Mayor. Administrative committees are as follows:[48]

Boards of Education

Prefectures and municipalities each have their own Board of Education. Members are appointed by the governor or mayor, with the approval of council, for four years. Boards are responsible to execute affairs concerning education, science and culture.

A superintendent of education is appointed by the board to manage the affairs. The superintendent is responsible for executing all affairs of the board under its direction and supervision.[49]

Public Safety Committees

Prefectural bodies, not established in municipalities, whose members are appointed by governors, with council approval, to serve three-year term, public safety committees supervise prefectural police headquarters and the services they provide.[50]

Election Committees

Election committees are established in every prefecture and municipality. Members are elected at council meetings from among electors and serve four-year terms. Election committees manage all local elections in their respective areas, as well as, election affairs at the national level. Municipal election committees look after the election affairs of governors and councillors in their prefectures.[51]

Thus, the structure of local government in Japan seems tidy and logical. It also appears comparatively efficient and to employ relatively fewer officials than local administrations in the USA and U.K. But local autonomy is strictly circumscribed and controlled by the centre. Each prefecture finds that it needs a strong liaison office in Tokyo, which had to spend most of its time negotiating with central government bodies to get necessary permissions and funds from the centre.[52]

Governors and Mayors are, although elected officials, come up through the local bureaucracy, in which they may have been placed from central government. This ensures that local affairs are in the hands of experienced executives, but it also tends to depoliticize and bureaucratize local administrations. Local autonomy in Japan is, thus not as great as it would seem on the surface, although despite various successful moves to decentralize administration, prefectures are run in a much more democratic way than they are under the pre-war system, where Governors were appointed.[53]

Governor and Mayor

The Governors and Mayors are elected to serve four year terms. They are not permitted to simultaneously serve as members of the Diet or local councillors, or to be regular officials. They cannot act as contractors to the local authority.

They are responsible for ensuring the overall consistency of the local authority's services and functions, and are authorized to represent the authority externally. Governors and Mayors, thus, exercise general control over other executive organs, such as administrative committees. Important powers given to local chief executives include rights to enact regulations, to draft budgets, to introduce bills, and to appoint members of administrative committees, as well as vice Governors, Deputy Mayors, a Chief Accountant, treasurer and other officials of their respective local authorities. In addition to these powers, they are responsible for the execution of all affairs of the local authority excluding those of the elected council and the administrative committees.[54]

Functional Responsibilities

The local governments in Japan have basically two kinds of functions: Delegated Functions and Entrusted Functions.

Delegated functions were entrusted to the heads of local government authorities, as agents of the Central Government or the upper tier of local government, according to statutes. This formed a key part of Japan's centralized administrative system. It had long been pointed out. This obscured the location of responsibility and obstructed the establishment of cooperative relations between central and local government. In accordance with the amendment of the Local Autonomy Law by the Omnibus Decentralised Act, which took effect in April 2000, delegated functions were abolished and the functions of local government were restructured into self governing functions and statutory entrusted functions.[55]

Statutory entrusted functions are certain previously delegated functions that have been restructured from the standpoints of convenience to the people, operational efficiency, and how best to allocate roles, between central and local government. Statutory entrusted functions are the functions, handled by local governments, based on statutes or cabinet order that should, in fact, be the responsibility of the central government (or prefectural government), but are entrusted to local governments to ensure their proper handling.[56]

According to the Local Autonomy Law, local governments cannot administer the judicial affairs, punishment and national disciplinary actions, national transportation and communication, postal services, national educational and training institutions, national hospital and medical treatment, national navigation, meteorology and waterways, and national museums and libraries. Local governments may deal with any matter, excepting the above, exclusively national affairs. The Local Authority Law specifies 22 activities as illustration of the scope of local government responsibilities. It also specifies the following four criteria to be employed in determining the responsibilities of prefectural government:[57] sphere of administration, the necessity of unified administration, communication and adjustment among municipal governments, and the administration, which deemed not be handled by the municipal government.

According to the Constitution, local governments have the right to enact their own regulation for the purpose of executing their wide ranging activities. Most of the items are imposed by the laws and ordinances of the national government to be performed by the local government.[58]

In Japan, the prefectural Governors and Mayors and administrative committees are appointed as agents of the national government. They are delegated with the administration of affairs, in accordance with the laws and ordinances. The system is known as Kikan-Inin-Jimu (agency delegated functions). It is executed by the organization, personnel and budget of the local government. However, the execution is subject to various restrictions, which limit the autonomy. On the execution of those activities, the competent minister directs and supervises the governor, and the competent minister and the prefectural governor direct and supervise the mayor of municipalities. This system is not fundamentally different from the Chihokan-Kansei. Local assemblies do not have any decision-making power over these activities, nor do they have the right to review official papers or to inspect and examine the execution of these administrative affairs.[59] They merely have the right to demand explanations from the chief executives and to express their opinions.

The prefectural and municipal governments are vested with the power to execute other affairs as provided by law. These affairs are normally known as Dantai-Inin-Jimu (affairs delegated to the corporation).

Local governments, in addition, have discretionary powers over services and regulation. However, in reality, local governments are confronted with a variety of obstacles, such as limited financial resources.

More specifically, the administrative activities flow in a vertical manner from national government bureaus through prefectural bureaus and down to the municipal decisions in charge.

Local authorities are responsible for administering local public services, including planning, construction and maintenance, as well as regulating and managing facilities in the following areas:[60]

(a) local courts and police,
(b) hospitals, welfare, burial arrangements and environmental protection,
(c) infrastructure, such as local roads, bridges, transport, land development, water and sewerage, gas and electric power supplies, parks and playgrounds, and
(d) education and culture, e.g. schools, laboratories, libraries, museums, sports facilities etc.

Major areas of local government expenditure are education, which take up more than a quarter of local spending; public works, which absorbs about a fifth of local expenditure; health; sanitation; social welfare; and public security.

Local Revenue

Local authorities are empowered to manage their own financial affairs, and sources of revenue are guaranteed, in a number of ways. Local tax revenues occupy a considerable part of the total revenue of local governments. In addition to local tax, local governments gain revenues from fees and charges and income from properties, but these revenues account for only a small portion of the total amount. More than 60 per cent of the final local expenditure is accounted for by the transfer, including local bond revenues from the national government.[61]

Local revenues include the distribution of local allocation tax grants, national treasury disbursements (subsidies) and local bonds.[62] The purpose of the distribution of local allocation tax grants is explained as a financial adjustment between the national government and local government and as a supplement for the general revenues of local government. The source of grants comes from the national tax revenue and claims 32 per cent of total amount of the corporate tax, personal income tax and liquor tax. The amount of subsidy is calculated on the discrepancy between the amount of basic financial needs and the amount of basic financial revenues.[63] The basic financial revenue is equivalent to 80 per cent of total local taxes, fees and charges, in the case of prefectural governments, and 75 per cent, in the case of municipal governments. The basic financial needs are determined by the necessary expenses, which each local government requires to carryout "rationalized and appropriate" administrative activities under a certain standard of conditions.[64]

Thus the financial situation of local government is deeply integrated with the financial and monetary policies of national government. The prefectural governments are under the control of the national government, while they, in turn, act as controlling organs, with respect to local allocation tax grants, national treasury disbursements, and local bonds, to the municipal governments.[65]

Local governments spend nearly three quarters of Japan's revenue. Appropriately 40 per cent of this, comes from central government allocations and the rest is met from local taxes and other local revenue. The Central Government has effective control on local government expenditure.[66]

Poorer prefectures benefit more than richer ones in the allocation of central government funds. Part of central government's allocation to local authorities is earmarked for specific purposes, but some allocations are made specifically for the performance of functions delegated to local governments. Local governments are permitted to do some deficit financing through the issuing of bonds, on their own guarantee, redeemable after a few years.[67]

Prefectures and municipalities are authorized to levy local income tax (inhabitants tax). This is in two parts. One part is based on total income, and the other part is a per capita tax. Prefectures can also levy corporate and business taxes, as well as, taxes on amusements, meals and automobiles. Prefectures and municipalities, in addition, levy taxes on tobacco, and municipalities, on electricity and gas supplies. Some income is derived from the issuing of permits and from the sale or leasing of public land.[68]

The Local Allocation Law requires local authority estimates to be determined by the cabinet, submitted to the Diet and subsequently published. The programme allows for verification that the local authority revenues will be sufficient to provide a given level of services, as well as, meet their delegation. It also helps local authorities match their economic and fiscal policies with those of the central government and acts as a guideline for fiscal management.

Local authorities are able to levy and collect local taxes under the provisions of the Local Tax Law. Local tax has many components. A local consumption tax was introduced in April 1997, and the total amount of revenue from this is accounted for as prefectural revenue. Local taxes account for approximately 42 per cent of the country's total tax revenues. Prefectural taxes make up 30 per cent of total prefecture revenues, while the municipalities represent 34 per cent.[69]

The Local Allocation Tax allows the Central Government to balance local authority revenues and guarantee a standard level of service. The system provides for certain percentage of national tax revenues to be set aside as a common revenue source for local authorities. The system rectifies inequity of financial capability among local authorities caused by uneven distribution of tax revenue resources. Of the annual total set aside for local allocation tax, 94 per cent is distributed to level out the differences in individual financial capability, the remaining 6 per cent is set aside for extraordinary cases, such as natural disasters.[70]

The Local Finance Law provides that local authorities should use revenues other than that from local bounds to finance their expenditure, but the law permits them to issue bonds to finance capital expenditures, such as construction of public facilities, and to cover the expenses of public enterprises. In accordance with the Omnibus Decentralization Act (April, 2000), starting in April 2005, the issuance of local bonds has been changed from the current system, in which central government permission is required, to a local consensus system.[71]

In addition, there are national government disbursements and a local transfer tax. There are three types of national government disbursements: national treasury obligatory shares, grants-in-aid, and payment for agential tasks. National treasury obligatory shares are payable for undertakings, that are carried out under the joint responsibility of the Central and Local Governments. National treasury grants-in-aid are distributed as subsidies for local undertakings (e.g. improvement of sewerage systems). National treasury payment for agential tasks are concerned with undertakings, which are, in fact, the responsibility of the central government, but are entrusted to local authorities for convenience and efficiency (e.g. election expenses for Diet members).[72]

There is also the local transfer tax. This was originally a direct source of income for all local authorities, but for greater convenience, collection was subsequently arranged nationally for redistribution to local government on an objective basis. The local transfer tax falls somewhere between local taxes and the local allocation tax, and a typical example is the local road tax on fuels, such as petrol.[73]

The Local Tax System in Japan may be summarized as under:

Local Taxes	Prefectural Taxes	Ordinary Taxes	— Prefectural Residents Tax (Individual, Corporation, Interest)
			— Business Tax (Individual, Corporation)
			— Local Consumption Tax
			— Real Estate Acquisition Tax
			— Prefectural Tobacco Tax
			— Golf Links Tax
			— Automobile Tax
			— Mine-lot Tax
			— Prefectural Non-Statutory Ordinary Tax
		Objective Taxes	— Automobile Acquisition Tax
			— Light Oil Delivery Tax
			— Hunting Tax
			— Water and Land Utility Tax

(Contd.)

		— Accommodation Tax (Prefectoral Non-Statutory Objective Tax)
Municipal Taxes	Ordinary Taxes	— Municipal Residents Tax (Individual, Corporation)
		— Fixed Assets Tax*
		— Light Motor Vehicle Tax
		— Municipal Tobacco Tax
		— Mineral Product Tax
		— Special Land Ownership Tax*
		— Non-Statutory Tax
	Objective Taxes	— Spa Tax
		— Business Office Tax*
		— City Planning Tax*
		— **Water and Land Utility Tax**
		— **Common Facility Tax**
		— **Building Land Development Tax**
		— National Health Insurance Tax
		— Non-Statutory Tax

Notes:

1. Figures marked with * among those for municipal taxes referred to metropolitan tax in the 23 special wards. Municipal taxes applying to corporations are imposed as metropolitan resident tax in the 23 special wards.
2. Bold indicates that the tax is not levied in Tokyo Metropolis.
3. Accommodation Tax is a Prefectoral Non-Statutory Objective Tax, which is a special tax levied by the Tokyo Metropolitan Government.
4. The Special Land Ownership Tax has been suspended since fiscal 2003.

Source: Tokyo Metropolitan Government, 2006.

Local Government Personnel

Most local government employees are on life time employment. That usually means the local government authority, the Governors or Mayors, employ the local government employees immediately after they graduate from university. Employees then have to work in the same organization until they reach retirement age. This system is called the career system.[74]

Local government personnel are classified either as "special" or "regular." Directly elected Governors, Mayors and councillors, as well as members of boards of education and other administrative committees, together with temporary or part-time advisers, researchers and so on, are "special." The Local Government Personnel Law, which defines the status of local government officers, does not apply on them. Others are classified as "regular" staff, to which the Local Government Personnel Law is applied.[75]

Unless provided for, by the law, local authorities are duty bound to introduce byelaws covering all personnel matters, based on the provisions of the Personnel Law.

The main responsibility for appointing local government staff rests with Governors and Mayors, council chairmen, members of administrative committees, prefectural chiefs of police and municipal fire chiefs. Prefectures, designated cities, special wards and some cities, with population of 150,000 and over, have personnel committees and the remaining municipalities have equity committees.[76] Both types of committees are independent of the employers and have been instituted primarily to improve working conditions and hear employees' complaints. They advise employers on personnel management, and, in most cases, give guidance on annual salary increases.

Local government staff appointments are based on competitive examinations in all local authorities with personnel committees. Appointments may be made by other means, if the committee permits or in municipalities, with an equity committee. Generally speaking, most local government officers are employed on the principle of lifetime employment. Equal opportunity is established in statutes. Recently, some local authorities have allowed the appointment of foreign nationals to positions, that do not exercise authority or do not have public decision-making power.[77]

Local authorities are obliged to make provisions for employee welfare, including leisure and recreation activities, medical checks, housing and convalescent care.[78]

The Local Government Personnel Law restricts some or all of the basic rights of employment for local government employees according to their duties, including the right to organize, to participate in collective bargaining, and to conduct labour strikes—all of which are guaranteed to other workers under the constitution. Although restricted, employees are able to maintain and improve working conditions via personnel committees. The Local Government Personnel Law gives staff the right to request the committee or its equivalent to act on their behalf, regarding salaries, working hours and related matters.[79]

Local authority employees are commonly assigned for a time to the central government or another local authority for training purposes.

Equally often, in the case of highly experienced staff, these exchanges take the form of retiring from local government and being re-employed at the central government or a different local authority. Likewise, central government officials are sent to local authorities, where they help build closer relationships between the central and local government, or between local authorities.[80]

Local-National Relationship

In Japan, local authorities are positioned within a unified system of national government comprised of central and local components. In a broad sense, central and local governments depend on and complement one another, at both the prefectural and municipal levels, within a region. The Omnibus Decentralisation Act establishment, in July 1999, has revised the comprehensive powers of control and supervision that central and prefectural governments had over municipalities, with involvement restricted to cases, where it is provided for in laws or the ordinances based on such laws. Interference is kept to a minimum, and must conform to certain basic patterns. Further more, the laws stipulate that the autonomy and independence of local authorities must be taken into account.[81]

The relations between national government and local government had been buttressed by the two system of law: Local Authority Laws and Chihokan-Kansei. This system was described as allocating "politics and rights" to the national government and "administration and obligations" for local government.[82] Fu and Ken as well as Shi, Cho and Son emerged as local authorities, with corporate power and responsibility, in accordance with the Local Authority Laws. They did have local assemblies elected by popular vote of limited suffrage. The Governors of Fu and Ken administer and represent Fu and Ken and were ordinary local agents of the national government. Although Fu and Ken were classified as local authorities, they, in reality, were more of the administrative regions of the national government. The local assemblies of Fu and Ken, composed of local magnates, elected by limited vote, had the right to approve the revenue and expenditure budgets. In reality, the major role of local assemblies was merely to agree to bear the expense of national administrative affairs.[83]

The relationship of Fu and Ken, with their subordinate authorities (Shi, Cho, Son) was similar. These subordinate authorities performed a wide range of national administrative affairs under the supervision and control of the Governors.[84]

Thus, the inter-governmental relations, established in the 1890s, were nothing but a highly centralised administrative system. Under such circumstances, local government meant the participation by local magnets, consisting mainly of landlord in national administrative affairs, in a limited form.[85]

Following the First World War, Japan experienced rapid urbanization and industrialization. In urban areas, governments were confronted with problems of housing, sanitation and transportation, while the rural area governments were faced with problems of poverty and stagnant tax revenues, stemming from the lopsided development of the local economy. As a result, although the relationship between the national and local government still remained within the framework of the dual system of Local Authority Laws and Chihokan-Kansei, political participation by the people gradually progressed and control by the national government shifted to financial aspects.[86]

The right to vote was expanded, and in 1925, equal voting rights for national political elections were granted to male citizens. These voting rights were also applied to election of assemblies of Fu, Ken, Shi, Cho and Son, in 1926. Together, restrictions were placed on the supervisorial and controlling powers of the Minister and Governors regarding the administration of local governments. In 1929, the assemblies of Fu and Ken were vested with regulation making power. These improvements brought an end to the classical system of local government fostered by the Meiji Government.[87] Although the centralized relationship between the national and the local government was preserved, the control of the national government moved in the direction of modernized financial control. During the depression from 1931 to 1934, the national government embarked on subsidy programmes for public work projects in the rural areas. General revenue sources were granted to Cho and Son (in1936) and Fu, Ken and Shi (in 1937).[88] In 1940, the system of local apportionment tax was established, which developed into the present local allocation tax grant system.[89] Thus, the financial management of local governments became deeply incorporated in national finance and the relationship between the national and local governments became closer.

Thus originally, the national government implemented the control measures by linking the local communities and bureaucracy. When such a relationship ceased to function, the national government intended to preserve penetration into local government through financial control. It appointed Governors, as local agents, to execute national administrative affairs and reinforced its control over local governments through subsidies and grants for financial adjustments.[90]

Since the acceptance of the Potsdam Declaration of 15th August 1945, the relations between the national and local governments experienced significant institutional change. Prefectural and municipal governments emerged as fully autonomous entities obtaining the dual representative organs of chief executive officers and their assemblies; both, elected by direct popular vote. The role of prefectural Governors shifted from that of local agents of the national government to representative organs of residents.[91]

Administrative organization of local governments is regulated by various enactments. The internal administrative organization of the prefectural government is guided by Local Autonomy Law. There is no provision that regulates the organization of the municipal government, as a whole.[92] In addition, local governments must establish special local administrative agencies. This is a new mechanism; the national government has introduced to control local governments under the post-War Constitution. Moreover, in the administrative areas of road transportation, social insurance and employment security, there exists Chihojimukan Seido (local administrative officials system).[93] These officials are national civil servants, working in local governments, performing Kikan-Inin-Jimu. Prefectural governors direct and supervise them, with respect to the execution of respective administrative affairs.[94]

In the 1960s, some of the functions of the prefectural government were transferred to the national government. The local offices of ministries and agencies of the national government were reinforced, and a number of projects were developed by national government corporations. The expansion of Kikan-Inin-Jimu and local projects, directly administered by the national government, have created highly centralized inter-governmental relations.[95]

As far as the financial relationships are concerned, the revenue, for which the local government has to rely on, is controlled, to a high degree, by the national government. Although local allocation tax grants are classified as general revenue of local governments, the national government is capable of guiding the overall policy direction of local governments through their allocation.[96]

As mentioned earlier, the national government delegates the execution of various activities to local governments. The Local Finance Law specifies that the total expenses for such activities concerning the interests of the whole nation are borne by the national government, while the expenses of such activities, which simultaneously concern the interests of the national and local governments, are borne by both. However, local governments are not allowed to give opinions in determining the ratio.[97]

In nutshell, the relationship between national governments and local government under pre-War system, can still be observed in present-day Japan. The current relations between national government and local governments were instrumental in promoting modernization, urbanization and industrialization, but are no longer relevant in present day Japan, which has transformed herself into an urban society.[98]

Under the principle of the present system of local autonomy, the central government, in its dealings with local authorities, is required to respect their independence and to limit the exercise of its administrative powers and involvement with local affairs only to cases requiring nation-wide comprehensive policies. Such involvement must be approved on a case-by-case basis, according to the law. Legislatively, the central government may intervene in local authorities affairs by legislation, enacted by the Diet, in so far as, it does not contradict the idea of local autonomy, stated in the Constitution. Judicially, all law suits involving local authority, must submit to the jurisdiction of the Court of Justice. Litigation between the central or local government, concerning the scope or execution of powers, may not be regarded as a law suit, in the strict sense of the word, but the way is open to submit such disputes to judicial proceedings.[99]

Administratively, intervention is the most common form of central government intervention in local affairs. It can also take the form of quasi-legislative intervention (cabinet orders, ministerial ordinances etc.) or quasi-judicial intervention (administrative appeals etc.),[100] but the most frequently used form of intervention is administrative. Administrative intervention can be divided into two types: non-authoritarian (advice, recommendations, notifications etc.), and authoritarian (permissions, indications etc). These types of interventions need to be based on statutes or cabinet order and must give consideration to the autonomy and independence of local authorities.[101]

If a local government has any objections to such an intervention, it can file for a review by the Central-Local Government Dispute Resolution Council.[102]

Direct Participation System[103]

The systems, allowing residents to participate directly in local authority affairs, supplement the usual indirect democratic process. This is carried out by a specified number of signatories, demanding the approval, amendment or abolition of bylaws, special audits, dissolution of the council, and the dismissal of Governors, Mayors and councillors.

Direct demands for approval, amendment or abolition of bye-laws must be supported by at least 1/50th of the electorate. The Governor or Mayor must call a special meeting of the council, within 20 days of receiving such demands, and submit the proposed bylaw along with his comments. The final decision rests with the council, which is not bound by the proposal. The direct demand provisions do not apply to local taxes, fees and charges.

Again, the signatures of a minimum 1/50th of the electorate must accompany a demand for the audit committee to investigate the authority's financial probity—the audit committee is the authority's auditing mechanism. Once the committee has finished its audit, it must formally publish the results.

One-third of all electors must sign the demand of dissolution of the council. On receipt the whole electorate is balloted, and a majority vote, in favour, would result in dissolution.

One-third of all electors must support the demand of dismissal of Governors, Mayors and councillors. After balloting the electorate, a majority vote in favour would result in dismissal. This same system also applies to Vice Governors, Deputy Mayors, Treasurers and Chief Accountants, election committee members, as well as, audit and public safety committee members. In these cases, however, the chief executive refers the demand to the council for a decision.

The present Constitution allows the enactment of bye-laws, specific to a particular local authority, but only on the condition that the majority of electors vote in favour. As tax payers, residents can ask the audit committee to investigate their local authority's expenditure, its acquisition, management or disposal of property, and relevant officers' decisions. Depending on the results of such investigation, they can also ask for the appropriate corrective or preventive action to be taken. If dissatisfied with the results, they have further right to take legal proceedings.

The Challenges Facing Local Government

Urbanization has continued apace for the last forty years, and though it may have slowed recently, it is generally accepted that it will continue. Of the more than 127 million people, who inhabit Japan's 377,000 sq. km., half of them live in just 14 per cent of the total land areas—three large urban areas (Tokyo, Kausai and Nagoya). The Tokyo area has a population of 33 million, the Kausai area has 18 million, while Nagoya area has 11 million.[104] Of these, Tokyo and Tokyo area have the highest concentration of population, and as a result the highest concentration of functions for the economy, information, education, culture and entertainment. This concentration has even spawned a newer term in Japan—unipolar concentration in Tokyo.[105]

In addition, perhaps the most formidable task facing Japan, is how to cope with its ageing population. Statistically, the population of Japan is ageing faster than anywhere else in the world. In 2003, one-fifth of the population was aged 65 or older, and this population is certain to rise.[106] The speed of ageing is not the same nationwide and significant local differences can be observed. The challenges faced by an ageing society are:[107] an increased need to build a new social system to match the changing pattern of family life, and the increased burden of those still employed; providing employment for the elderly; financial stability and meaningful lives for the elderly; and the health care of the elderly.

Central and Local Governments must work closely together to find solutions. Local Government needs to develop appropriate policies based on changes in the population structure, rather than rely on conventional welfare planning.[108]

Unfortunately, the excessive concentration of people and business pursuing economic efficiency, the main urban areas brought about a number of problems, including air and water pollution, noise, subsidence, traffic congestion, soaring land prices, the loss of local traditions and the spread of an 'efficiency-first' attitude.[109] Rural and fishing communities are losing many of their young people and most of their workforce to the large cities, leaving only children and the elderly and putting the community existence at risk. Policies to revitalize local communities are needed, if a proper balance between urban and rural development is to be maintained. The central government has made five National Comprehensive Development Plans since 1962 and promoted many relevant policies.[110] While local authorities have implemented diverse measures in line with Central Government's policies, they also began actively rolling out independent measures.

Rapid improvements in transport and communications, of late, have enhanced the mobility of people, goods and information to a global level, resulting in the building of close relationships that reach beyond conventional boundaries and an increase in mutual assistance. Domestic daily life is increasingly influenced by international factors. International relationships, once the preserve of national government, are now common place for local authorities, private organizations, as well as, for ordinary individuals. Local authorities are responsible for overall regional administration and possess the necessary expertise and technology. With the use of these resources, international exchange has the potential to evolve from "exchange" to "cooperation."[111] Local governments have established the Council of Local Authorities for International Relations to assist local authorities in their international dealings and to promote, among others, the JET Programme, which invites to Japan young people from around the world to help as foreign language teachers in Japanese schools.[112] In the future, local authorities will need to define their own objectives of international involvement and exchange, establish a system to promote citizen-led programmes, compile associated information and knowledge, and equip individuals with adequate skills to cope with this trend.[113]

A Better Quality of Life

Local authority urban programmes are increasingly moving away from "hardware" activities, such as road construction and the development of parks, to comprehensive improvement and maintenance of the residential environment, including "software" activities.[114]

In the background are the negative aspects of the progress of national development and urbanization, that accompanied the country's high economic growth. Some of Japan's formerly rich green areas have been lost. There has been water pollution, deterioration of the waterside environment, collapse of urban and rural communities, and loss of traditional culture. Many areas have lost their once beautiful scenery.[115]

This shift in emphasis has grown from the awareness that Japan's economic miracle was achieved at the cost of something very precious.

Administrative policies with the foregoing emphasis may be collectively called, amenity-related programmes. Creation of comfortable urban environments; protection and nurturing of urban beauty and charm; preservation of urban areas with historic value; creation of urban landscapes; protection and preservation of clean water, beautiful greenery and skies; promotion of city planning that gives appropriate priority to the natural environment—all these are included in amenity-related programmes.[116]

The beginning of amenity-conscious administration can be traced back to the late 1960s, when people became aware of the destruction of environments with historical heritage, and citizens' movements for preservation (in a form similar to a national trust) sprang up across the country. As a result, municipalities adopted independent bye-laws and implemented policies to protect areas with historic value.[117]

This, in turn, led to the enactment of similar legislation, and revision of associated laws at the national level. In addition to the protection of areas with historic value, an increasing number of local authorities are presently adopting bye-laws and plans concerning tree preservation, promotion of tree planting, and protection of noted clean water sources as part of conservation of natural environment. They are also enacting byelaws for the protection of urban landscapes, including roads and streetscapes.[118]

Innovative local authorities have implemented policies that actively promote the creation of quality urban areas, in addition to the emphasis on environmental conservation, which is more or less a preventive measure.[119] Many authorities are also adopting environmental policies that take into account the global environment as well as their local environments, as part of their amenity-related programs. Global-oriented local environmental policies ranging from waste recycling and construction of recycling facilities to combating global warming will become even more important in the future.[120]

Cultural Promotion

Culture-related services were introduced around 1978, when the key phrase was "the age of localism."[121] As the nation's economy grew, local areas found themselves increasingly reliant on one-way flow of economic activities and information from Tokyo. In an effort to counter this situation, the revival of local life-styles, traditions and cultures was promoted.[122] The following sections give some idea of the range and scope of local authorities' activities in this area.

Residents' Participation and Access to Information

As Japan's society has grown more complex, and people's thinking and sense of values become increasingly diverse, local authorities have seen the need for new ways of keeping in touch with their respective communities. It is no longer enough to rely on outmoded and ill-used systems, neither of recall and residents' votes, or simply to rely on elected members and the council process.[123]

Today a variety of methods are used to guarantee that popular opinion is considered fully when projects or services are planned and implemented: symposiums or informal gatherings are held in each area, questionnaire surveys are undertaken, and people are encouraged to voice their opinions and ideas.

To reflect popular opinion directly in day-to-day services, in addition to project planning and execution, especially at the municipal level, informal meetings with the Mayor are held, citizens' committees are organized and suggestion boxes are made available to give everyone a chance to voice their opinions.[124]

Prefecture and municipal governments have recently enacted disclosure of information bye-laws and, at the behest of local citizens, are actively making government information available. By allowing access to information, local authorities are also helping to maintain public relations by letting residents confirm that the administrative work is being done appropriately.[125]

In-Step with Advances in the IT Revolution

The IT revolution is sweeping through all parts of society, from the economic and industrial sectors to government administration, which lays the foundation of society. This can be seen in the sophisticated application of information technology in the development of "e-government" and "local e-governments."[126] With the establishment of the Basic Plan for the Computerization of Government Administration in 1997, and the approval of the e-Government Construction Plan in July 2003, concrete action to develop an e-government and local e-government has been planned for systematic implementation.[127]

As part of this project, a Local Government Wide Area Network (LGWAN)—a general administrative network, that interconnects approximately 3,200 local governments throughout Japan—has been developed to facilitate smoother communication among government entities, establish a foundation for advanced information use through sharing, and connect local government organizations throughout the country.[128] In addition, it has been connected with the interministerial network, "Kasumigaseki WAN", for data exchange with national government organizations.[129]

At the same time, advances in the IT revolution have increased the need for stricter security measures, with those against cyber attacks, web page tampering, internet crimes, and cyber terrorism emerging as international issues. In the present sophisticated information society and amid continuing advances in information technology, security and reliability are in great demand along with convenience. To guarantee these needs are met, a multifaceted approach to development in terms of system, technology, management, etc. is necessary. At the same time, a mechanism adapted to the new IT society is needed as well. Local government entities must increasingly be able to adapt accordingly and keep in step with advances in the IT revolution in the future.

REFERENCES

1. http://web.japan.org; Abes, H., Shindo, M. and K. Sadefumi (1994). *The Government and Politics of Japan*, Tokyo University Press, Tokyo.
2. Shindo, Muneyuki (1982). *Relations between National Government and Local Government in Public Administration in Japan*, Seushu University
3. http://web.mofa.go.jp; Apter, D. E. and Nagayo, S. (1984). *Against the State: Politics and Social Protest in Japan*, Harvard University Press, Cambridge, MA.
4. Constitution of Japan as depicted http://web.japan.org
5. Shindo (1982). *op cit.*; Bachtler, John (1996). *Regional Problems and Policies in Japan*, Berman Assoc.
6. http://web.japan.org; Austin, L. (ed.) (1976). Japan: *The Paradox of Progress*, Yale University Press, New Havel, CT.
7. Abes, Shindo, *et al.*, *op cit.*

8. Rowat, Donald C. (ed.) (1980). *International Handbook on Local Government Reorganization*, Greenwood Press, Westport.
9. *Ibid.*
10. *Ibid.*; Allinson, G.D. (1975). *Japanese Urbanism: Industry and Politics in Kariya*, 1872-1972, University of California Press, Berkeley.
11. Japan Local Government Center (CLAIR), Tokyo; Kubota, Jiro (2004). Local Government Innovations in Japan, in Local Government in Japan, Council of Local Authorities for International Relations, Tokyo.
12. Semeis, Gyosei, *Population Statistics and Administrative Services*, Government of Japan, Tokyo.
13. Tsuji, K. (ed.) (1984). *Public Administration in Japan*, Institute of Administrative Management and University of Tokyo Press, Tokyo
14. Rowat, *op cit.*
15. Laxmikant, M. (2001). *Public Administration*, Tata McGraw Hill, New Delhi.
16. Gyosei (2001). *The Origins and System of Local Government*, Tokyo.
17. *Ibid.*
18. Laxmikant, *op cit.*
19. Tsuji, K.,(ed.) (1984). *Public Administration in Japan*, Institute of Administrative Management, University of Tokyo Press, Tokyo.
20. An Introduction to Local Administration in Japan, 1990, CLAIR.
21. Toshiro, Ku (1988). Japan, in Donald C. Rowat (ed.), *Public Administration in Developed Democracies: A Comparative Study,* Marcel Dekker Inc., New York.
22. http://web.jiia.or.jp; Maass, Arthur (1959). Division of Powers: An Areal Analysis, in Area and Power: A Theory of Local Government, Free Press, Glencoe, IL.
23. Toshiro, *op cit.*
24. Administrative Management Agency (1982). *Administrative Management in Japan*, AMA, Tokyo.
25. Pernpel, T. J. (1982). *Policy and Politics in Japan: Creative Conservatism*, Temple University Press, Philadelphia.
26. http://web.japan.org; Okimoto, D. (1984). Political Inclusivity: The Domestic Structure of Trade, in T. Inoguchi and D. Okimoto, (eds.), *The Political Economy of Japan*, Vol. 2, Standford University Press, Palo Alto, C A.
27. Pernpel, *op cit.*
28. Hyoe, M. and Johannes, H. (eds.) (1979). *Politics and Economies in Contemporary Japan*, Japan Cultural Institute, Tokyo.
29. *Ibid.*
30. Ward, R.E., and Ruston, D. (eds.) (1964). *Political Modernization in Japan and Turkey*, Princeton University Press, Princeton, N.J.
31. *International Review of Administrative Sciences*, 48 (2), 1982, 115-262.
32. Christopher, *op cit.*; Kitayama, T. (1995). Local Governments and Small

and Medium Sized Enterprises, in Hyung-Ki Kim, Michio Muramastu, T. J. Pempel, and Kozo Yamamura, (eds.), *The Japanese Civil Service and Economic Development: Catalysts of Change*, Oxford University Press, Oxford.

33. Rowat, Donald C. (ed.) (1980). *International Handbook on Local Government Reorganisation*, Greenwood Press, Westport.
34 http://web.mofa.go.jp; McKean, M. A. (1981). *Environmental Protest and Citizen Politics in Japan*, University of California Press, Berkeley and Los Angeles.
35. Rowat, *op cit.*
36. *Japan: A Pocket Guide* (2002).
37. Hyoe, M. and Johannes, H. (eds.) (1979). *Politics and Economies in Contemporary Japan,* Japan Cultural Institute, Tokyo.
38. Rowat, *op cit.*
39. Dowdy, Edwin (1973). *Japanese Bureaucracy: Its Development and Modernisation,* Cheshire, Melbourne.
40. Christopher, R. C. (1983). *The Japanese Mind: The Goliath Explained,* Fawcett Columbine.
41. Overview of the Nation's Cities, Towns and Villages (2004). Administrative Improvement Division of the Ministry of Internal Affairs and Communications.
42. MacDougall, Terry E. (1975). *Political Opposition and Local Government in Japan*, Ph. D. Dissertation, Yale University, New Haven, CT.
43. Gyosei (2001). *The Origins and Systems of Local Government*, Tokyo.
44. Laxmikant, M. (2001). *Public Administration*, Tata McGraw Hill, New Delhi.
45. Ward, R.E. (1978). *Japan's Political System*, Prentice Hall, Englewood Cliffs, N.J.
46. Yanaga, C. (1968). *Big Business in Japanese Politics*, Yale University Press, New Haven.
47. The Challenges Facing Local Government; www.clair.or.jp/e/
48. http://web.nira.go.jp; Reed, S. (1986). *Japanese Prefectures and Policy-making,* University of Pittsburg Press, Pittsburg.
49. Institute of Local Government, Outline of Japanese Local Autonomy System, 1994.
50. *Ibid.*
51. http://web.nira.go.jp; Ozawa, I. (1994). *Blueprint for a New Japan: The Rethinking of a Nation,* Kodansha, Tokyo.
52. Christopher, R.C. (1985). *The Japanese Mind: The Goliath Explained,* Fawcett Columbine.
53. Yanaga, *op cit.*
54. The Challenges Facing Local Government; www.clair.or.jp/e/; Council of Local Authorities for International Relations, Tokyo.
55. *Ibid.*

56. *Ibid.*
57. Constitution of Japan.
58. Rowat, *op cit.*
59. Pernpel, *op cit.*
60. Ward, *op cit.*
61. Tsuji, *op cit.*
62. http://web.nira.go.jp; Myriad Leaves (2006). The Newsletter of the Japan Local Government Centre, London, June.
63. Laxmikant, *op cit.*
64. Hyoe, *op cit.*
65. Mohanty, B. (1999). *The Glimpses of Local Government*, Gyanjuga, Bhubaneswar.
66. Rowat, *op cit.*
66. http://web.jiia.or.jp; *The Challenges Facing Local Government*; www.clair.or.jp/e/
68. Ward, *op cit.*
69. Ministry of Internal……*op cit.*
70. *Ibid.*
71. http://web.japan.org; Stevens, A. (2004). Local Government in Japan, Council of Local Authorities for International Relations, Kasumigaseki Chiyoda—ku, Tokyo.
72. Cyoesei (2001). *The Origins and Systems of Local Government*, Tokyo.
73. Laxmikant, *op cit.*
74. Kubbota, J. (2004). *Local Government Innovations in Japan*, Council of Local Authorities for International Relations, Tokyo.
75. Shindo, M., *Relations between National and Local Government in Public Administration in Japan*, Seushu University.
76. Dowdy, *op cit.*
77. *Ibid*; *The Challenges Facing Local Government*; www.clair.or.jp/e/
78. http://web.nira.go.jp; *The Challenges Facing Local Government*; www.clair.or.jp/e/
79. Dowdy, E. (1973). *Japanese Bureaucracy: Its Development and Modernisation*, Cheshire, Melbourne.
80. Ward, *op cit.*
81. An Outline of Local Government in Japan, Council of Local Authorities for International Relations, Tokyo.
82. http://web.japan.org; Vogel, E. (1979). *Japan as Number One*, Harvard University Press, Cambridge, MA.
83. Ward, *op cit.*
84. Ministry of Internal…... *op cit.*
85. http://web.mofa.go.jp; Hirashima, A. (2004) *Economic Development and Human Security*, Ministry for Public Management, Home Affairs, Posts& Telecommunications, Tokyo.
86. Pernpel, *op cit.*

87. http:://web.jiia.or.jp; Gyosei (2001). *The Origins and System of Local Government*, Tokyo.
88. *Ibid.*
89. Local Finances White Paper (2002). Ministry of Internal Affairs and Communications.
90. Rowat, *op cit.*
91. Laxmikant, *op cit.*
92. Ministry of Internal......*op cit.*
93. Rowat, *op cit.*
94. *Local Autonomy Law*, Ryosho-Fukyukoi.
95. Council of Local Authorities for International Relations, Tokyo; http://www.clair.or.jp
96. *Political Economy*, Sukan Suppan.
97. Hyoe, *op cit.*; Kitayama, Toshiya (2001). *Local Government Policy Initiatives in Japan*, The World Bank, Washington, D. C.
98. Shindo, *op cit.*
99. Gyosei, The Laws and Regulations of Japan; Samuels, Richard J. (1983). *The Politics of Regional Policy in Japan*, Princeton University Press, Princeton, NJ.
100. http://web.japan.org; Mac Dongall, T. (1988). *Towards Political Inclusiveness: The Changing Role of Local Government in Japan*, Stanford University Press, Japan.
101. Modern Japan (a Concise Survey); Council of Local Authorities for International Relations, Tokyo.
102. http://web.japan.org; Mizuno, K. (2002). Leading by Example: Local Government in Japan, *ISO Management System*, May-June.
103. *The Challenges Facing Local Government*; www.clair.or.jp/e/; Council of Local Authorities for International Relations, Tokyo.
104. http://web.japan.org; *The Challenges Facing Local Government*; www.clair.or.jp/e/; Council of Local Authorities for International Relations, Tokyo.
105. Ward, *op cit.*
106. http://web.japan.org; Ozawa, *op cit.*
107. Hyoe, M. and Johannes, H. (eds.) (1979). *Politics and Economies in Contemporary* Japan, Japan Cultural Institute, Tokyo.
108. Laxmikant, *op cit.*
109. http://web.jiia.or.jp; Gyosei, *op cit.*
110. Tashiro, K. (1988). Japan, in Donald C. Rowat (ed.), *Public Administration in Developed Democracy: A Comparative Study,* Marcel Dekker Inc., New York.
111. Yanaga, *op cit.*
112. Pernpel, T. J. (1982). *Policy and Politics in Japan: Creative Conservatism*, Temple University Press, Philadelphia.
113. Japan Cultural and Information Centre, New Delhi.

114. http://web.japan.org; Reed, *op cit.*
115. Japan Cultural...*op cit.*; Samuels, R. J. (1987). *The Business of the Japanese State*, Cornell University Press, Cornell, NY.
116. Christopher, *op cit.*
117. Kubota, Jiro (2004). Council of Local Authorities for International Relations Japan; JLGC review (2005). The Japan Local Government Centre, London.
118. Shindo, *op cit.*
119. Kubota, J., *op cit.*; Stevens, Andrew (2004). Japanese bureaucrats outraged by cuts in local government subsidies, www.clair.or.jp/e/
120. Pernpel, *op cit.*
121. http://web.nira.go.jp; Okimoto, *op cit.*
122. Japan Cultural...*op cit.*
123. Yanaga, *op cit.*; *Council of Local Authorities for International Relations*, Tokyo.
124. Ministry of Internal....... *op cit.*
125. *Ibid*; www.clair.or.jp/e/
126. http://web.mofa.go.jp; Gyosei, *op cit.*
127. *Council of Local Authorities for International Relations*, Tokyo; The Japan Local Government Centre, London.
128. http://web.japan.org; Hirashima, *op cit.*
129. Profile of Nation; *Council of Local Authorities for International Relations*, Tokyo.

Chapter 6

Russian Local Government

The Russian Federation

Russia is a federative state, consisting of eighty-nine subjects, which are grouped into twelve economic zones. These include twenty-one republics, six *krais*, forty-nine *oblasts*, two federal cities (Moscow and St. Petersburg), one autonomous oblast and ten autonomous districts. Each republic is an ethnic administrative unit. *Krais* are territorial units, which incorporate smaller ethnic administrative units, and *oblasts* are territorial units based on and named after large cities. Each of the 21 republics has its own constitution and its own president. *Krais*, *oblasts*, cities with federal status, the autonomous regions and autonomous areas have charters and governors, as heads of administration.[1] Despite the diversity of categories, all subjects of the Federation have equal status, pursuant to the 1993 Constitution of the Russian Federation. The Russian Federation has made few changes in the Soviet pattern of regional jurisdiction. As the power and influence of the central government have diluted, Governors and Mayors have become the only relevant government authorities in many jurisdiction.

The Federative Treaty (signed in March 1992 by President Yeltsin and most leaders of the autonomous republics and other ethnic and geographical sub-units), an integral part of the Constitution, allows for bilateral agreements between the central government and member regions, which grant regions special rights and obligations. The classification of regions as republic, *krai* or *oblast* is derived from historical reasons, and does not generally provide any indication of status. The federal government, recognizing the risks in continuing to develop asymmetric federalism, eventually revoked most privileges previously granted to individual regions. To signal a return to a policy of uniform federalism, the State Duma of the Russian Federation passed a law, in 2000, mandating that all regions bring their legislation into conformity with the Constitution and with federal legislation.[2] Nonetheless, complete uniformity will be difficult to attain in a country as large and diverse as Russia.

The Russian governmental system has three types of structure. The first one is the federal structure, which consists of federal ministries, state committees and other agencies with nationwide authority operating through a hierarchical network of territorial bodies subordinated to them. Federal jurisdiction includes issues, such as finance and the budget, management of federal property, state security, defense, law enforcement etc. The Constitution provides for a single system of executing power in the Russian Federation. The second type is the system of governments of the subjects of the federation. The republics have their own republican ministries and prime ministers, while other subjects have administrations sub-divided according to their areas of authority and the heads of the administrations. The third type of government structure is the system of local self-government. Its organization is defined by the administration of the subject of the federation, based on the principles defined in the federal law. Units of local self-government operate in raions (districts), cities and towns, selsovets (groups of villages) and villages. The status of *raion* self-government is not entirely clear.[3]

Regional Structure

Regions are divided into cities and rural areas (*raions*). This territorial division was largely inherited from the former Soviet Union, though several jurisdictions had existed previously. *Raions* are divided into smaller units, such as sub-*raion* towns, townships, villages and rural districts. Sub-*raion* towns may be composed of townships and rural districts. Rural districts themselves may include several small rural settlements. The territorial structure of Russian Federation subjects is, therefore, generally composed of three or four levels,[4] as shown under:

Territorial Division of Regions

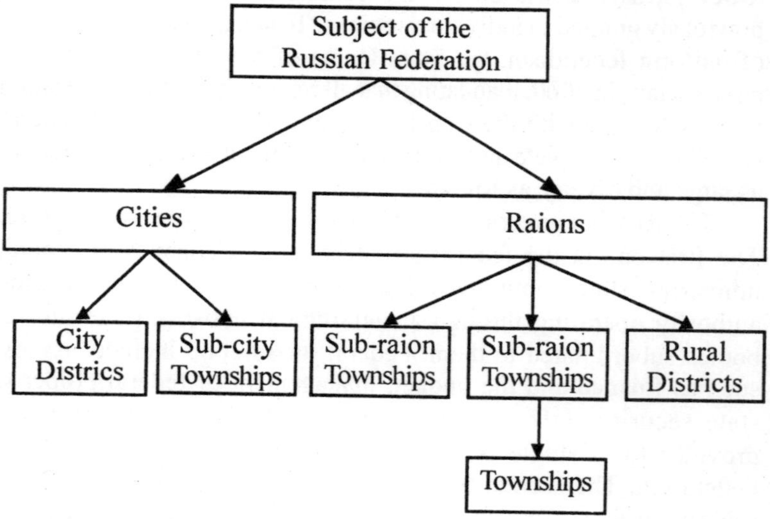

Local Government

The law defines the municipality, the primary unit of local government, as any populated territory (city, town, township or any combination of these on a contiguous territory), which is self-governed and possesses municipal property, a budget and an elected local government body. In conformity with the Constitution, the law allows self-governments to be established at a variety of territorial levels from raions to towns or villages, irrespective of population size.

This law also grants uniform legal status to all local governments, thereby establishing one of the distinctive features of the Russian model of local self-governance. All local governments—*raions*, towns and townships in rural districts—enjoy the same institutional and administrative rights, without subordination of one municipality to another. Accordingly, the entire territory of the Russian Federation should be divided into local government jurisdictions without overlapping.[5] This model of municipal equality distinguishes Russia both from the previous Soviet system and from the majority of former Soviet Union countries who chose to build the institution of local self-government upon the foundations laid in the pre-reform period.

Prior to local government reform, the hierarchy of territories reflected the hierarchy of administrative subordination. With the transition to a more decentralized structure, settlements of all sizes were granted the right to establish local governments and register as municipalities with equal status to one another. Reform thus meant the transition from a three-tier hierarchy of jurisdictions within the regional state administration to a two-tier system made up of the regional government and local governments, with no administrative subordination between the two. The system of municipalities was superimposed over the previous structure, which often resulted in peculiar organizational forms in which village-level municipalities are subordinated to *raion*-level municipalities. Since the breakdown of regional territories into municipalities has not yet been finalized, federal agencies with territorial branches have been slow to revise their internal organization according to the new municipal division.[6]

Territories with Special Status

Two regions, the federal cities of Moscow and St. Petersburg, enjoy special rights with respect to local self-government. Both city governments are entitled to determine the property, budgetary expenditures and revenue sources of local governments within their jurisdiction. St. Petersburg has jurisdiction over one hundred local governments, which enjoy very little autonomy; Moscow has none.

In addition, about forty territories are classified as restricted access territories ("*zakrytye administrativnoterritorialnye obrazovanya*" or ZATOs) and fall under the jurisdiction of the federal government. By federal law, ZATOs can be urban or rural settlements, whose territorial boundaries may overlap regional or *raion* boundaries. The boundaries and administrative subordination of ZATOs are determined by the federal government, as are the rights and responsibilities of regional governments with respect to the ZATOs located in their territory. ZATOs are financially independent from the regional governments, as they receive inter-governmental transfers directly from the federal government. ZATO residents can also form local governments. Generally speaking, regional laws apply across the entire territory of the region, including ZATOs, with the exception of fiscal laws; in fiscal matters ZATOs are federal territories. Until recently, ZATOs were allowed to retain all taxes collected in their territories, including the regional and federal tax shares. Starting from 2000, all but two ZATOs are mandated to remit federal taxes, as well as levies accruing to earmarked budgetary and extra-budgetary funds of the federal or regional government, to the respective government or fund in accordance with the federal and regional legislation. Any financing gaps between the expenditure needs and revenues of ZATOs are covered directly from the federal budget.[7]

Local Government Reform[8]

The Soviet Period

The first step towards democratizing local government was taken at the end of the 1980s, while Russia was still a member of the Soviet Union. In an experimental move, some *raions* were allowed to field more candidates than were vacant offices in the 1987 elections to local soviets. Altogether 26,000 candidates competed for 4,700 councillor seats in the pilot *raions*, which made up about five per cent of total *raions*. In all other respects, local governments remained part of the same centralized administrative hierarchy, which was completely subordinated to the party apparatus. The pertinent features of !ocal governments in the early years of transition were that:[9]

- No distinction was made between the local and the state levels of government;
- Local government jurisdictions exactly replicated existing administrative-territorial divisions; and
- Local governments were subordinated to state and party authorities.

The next landmark event was the amendment of the Constitution of the Soviet Union and the Law on Elections of USSR People's Deputies in 1988. The most important amendments in terms of local government were those which established the right of voters to nominate candidates, guaranteed the right of local soviets to exercise control over local state agencies and limited the term of the officials appointed by local soviets.

The first law to use the term "local self-government" was the Law on General Principles of Local Self-Government and Local Economy in the USSR (April 1990), which opened the door for sweeping changes to the local government role in developing a civil society. Most importantly, this law established:[10]

- Guarantees, that local authorities are autonomous, independent and elected by popular vote;

- The scope of competencies of local soviets;
- The transfer of communal property to local soviets; and
- Revenue sources of local soviets, including fixed shares of federal tax revenues and a list of own taxes, levies and duties to be introduced at the discretion of the local soviet.

The stipulation that local authorities be elected by popular vote applied only to representative bodies. The basic unit of local self-government established by this law coincided with lowest administrative tier that existed at the time, which was a rural district, a township, a sub-*raion* town or a city district. The first law on local self-government to come into force after independence was passed in July 1991, while Russia was still part of the Soviet Union. The progressive feature of this law was the requirement that not only representative bodies but also heads of local administrations be democratically elected. This law also decreed the dissolution of the executive committees, or lowest level tiers in the hierarchy of state power.

The Post-Soviet Period

In the early years of independence, the legal framework for local self-governance in Russia evolved primarily through amending the Law on Local Self-Government in 1991 in the Russian Federation. The harmonization of this law with other legislative acts, particularly the Law on the Tax System in the Russian Federation eventually diluted the effect of the law, limiting the autonomy of local authorities over local revenues.[11]

The dissolution of the Supreme Council of the Russian Federation and the passage of the new Constitution in 1993 marked the beginning of a revolutionary phase in the development of local self-government in Russia. The "municipal revolution" originated in the center, fuelled by a desire to counterbalance the growing political opposition of the regional elite. New departments of federal agencies were specifically commissioned to provide support to the lowest tier of the state hierarchy, the autonomous local governments. These local governments and their leaders, independent from regional administration, represented invaluable allies to Russian reformers charged with implementing the often unpopular policies of the federal government.[12]

Constitutional Basis of Local Government[13]

The Constitution lists local self-government among the fundamental institutions of the constitutional order, along with state power, a federal system of government, republican rule and other provisions of the Constitution. It lists local government bodies among the institutions through which the people exercise their will, together with direct democracy and democracy exercised via bodies of state power, besides providing for municipal ownership of land.

Article 12 unequivocally determines that "local self-government bodies do not form part of the system of state power." The Constitution instituted a legal regulatory framework in place of the previous administrative subordination of local authorities to regional ones. One chapter (8) of the Constitution is entirely devoted to local self-governance. Article 130 states that "(1) Local self-government in the Russian Federation shall ensure the independent solution by the population of the issues of local importance, of possession, use and disposal of municipal property. (2) Local self- government shall be exercised by citizens through a referendum, election, and other forms of direct expression of the will of the people, through elected and other bodies of local self-government." Article 131 reads that "(1) Local self-government shall be administered in urban and rural settlements and in other areas with the consideration of the historical and other local traditions. The structure of local self-government bodies shall be determined by the population independently. (2) Changes in borders of areas in which local self-government is administered shall be made with the consideration of the opinion of the population of the corresponding areas."

Further Article 132 provides that "(1) The local self-government bodies shall independently manage municipal property, form, adopt and implement the local budgets, introduce local taxes and dues, ensure the protection of public order, and also solve other issues of local importance. (2) The local self-government bodies may be vested by law with certain state powers and receive the necessary material and financial resources for their implementation. The implementation of the delegated powers shall be controlled by the state." Article 133 ensures that "Local self-government in the Russian Federation shall be guaranteed by the right for judicial protection, for a compensation for additional expenses emerging as a result of decisions adopted by state authority bodies, by a ban on the limitations on the rights of local self-government fixed by the Constitution of the Russian Federation and the federal laws."

Thus these four articles of the Constitution of the Russian Federation collectively provide the following guarantees:

- Local communities possess autonomy in addressing issues of local importance,
- Local self-government may follow a diversity of organizational models,
- Regional authorities must take into account the preferences of local communities, when determining the boundaries of local government jurisdictions,
- Local governments possess financial autonomy (albeit limited), with discretion over the management of municipal property and the implementation of local budgets,
- Adequate funding is guaranteed for the performance of additional state functions delegated to the local government by the decision of federal or regional state authorities, and
- Local governments will be reimbursed for the costs of implementing federal mandates.

According to the Constitution, the establishment of general principles of local government organization is the joint responsibility of the federal center and the regions. To fulfil this responsibility, federal authorities have passed a number of laws on local government organization. These include:

- Law on General Principles of Local Self-Government (28 August 1995).
- Law on the Constitutional Right to Local Government Elections (26 November 1996).
- Law on Electoral Rights and Referenda (19 September 1997).
- Law on Local Government Finance (25 September 1997).

Legal Basis of Local Government[14]

The fundamental principles of Local Self-Government in Russia are set forth in the federal Law on Local Self-Government in the Russian Federation. This law is distinct from its Soviet predecessors in the sense that it determines the general principles of local self-governance, rather than a system of local government bodies.

A major objective of federal policy on local self-government was to encourage the regions themselves to hold municipal elections and adopt the necessary laws to develop systems of local government.

In late 1996, the federal Law on the Constitutional Right to Local Government Elections was passed to prevent a surge of regional resistance to the establishment of local self-governments. The provisions of the law essentially constituted federal intervention in affairs of those regions that failed to comply with the federal legislation. Where regional administrations did nothing to organize local elections, the right to convene elections was assigned to the courts. Rules governing the conduct of local elections were outlined in a separate annex to the law.

The federal Law on Electoral Rights and Referenda was passed in 1997 to guarantee the right of citizens to hold local elections on the basis of the Law on Local Elections even in the absence of regional laws.

The federal Law on Municipal Service completed the legislative framework of local self-government, as conceived by the Yeltsin Administration. However, at the very start of the Putin Administration in 2000, the Law on Local Self-Government was significantly amended. The core of the amendments was a reversion to vertically imposed administrative control over the public sector.

Article 49 of the amended Law on Local Self-Government establishes that the Russian President or regional governor is entitled to dissolve the local council, discharge the mayor, convene new elections and appoint an interim mayor in cases where the court finds that local government decisions violate the Constitution, federal or regional legislation and the mayor or local government do not remedy the decision in question.[15]

Prior to these amendments, the law had provided for dissolution of the local government body and dismissal of the mayor, but the previous procedure was more complicated and necessitated additional court proceedings. Unfortunately, the new authorities have opted to strengthen administrative levers rather than improve enforcement of court rulings.

Regional Legislation on Local Government

According to the principle of joint jurisdiction set forth in the Constitution, regional-local relations are established by regional laws within the framework of existing federal legislation. The Law on Local Self-Government lists issues to be regulated by regional laws, including the following:[16]

- procedures for determining the territorial boundaries of municipalities,
- procedures for holding municipal elections,
- procedures for the registration of municipal charters,
- procedures for the transfer of property to municipalities,
- regulation of the fiscal relations between the region and its municipalities and the equalization of the fiscal capacity of municipalities,
- delegation of certain state powers to local government bodies and the transfer of the financial resources necessary to support their execution, and
- municipal services and other issues.

The development of regional legislation on local self-government has been in progress since 1996 and is far from complete. In reforming local self-government, different regions have displayed varying attitudes towards relinquishing administrative control. These can be broken down into the following responses:[17]

Constructive Response

This category includes those regions, which recognize the advantages of developing independent public administration at the local level and have unconditionally complied with the implementation of local self-government according to constitutional principles. In most of those regions, municipal elections had been held prior to adoption of the Law on Local Self-Government. Their legislators have been very active in developing laws on municipal issues, in many cases preceding federal legislation.

Obstructive Response

This category includes regions where self-government is either non-existent or confined to the level of small townships and deprived of any legal basis. Issues assigned to local self-governments by federal legislation are instead handled by territorial branches of regional state administrations in cities and *raions*. In some cases, mayors may be elected in cities and *raions*, but are subject to removal from office by the regional government, which also retains the authority to annul their decisions. Legislation on municipal issues in these areas is either in its infancy or in conflict with federal legislation. In some regions, local government bodies do not exist, nor have they been even provided for in regional legislation. Most of the regions in this group are ethnic autonomies. Their leaders avoid publicly refusing to comply with the Constitution, instead emphasizing the need to maintain control over territories or arguing that the population lacks managerial personnel and is generally unprepared for new forms of government organization.

This group consists of regions, which view local self-government as an inescapable evil. Although they refrain from committing any outright violations of federal legislation, they employ numerous delaying tactics to slow the process down. Local government bodies were not formed in these jurisdictions until 1997. Relevant legislation is in its inception and is heavily borrowed from other regions rather than a product of local effort. This is a fairly large group of regions, which have increasingly tended to join one or the other of the categories. Since the attitudes of regional authorities vary so widely, the quality of regional legislation on local self-government leaves much to be desired and often contain norms that run counter to the Constitution and federal legislation.

Levels of Self-Government[18]

Before the launch of local government reform, Russia possessed a rigid administrative hierarchy in which smaller territorial units were subordinate to the larger territorial units in which they were located. Depending on area, population size and density and administrative and territorial status, sub-regional units made up the following hierarchy: regions—*raions* and cities subordinated to regions— cities subordinated to *raions*—townships and rural districts. The recently created municipalities were formed at different tiers of the former administrative and territorial hierarchy, depending on the region. In some regions, they were established at the level of former cities and raions, in others at the level of rural districts and in some others, a combination of the two. In some regions, former *raions* were transformed into territorial branches of the regional administration, making up a second tier of the regional state administration (region—*raions* and cities). In other regions, raions became municipalities, often with a two-tier structure themselves (cities and *raions*—townships and rural districts). It is possible to distinguish the following three basic types of local public administration:

Type I

A one-tier regional state administration together with one-tier local government administrations.

In this model, local government bodies are generally made up of large cities and *raions* and enjoy full fiscal rights stipulated by federal legislation. Regional authorities determine regional- local fiscal relations through deciding upon transfers and local shares of tax revenues. In a number of regions, municipalities consist of sub-*raion* cities and rural districts, in which case the regional authorities must deal with hundreds of sub-*raion* municipalities.

Type II

A two-tier regional state administration together with one-tier local government administrations where local governments are deprived of important rights.

This structure is similar to the previous one, with the exception that municipalities formed at the sub-*raion* level are deprived of some powers established by federal legislation, particularly budgetary rights. The authority to set local taxes is vested in territorial branches of the regional administration, which do not have elected bodies. Municipal budgets are incorporated in the regional budget in the form of expenditure plans.

Type III

One-tier structure regional state administration together with a two-tier local government structure in which some local governments are subordinate to others, in violation of federal legislation.

The first-tier of local governments is comprised of big cities and *raions*; the second level of sub-*raion* cities and other populated areas within cities or *raions*. Both first and second-tier governments are elected by local residents. First-tier local governments engage in direct financial relations with the regional authorities. In contrast, financial relations between second-tier local governments and regional authorities are indirect, mediated by the first-tier local governments. First-tier local governments are responsible, among other things, for the distribution of regional grants to second-tier governments and for dividing the local shared revenue from regional or federal taxes. In this model, first-tier local governments essentially perform the function of the regional state authorities.

If the second-tier municipalities cover the entire territory in the jurisdiction of the first-tier municipality, the latter is usually made responsible for maintaining social infrastructure facilities that service the entire area. In these cases, local taxes are usually established by the second-tier municipalities. Sometimes, however, smaller municipalities delegate their taxation authority to the *raion*-level municipality, in which case the *raion* typically sets uniform tax rates for all municipalities located within its boundaries.

In cases where the boundaries of the first and second-tier municipalities do not coincide exactly, the first-tier municipality is responsible for performing all local government functions outside the jurisdiction of the second-tier municipality. Local taxes, in this case, are established by local self-governments of both levels. This model was dubbed as the "*matrioshka*-doll" system.

The above-mentioned types of municipal organization can be combined within regions. For example, Tyumen *oblast* has 295 municipalities; of these, four are large cities, two are *raions*, and the rest are small townships. In Vladimir oblast, eighteen municipalities at the *raion* level have a "matrioshkadoll" structure, while the remaining seven municipalities follow the one-tier model. The second-tier municipalities in the Vladimir oblast are individual areas that have opted for local autonomy. However, regional authorities are unwilling to recognize them as full-fledged participants in inter-governmental fiscal relations and deal with them through the first-tier bodies of local self-government.

At present, there are about 29,500 local administrations in Russia, of which 12,261 are officially registered as municipal entities.[19] Of these, only 11,691 have elected representative authorities,[20] only 1,209 municipalities are endowed with municipal property and only 4,500 have fully independent budgets.[21]

Local Politics

With the exception of central regional cities, where local and regional politics are closely interwoven, the political process at the local level is virtually non-existent, generally limited to the organization of local elections and referenda on forming or merging municipalities. Debate over local policy issues occurs between the local administration and the regional authorities, rather than between the local administration and political parties or local interest groups. The reason for this state of affairs is clear: financially, local governments in Russia are strongly dependent on the governments of higher levels and therefore seek to please the regional bosses rather than voters. Due to the lack of local financial autonomy, a local government which does not fulfil its election promises to the local constituency may always assign the blame to the failure of the regional administration to provide adequate funding. The strength or weakness of local policy makers is thus determined almost exclusively by their ability to negotiate with the region.[22]

Regional grants are traditionally allocated to localities to maintain existing social infrastructure facilities inherited from the old system, such as schools or kindergartens.[23] Therefore, local leaders refuse to close down vacant or underused facilities, even in dire financial circumstances, since any reduction in the number of social facilities on the local government's balance sheet deprives them of leverage to increase regional grants in negotiations with regional authorities. Preservation of existing facilities at any cost becomes the single most important policy objective of local governments regardless of their actual usefulness to local constituency. Between elections, local officials are accountable to the regional authorities rather than to voters.

Public Participation in Decision-Making

Referenda and citizen assemblies are stipulated in Article 4 of the Law on Local Self-Government as forms by which citizens can directly express their will. The municipal charter establishes procedures for holding local referenda or assemblies in accordance with regional legislation. According to Article 22(5), "a decision made by local referendum does not require approval by bodies of state power, state officials or local self-government bodies. If a regulatory act must be issued in order for such a decision to be implemented, the relevant local government body shall pass the required act."[24] Procedures for holding referenda are also addressed in the Law on Guarantees of Electoral Rights and Referenda.

In addition, Article 25 of the Law on Local Self-Government grants citizens the right to legislative initiative on issues of local importance: "Bills on issues of local importance submitted by the citizenry to local government bodies are subject to mandatory consideration at open sessions attended by representatives of the public, and the results of such consideration shall be made public." [25]

Despite their statutory right to participate in decision making, however, citizens very rarely display legislative zeal. Legislative attempts often encounter administrative difficulties as well.

Local Councils

According to the Law on Local Self-Government, the name of the representative local government body is established in accordance with the laws of a respective region, subject to ethnic, historical and local traditions. Common names include City (*Raion*) Duma, Council of Representatives and Council of Deputies. A local council consists of representatives elected on the basis of universal, equal and direct suffrage in compliance with federal and regional legislation. Hence, bodies of local self-government can be elected or appointed. According to the Law on Local Self-Government, an elected representative body, usually a local council, is mandatory for a settlement to be recognized as a municipal entity or self-governing territory, although citizen assemblies are also permitted to exercise the powers of representative bodies.[26]

A municipal charter may provide for a position of mayor, an elected official to direct the execution of local self-governance in the municipality. There is no federal law on appointed bodies of local self-government or on the internal organization of executive bodies of local self-government.

The Constitution charges the Federation and its subjects jointly to establish the general principles of state administration and local government organization. The regional and federal state authorities follow one structure of administration, with regional government bodies reproducing the major features of federal government bodies. The structure of local governments, on the other hand, is determined entirely at the discretion of the population, according to Article 131 of the Constitution.[27] Thus, both federal and regional legislations establish only general principles of organization for local self-government, while actual structures may vary among municipalities.

Terms of office for local councils differ by region and municipality, usually as established by regional legislation. The mandate for local councils is typically four years, but in some regions it may be two years for selected municipalities. In some Republics the mandate for some local councils is five years.[28]

Mayor

In addition to other elected local government officials, the municipal charter may stipulate an official to head the executive branch of local government. Titles vary, but the position is most frequently referred to as "mayor" or "head of local administration". Mayors may either be elected by citizens or chosen by the local council from among its members. If elected directly by the citizens, the mayor may be entitled under the municipal charter to be a member of the local council and preside over its meetings. Both the scope of mayoral responsibilities and the term of office are established by municipal charter. The mayor is directly accountable to citizens and may also report to the local council, if prescribed by the charter.

Structures of Local Government

The Law on Local Self-Government provides for the following models of local self-government:[29]

- A local council and an elected mayor, who is not a member of the local council;
- A local council and a mayor, who is a member of the local council;
- A local council, the chairman of which is the Mayor;
- A local council, an elected mayor, who is not a member of the local council, and a municipal manager, hired by the mayor, with the consent of the local council;
- A local council and a municipal manager, hired by the council, on a contractual basis;

- A citizen assembly and elected elders; and
- A local council, with committees to oversee individual areas of executive activity, and no Mayor.

The Law on Local Self-Government delegates to regions the right to establish the legal framework for local administrations, including their powers, procedures for establishment, terms of office, organization of activities, names of bodies, officials and elected persons of local self-government. Although the structure of local governments may vary from region to region, in practice, the distribution of power tends to be similar. Most regions follow the "strong mayor/weak council" model, which can take many forms. A classic version is, when the elected mayor also chairs the local council. Another variant is when the mayor is elected by the local council from its members. The "weak mayor/strong council" is a less common pattern, encountered mainly in rural areas. The combination of citizen assemblies and elected elders is encountered only in rural settlements, with a small population, generally at the sub-municipal level.[30] The hiring of managers on a contractual basis occurs rarely and, is the exception, rather than the rule.

Quite frequently mayors are, to all intents and purposes, appointed by regional governors. Mayors in Saratov *oblast*, for instance, are elected by the local council but nominated by the governor. Not once have council members voted against candidates proposed by the governor. If the candidate is not a council member at the time of elections, he or she is appointed to act as the head of local government until council elections are held.[31]

As of 1 September 2000, over 12,261 municipalities[32] were registered in Russia, of which only 11,691 have elected representative bodies. In over 7,000 municipalities, the mayors were elected directly by the citizenry by secret ballot. In more than 3,600 of these municipalities, the mayor both manages the local administration and presides over council sessions as a member of the local council. In 4,519 municipalities, elected officials were chosen from among local council members, including nominees proposed by the regional government administration.[33] In eighty-nine municipalities throughout five regions, the head of the local government is hired by the council on a contractual basis.[34]

Functional Jurisdiction

The 1993 Constitution presents a daunting list of powers reserved to the center. Powers shared jointly between the federal and local authorities are less numerous. Regional jurisdictions are only allocated powers not specifically reserved to the federal government or exercised jointly. Those powers include managing municipal property, establishing and executing regional budgets, establishing and collecting regional taxes, and maintaining law and order. Many sub-national jurisdictions have their own constitutions, however, and often those documents allocate powers to the jurisdiction inconsistent with provisions of the federal constitution.[35]

According to the glossary of the Law on Local Self-Government, "Local self-government bodies refer to elected and other bodies empowered to solve issues of local importance which do not constitute part of state administration."[36] This definition is based on the provisions of the Constitution which state that:

1. Local self-government shall be exercised by citizens through their direct will and through elective and other bodies of local self-government;
2. Bodies of local self-government shall have autonomy in managing the municipal property, in formulating, approving and executing their local budget, in establishing local taxes and fees, and in deciding on other issues of local importance; and
3. Bodies of local self-government are not incorporated into the system of bodies of state power.

Local governments in Russia are responsible for the following functions:[36]

- local development,
- maintaining municipal housing and public utilities,
- establishing and maintaining municipal educational institutions,
- establishing and maintaining municipal health care and sanitation institutions,[38]
- establishing and maintaining municipal law enforcement authorities, maintain public order,
- the preservation of the local historical and cultural traditions,
- regulating planning and development,

- organizing, maintaining and developing municipal services, such as electricity, gas, sewerage, heating and water supply,
- organizing subsidized fuel deliveries to households and municipal institutions,
- constructing and maintaining local roads,
- improving land and municipal parks,
- waste disposal,
- funeral services and crematories,
- establishing and maintaining municipal archives,
- public transport and communications,
- fostering the provision of trade, catering and consumer services,
- effectively managing cultural institutions,
- conserving historical and cultural monuments in municipal ownership,
- organizing and maintaining the municipal information service,
- effectively managing municipal mass media,
- effectively managing athletic institutions and support of sports activities,
- welfare services and promotion of employment,
- protecting the environment, and
- organizing the municipal fire department and promoting fire safety.

As shown above, municipalities are charged with the responsibility to finance and deliver a fairly wide range of public services. However, this list of functions is not mandatory for each and every municipality, since the basket of public services offered by local governments in Russia traditionally depends on the availability of the relevant social infrastructure facilities. Likewise, the delineation of service provision responsibilities between federal, regional and local authorities depends on the distribution of property in social infrastructure facilities among the three levels of government.

In some cases where the failure of local governments to support inter-municipal service provision becomes too visible, regional governments assume responsibility for the facility in question.

Finally, the law details the scope of regional authority with respect to local self-governance and lists the responsibilities of local governments. Many of the responsibilities are stated as the obligation to maintain infrastructure facilities that were transferred to municipal ownership, rather than the obligation to perform local functions. Unlike many countries with strong institutions of local government, local governments in Russia are responsible for the delivery of public services such as education and health care. However, the law allows local governments to limit service delivery according to the capacity of its inherited social infrastructure facilities. Therefore, the assignment of expenditure responsibilities between the regional and local governments depends on the delineation of property between the two levels of government.[39]

In recent years, it has become increasingly common to contract municipal service provision out to private sector enterprises and local administrations have accordingly set up departments of municipal contracts. Some municipalities may also establish departments of public works to address employment maintenance or job creation problems.

Local Finance

Local finances are regulated by the Constitution of the Russian Federation, the Federal Law on the General Principles in the Local Self-Government in the Russian Federation, the Federal Law on the Financial Basis of Local Self-Government in Russian Federation, the Budget Code of the Russian Federation, the Tax Code of the Russian Federation, as well as other federal laws, constitutions, charts, laws of the federation subjects, municipality charters and various local government's legal acts. According to the Federal Law on the Financial Basis of Local Self-Government in the Russian Federation (1977), municipal finances are characterized as a total sum of financial resources formed and used to satisfy the diverse needs of the local community. Municipal finances are based on the following principles: independence, state financial support, and publicity. Thus municipal finances, along with the municipal property and federal property objects handed over to the municipalities; provide the economic foundation of local government in Russia.[40]

The principal law governing financial systems at the local level is the 1997 Law on Local Government Finance. The development of local self-government in the Russian Federation was not supported by the transfer of genuine fiscal autonomy to the local level. Although local governments form their own budgets, their autonomy over revenues is very limited. Yet in the majority of regions, a sizeable portion of consolidated budget expenditures has to be paid by municipalities. In 1999, the municipal share amounted to twenty-eight per cent of the national consolidated budget and fifty-three per cent of the sub-national budget.[41]

As local tax and non-tax revenues can cover only a small portion of local spending needs, the resulting financing gap is covered by the regional governments through grants and shared revenues from federal and regional taxes. In 1999, about twenty-four per cent of local budget expenditures were financed with grants (transfers, subsidies, subventions and mutual settlements) from higher-level budgets; when combined with shared taxes, they accounted for roughly sixty-nine per cent of local budgets. [42]

As the local proportion of shared taxes vary from year to year, local governments cannot predict the amount of revenue that will be available to them, and in effect bear no responsibility for forming and executing their budgets, or for the quality and quantity of services provided to the public.

Municipal finances include: local budgets, municipal extra-budget funds, state and municipal securities owned by a local government, and other financial resources owned by a local government. In their efforts to develop local self-governance, federal authorities attempted to ensure the financial autonomy of local budgets. Revenue sources for local budgets were determined in 1991 by the Federal Law on Taxes. However, revenue from the local taxes and fees enumerated in this law rarely covered more than twenty per cent of local expenditure needs, even including the usually insignificant share of federal taxes permanently assigned to local governments. The regional government had to cover the resulting financing gap with inter-governmental transfers.[43]

Local governments were heavily dependent on regional administrations due to the regional authority to regulate local revenues. The Law on Local Government Finance in the Russian Federation sought to ensure stable revenues for local budgets by restricting the latitude of regional administrations in disposing of their revenue sources. The law was passed in September 1997 only after the president overcame the veto of the Upper Chamber of the Russian Parliament, which is composed of governors and the heads of regional representative bodies.

Local budgets are at the core of municipal finances. The municipal budget is a centralized financial resource fund, local government carryout its drafting, approval, and exercise control over its execution independently. Local legislatures are granted the right to set up local taxes, levies and tax exemptions in accordance with federal legislation. The formation of a local budget is based on uniformed methodology, budget classification, as well as state minimum social standards and social norms provided by federal and regional government bodies. In this sense, local governments' fiscal autonomy is restrained within the frames of federal and regional legislation.[44]

The Law on Local Government Finance is an important milestone in the establishment of a full-fledged institution of local finance. In its provisions, the law establishes the following principles for the municipal budget process:[45]

- maximum levels of municipal debt,
- limits on the ability of local authorities to undertake financial risks, such as speculating in stock markets or contributing local budget funds to bank capital,
- the right of municipalities to set up their own treasuries and tax administrations,
- a fixed proportion of federal taxes to be shared with local governments, applied on average within a region,
- requirements that inter-governmental transfers from regional to municipal budgets be calculated according to a formula, and that allocation of equalization transfers and proportions of shared tax revenue be determined according to a standard methodology, and
- prohibition of the reduction of transfers to municipalities, if own municipal tax revenues are greater than predicted.

Due to the vast disparity in revenues across regions and across municipalities, the Law on Local Government Finance has unfortunately failed to ensure financial autonomy for most local governments.

Eventually, the adopted version of the law established fixed rates of shared taxes to be averaged over all municipalities within a region. Accordingly, regions may establish different rates for different municipalities, potentially allowing richer municipalities to retain no federal taxes whatsoever, while allowing poorer localities to retain one hundred per cent of the regional share of federal taxes. Hence, budget revenues are equalized among municipalities through redirecting financial revenues from rich to poor municipalities, while transfers from the regional budget are used for narrowing the remaining disparity.[46]

Furthermore, the Law on Local Government Finance does not establish standards for regions to distribute funds received from the federal government for equalization purposes. Nevertheless, these grants are substantial; in subsidized regions, those resources may exceed by far the total tax collections in that jurisdiction.[47]

The municipalities do not have the financial independence that they are supposed to have in their capacity as the units of local self-government. Local taxes or shared tax revenues account for only a small fraction of self-government budgets. Otherwise, the municipalities are forced to buy for subsidies from either the federal government or the governments of the subjects of the federation. These governments then begin to encroach upon the authority of the municipality. This essentially leads to a restoration of the Soviet type system.[48]

Local autonomy over expenditures is narrowly constrained by federal mandates that entitle various population groups to benefits and subsidies. These entitlements are prescribed in over 150 federal legislative acts, forty-five of which were passed before 1992. Local authorities are mandated to pay thirty-seven types of subsidies from local budgets, with eligible groups comprising a large proportion, if not the entirety, of the local population.

Responsibility for most of those entitlements and subsidies was assigned to local governments by federal legislation from the outset. The funds required for these federal mandates are estimated to outrun all revenues of most municipalities, including transfers.

Revenue Sources

The standard classification of government revenues and expenditures currently in effect lists the following categories of local government revenues:[49]

(i) local taxes and fees,
(ii) permanently assigned taxes and fees,
(iii) shared tax revenues (at rates decided annually),
(iv) non-tax revenues,

(v) grants from higher-level budgets:
- (a) transfers,
- (b) subsidies,
- (c) subventions,
- (d) mutual settlements.

Local Taxes and Fees

Prior to 1998, local governments were entitled to levy twenty-three local taxes. However, a regional sales tax was introduced in 1998, replacing sixteen of the local taxes. Local governments were instead assigned sixty per cent of sales tax collections, which often fail to compensate for the loss of revenue from the repealed taxes. Revenues from local levies, in 1999, amounted to thirteen per cent of all revenues for municipalities.[50]

Even prior to the introduction of the regional sales tax, local taxes failed to ensure fiscal autonomy for municipalities, since the rates of taxation were virtually legislated by the federal government. Furthermore, the list of local taxes was exhaustive, barring municipalities from introducing new taxes at their own discretion. Local governments could exercise some autonomy in determining the tax base and rates for a very limited number of taxes, such as the tax on the construction of manufacturing facilities in health resort areas and fees for the right to engage in trade, parking, race course participation, the right to shoot movies and TV films, street cleaning and setting up gambling establishments.[51]

The fee for street cleaning, levied on gross sales of enterprises, has become a significant source of own budget revenue for a number of municipalities. In some cases, revenues from this tax amounted to twenty-five per cent of all tax collections, clearly more than was spent on street cleaning.

Article 15 of the Russian Federation Tax Code, which determines the list of local taxes and fees, has not gone into effect. However the list, which contains only five local taxes, is indicative of the intentions of federal legislators towards local taxes. Local taxes specified are:[52]

- (a) land tax,
- (b) personal property tax,
- (c) inheritance and gift tax,
- (d) advertisement tax, and
- (e) local license fees.

This article also stipulates that once a region institutes the immovable property tax, local governments in its jurisdiction will cease to levy the land tax and personal property tax.

Non-tax Revenues

The main sources of local non-tax revenues are:[53]

(i) revenues from use of municipal property and activities, and
(ii) revenues from sales of municipal land and intangible assets.

These revenues are an independent source of local budget revenues. Starting from 1999, the budget classification treats part of the revenues from sales of public property as a source of deficit financing, since these are non-recurring revenue sources.

In addition to the local tax and non-tax revenues mentioned above, the Law on Local Government Finance allows local governments to collect "self-imposed charges" or voluntary lump-sum contributions from citizens, in accordance with the municipal charter. Due to the system of budget reporting, it is difficult to estimate the significance of these contributions in total revenues. If any municipalities collect these contributions, they are most likely used as a revenue source for forming extra-budgetary funds, rather than as a source of budget revenues.[54]

Federal and Regional Tax Revenues Permanently Assigned to Local Budgets

According to the Law on the Tax System, the following federal tax revenues are assigned to localities on a permanent basis:[55]

(i) royalty for use of subsoil resources (local government share fixed according to type of resource),
(ii) stamp duty (one hundred per cent),
(iii) state fee (one hundred per cent),
(iv) inheritance and gift tax (one hundred per cent), and
(v) income tax on individuals engaged in entrepreneurial activities (one hundred per cent).

Regional tax revenues assigned to localities under this law include:

(a) enterprise property tax (fifty per cent).
(b) sales tax (sixty per cent).

Shared Tax Revenues

Shared taxes are a principal tool of inter-governmental fiscal regulation at the regional level and account for the largest amount of revenues distributed from regional budgets to localities. Local revenues from shared taxes are general purpose grants extended from a higher-level budget, similar to subsidies or equalization transfers. Regional governments determine both the applicable taxes and the proportion of tax to be shared between the region and municipalities.

Regions may choose to divide their share of the following federal taxes with localities:[56]

(i) value added tax,[57]
(ii) personal income tax,
(iii) enterprise profit tax, and
(iv) excises, assigned on share by federal authorities to subjects of the Russian Federation.

They may also share the following regional taxes:

(a) enterprise property tax (within the fifty per cent share assigned to the regional level),
(b) forest tax,
(c) payments for water,
(d) education tax, and
(e) sales tax (within the forty per cent share assigned to the regional level).

Under the Law on Local Government Finance, the region may distribute its shared federal taxes differently among its municipalities, but the total share of localities in a particular federal tax should not fall below an established minimum which varies by type of tax:[58]

(a) fifty per cent of the personal income tax,
(b) five per cent of the enterprise profits tax,[59]
(c) ten per cent of VAT,
(d) five per cent of excises on alcoholic beverages, and

(e) ten per cent of excises on other goods.

However, the minimum requirements, highlighted above, do not assist municipalities in estimating their next year revenues from tax sharing, since regions may allocate these percentages differently among municipalities at their discretion.

The Law on Local Government Finance requires that the local proportion of shared taxes be determined by formula and that shared taxes and equalization transfers be allocated to municipalities using a standard methodology. These requirements imply that both regional/ local tax sharing and equalization transfers to localities from the regional government are general purpose regional grants, but transferred to localities through different channels.[60] In practice, however, these requirements are not enforced, and regional authorities make no attempt to allocate those funds using a single equalization methodology.

Special and General Purpose Grants

Grants to localities from the federal and regional budgets include equalization transfers (subsidies), subventions and mutual settlements. Equalization transfers are distributed to localities for the sole purpose of equalizing fiscal capacity, meaning that local governments are free to spend these revenues at their own discretion. Regional governments determine the size of the transfers and sources of revenue for the equalization fund within the regional budget. Under the Law on Local Government Finance, equalization transfers should be allocated across municipalities using a fixed formula with parameters including population size, the proportion of various age groups (such as school-age children and pensioners) in the municipal population, per capita fiscal capacity before equalization and other local features. However, in the majority of regions, distribution of equalization transfers is negotiated rather than formula-driven.[61]

Subventions are distributed to municipalities from the federal or regional budget for specific purposes. These are subject to re-payment in case of failure to use them for their intended purpose within the established time limit. Federal legislation does not specify purposes for regional subventions to localities or procedures for distributing subventions among localities.

Regions rarely use subventions as a means of transferring financial resources to municipalities as the inadequacy of transferred funds would be immediately apparent. Instead, they excuse themselves by claiming that the execution of federal and regional mandates was taken into account in determining the size of equalization transfers distributed to local budgets. In cases where they are utilized, subventions from regional budgets are provided primarily for the execution of federal mandates,[62] and occasionally for the execution of regional mandates.[63]

Mutual settlements are another variety of special purpose grant, transferred to municipalities by regional governments in order to reimburse them for cost increases or revenue losses caused by regional government decisions made during the budget year, after local budgets were approved. Grants provided to local budgets under this category include funds to cover costs of housing maintenance, utilities and other facilities transferred to municipalities. Municipalities may also receive additional earmarked assistance under this category, not provided for in the budget, to finance other expenditures or write off debts on budget loans. There is no prescribed method of allocating those additional financial resources across municipalities.

The method of allocating inter-governmental transfers to municipalities varies across regions. Most regions estimate local expenditure needs and revenue capacity and allocate transfers to cover the resulting financing gap. The region and individual local governments then negotiate the actual figures, with the local government claiming higher expenditure needs and lower anticipated revenue than the regional estimates. In this process, both parties usually refer to historic tax collections and expenditures or estimates derived from previous years' data.

In June 2000, the federal Ministry of Finance approved a document entitled "Provisional Methodological Recommendations for Russian Federation Subjects on the Regulation of Intergovernmental Fiscal Relations". The Recommendations advise regional administrations to use the following guidelines for allocating grants:[64]

(i) Formula-based equalization of per capita fiscal capacity should be employed rather than the principle of balancing own revenues and "needs" of local governments;
(ii) Revenue capacity should be estimated based on the taxable resources of a municipality rather than past revenue collections;

(iii) When measuring per capita fiscal capacity, objective differences in demand for public services and their costs should be considered. These include the demographics of a population, the cost of living, the duration of the heating season, population density, etc. Expenditure needs should no longer be estimated based on the existing social infrastructure; and
(iv) The total sum of shared taxes and equalization transfers intended for municipalities should be estimated during a single process.

These principles allow regions great flexibility in selecting formalized distribution methods. Using a formalized methodology to allocate grants will ensure predictability of transfer amounts, save time spent in negotiating local budget targets and create incentives for local governments to raise additional revenues and use budget resources more prudently.

It should be emphasized that, under the current federal legislation, regional governments are free to choose the method of intergovernmental fiscal relations within their boundaries; the federal government may only advise.

Municipal Personnel

Municipalities may determine personnel policy with respect to municipal employees and of local budgetary institutions. The only exceptions are heads of local line departments, who must usually be approved by officials of the relevant regional department.

According to Article 4 of the Law on Local Self-Government, the regulation of municipal service falls under the competence of the state administration. Article 3 establishes that citizens of the Russian Federation have equal opportunity to municipal employment.[65] Before the adoption of the Law on Foundations of Municipal Service in the Russian Federation, employees of municipal government organizations fell under the scope of the Federal Law on Foundations of the State Service in the Russian Federation, despite the fact that local government is outside the system of state administration. The adoption of the Law on Municipal Service in early 1998 meant that employment in the local government brought the same high level of benefits and social insurance as employment in the state government.[66] Municipal employees fall into the following categories:[67]

(i) Elected officials,
(ii) Full-time employees,
(iii) Part-time employees
(iv) Appointed officials,
v) Staff of local governments, and
(vi) Staff of local budgetary institutions.

Elected Officials [68]

The term "elected official" primarily refers to the mayor and local council members. Although the law provides for the existence of other elected officials, in practice they are rarely encountered, if at all. Elected local officials are not currently required to meet any professional qualifications. The only restriction imposed by federal legislation on elected local officials is that they cannot simultaneously perform the functions of hired or appointed municipal employees.

Some regions (Rostov and Ryazan) have introduced a ban on combining an elective local office with membership in the regional legislative assembly, although no such federal restriction exists. Under the same law, local government officials are subject to early termination by regional authorities, if a court finds a breach of law or of the provisions of municipal charter. In practice, elected local officials are rarely removed from their posts due to a court ruling. When a mayor is removed, it is usually a mayor who had effectively been appointed by the regional governor in the first place. No correlation has been established between the re-election of mayors or local council members and their administrative performance.

Members of local councils can be either full-time employees on the government payroll or part-time officials, who do not receive compensation for their position and continue to perform their previous jobs. Full-time officials are commonly prohibited from holding another income-generating office.

Elected officials are generally accorded immunity from legal prosecution by regional legislation. Additional social guarantees for elected local government officials may be established in regional legislation.

Appointed Officials

The Law on Local Self-Government provides the following definition: "municipal service shall be understood to mean full-time professional employment in local government bodies for exercise of their powers."[69] Hence, municipal service applies only to employment in local self-government bodies, as opposed to other public institutions. It is a full-time job paid for from the budget, though not necessarily the local budget.

Local Government Staff[70]

The Law on Municipal Service also states that legal regulation of municipal service shall be prescribed in the municipal charter as required by federal and regional laws. These regulations include qualification requirements, municipal employee status, terms and conditions of municipal service and administration of municipal service. Regional laws usually establish limitations on the level of wages for municipal employees. Since, the majority of municipalities are subsidized from the regional budget, the regional government wishes to prevent municipal employees from earning more than their regional counterparts.

The status of all staff working under contracts is addressed by the federal Labour Code and similar regulations. Personnel departments of local administrations or councils are responsible for hiring their employees, whose professional requirements are established according to the municipal charter. Individuals, not working in local administrations but providing technical support to local self-government activities, are not considered to be municipal employees. In order to ensure equal opportunity for municipal employment, vacant municipal positions must be publicly announced according to procedures stipulated in the municipal charter.

Staff of Budgetary Institutions[71]

Under Russian legislation, individuals employed by budgetary institutions do not fall into the category of municipal employees. Terms of their remuneration, social guarantees, etc. are established in the Law on the Uniform Schedule of Wages for Workers of Budget Organizations. Hence, salaries paid to budgetary institution employees by local governments cannot be below the federal statutory level. However, local governments are entitled to pay fringe benefits to budgetary institution employees, in addition to their regular salaries. The federal schedule of rates sets basic rates and allowances for employees if a budgetary organization is located in the Far North or equivalent territory. Local authorities are entitled to pay local allowances to employees of municipal budgetary institutions (primarily schools, outpatient clinics and hospitals) in addition to their wages, but rarely exercise their right due to lack of financial resources.

Personnel Training[72]

The new role of local governments in Russia necessitates qualified personnel, modern information technologies, and new methods of work and workflow organization.

Training and re-training of local government employees may take place in both traditional state owned educational establishments and new training institutions such as colleges and long-distance training and consulting centers. Municipalities, regions and the federal government are all contributing to the creation of a pool of information to assist local policy-makers. The outcome of their efforts includes periodicals for local governments, publishing houses that specialize in literature for local governments and dissemination of software and information systems.

Nevertheless, these elements do not yet form an integrated system of professional training, information and methodological support for local governments. State establishments of higher education for training personnel in local self-government are available only in forty-two out of eighty-nine regions, with no professional training of municipal personnel occurring in the other regions.

It is hard to predict which of the two tendencies—centralization or decentralization—will eventually prevail. Despite growing public awareness, the higher demands on governments by the citizenry and the diminished degree of awe for official status in recent years, the beginnings of civil society in Russia are still too weak to be effective. Whether the institution of local self-government will survive is fully dependent on the political course taken by federal authorities.

Local Government Involvement in Profit Enterprises

The Law on Local Self-Government gives local self-governments the right to establish for profit enterprises, agencies and organizations, and deal with issues of reorganizing and liquidating such enterprises. More and more local governments in Russia are setting up municipal companies purely for profit reasons. Local governments are usually nominal owners, often with only a permit for operation serving as their contribution to the stock, but occasionally they may establish companies entirely at their own initiative.[73]

Local administrations have also shown a tendency to contribute municipal property (land or buildings) to the authorized capital of profit enterprises.

Although it is not illegal for Russian municipalities to engage in commercial activities directly or through municipal enterprises, existing limitations make it difficult without violating the law. In addition, revenues from such activities are a liability for local governments, as their inclusion in the budget may lead to a reduction of financial transfers from above. In order to hide commercial revenues, municipalities generally set up various extra-budgetary funds not reflected in budget execution reports.[74]

Federal-Regional-Local Relationships

Under the 1993 Constitution, the republics, territories, *oblasts*, autonomous *oblast*, autonomous regions, and cities of federal designation are held to be "equal in their relations with the federal agencies of state power." Equal representation in the Federal Council for all eighty-nine jurisdictions furthers the equalization process by providing them meaningful input into legislative activities, particularly those of special concern.[75]

According to federal legislation, local government authorities are free to decide on methods of service delivery for public services that fall within their competence. Regional infringements upon the basic rights of local self-governance commonly take the following forms:[76]

(a) establishing municipal boundaries without prior consent;
(b) adopting the Model Charter of a Municipality as regional law;

(c) stipulating that the mayor be elected only from among candidates nominated by the regional governor; and
(d) requiring that appointed heads of municipal line departments be approved by the regional governor or the head of the respective regional department.

In most subjects of the Federation, local self-governance was developed in conformity with the preferences of regional authorities. Consequently, municipalities and their boundaries were established according to the will of regional authorities. Any local attempts to establish new municipalities without approval of regional authorities are nipped in the bud.

In January 1998, after considering other infringements by regions on the principle of local administration, the Constitutional Court ruled that a body of public power should be of either state or municipal nature, depending on the scope of issues falling under its competence. The Constitutional Court thus reaffirmed that government bodies which create the local budget, introduce local taxes and establish procedures for managing municipal property shall be recognized as bodies of local self-government, regardless of their name. As such, they are separate from bodies of state power and are formed through elections by local residents.[77]

Fiscal Relations between Regional and Local Authorities

As noted earlier, local governments are heavily dependent on regional authorities for the transfer of intergovernmental funds. A survey[78] of local budgets, conducted in 1999, revealed that only two municipalities covered their expenditures exclusively from local and permanently assigned revenues without additional financial assistance from the regional government.

The fact that there are almost no self-sufficient municipalities in Russia is the result of insufficient local and assigned revenues, as well as the fact that regional governments derive advantages in exercising firm financial control over localities. In order to increase their share of tax collections, local governments apply informal pressure on taxpayers, resulting in larger regional tax collections.

Since functional responsibilities are divided between regional and local authorities according to ownership of social infrastructure facilities, it is quite common for a territorial branch of the regional administration to be responsible for projects or facilities in a particular municipality. If there are no conflicts between regional and local authorities on the ownership of social infrastructure facilities, bodies of local self-government and territorial branches of state power operate in parallel and autonomously.

Territorial branches of regional state administration are found at the *raion* level only when local self-government is established at the sub-*raion* level. In such cases, the regional center may delegate responsibility for relations with local governments to the territorial branch.[79]

Control, Audit and Supervision of Local Government

The federal control over the operation of the subjects of the federation and local self-governments is executed by the Representative of the President, nominated by the heads of the presidential administration appointed by and directly subordinate to the President. He controls the operations of the bodies of local government. He makes statements of isolations of presidential decrees and government resolutions and submits them to the bodies of local government. He also informs the Prosecutor's Office about these isolations. The Representative of the President has no right to interfere with the operation of local government. Federal government or government of the subject cannot limit the subjects of local self-government defined in the Constitution or federal legislation.[80]

The Constitution was followed by a number of other laws, also initiated at the central level, to establish procedures for the formation and operation of local governments. All of these laws were directed at strengthening the autonomy of the lowest tier of public administration. After establishing a federal relationship between the central and regional levels of government, the Central Government curtailed regional rights over local governments by establishing a similar, though weaker, federal relationship between the center and the regions at the sub-national level. The majority of regions benefited from the federalization of their relations with the center, but was reluctant to relinquish power over sub-regional territories. They preferred paternalistic relations with the local governments to decentralization; rather than employ their newly assigned methods of control, legislative initiative and law enforcement; they opted to reinstate the vertical axis of executive power.[81]

By strengthening the vertical axis of power, the policies pursued under President Putin from the start of his term echoed the governors' preference for centralization. The Office of the President became the source of legislative initiatives and administrative decisions that led to reinforcement of administrative methods of control in the Russian Federation at all levels of power.

Regional Supervision

The Constitution introduced a fundamentally new type of intergovernmental relations, as regulatory interactions replaced direct administrative subordination. However, many regional officials often manifested fierce resistance to the idea of local self-governance and did not abandon the administrative approach in their relations with lower-level governments. These authorities were unable or unwilling to make use of new control mechanisms which emphasized legislative activity and enforcement of laws through the courts.

In the Republic of Tatarstan, local self-government is set up only in rural areas, not in cities. This resistance to the new model explains why governors embrace a "return to the vertical hierarchy of power," most of these governors support the recently amended Law on Local Self-Government, which establishes broader rights to dissolve local councils and dismiss Mayors, if local legislation is found to be inconsistent with the Constitution, federal legislation or legislation of subjects of the Federation.

As in Tatarstan, local self-government in Bashkortostan mainly operates at the sub-*raion* and village level; cities and *raions* are governed by state authorities that are appointed and dismissed by the government of the Republic.[82] Otherwise, provisions of the Law on Local Self-Government still apply whereby local self-government bodies are independent and accountable only to the law and their constituency. The amended law also entitles the federal government and regions to delegate certain federal or regional powers to local governments and monitor their execution, provided that they also transfer the necessary material and financial resources.

Although the Law on Local Self-Government declared extensive local autonomy, both financial and administrative, the legislative trend in recent years has been to clamp down on local autonomy, particularly in the financial sphere. With the adoption of the new Tax Code, the local tax base has been drastically reduced. At present more than seventy per cent of local budget revenues come from federal and regional shared taxes and local governments are utterly dependent, financially and administratively, on regional authorities.[83]

Financial Audit

Independent financial audit of local authorities has not yet gained ground in Russia. Regional and local financial bodies ceased to be departments of the federal Ministry of Finance in 1998, and are now subordinated to the regional or local government. However, as part of the Russian state administration, regional administrations must follow directives from the federal center, including the Ministry of Finance. Federal approval of regional budgets is not required, but regions must submit reports on the execution of consolidated (regional plus local) budgets to the Ministry of Finance. Both the adoption and execution of local budgets are considered by federal legislation to be matters of local significance; municipalities need only report to their residents. Therefore, although regions require local budget data for their consolidated budget reports to the Ministry of Finance, they technically have no right to request the local government to file budget execution reports.

Nevertheless, local governments have continued to file local budget execution reports with regional financial authorities. In addition to local budget execution reports, regions also require that local governments submit their draft budgets for the new fiscal year in order to allocate equalization grants.

The federal Budget Code establishes the regions' right to request this information, but also states that any local government not wishing to compete for regional grants is not required to report budget information to regional authorities. However, local governments seldom refuse to do so.

The Russian Budget Code stipulates the right of local councils to exercise financial control during discussion, approval and execution of local budgets. It also grants local councils the right to create auditing commissions to perform "external" audits of local budgets. Local governments do establish auditing units, but it would be an exaggeration to call them external. Occasionally, local governments initiate external audits, hiring independent auditing firms with a view to making their territories more attractive to foreign investors.[84]

Under the Budget Code, regional authorities are entitled to monitor local spending only where local governments are grant recipients, a right that only applies to funds received from the regional budget. However, regional authorities rarely exercise any control over local spending even on such a limited scale.

Legal Control

The Office of the Public Prosecutor in Russia is a single federal system of state administration, whose territorial branches monitor the compliance of regional and local regulatory and legislative acts with federal legislation. The Public Prosecutor's Office plays a fairly active role in ensuring compliance of local government acts with federal legislation. The violations discovered are often a product of imperfect federal and regional legislation that does not clearly delineate functions between federal authorities, regional authorities, raion branches of regional administrations and local governments. Many infringements have to do with financial matters, such as the distribution of proceeds from the privatization of municipal property or the funding of federal mandates.

Challenges Before Local Government [85]

Although local government has already become an integral part of the public administration system in the Russian Federation, it still remains burdened with many complicated problems. Some of these problems are summarized as under:

Legal Foundation

The Constitution of the Russian Federation, the Federal Law on General Principles of Local Self-Government Organization in the Russian federation and a number of other federal laws provide the general basis for the functioning of local government in Russia. However, they do not settle a wide range of specific legal issues related to local government. Some of these issues are regulated by regional and sectoral legislation. There is not adequate coordination or mutual adjustment among the legal acts regulating local government issues. All of the issues that need legal regulation have not yet been resolved. In many cases, regional governments are either reluctant to pass the necessary laws on local government or adopt legal acts concerned with local government issues that contradict the relevant federal legislation.

Territorial Base

It is obvious that the competition among local and regional governing elites has seriously distorted the process of developing local government's territorial organizational models. The agreement on municipalities' territorial configuration has often been reached either on the basis of a compromise or without regard to the principles of efficiency for local government. As a result, the territorial organization of local government in a number of regions does not comply with local government's goals and functions.

Local Governments' Competence

Most of the conflicts between the different tiers of public government in Russia arise from the vagueness of their range of authority. Inaccurate norms in the Federal Laws on General Principles of Local Self-Government Organization in the Russian Federation allows federal and regional governments to interpret the authority of local governments at their own choosing. Therefore, local governments, as the most vulnerable layer in the public administration system, get more responsibilities and fewer rights.

Financial and Economic

The most critical problems for the functioning of local government in Russia are related to its financial and economic foundation. In spite of the fact that legislation provides for the fiscal autonomy of local government, local governments' own revenue comprise less than 30 per cent of their local revenue on average. This means that the existing fiscal model encourages large scale distribution and redistribution processes among levels of public government. At the same time, the mechanism for regulating intergovernmental fiscal relations is not properly defined and suffers from frequent and erratic reform. These reforms, as a rule, result in further decentralization of expenditure responsibilities as well as further centralization of financial resources.

Under the current fiscal model, local governments actually do not have sustainable sources of revenue to cover their vital expenditure items, nor can they schedule their financial resources and expenses and advance. This dynamics hinders the long-term progressive development of the territories. What makes things even more complicated is the fact that the central and regional governments tend to rid themselves of burdensome social mandates by imposing them on local governments, without any sort of financial provisions.

REFERENCES

1. Lipman, M. and Lapteva, L. (1994). Russia, Commissioned by the Institute for Local Government and Public Service, Moscow.
2. As of October 2000, only the republics of Bashkortostan and Tatarstan retained individual privileges not stipulated in the Constitution.
3. Auty, Robert, and Dmitry O. (eds.) (1976). An Introduction to Russian History, 1: *Companion to Russian Studies*, Cambridge University Press, Cambridge.
4. Chew, A. F. (1970). *An Atlas of Russian History: Eleven Centuries of Changing Borders,* Yale University Press, New Haven.
5. Goskomstat, 1994 Census; Ryan, M. comp. (1993). *Social Trends in Contemporary Russia: A Statistical Source Book*, St. Martin's Press, New York.
6. *Ibid*; Petersson, B.O. (2001). *National Self Images and Regional Identities in Russia*, Ashgate.
7. Dmytryshyn, B. (1977). *A History of Russia,* Prentice Hall, Englewood Cliffs, N.J.
8. The only exception is the federal Ministry of Finance, which gave up its regional, city, and raion offices with transition to the decentralization of local government. All local branches of the Ministry of Finance were officially transformed into the financial departments of regional or local governments.
9. Hittle, J. M. (1979). *The Service City: State and Townsmen in Russia, 1600-1800,* Harvard University Press, Cambridge.
10. USSR (1990). *General Principles of Local Self-Government and Local Economy in USSR,* Government Publication, Moscow.
11. Government of Rusia (1991). *Law on Local Self-Government in Russian Federation*, Moscow.
12. Orlovsky, D. T. (1981). The Limits of Reforms: The Ministry of Internal Affairs in Imperial Russia, 1807-1881, Harvard University Press, Cambridge
13. Costitution of Russian Federation, 1993.
14. Rogger, H. (1987). *Russia in the Age of Modernization and Reform, 1881-1917,* Longman, London.
15. Law on Local Self-Government, 1991.
16. *Ibid.*
17. Mitrokhin, S. (1999). "Implementation of the Municipal Project in Russia: Some Aspects of Federal Policy".

18. Cohen, S. F. (1985). *Rethinking the Soviet Experience: Politics and History Since1917*, Oxford University Press, New York.
19. Zamotayev (1999). as quoted in Mitrokhin, *op cit.*
20. Goskomstat (2000). *Forming Local Self-governance in the Russian Federation.*
21. In the Ingush Republic, for example, heads of municipalities have been appointed by decrees of the President of the Republic.
22. Goldman, M. I. (1983). Economic Problems in the Soviet Union, *Current History*, 82, October.
23. Goskomstat (2000). *Forming Local Self-governance in the Russian Federation.*
24. Law on Local Self-Government, 1991.
25. *Ibid.*
26. Walker, E. W. (1995). Federalism Russian Style: The Federation Provisions in Russia's New Constitution, Problems of Post-Communism, July- August.
27. Constitution of Soviet Federation, 1993.
28. Ovchinnikov, B. (1999). "Municipal Elections: Tendencies and Patterns"; Teague, E. (1994). Russia's Local Elections Begin, *RFE/RL, Research Report*, 3(7), February.
29. Law on Local Self-Government, 1991.
30. *Ibid.*
31. Grushin, D. (1999). "Ethnicities and Local Government", New Haven, Yale University Press.
32. Goskomstat (2000). *Forming Local Self-governance in the Russian Federation.*
33. For example, in Saratov oblast.
34. For example, in some municipalities in Voronezh oblast.
35. Lankina, T. (2000). Municipal Government in Russia's Regions, Centre for International Security and Cooperation, Stanford University, Stanford, CA; Dating Russia.com
36. Law on Local Self-Government, 1991.
37. *Ibid.*
38. Health care is financed by the municipal, regional or federal budget as well as from the mandatory medical insurance fund. This dual financing scheme generates difficulties in delineating powers.
39. City of Petrozavodsk Administration, http://www.petrozavodsk.ru
40. Danielian, Armen, Local Government in Russia: Reinforcing Fiscal Autonomy, Local Government and Public Service Reform Initiative.
41. Law on Local Government Finance, 1997.
42. *Ibid.*
43. Law on Taxes, 1991.
44. Danielian, *op cit.*
45. Law on Local Government Finance, 1997.
46. Economy of the Russian Federation in 1990, Statistical Reference Book, Republican Information Publishing Centre, Moscow, 1991.

47. *Ibid.*
48. Lipman, *op cit.*
49. Treadgold, D. W., (1987), *Twentieth Century Russia*, Westview Press, Boulder, Colorado.
50. *Ibid.*
51. *Ibid.*
52. Russian Federation Tax Code.
53. *Ibid.*
54. Law on Local Government Finance, 1997.
55. Law on Tax System.
56. Rowland, R. H. (1994). Declining Towns in the Former USSR, *Post-Soviet Geography,* 35(6), June.
57. Starting from 2001, municipalities have been receiving five per cent of collections from the enterprise profits tax.
58. *Russian Regions Today: Atlas of the New Federation*, 1994, International Center, Washington.
59. In Vladimir oblast, subventions from the oblast budget in 1999 were provided primarily for payment of child benefits to low-income families, while in Leningrad oblast they were designated for subsidies to eligible groups for housing, utilities and free medicine.
60. Law on Local Government Finance, 1997.
61. Saikal, Amin, and William Malrey (1995). *Russia in Search of Its Future*, Cambridge University Press, Cambridge.
62. Vladimir Oblast; Wallich, C. (1992). *Fiscal Decentralisation, International Relations in Russia*, World Bank, Washington.
63. In Leningrad oblast, subventions to local budgets in 1999 were used to support the State Service of Medical and Social Examination. In Altai krai local budgets received subventions for maintenance of inter-raion budget agencies.
64. Ministry of Finance (2000). Provincial Methodological Recommendations for Russian Federation subjects on the Regulation of Intergovernmental Fiscal Relations.
65. Law on Local Self-Government, 1991; Teague, E. (1994). Russia's Local Elections Begin, *RFE/RL, Research Report*, 3(7), February 18.
66. Law on Foundations of Municipal Service in the Russian Federation, 1998.
67. Lapidus, G. W. (ed.) (1995). *The New Russia: Troubled Transformation*, Westview Press, Boulder, Colorado.
68. *Ibid.*
69. Tolz, V. (1994). Problems of Building Democratic Institutions in Russia, *RFE/RL Research Report*, 3(10), March 4.
70. Law on Municipal Service; Nove, A. (1990). *The Soviet Economic System*, George Allen and Unwin, London.
71. Law on Foundations of Municipal Service, *op cit.*
72. Hewett, E. A. (1988). *Reforming the Soviet Economy*, Brookings Institution, Washington.

73. This refers to commercial banks established with assistance from municipal capital. One example is *Dom-bank,* which operates in Domodedovo raion of Moscow region. The raion administration originally held a small share (one percent) in the bank capital. The administration and committee for property management presently hold a controlling block of shares (fifty two per cent).
74. Starting from 2001, all VAT revenues are due to be consolidated in the federal budget.
75. Lankina, *op cit.*
76. Law on Local Self-Government, 1991.
77. World Bank, 1995, *Statistical Handbook* 1994: States of the Former USSR, Washington.
78. This study was undertaken by the Georgia State University under the Fiscal Reform in Russia Project sponsored by the United States Agency for International Development.
79. Aslund, A. (ed.) (1994). *Economic Transformation in Russia*, Pinter, London.
80. Lipman, *op cit.*
81. Hanson, Philip (1996). Structural Change in the Russian Economy, *Trasition*, 2(2), January 26.
82. Constitution of Russian Federation, 1993; Wallich, C. (ed.) (1994). *Russia and the Challenge of Fiscal Federalism*, World Bank, Washington.
83. Law on Local Self-Government, 1991.
84. Russian Budget Code; International Monetary Fund, World Bank, Organisation for Economic Cooperation and Development and European Bank for Reconstruction and Development, 1991, A Study of the Soviet Economy, World Bank, Washington.
85. Danietian, *op cit.*; Saikal, A. and William Maley, (eds.) (1995). *Russia in Search of Its Future,* Cambridge University Press, Cambridge; Wallich, C., (ed.) (1994). *Russia and the Challenge of Fiscal Federalism*, World Bank, Washington.

NB. Other materials used are working materials of government agencies and other research institutions, and were obtained through websites............ Code of Legislative Acts of the Russian Federation, M.A. Krasnov, Introduction to Municipal Law, Law University Publishers with the Institute of State and Law, Moscow, 1993, Russian Federation issues 1-5, 1994 section on Local Self-Government, and others.

Chapter 7

Emergence of Local Government in India

Age of Imperial Unity

The ancient India was purely a rural country. The administrative structure differed from empire to empire, and even from king to king in one kingdom. However, the main administrative unit of local administration was village. Thus for effective and smooth administration, the rural collective life was promoted by organizing every village with a number of common administrative units, known as '*Sangrahara*', '*Kharwatika*' and *Mahagrama* or '*Sthaniya*'. According to Manu, the king appointed lords of ten, twenty, hundred and thousand villages.[1] Similar divisions are also hinted at by Kautilya, who mentions a royal official, called '*Gopa*', who looked after five or ten villages and another called '*Sthanika*', who supervised one quarter of *Janapads* or districts. The chief executive officer of the village administration was called '*Gramani*' or '*Gramika*', who was appointed by the king. He carried out the village administration with the help of village elders. He was in some cases elected and, in few other cases nominated. He was vested with magisterial authority. He was assisted by a number of officials, selected by the people, among them accountant was the most important. The chief functions of the village headman included as leader of the village militia, defence of village, collection of revenue, custodian of village records, presiding over the village council and guiding its deliberations, to carry on correspondence with district and central authorities and to organize works of public utility.[2]

Kautilya, in spite of being staunch supporter of strong and absolute monarchy, allowed the village community to have freedom from central control. His ideas helped them in their healthy existence.[3]

He gives a vivid account of urban administration, dominated by central organization of a monarchy. The direct control and participation of the state officials was felt in town administration under a '*Nagarka*', who was also called '*paramukhya*'. '*Nagarka*' was responsible for city administration with the help of '*Gopa*' and '*Sthanika*'. His main duties were to maintain peace in the city, to keep watch over the whereabouts and conduct of the newcomers, to take charge of foreigners and to keep an eye on brothel keepers, to keep census of inhabitants with their income and expenditure, to ensure good sanitary conditions, to protect people from the ravages of fire and epidemics, to guard the city and prevent the persons from moving at night, to keep drains and waterworks in proper order, to help foreigners in distress, and to take charge of lost articles. The '*Nagarka*' had a regular office having various officials. City guards were strictly controlled. The town was also the seat of judicial administration. The city elders retained wide powers. The municipal administration was conducted efficiently.[4] The city was built on a thought out plan. The strict municipal regulations were in the interest of the public. Kautliya mentions different types of committees and specialists, which appear fully relevant in modern times. According to Strabo, many duties of '*Nagarka*' were discharged by Boards of Five (Panchayats). Strabo enumerates six such Boards.[5]

The Classical Age

The Pallavas

The material relating to provincial and local governments in this period is very scanty. The development of local self-governing institutions such as '*Sabha*' or the Assembly, was a later growth in Tamil Nadu under the Pallavas (not earlier than 8th century A.D). Side by side with the working of the village 'Sabha' or 'Nadu', 'Ur' is also referred to in various inscriptions. 'Nadu' was an administrative unit larger than village and smaller than 'Kottam'. 'Viyavan' a hereditary office was village head. 'Viyavan' was entitled to certain remuneration from village and was therefore held in esteem. Every member of the village was liable to pay a small fee for the maintenance of the 'Viyavan', who held office and discharged his duties in the interest of the village people.[6]

The village assembly was variously known as '*Sabha*' and '*Mahasabha*'. Its members were called '*Perumakkal*' or greatmen.

According to Minakshi, *Sabha* was placed in charge of several kinds of work. They controlled, as a body, a number of committees of 'Variyams' and carried on the village administration. The assembly being a larger body exercised control over the committees.[7]

The Cholas

Though there was corporate activity in economic and religious life and in territorial divisions like '*Nadus*' and '*Nagarams*' (town) during the Cholas, it was the village assembly that exhibited the greatest and the most comprehensive group activity. The village and town assemblies, while those of Nadus were representative institutions. Of the two kinds of assemblies called 'Ur' and '*Sabha*' or '*Mahasabha*', which were the gatherings of the adult male members of the local community, the former was of the general type and the latter was the assembly of the 'agrahara' or Brahamana settlement.[8]

The lowest unit of the local administration, the self-governing villages, was of two principal types. The first type had an assembly called 'Ur' and an executive body, called the 'alunganam' (ganam). The second type, which was specially represented by villages of Brahamanas, had an assembly called '*Sabha*' and various committees (Variyams) of the same to carry out its executive works. '*Sabhas*' exercised a wide range of powers. They kept their own records relating to the rights of the villagers. They decided disputes and granted lands for maintenance of services and sacred teachings in the temples. They founded and maintained hospitals and took charge of all charitable endowments in the village. They controlled a number of taxes, which they could assign or remit at their pleasure.[9]

According to the regulations of AD 921, each of the villages was to nominate persons possessing certain qualifications. Village assemblies were autonomous. The '*Mahasabha*' possessed proprietary rights over communal lands and controlled the private lands within its jurisdiction. The committees looked after the village administration with the assistance of paid officials.[10]

Medieval Period

Delhi Sultanate

During the Sultanate period village was the basic unit of administration and it was permitted to maintain its traditions of self-governance.

The government entrusted it with the responsibility of maintaining peace in the area under its control. The village dealt with the administration through its headman, and maintained an accountant called '*Patwari*' to keep its records of cultivation, produce, assessment and payment of the state demand. The headmen, some of whom were hereditary, were given a small percentage of revenue, which they had helped in realizing.[11]

'*Kotwal*' was the custodian of peace and order. He was responsible for maintenance of public utilities and prevention of nuisance. Another officer of the municipal police was the '*Muhtasib*', whose duties were to keep a strict watch over the conduct of people, to control the markets and to regulate weights and measures.[12]

Maratha Administration

The changes at the upper levels in the state did not affect much of its organization at the lower levels, where government impinged on the masses. The self-sustained village remained the primary unit of administration. Each village had a headman, the 'Patel', who came from peasant stock and who combined the functions of revenue officer, magistrate and judge, and acted as intermediary between the village and the government officials. Though he held his office by a grant from the government, his office was hereditary and was to the subject of sale and purchase. The '*Kulkarni*' or village clerk or record keeper, who was always a Brahmin, was second in importance to the Patel. He was often expected to share the Patel's responsibility for the good behaviour of the village community. The '*Mahar*' was another important functionary of the community. He was the watchman and messenger of the village.[13]

As a revenue officer 'Patel' allotted the lands to such cultivators, who had no landed property of their own, and fixed the rent, which each had to pay. He collected the revenue for the government from all the *ryats*, conducted all its arrangements with them and exerted himself to promote the cultivation and prosperity of the village.[14]

Mughal Administration

The Mughals divided the face of whole country into villages for administrative purposes. Each member of the brotherhood held in separate possession of the land, which he cultivated and enjoyed the fruits of his labour. In managing the affairs of the village, the members acted as body, their agents being the 'headmen' chosen from among them according to the custom of the locality. The headmen could let to tenants the land not required by the members of the brotherhood, and they represented the village in its dealings with the administration. The extent of their powers varied in different regions but they were everywhere important. Each village had a hereditary registrar or accountant, who maintained records of cultivation, receipts and payments, and assisted the headman in the performance of the duties.[15]

Villages were grouped into larger units, known as '*Paraganas*'. There was a headman (*chaudhari*) in each paragana, who received orders from the administration and exercised some sort of local jurisdiction. There was also a registrar or accountant (*Kanungo*) for the paragana. He was the repository of local agrarian knowledge and the interpreter of local customs on whom foreign administrators relied.[16]

The Mughal administration was concentrated in the provincial capital. It was city government living and working in cities and mainly concerning itself with the inhabitants of the cities and their immediate neighbourhood. The villages were neglected and despised, and the village life was left pretty much to their own devices, uninfluenced by and indifferent to the government of the province, so long as they paid the land tax and did not disturb the peace.[17]

Thus, local government institutions have always existed in India in one form or the other since ancient times. The modern form of local government however owes its genesis to the British rule in the country.

British India

As far back as 1687, Directors of the East India Company ordered that a corporation consisting of European and Indian members be formed at Madras (now Chennai) for the purposes of local taxation. This corporation had a mayor, twelve aldermen and sixty burgesses. It was superseded by the Charter of 1726. The early records of the East India Company bear evidence to the fact that the officer, who had the charge of the presidency town police, exercised municipal functions also.[18] The organization was comparable to the Mughal institution of '*Kotwal*', a police magistrate also, who united in his office the duties of a municipal chairman.

The system of voluntary taxation perhaps dictated the expediency of popular concurrence for the arrangement made by Hastings in 1773. Accordingly, the whole town of Kolkata (Calcutta) was divided into a number of wards. Each ward was placed under a '*Kotwal*', appointed with the general approval of the people. Below him was a '*Thanadar*', who was assisted by a 'naib' or deputy and a number of 'pikemen', whose duty was to patrol the town at night. '*Kotwal*' also controlled the market and levied assessment on the inhabitants in keeping with the usage of the country, the laws of their religion or castes or their voluntary consent. In doing so, he obtained the concurrence of the principal householders and kept a regular account. At the head of all the divisions, was placed a European employee of the Company i.e. Superintendent of Police, who exercised both police and municipal functions.[19]

The Governor General-in-Council enacted a set of regulations in 1780. The objects of these reforms were to perfect the municipal administration for the town of Calcutta (now Kolkata). Provisions were made to establish a body of thirteen commissioners chosen by the Governor General-in-Council. The commissioners, subject to the approval of the Governor General-in-Council, were authorized to assess the annual rent of every holding in the town, and separate collectors were appointed to realize municipal taxes. They were also authorized to take cognizance of any offence committed against municipal law.[20]

The Act of 1847 vested the collection and disbursement of assessment in a Board of Seven Commissioners, to be called Commissioners for the improvement of the town of Calcutta (Kolkata). This replaced the Justices of Peace. Out of seven, three commissioners were appointed by the Governor of Bengal, while remaining four were elected by the rate payers, one from each of the four wards in which the town of Calcutta was divided, later on they were allowed extensive powers of conservancy and sanitation as well. The Calcutta Municipal Commissioners were declared a body corporate. The Act of 1852 reduced the number of Commissioners to four—two nominated and two elected.[21]

In the case of Bombay (now Mumbai), the Act of 1845 established an executive body called the Board of Conservancy, consisting of seven members—two being *ex-officio* and five elected by the Justices (3 were to be Indians).[22]

India Under British Crown

The Presidency Towns

Perhaps under the stress of changing circumstances the British masters did not realize the importance of indigenous institutions of the country, but built up gradually a new system of their own. In Bengal, Regulations, passed in 1816 and 1819, authorized the government to levy money for the construction and repairs of roads, bridges and drains and for the maintenance of ferries. The government worked in such matters with the assistance of local consultative committees, with the Magistrate as secretary in the respective districts. Voluntary funds for local improvements were raised in Madras (now Chennai) and Bombay (Mumbai). An Act of 1869 authorized the Bombay Government to make provisions for expenditure on matters of local public utility and to form committees for administration of such funds not only in the district as a whole, but also in the sub-divisions.[23]

The legislation of 1856 attempted to coordinate the municipal and police administration of the Presidency towns on a uniform basis. The Madras Act of 1867 divided the city into eight wards, to each of which the local government appointed four commissioners. In addition, a President was also appointed by the government. The executive function was vested in him. Calcutta and Bombay reverted, in 1885, to the system of administration by Justices of the Peace, as a consultative and controlling body with a salaried chairman as their executive officer.[24]

Lord Mayo's decentralisation scheme of 1870 was a significant step in the direction of local self-government. In the following years, Acts were passed in different provinces providing for the levy of rates and the constitution of local committees to administer the funds. These committees with an official chairman for each, were constituted by official and non-official nominees of the government and were under its control. They acted mostly as government agencies. Act of 1872 constituted two representative bodies in Bombay. The first body was the Municipal Corporation of the City of Bombay consisting of sixty-four persons—32 were elected by the rate payers, 16 nominated by the government and 16 elected by the Justices of the Peace. Their term was two years. They elected one chairman for a year. The second body was the Town Council. It consisted of twelve members, of whom eight were elected by the corporation out of their own members, while four were nominated by the government from among the members of the corporation itself. They also held office for two years. The government appointed one of its members as chairman.[25]

The function of the corporation was to exercise a general control over all municipal affairs. The council was to secure clear administration of the municipal fund. It was a sort of finance committee of the corporation, whose duty was to control expenditure and prepare annual budgets. The municipal commissioner, an ICS officer, controlled, in fact, the entire executive administration of the corporation.[26]

The Calcutta Municipal Corporation Act 1876 established the Corporation of the Town of Calcutta, consisting of 72 members (commissioners), of whom 48 were elected by the rate payers and 24 appointed by the local government. Their term was three years. In addition, the Bengal government appointed a chairman, and one vice-chairman appointed by the commissioners. The chairman was the Commissioner of Police and the Municipal Commissioner as well.[27]

The Madras Act of 1878 empowered the rate payers to elect half of the 32 commissioners. The position of the President remained the same. There were two Vice-Presidents one to be an engineer, who presided over the department of public works and sanitation, and the other controlled assessment and collection of rates and taxes. The president and vice presidents were to be commissioners, *ex-officio*. These 34 together constituted the Municipal Commissioners for the City of Madras, a body corporate.[28]

The liberal administration of Lord Ripon is memorable for its famous Resolution of 1882 on Local Self-Government. Making allowance for local peculiarities, a network of Local Boards was to be maintained and extended throughout the country. The smallest administrative unit, the sub-division, the 'taluk' or the 'tehsil', was ordinarily to form the maximum area to be placed under a Local Board. It was laid down in the Resolution that the Local Boards "must everywhere have a large preponderance of non-official members. In no case ought the official members to be more than one-third of the whole."[29] The non-official members were to hold office for at least two years and they were to act as Chairman of the Local Boards. Provision was, however, made for control of the Provincial Government over the Local Boards. In first place, sanction of the executive authorities was required for the validity of certain Acts. In the second place, the Provincial Government was to have power either to set aside altogether the proceedings of the Board. Further, the appointment of Chairman was to be subject to the approval of the Government.[30]

Lord Ripon's Government took an important step also, in regard to municipal administration of towns. The first attempt to introduce municipal government, outside Presidency towns, was made by an Act passed in 1842. This Act, applicable only to Bengal, was to enable "the inhabitants of any place of public resort or residence to make better provision for purposes connected with public health and convenience". The Act of 1842 was repealed in 1850 and the Act for municipal administration of county towns was applicable to the whole of British India. This Act was permissive in nature. The Act was partially in-operative in the states of Madras and Bengal, though it was considerably used in Bombay and the North-Western Provinces. Gradually, there was growing consciousness about the need for further municipal legislation, and Acts were passed for Madras, in 1865, for Bengal, in 1864 and 1868, for Punjab, in 1867 and for the Central Provinces, Awadh and North-Western Provinces in 1868. These Acts provided for elections in constituting municipalities and also the levy of local taxes. But nowhere was the election introduced, except to some extent, in Punjab and the Central Provinces. On the whole, nothing like a responsible municipal government had as yet come into being. In most cases, the members of the Municipalities were virtually under government control. In many places, services admirably adopted for local government were reserved in the hands of the central administration, while everywhere heavy charges were levied on Municipalities in connection with the police, over which they had necessarily no executive control.[31]

Lord Ripon's Resolution of 1882 provided for the introduction of principles of self-government in the municipalities. According to it, the actual municipal administration was to be transferred to the elected representatives of the people, working under a non-official chairman, though the ultimate supervision, control and superintendence remained with the government. It was further proposed that the charges for the maintenance of the town police, hitherto paid out of municipal revenues, should be met by Government, and Municipalities should spend equivalent sum on education, medical relief and local works of public utility. Acts were passed in 1833-34, which modified the Constitutions, powers and functions of the municipal bodies and provided for the compulsory election of a larger proportion of municipal commissioners varying from one-half to three-quarters. Provision was also made for the election of a chairman in place of the Executive Officer, who had hitherto held the post. But for several years, the District Officer continued to be elected as the Chairman at many places. Gradually, however most of the Municipalities came to elect a non-official as Chairman.[32]

The Madras Act of 1884 provided the election of three-fourth of the commissioners and one-fourth to be nominated by the Governor-in-Council. Another feature was to establish a standing committee. It consisted of five members, the president, the vice-president and two of the ordinary commissioners. Its function was to control municipal expenditure.

The City of Bombay Municipal Act of 1888 defined municipal authority as consisting of a Corporation, a standing committee (in place of town council) and a Municipal Commissioner. The members were now called councillors. They were 72 in number—36 elected at ward elections, 16 by the justices, two by the fellows of Bombay University and two by the Bombay Chamber of Commerce. The remaining 16 were appointed by the Local Government. They were elected for three years.

The Calcutta Corporation Act of 1888 increased the strength to 72—fifty elected by the rate payers, four by the Bengal Chamber of Commerce, four by Calcutta Traders Association and two by the Commissioners for the Port of Calcutta. The Government was to nominate fifteen members only. The Act established a General Committee, consisting of 18 members –12 being elected by the elected commissioners and six nominated ones. The Chairman of the corporation was the President of the General Committee and the Vice-Chairman its *ex-officio* member. It was essentially the budget and finance committee of the Corporation.

The Act of 1899 created three authorities—the Corporation, the General Committee and the Chairman, each of them being made independent within its own sphere. The entire executive powers vested in the Chairman. The corporation was reduced to the position of a mere deliberative assembly.

The Act of 1904 consolidated the Constitution of the Madras Corporation. It vested the municipal government in a nominated salaried President and 36 commissioners –20 were to be elected at ward elections, while of the remaining 16, three were to be appointed by the Madras Chamber of Commerce, three by the Madras Traders Association, two by such corporate bodies as of the local government directed, and eight by the Local Government itself. The standing committee was to consist of eight members, all of them being commissioners elected annually by the corporation. The President of the Corporation was to be the President of the committee also. The entire executive responsibility of the corporation vested in the President. The President became subject to popular control under the Madras City Municipality Act of 1919. It provided for a council of 50 members, who elected their President from amongst themselves. The Act of 1933 designated the President as the Mayor. In Bombay, it was done by the Act of 1931.

Thus through various measures, municipal administration in the Presidency towns had developed a few important features. A limited electorate, a strong executive in the hands of a government official, certain safeguards for control over finance and auditing of accounts, and statutory provisions for such works as sanitation, water supply etc. The government had the right to interfere in cases of mismanagement or negligence. There was no real self-governance in the municipalities and government control was maintained over them in many respects. There was however, a growing consciousness in the country for making municipalities self governing and efficient.

District Municipalities

The history of municipalities in British India, outside the Presidency towns may be divided into four phases:[33]

1. Development upto 1850, essentially a phase of voluntary associations;
2. The period 1851-81, when the element of election was introduced with an emphasis on administrative efficiency and extension of municipals services;
3. The period 1881-1919, a phase of development, where efficiency was to be subordinated to the political consideration injected in 1882; and
4. From 1919 to 1947, a period of democratization.

First Phase (Up to 1850)

In the early years of its rule the Company's Government in Bengal maintained the Mughal pattern of '*Kotwali*', established in large towns, each containing a certain number of '*barkandazis*' (armed guards), '*chaukidars*' (watchmen) and '*domes*' (scavengers). Both police and municipal functions belonged to the Government, who exercised them through the agency of '*Kotwal*'. In 1812, the Banaras system was introduced. To give stability, 'thanna' engagements were prepared and signed by the contractors, who themselves fixed their quota and appointed their members to be a 'Panchayat'.[34] The members were authorized to realize the contribution and disburse the wage of the '*chaukidars*', who were nominated, appointed and maintained by the community for its own benefit and protection.

The legislation of 1842 firstly introduced the taxation for municipal purposes outside the Presidency towns. It enabled the inhabitants to make better provision for purposes connected with public health and convenience. The people however, did not favour and refused to pay levy.[35] The next attempt made in 1850 was permissive in nature. The provision for taxation made was indirect methods. It retained the 'panchayat' system as an agency of assessment and continued to apply part of that assessment to municipal purposes.[36]

Second Phase (1851-81)

The Towns Improvement Act, 1865 in the Madras state provided for the compulsory levy of rates for both police and municipal purposes, including construction, repairing and cleaning of drains, making and repairing of roads, and preserving the public health.[37] One-fourth of the amount raised for these purposes was to be met by the Government as a grant-in-aid.

The Act of 1871 withdrew the grant-in-aid to the municipal funds but relieved the municipalities of the cost of maintaining the town police. In 1879, the right to elect municipal commissioners was first conferred on four towns.[38]

The Bombay Presidency Act of 1873 divided the existing municipalities into:

(i) cities, where the elective system was made permissive in regard to 2/3 of the commissioners, and
(ii) towns, where all the commissioners were to be nominated.

The District Officer was the *ex-officio* president of all the municipalities,[39] while the Assistant or Deputy Collector of the 'Taluk' was to be Vice-President.

In Bengal, the modern municipal system was introduced under the Act of 1869. It did not repeal the 1850 Act and empowered to set up municipality consisted of four *ex-officio* and seven nominated non-official commissioners, with the District Officer as Chairman. The Act of 1868 brought elective principle, for the first time, as regard 2/3 of the members, chairman and the vice-chairman. The Act of 1873 provided for an elected chairman. It divided the municipalities into four classes on the basis of the law enforced[40] i.e., (i) First class (1864), (ii) Second class (1868), (iii) Unions (1856) and (iv) Stations (1850).

From the preceding account of the development of municipal government in India prior to 1882, there emerge three broad conclusions.[41] First, that although the idea of self governing municipal institutions was not absent, the immediate object was to create, through a process of decentralisation, municipal and other local agencies that might relieve the Government of India, both financially and administratively. Secondly, that the changeover from a voluntary to a compulsory system of local taxation introduced a degree of direct official control over municipalities that rendered the permissive provisions of the elective principle on the whole nugatory. Thirdly, stress was laid on the extension and efficient administration of municipal services.

Third Phase (1881-1919)

Lord Ripon heralded a new era in the history of local government in India. His contributions were mainly two:[42] First, he introduced the decentralized system of finance on a uniform and extended basis. Its object was to secure the transfer from the provincial to local heads such additional items of receipts and charges as might equalize local and municipal taxation. Secondly, he injected a political element in self-government policy. He wanted to enforce the elective system as the instrument of political education.

The Bengal Act of 1884 abolished the distinction between city and town municipalities and provided that at least half of the commissioners are elected, officials in no case exceeding one-fourth. The president was either to be elected by the commissioners or appointed by the Government. The Act III of 1884 excluded from its operation in Unions and Stations. In the remaining two towns, two-third of the Commissioners were to be elected. The chairman was to be elected in most cases.[43]

Lord Ripon's reform, however, introduced elections, based on communal basis. The Royal Commission on Decentralisation (1907) indirectly revived Ripon's emphasis on popular local self-government. The Morley-Minto Reform (1909) introduced separate communal representation in the supreme Legislative Council; a provision for council election on a communal basis involved the municipalities in communal politics. The Decentralization Commission emphasized the strengthening of the executive with the growth of municipal autonomy.[44] As such, local government became a transferred subject administered by the provincial legislature.

Fourth Phase (1919-1947)

Most of the legislations enacted during this period were to democratize the municipal government in the country. Moreover, local government had not taken root before it was overwhelmed by anti-imperialist and communal politics. Since its development in the past had proceeded as part of a process of administrative devolution with the object of assisting the Government in the discharge of its local functions, there was much self-government except the elective representatives of a local community, with powers to levy taxes and exercise patronage. There would have been an element of continuity and some substance of self-government, if the traditional 'Panchayat' system, which was rooted in the community and based on custom, had received statutory recognition. Modern municipalities did not grow from below; they came in, primarily, as a source of taxation.[45] The distance between them and the community remained.

Rural Boards

Rural Boards like municipalities did not grow indigenously. They did not owe their origin to traditional institution of village communities and 'panchayats'. The Government created modern local bodies for the administration of local funds, raised executively in the beginning but made statutory later, to meet a number of local requirements, the most important of which was initially the construction and maintenance of roads.[46]

Indian States

There was also a beginning of local self-government in the Indian States. In 1862, a municipal committee was constituted at Bangalore as an experimental measure, and was later followed by more municipalities at the district and 'Taluk' headquarters, their number finally rising to 83, in 1881. Jaipur and Indore States established municipalities in their capitals, in 1868. A year later, municipal administration was introduced in Hyderabad city and its suburbs also. Finally, in 1877, municipalities were established in all towns of the Baroda State containing a population of 10,000 people and over, excepting Dhaka. But all the members of all these bodies were nominated though non-officials too were included, among them. Local self-government was no where introduced save in Mysore. The municipalities were no more than local committees dealing with lighting and sanitation, while in some cases, these were entirely managed by the State.[47]

The efforts to extend local government in the states were continued. Progress of the municipalities in Mysore was duly maintained and their number rapidly increased. In 1892, the system of electing some non-official members was introduced. The system of municipal taxation and finances was revised, and new sources of municipal income were allotted to these bodies. The conditions in other states were not so advanced. In Hyderabad State, more municipal committees or local boards were established but no real advance was made and the members were still being nominated. In Travancore State, a start was made only in 1900, when an enactment was passed. In Malwa, the municipal self-government was still not common. The Gwalior State made a beginning by establishing a municipal board in Gwalior, in 1887, and by 1905, as many as 48 of its members were being elected out of the total of 80. More municipalities were opened by the Gwalior and Indore States in populous towns. In Rajputana, municipal committees had been established at Jodhpur and Bikaner, in 1884 and 1889, respectively. But Rajputana still did not contain any municipality in the true sense of the term, enjoying the corporate privileges of local self-government, and all the members were still being nominated. The conditions in the Baroda State had however, rapidly progressed. The Maharaja was most anxious to preserve as much of the ancient self-government in the villages as was possible.[48]

Post-Independence Scenario

Local self-government played an important role in the Independence Movement. After Independence, the Constitution of the country was framed on federal principles (although word 'federation' was not mentioned). The Constitution divides the government functions in three lists:[49] Union, State and Concurrent. Local government is put in the State List and is governed by the State Statutes or in the case of Union Territories, by the Union Parliament.

After Independence, many leaders, especially Gandhiji felt the need of reviving the traditional local government system. With the formation of the First Five Year Plan and introduction of the Community Development Programme, in 1952, the question of grass-root level development became important and a high power committee was set up to consider the question of establishing Panchayat Raj in rural area. To examine this institutional issue, another committee headed by Shri Balwantrai Mehta (known as the Mehta Committee) was set-up. This Study Team, after a thorough examination of the Plan projects in operation in the field, submitted its famous report in 1957. The three-tier Panchayati Raj system of self-government in rural India was set up on the recommendations of the Mehta Committee. Panchayat system developed differently in different states because of local peculiarities.

In 1958, the National Development Council (NDC) of Government of India stated that there should be a three-tier (three levels) structure of local self-government from the village to the district, with the village at the bottom and the district at the top.[50]

The Constitution of India promoted the establishment of village panchayats but entrusted local self-government as a subject to the states. Although this directive principle was followed to some extent, it was not universally adopted. However in 1992, the 73rd and 74th Amendments to the Constitution gave recognition and protection to local governments.

Under the compulsions after Independence, local level administration was completely restructured and overhauled. Many important changes were introduced in keeping with the democratic constitution. Substantial executive powers and allocation of resources were granted to the municipalities. Local government has been sought to be integrated with planned development of the country. Many new schemes have been introduced from time to time to augment civic services and improve urban infrastructure. Attempts have been made to improve urban living conditions with specific emphasis on slums and poverty pockets in urban areas. Institutional changes like Mayor-in-Council type of political executive and municipal personnel enactment have been brought about in many states. Also, municipal financial situation has been sought to be improved by introducing regular grants-in-aid and other resource transfer policies by state governments. Provision for more funds has been recommended by the State Finance Commissions and the Central Finance Commissions as well.

Recent years have witnessed an increasing interest and a growing consciousness of the need and importance of local self-government as not only provider of services but facilitator as well to the local community, as well as an instrument of democratic self-government. Local government is an integral part of the national government structure, the level of government closest to the citizens and in the best position both to involve them in the decision making process of improving their living conditions and to make use of their knowledge and capabilities in the promotion of all round development. There are two types of local government in the country: urban local government and rural local government. Urban local government manifests in Municipal Corporations, Municipal Councils, Town/Nagar Panchayats/Notified Area Committees. Rural local government operates through *Zilla Panchayats (Parishads)* (at the top of the tier), *Taluka (Kshetra) Panchayats* (at intermediary level) and *Village (Gram) Panchayats* (at grassroot level).

Thus, the local self-government existed in India since ancient times but it owes its present structure and style of functioning to the British rule, which formed a base for further development after Independence in India.

REFERENCES

1. Agarawal, V.S. (1953). *India as Known to Panini*, Lucknow.
2. Banerji, P.N. (1961). *Public Administration in Ancient India*, Calcutta.
3. Singh, U.B. (1998). *Administrative System in India*, APH, New Delhi.
4. Rao, M.V.K. (1958). *Studies in Kautilya*, Delhi.
5. As quoted in Kumar, U. (1990). *Kautilya's Thought on Public Administration*, National Book Organ, New Delhi.

6. Ghoshal, U.N. (1988). Political Theory and Administration Organization in the Classical Age, in R.C. Majumdar (ed.), *The History and Culture of Indian People*, Vol III, Bhartiya Vidhya Bhawan, Mumbai.
7. Minakshi, C. (1950). Administration and Social Life under the Pallavas, in K.A.N. Sastri (ed.), *A Comprehensive History of India*, Historical Series No. 13, University of Madras, Chennai.
8. Santhianathaier, R. (1988). *The Cholas*, in R.C. Majumdar, *op cit.*
9. Ghoshal, U.N. (1988). Political Theory, Administrative Organization Law and Legal Institutions, in R.C. Majumdar (ed.) *op cit.*
10. *Ibid.*; Singh, S.N. (1987). *Issues in Local Government*, National, New Delhi
11. Qureshi, I.H. (1988). Islamic Political Theory, Administrative Organization, Law and Legal Institutions, in R.C. Majumdar (ed.) *The History and Culture of Indian People*, Vol. No. VI, Bhartiya Vidhya Bhawan, Mumbai.
12. Sharma, S.R. (1988). Political Theory, Administrative Organization Institutions, in R.C. Majumdar (ed.), *op cit.*
13. Dighe, V.G. and Qanungo S.N. (1988). Administrative and Military System of the Marathas, in R. C. Majumdar (ed.), *op cit.*
14. *Ibid.*
15. Sarkar, J.N. (1952). *Mughal Administration*, IV ed., Sarkar & Sons, Calcutta.
16. Mukherjee, R.K. (1958). *Local Government in Ancient India,* Motilal, Delhi.
17. Mahajan, V.D. (1972). *British Rule in India and After*, S.Chand & Co., Delhi.
18. McSwite, O.C. (2002). *Invitation to Public Administration*, M.E. Sharpe.
19. Kaye, J.W. (1953). *The Administration of the East India Company*, Longman, London.
20. Mishra, B.B. (1955). *The Central Administration of the East India Company (1773-1834)*, Manchester.
21. Coupland, R. (1943). *The Indian Problem (1833-1935)*, Part I, Report, London.
22. *Ibid.*
23. Panikkar, K.M. (1929). *The Evolution of British Policy Towards Indian States (1774-1858)*, The Calcutta University Readership Lectures, Calcutta University.
24. *Ibid.*
25. Singh, U.B. (1998). *op cit.*
26. *Ibid.*
27. Datta, K.K. (1960). *An Advanced History of India*, McMillan, New Delhi.
28. Chandar, A. (1958). *Indian Administration*, London.
29. Datta (1960). *op cit.*
30. Majumdar, B.B. (1934). *History of Political Thought*, Calcutta.
31. Majumdar, R.C. and Datta, K.K. (1988). The Administrative Organization, in R.C Majumdar (ed.), *History and Culture of the Indian People*, Vol. IX, Bhartiya Vidya Bhavan, Bombay.
32. Datta (1988). *op cit.*
33. Singh, U.B. (1998). *op cit.*
34. Curzon, Lord (1925). *British Government in India*, Vol. 2, London.

35. Argal, R. (1954). *Municipal Government in India*, Allahabad.
36. Singh, U.B. (1998). *op cit.*
37. Majumdar (1988). *op cit.*
38. Datta, K.K. (1960). *An Advanced History of India*, Part III, Macmillan, New Delhi.
39. Argal, *op cit.*
40. Khera, S.S. (1960). *District Administration in India*, New Delhi.
41. *Ibid.*
42. Curzon, *op cit.*
43. Khera, *op cit.*
44. *Ibid.*
45. *Ibid.*
46. Mukherji, P. (1915). *Indian Constitutional Documents*, Calcutta.
47. Panikkar, K.M. (1929). *The Evolution of British policy towards Indian States (1774-1858)*; The Calcutta University Readership Lectures, Calcutta University.
48. Mohanty, B. (1999). *Glimpses of Local Government*, Gyanjuga, Bhubaneswar.
49. Constitution of India (2005). 27th ed., EBC, Lucknow.
50. Mohanty, *op cit.*

Chapter 8

Urban Local Government in India

Introduction

The growth of cities offers many problems relating to the people residing within municipal limits. Some of the problems like public safety, health and hygiene and environmental problems require organized attempts to be solved through mutual efforts. This led to the idea of constituting municipalities to take care of the day-to-day problems and solve them at local level. The word 'municipality' is derived from Latin word 'Municipium munus', which means a duty or privilege and care to take. Similarly, the word 'corporation' is derived from Latin word 'corporate', which means to form into a body. The Municipal Institutions took concrete shape in the Roman Empire because the main function of the Municipalities was to perform certain services to Romans.[1]

Urban local bodies are supposed to be formed as democratic institutions based on the principle of self-government and should represent people's desires and strengths. Due to rapid urban growth during the 20th century, the urban quality of life has deteriorated and creates an urgent necessity for having vibrant and efficient urban local government system that can deliver adequate services and improve living conditions.[2]

Evolution

Urban local government is synonymous with municipal government and has a long history. Modern municipal bodies are the creation of the British. The credit goes to Sir Josia Child for creating the base of modern local government system in India. The Memorandum on the Development and Working of Representative Institutions in the sphere of Local Government says that "*Local Self-Government in India in the sense of representative organizations responsible to a body of electors enjoying wide powers of administration and taxation and functioning both as a school for training in responsibility and vital link in the chain of organism that make up the Government of the country is a British creation*".[3]

The first such body called a Municipal Corporation was set-up in the former Presidency Town of Madras (now Chennai) in 1687, and was followed by the establishment of similar corporations in Bombay (now Mumbai) and Calcutta (now Kolkata), in 1762. The Charter Act of 1793 placed these local self-government institutions on statutory basis by giving power to the Governor-General to appoint Justices of Peace for the Presidency Towns. Municipalities were established in many other towns with the power to impose direct taxes on local residents. The Act of 1850 realized the futility of direct taxation for local purposes. The municipalities had no scope for self-government because of many limitations.[4] The creation and development of local bodies during 1840 and 1853 was more or less shot in the air, without any constructive outlook and formidable logic, as is evident from the fact that the elective principle introduced earlier was scrapped in the year 1856. The Municipal Committee system was tried for discharging the municipal functions. The growth of municipalities during this period was like mushrooms as even small places having a population of 800 were granted municipalities.[5]

Lord Mayo's Resolution of 1870 encouraged the introduction of an elected President in the municipalities. The Taxation Enquiry Commission (1953) observes that "It was implicit in the decentralization as then conceived that the emphasis was on the 'local' rather than on the 'self-government' aspect of Local Self-Government".[6] In pursuance of this resolution, so many Municipal Acts were framed. "Thus by 1880 the number of local self-government had been put in progress only in the cities of Calcutta and Bombay and in a few towns of Central Provinces and North Western Provinces. Elsewhere although framework of local administration and local taxation existed, control was firmly in the hands of servants of the Government".[7] However, in their present form and structure, the municipal bodies owe their existence to Lord Ripon's Resolution on local self-government, adopted on 18 May 1882.

The Independence opened a new chapter for India not only to regain the paradise lost but to march steadily on the path of peace, progress and prosperity. The structure of municipal bodies has remained, by and large, the same even though the number of urban areas has increased and their problems have become more and more complex.

There are two kinds of statutory provisions creating a municipal authority. Either the statute itself may establish a municipal authority,[8] like the Bombay Municipal Corporation Act (1888), the City of Nagpur Corporation Act (1948) and the Delhi Municipal Corporation Act (1957), or it may empower the State Government concerned to create a Municipality (Municipal Authority, Municipal Council or Municipal Board), such as the U.P Municipalities Act 1916, Bombay Provincial Municipal Corporations Act (1949) and the Gujarat Municipalities Act (1964). The extent of the municipality's powers, as well as the extent of government control over a Municipality depends on the statute enacted for its creation. Presently, the statutes confer wider controlling and supervisory powers on the state government. This is due to two reasons:[9] firstly, the Constitution does not demarcate the powers and the duties of the municipal authorities and secondly, in the absence of any clear-cut demarcation, it is obvious that state governments control municipal authorities, more so, local government is a state subject.

The attention on the overall development of local bodies got priority over the First Five Year Plan. In August 1948, a Conference of State Ministers of Local Government was convened with a view to sort out the problems relating to local bodies. The Finance Enquiry Committee was constituted, in 1951, to suggest ways and means to improve the financial health of local bodies. Similarly, the Taxation Enquiry Commission was appointed, in 1953-54, to suggest *interalia* measures for improving the financial condition of local bodies. The Local Self-Government Ministers' Council was constituted in 1954. Again a committee of Local Self-Government Ministers, known as Zakaria Committee (1963) was also constituted to suggest improvement in the financial structure of local bodies.[10]

In view with the problems faced by urban local government bodies, the Rural-Urban Relationship Committee, was set-up by the Government of India in 1963, pointed out that local government can no longer remain merely instruments of political education and civic conscience. Instead they have to become institutions for the promotion of social and economic development of local communities as well as an integral part of the National Government.[11] The Committee also made significant recommendations on various aspects of local government like the criteria for constitution of municipal bodies with the need for a clear delineation of powers, functions and resources of urban local bodies.

The Committee for Augmentation of Financial Resources of Urban Local Bodies (1963) (popularly known as Zakaria Committee) feels that "*it is the rural sector which has been engaging the main attention of the Government. After Independence two committees viz. Local Finance Enquiry Committee, 1949 and the Taxation Enquiry Commission, 1953 examined the problems of finances of urban local bodies....... But the recommendations made by them have hardly been implemented in any state*".[12] The Committee further notes that "*local bodies have suffered from neglect over all these years and their aims and problems, unfortunately have been regarded as inferior to those of State and National Governments. Unless local bodies are given proper attention, it will not be possible to look at urban areas in their proper setting in the country's political and economic life.*"[13]

As far as the Municipal Government is concerned, it is assumed to be a State Function. Entry 5 of the State List in the Seventh Schedule of the Constitution of India gives legislative power to the State with regards to municipal laws, establishments, constitution and powers of local government.[14] Except for recognizing local self-government as an essential part of the system of the country's government, the Constitution does not confer any independent status or powers to local government bodies except a mention in the Directive Principles of State Policy.[15] In this backdrop, the Union Government introduced in Lok Sabha the Constitution (65th Amendment) Bill in 1989, which could not be passed and lapsed due to dissolution of Lok Sabha. Another Bill (72nd) was introduced by the succeeding National Front Government and met the same fate. Again 72nd Amendment Bill was introduced in 1991 and was passed in 1992. It was ratified by majority of states and after the Presidential assent came into force with effect from 1st June 1993 in the name of the Constitution (74th Amendment) Act, 1992.

The Constitution (Seventy-Fourth Amendment) Act, 1992

It was the first serious attempt to ensure stabilization of democratic municipal government through constitutional provisions. A new chapter (Part IX A) has been added to the Constitution and in all 18 Articles has been inserted. Initially the provisions were not applicable to the Scheduled Areas and Tribal Areas as referred to in Article 244, but by the provisions of the Municipalities (Extension to the Scheduled Areas) Act 2001 the provisions of 74th Amendment were extended to the Scheduled Areas as well with certain modifications.

The Constitution (Seventy-fourth) Amendment Act (CAA) seeks to introduce fundamental changes in the urban local bodies.[16] Its main features are:

(i) Bringing uniformity in urban structure in the country;
(ii) Granting a fixed life of five years to municipalities;
(iii) Reservation of seats for the members of Scheduled Castes and Scheduled Tribes and one-third of seats for women in municipal bodies;
(iv) Restrictions on the power of state governments to do away with democratically elected municipal governments;
(v) Holding of periodical and timely elections; if a municipality is dissolved for any reason, it should be reconstituted within 6 months;
(vi) For conducting regular elections after every five years, constituting State Election Commission in every state;
(vii) Specifying by law the sources of municipal finance and their periodic review by a statutorily constituted State Finance Commission and by making it obligatory on the part of the Central Finance Commission to recommend measures needed to augment state resources to assist the municipal governments;
(viii) Specification by law of the powers and responsibilities entrusted to municipalities and ward committees;
(ix) Introduction of the Twelfth Schedule which lists the functions of the urban local bodies, covering planning, regulation and developmental aspects;
(x) Proposed establishment of ward committees in areas having a population of over three lakhs; and
(xi) Establishment of District and Metropolitan Planning Committees responsible for the preparation of development plans at district and metropolitan levels, respectively.

The Amendment envisages enabling people to participate in development processes at ward, municipal, district and metropolitan (regional) level. The empirical evidence of such optimism could be realized only after implementing the provisions of the Amendment in true spirit.

Municipal Structure

The structure and composition of the municipalities vary widely. There is generally no accepted set of criteria with reference to urban agglomerations resulting in wide differences of definitions and structures between states. The Constitution seeks to bring some uniformity in the constitution of the municipal bodies by classifying them as follows:[17]

- *Nagar Panchayat*, to be constituted in rural-urban transition areas. These have been conceived to properly channelize the growth impulses in such settlements and also to bring some sort of order in their growth and provision of services;
- *Municipal Councils* for smaller urban areas; and
- *Municipal Corporations* for larger urban areas.

Urban local government is not hierarchical. As an institution, all the three units enjoy autonomy. The Municipal Corporation however, enjoys greater autonomy than other forms of local government. It enjoys the power of dealing directly with the state government whereas the municipalities have no direct access to the state government and are answerable to the state government through District Collector and Divisional Commissioner and Director of Local Bodies.[18]

In the early days, the municipal institutions in the district towns were modelled closely on the Britishounciliar system of local government. But, the Presidency towns viz. Bombay and Madras, grew up an exotic type of municipal government, which had later become the model of big city government in India. The third Presidency town viz. Calcutta threw up another unique type almost diametrically opposite to the Bombay model.[19] Prior to the introduction of the Calcutta Municipal Act, 1923, the Calcutta Corporation was governed by the Mackenzie Act of 1899, which provided for three distinct authorities viz. a Government appointed chief executive, a general committee and the corporation or the city council. All executive functions were concentrated in the hands of the chief executive who enjoyed considerable independence of the corporation and its committees. It is an irony of the history that the Bombay model of municipal government which set up the ideal of big city government in India was cast in the same mould as the Mackenzie Act.[20]

Municipality

A municipality is a politic and corporate body constituted by the incorporation of the inhabitants of a city or town. Normally, Municipal Councils cover smaller areas than the Municipal Corporations. The State Government can, by notification, propose an area, except a military cantonment, to be a municipality, define its territorial limits and make alterations in them. As for structure and organization, there is a great measure of uniformity between municipalities of different states. There are at the same time significant differences in the degree of control exercised by the State Governments, the delegated powers of taxation, the scope and varieties of functions, efficiency of tax collection and general municipal administration. They enjoy more or less the same powers in the sphere of taxation etc. as do the corporations though the extent of state control here is relatively larger. But in terms of actual performance, barring a few exceptions, municipalities lag behind the corporations.[21] The Municipal Council, the President, the Committees and the Executive/Chief Officer constitute the main components of the structure of municipal government. The Municipal Council makes laws that are called bye-laws within the framework of the municipal act for the civic governance of the city or town. The size of every Municipal Council varies from state to state; the municipal acts prescribe both the maximum and the minimum number of councillors.

Like other partners in the Indian Union, Municipalities also have deliberative and executive wings. In general, deliberative wings of Municipal Corporations comprise the Corporation, the Standing Committee, the Corporators and the Mayor, whereas the executive wings comprise the Municipal Commissioner, the Deputy/Assistant Municipal Commissioner, the Municipal Engineer and subordinate administrative staff. In other two forms of local bodies as well, deliberative wing consists of elected President/Chairman, Councillors, and the executive wing has Executive Officer/Municipal Officer, Engineers and other subordinate staff.[22]

What chiefly distinguishes a corporation from a municipality is the almost complete separation of the deliberative functions from the executive functions and vesting of all executive authority in a Municipal Commissioner, who is relatively independent of the elected body. As a class they have wider functions and larger powers than municipalities.[23] They enjoy relatively more autonomy in matters like formulation of budget and sanction of municipal works and have larger revenue resources partly because of wider devolution but mainly because their jurisdictions have relatively broader and stronger economic base. All these factors account for their having higher standards of civic services and better administration.

Deliberative Wing

This is the General Body of the Municipality, comprising of elected and other members (councillors). Councillors are people's representatives and thus articulate the wishes of the population. The council is elected for a fixed term of five years. The 74th Constitution Amendment Act provides that every Municipality shall have the following categories of councillors:

- Directly elected councillors;
- Nominated councillors;
- *Ex-officio* councillors/members.

The number of elected councillors is to vary according to the size of the population of the territorial area of the Municipality concerned. Nominated councillors are to be nominated by the State Government. The nominated councillors shall be persons having special knowledge or experience in municipal administration. The *ex-officio* members consist of the members of parliament or state legislature.

Mayor

The Mayor in the Municipal Corporation is a representative elected, either by the councillors from amongst themselves for fixed but renewable term, or directly by the people.[24] The Mayor exercises administrative control over the secretariat of the corporation. Furthermore, some statutes specifically empower him, in case of an emergency, to direct the execution or stoppage of any work or any act. The Mayor in India is bereft of any executive authority. The indirect election of the Mayor combined with his short tenure makes him more a figurehead than an active functionary. A directly elected mayor comparatively has more executive and financial powers.[25] He convenes and presides over the meetings of the corporation and is responsible for the conduct of business.

Chairman/President

The council elects, from among the councilors, a President (Chairman) whose term may be co-terminous with that of the council. In a number of states the term of the President varies from one to three years and is not co-terminous with that of the council. In a number of states,[26] the President (Chairman) is elected directly by the people for five years. The President occupies an important position in the municipal administration and enjoys considerable authority and power both in the deliberative and executive organs of the municipality.[27] He convenes and presides over the meetings of the council and gives his rulings on all controversial matters. He also holds the power to take disciplinary actions against offending councillors and can suspend or adjourn any meeting in case of pandemonium.

The President not only guides the deliberation of the council but also executes its decision as its Chief Executive Officer. He is aware of day-to-day administration and he is supposed to convey to the council the working of the administrative machine. He is also the chief spokesman and the link person with the government. The President enjoys power and exalted position but his power depends on the support of the majority. The indirectly elected President being dependent on the council, faces a lot of pressures and influences in exercising his executive authority.[28]

Committees

Various statutory and non-statutory committees that are set-up by the council do most of the works of the corporation. Statutory committees (which are set-up by the statute), include executive committee, standing committee, planning committee, health committee, education committee, ward committee, etc. Non-Statutory Committees include transport committee, women and child welfare committee etc. The number and composition of the committees vary from state to state. The most important committee, both regarding power and range of functions allotted is the Standing (Executive) Committee of the Corporation. It acts as the steering committee exercising executive, supervisory, financial and administrative powers.[29] The Standing Committee consists of members in varying numbers elected through system of proportional representation of councillors or othewise.

Executive Wing

The Municipal Commissioner is the Chief Executive Officer and head of the executive wing of the Municipal Corporation. All executive powers are vested in the Municipal Commissioner. Although Municipal Corporation is the legislative body for laying down policies for civic governance of the city, it is the Commissioner who is responsible for execution of the policies.

The Commissioner belongs either to Indian Administrative Service or State Civil Service appointed on deputation. However, his tenure in a corporation may get either extended or reduced. The Commissioner's powers are classified into two broad categories:[30] those listed in the statute creating the corporation and those delegated by the Corporation or the Standing Committee.

In smaller municipalities, the Executive Officer/Chief Municipal Officer heads the executive wing comprising of all the supporting staff.

Functional Domain

Local Bodies are expected to have a profound impact on the performance of the economy of the country by utilizing local resources and tapping human potentialities to the fullest. In the present context of Indian economy, with massive urban growth and the economic liberalization, heavy responsibility is placed on urban local bodies. They are responsible for the improvement of the efficiency of programmes and services, to mobilize local resources and to provide coherent planning and delivery of services at the local level.

The local bodies as a democratic unit of Government at city level are primarily responsible to make the lives of citizens worth living by making the environmental atmosphere of the local areas safe and sound. They have been made responsible to shoulder the responsibility of making environment and sanitation safe and sound by providing necessary infrastructure for the better health and hygiene of the citizen.[31]

All Municipal Acts in India provide for functions, duties and responsibilities to be carried out by the municipal government. Urban local bodies are basically service organizations but they perform certain regulatory functions, e.g. regulation of dangerous trades, buildings etc.; some development functions, e.g. construction and maintenance of public streets and a few maintenance and general functions as well. These are divided in two categories obligatory and discretionary.[32]

Obligatory Functions

- Supply of pure and wholesome water,
- Construction and maintenance of public streets,
- Lighting and watering public streets,
- Cleansing public streets, places and sewers,
- Regulation of offensive, dangerous or obnoxious trades and callings or practices,
- Maintenance or support of public hospitals,
- Establishment and maintenance of primary schools,
- Registration of births and deaths,
- Removing obstructions and protections in public streets, bridges and other places, and
- Naming streets and numbering houses.

Discretionary Functions

- Laying out of areas,
- Securing or removing dangerous buildings or places,
- Construction and maintenance of public parks, gardens, libraries, museums, rest houses, leper homes, orphanages and rescue homes for women, etc.,
- Planting and maintenance of roadside and other trees,
- Housing for low income groups,
- Making a survey,
- Organizing public receptions, public exhibitions, public entertainment, etc.,

- Provision of transport facilities with the municipality,
- Promotion of welfare of municipal employees,
- Providing music for the people, and
- Slum improvement and poverty alleviation.

The Constitution provides that the State may endow the municipalities the power and authority to enable them to function as institution of self-government. The state may devolve powers and responsibilities upon municipalities with regard to the preparation of plans for economic development and social justice and the performance of functions and the implementation of schemes as may be entrusted to them including those in relation to the matters listed in the Twelfth Schedule.[33]

Thus the functions of the municipality, including those listed in the Twelfth Schedule are left to the discretion of the State Government. The local bodies have to be bestowed with sufficient powers, authority and responsibility to discharge the additional functions entrusted to them by the Constitution. However, the 74th Act fails to provide any powers directly to the municipalities and it has left it to the discretion of the state government. Some of these functions mentioned in Twelfth Schedule are of highly technical nature and are likely to render municipal bodies ineffective. The Constitution Amendment Act has a provision regarding devolution of powers and responsibilities. However, the devolution of powers commensurate with such responsibilities is left to the discretion of the concerned State Government. The functions given in the Twelfth Schedule are as under:[34]

1. Urban planning, including town planning.
2. Regulation of land use and construction of buildings.
3. Planning for economic and social development.
4. Roads and bridges.
5. Water supply for domestic, industrial and commercial purposes.
6. Public health, sanitation, conservancy and solid waste management.
7. Fire services.
8. Urban forestry, protection of environment and promotion of ecological aspects.
9. Safeguarding the interests of weaker sections of society, including the disabled and mentally retarded.

10. Slum improvement and upgrading.
11. Urban poverty alleviation.
12. Provision of urban amenities and facilities such as parks, gardens, playgrounds.
13. Promotion of cultural, educational and aesthetic aspects.
14. Burials and burial grounds, cremations, cremation grounds and electric crematoriums.
15. Cattle pounds; prevention of cruelty to animals.
16. Vital statistics including registration of births and deaths.
17. Public amenities including street lighting, parking lots, bus stops and public conveniences.
18. Regulation of slaughter houses and tanneries.

Thus, urban local governments in the country are required to provide for services irrespective of their administrative capacity to do so and have to face unexpected new terms of their own as a consequence of new sets of standards. In pursuing decentralization objectives, it is important to ensure that existing municipal structures are updated to undertake added responsibilities. Where the administrative functions of State Government for development of urban infrastructure are transferred to the local level, it will become necessary to examine whether local government is capable of handling such responsibilities. If such capacity does not exist or is inadequate, it needs to be created or strengthened.

Municipal Finances

The basic problem of local government in India is finance. In a sense, scarcity of resources in India is not a phenomenon peculiar to local bodies. As a matter of fact the entire economy is constrained for resources. But within an environment of overall scarcity the sense of denial and deprivation is most persuasive and acute in the case of local bodies. The paucity of resources at the local level is all the more agonizing because it is at the grass roots of democracy that the dissatisfaction about the frustrated needs of the people is most keenly felt and articulated.[35]

Municipal bodies are prescribed to perform a vast array of functions for which adequate financial resources should be available.

However, there is no separate list of taxes exclusively for municipal bodies. Although many commissions, like the Local Finance Inquiry Committee (1951), Taxation Inquiry Commission (1953-1954), Rural-Urban Relationship Committee (1963), National Commission on Urbanization (1985-88) had been set-up, from time-to-time, to look into the issue of municipal finance, municipal finance was left to the discretion of the respective state governments to specify the matters relating to imposition of taxes.

Municipal Revenues are basically of the following types:

(i) Tax revenue;
(ii) Non-tax revenue;
(iii) Grants-in-aid; and
(iv) Borrowings or loans.

Tax Revenue

Major taxes levied by urban local government are the following:

- Tax on property, including service levy for water supply, conservancy, drainage, lighting and garbage disposal.
- Tax on entry of goods into a local area for consumption, use or sale therein, popularly known as octroi and terminal taxes.
- Tax on professions, callings and employments.
- Tax on vehicles (other than motor vehicles).
- Theatre or show tax.
- Tax on advertisements.

The scope of taxation of Municipal Corporations is broader than their counterparts. They are generally empowered to impose or increase taxes within the limits laid down in the State Acts.

Property Tax

Under the Act of 1865, the Municipalities in India during the British period were authorized to impose a cess on land and a tax on houses in Sind. Later on, Municipalities in Madras and Bombay were also authorized for the imposition of tax on houses in the year 1866 and 1865 respectively. The Municipalities in Bengal, Burma (presently

Myanmar), Central Provinces (Madhya Pradesh) were also authorized to impose the tax on houses by various Acts passed between 1883 and 1885.[36] Later on, efforts were made to improve the administration of local bodies by augmenting their financial resources. With the passage of time the tax on lands and buildings occupied key position in the financial structure of the local bodies. Tax on properties owes its existence to Entry no. 49 of List II in the Seventh Schedule of the Constitution.[37]

Generally, property tax is the largest single source of revenue for municipal bodies in the states where there is no provision for octroi. Property tax is levied on buildings and lands. Its basis of taxation is the annual rental value or market rent. A municipal body can impose, suspend, reduce or abolish the tax and partly/wholly exempt any person or class of persons of any such tax on any property or description of property by a resolution passed at a special meeting and confirmed by the state government.

Property tax is a composite tax. Its main components are general (house/holding) tax, water tax, lighting tax, conservancy tax, drainage tax, fire tax, etc. It is levied on the basis of the annual rental value of the land and buildings. The annual rental value is derived either on the basis of rent or on the basis of area. The buildings used for commercial purposes are generally evaluated on the basis of capital value.

In almost all the states, property tax is at present based on the annual rental value of lands and buildings i.e. it is either based on the actual rent which the landlord receives for the building or it is based on reasonable rent which a hypothetical tenant may be expected to pay to the landlord or fair letting value. There have been several judicial decisions according to which the Standard Rent fixed under the Rent Control Act should be deemed to be the reasonable rent for purposes of assessment of the property for municipal taxation. As a result of these decisions, the annual rental value of almost all urban properties has remained frozen and the property tax which normally should have been a very flexible and growing source of income for the urban local bodies has not been yielding the expected results. In England the Rent Control Act does not in any way restrict the evaluation of a property for levying rates. The rent prescribed by the Rent Control Act restricts only the rent that any occupier has to pay to the owner of the premises.[38]

Octroi

It is the tax levied on entry of goods into a local area for consumption or sale therein. Octroi is the most traditional tax and a major source of local revenue. The origin of octroi as a local tax can be traced, as far back as the '*chungi*' of the Mughal period, the Sikh '*dharat*' and the '*muhtaraja*' of Maratha towns. Historically, octroi has been an important and traditional source of revenue to local government. In its present form this is one of the oldest in India and is considered as a traditional source of local revenue. This tax is also one of the most important sources of local revenue and accounts for approximately one-fourth of the total tax revenue of all local bodies in the country. It accounts for about 60 to 80 per cent of total revenue of the urban local bodies where it is imposed. In the states of Rajasthan, Gujarat, Punjab and Maharashtra for example, this tax is the major source of revenue. [39]

Octroi as a local tax has been subjected to much criticism. Sir Charles Trevelyan described it as the "remains of barbarous system of universal taxation". Sir Joshia Stamp described it as "*In my judgment both theoretical and on the result of experience no country can be progressive that relies to any extent upon octroi which has nearly every vice.*"[40] Due to scathing criticisms from many fronts, the states of Uttar Pradesh, Orissa, Andhra Pradesh, Assam, Karnataka, Kerala, Madhya Pradesh, Nagaland, Sikkim, Tamil Nadu, Tripura, Himachal Pradesh, Manipur and Meghalaya have abolished octroi. The state of Gujarat has taken a policy decision to abolish octroi and introduce an entry tax. There is a serious thinking in a few states to reintroduce the levying of octroi.

Non-Tax Revenue

Non-tax revenue consists of receipts from fees and fines, incomes from remunerative enterprises and other miscellaneous sources. Every Municipal Act has provisions for issuance of licenses. Likewise, every local authority is empowered to charge and collect fees, both regulatory (for licenses issued) and for services provided.

There is a vital difference between tax and fee: tax is a compulsory levy, while a fee is a charge made in return for a benefit allowed or conferred. When the service is extensively used and it takes on the character and form of a public utility, then the fee charged is called a user charge or user fee. Normally a user fee is to be charged for public utilities, parking, entry fees for play ground, swimming pools etc.

Grants-in-Aid

The system of giving grants-in-aid to local authorities to perform their functions has developed out of necessity. As the central and state governments burden local authorities with more and more functions, they have a moral obligation to assist them to carry out these functions particularly when the principal sources of revenue have already been tapped by them. The principle that grants-in-aid should form one of the important sources of revenue of local authorities has been accepted all over the world.[41] Presently, it is an important element of municipal finance in the country.

There are two types of grants: recurring and non-recurring. The former are given by state government to meet the gap in their recurring expenditure and they are paid annually. Non-recurring grants are provided for meeting the initial capital expenditure of specific projects. Recurring grants may further be divided as General Purpose Grants (GPG) and Specific Purpose Grants (SPG). The general purpose grants are intended to augment the revenue of the local bodies for discharging their normal functions. There are no conditions attached to them. The special purpose grants are used for specific requirements, e.g. the increase of wage bills due to inflation, education grants, public health, road maintenance etc. These are intended to induce local action in desired fields as part of a national or state level policy and in providing the desired measure of control over the quality of the services.

It is true that excessive dependence on grant will undermine the financial responsibility of the local bodies and lead to extravagant expenditure. It is also true to some extent that the state aid to local bodies leads to centralization and to certain amount of interference by the state in their autonomy. It is also alleged that grants tend to support public services of certain localities at the cost of others. There is no denying the fact that in spite of these drawbacks, the system of grant-in-aid has now come to stay. Grants also serve the very important purpose of shifting the burden of equally rising costs from regressive local taxation to the more progressive State and National taxes. In the state-local government relationship local government must inevitably be in the position of junior partner. It should be possible to increase grants and at the same time leave the portion of expenditure to be found from own resources of the local authorities at a sufficiently high level to ensure that local authorities still have an important financial stake and remain partners and not become agents of the state government.

Borrowings, Loans and Bonds

Municipal bodies can borrow from the state government and other agencies when they cannot afford to meet their expenditures with their existing revenues. The borrowing power of a local government is regulated under Local Authorities Loans Act of 1914. This Act provides that Municipal Corporations can borrow for development activities and for payment of debt charges. Local bodies are permitted to borrow for the construction of municipal works, provision of relief and the establishment or maintenance of relief work in times of scarcity or famine; prevention of the outbreak of any dangerous epidemic disease; acquisition of land; repayment of outstanding loans etc.[42]

The maximum period for which loans can be borrowed by municipal corporations is sixty years as compared to thirty years for municipalities. Municipal corporations can raise loan on the security of their immovable properties whereas municipalities can borrow on the security of their funds only. However, prior permission of the state government is necessary for such borrowings.

Financial instruments issued by municipal bodies to raise resources from capital markets are commonly known as municipal bonds. Municipal bonds are issued by local governments who finance, construct and deliver a variety of urban infrastructure projects and services, the benefits of which accrue for several generations. Municipal bonds may be of several types with fixed or variable interest rates. Municipal debt may be raised for project financing, equipment financing or to meet cash flow requirements. Such debt may also be raised to meet extraordinary expenses of a non-recurring nature. Municipal bonds act as an effective instrument for mobilizing adequate resources in order to enable municipalities to meet their financial needs of infrastructure development and basic amenities. There may be two types of municipal bonds,[43] viz., general obligation bonds and revenue bonds. General obligation bonds are backed by a pledge of full faith and revenue raising powers of the municipal corporation. The use of these bonds may be appropriate for financing general municipal functions where it may not be possible to ensure direct cost recovery for specific projects like roads, street lighting, public health etc. Revenue bonds are primarily backed by the user fees or basic charges paid by the user of a particular service. These are normally off-balance sheet liabilities of municipalities. They are used primarily for funding revenue producing public services, such as housing, water supply, toll highways, ports, air ports etc.

Finance Commission

With the increasing pace of urbanization, municipal bodies are finding it difficult to deliver the required level of services. Moreover, with the Constitution Amendment Act (1992) and the addition of eighteen functions in the Twelfth Schedule, the functional responsibilities of municipalities have increased beyond the provisions of only civic amenities. Local Bodies are expected to play a crucial role in the preparation of plans for local development and in the implementation of development projects. In view of this, proper assessment of resources of the municipal bodies is required. Thus, the Seventy-Fourth Constitution Amendment Act proposes the setting up of State Finance Commission. The Governor of the State constitutes a State Finance Commission after every five years. The State Finance Commission is required to formulate the principles for the following aspects:[44]

- Distribution between the state government and municipalities of the net proceeds of the taxes, duties, tolls and fees leviable by the state;
- Allocation of a share of such proceeds between the municipalities at all levels in a state;
- Determination of taxes, duties, tolls and fees to be assigned or appropriated by the municipalities;
- Grants-in-aid to municipalities from the consolidated fund of the state; and
- Measures needed to improve the financial position of municipalities.

Under the new dispensation, it is at the discretion of the Governor to refer any other matter to the Finance Commission. This Commission chalks out its own procedure within the framework of powers given to it by state law. Another important aspect is that the Governor has to present to the state legislature every recommendation made by the Finance Commission along with explanatory notes on the actions taken.

The setting up of a Finance Commission as proposed by the Constitution Amendment Act has thus helped the urban local bodies to a great extent, to deliver the increased level of services, which are required in the context of increasing urbanization. The additional responsibilities allotted to them under the Twelfth Schedule also make it imperative to make regular assessment of financial resources of the local bodies.[45] Regular assessment of financial resources would help in the proper channelization of resources as well as the devolution of resources from state to local government and give the local bodies a firm footing.

The Constitution further mandates the Central Finance Commission to consider the recommendations of the State Finance Commission while devolving fund to the State. This necessitates the State Finance Commission to devolve more funds to local governments. A detailed study of fiscal devolution by state finance commission of major states in the country can be seen in my book entitled Fiscal Federalism in Indian Union.

Municipal Personnel System

The efficiency of any organization and its capacity to accept additional responsibilities largely depends on the calibre of the personnel it has on its pay roll. In the wake of the phenomenal increase in the economic and trading activities and the accelerated growth in urban population, the city governments are increasingly called upon to undertake diversified functions. It is imperative on the part of the municipalities to systematize personnel planning with proper imagination so that a crop of talented and competent personnel may emerge capable of translating plans and programmes into action.[46]

Generally, there are three types of municipal personnel system in practice.[47] These are separate, unified and integrated.

Under the separate system, each municipality has its own personnel system. The personnel in this system are appointed by the municipality and dismissed by it. Such personnel are not transferred to any other municipality. This system has inherent advantages including ensuring the loyalty and effective performance of the employees; employees being local develop more interest in local affairs; attracting talents from local community; relatively economic as financial compensation are determined locally depending upon the municipality, and contributing to local self-government by allowing local authorities to manage its human resources locally.

This system has a number of disadvantages as well. The non-availability of competent people at local level encourages spoils system. The restricted opportunities for promotion, especially for higher level of officials result into frustration. And importantly being local, the personnel develop some kind of local vested interests. The complex nature of municipal administration may not afford feeling of personalized allegiance which is bound to hamper impartial delivery of urban services.[48]

No state has exclusively separate personnel system. In Uttar Pradesh, prior to 1966, the municipalities followed pure separate system of personalization wherein Council and President of Municipality had power to appoint and dismiss its employees.

A unified municipal system forms a single career service for the entire state. Appointment, transfers, promotion and dismissal of personnel are administered by a state level agency. Only a certain categories of municipal employees are included in such type of service, the remaining classes are arranged under separate like system. It involves objective criteria and merit for appointment and promotions. The staff is protected against arbitrary disciplinary measures. Such a system facilitates the creation of state wide career services based on merit and enables municipalities to obtain the services of qualified persons. It involves certain degree of state control over municipal personnel matters and lessens nepotism and favoritism in appointments and promotions.

This system has a number of disadvantages as well. The part of employees belonging to unified services arises new problems in relationships with employees recruited other wise. There are possibilities of conflict between the unified service agency and municipal councils.[49] Members of the unified services are also likely to be confused as to their relationships with municipality they serve.

Andhra Pradesh has followed this system since 1955 with municipal cadre for municipal commissioners, deputy commissioners, assistant commissioners, municipal secretaries, assessors, engineers, health officers etc. The state of Tamil Nadu has accepted the unified system since 1956 with state wide service of municipal commissioners. Rajasthan has adopted this system since 1963 through the Rajasthan State Municipal Service constituted for municipal commissioners, executive officers, secretaries, revenue officers, health officers, engineers etc. Uttar Pradesh also has unified system for 76 categories of staff since 1966. Madhya Pradesh has a unified personnel system.[50]

The integrated personnel system is a system in which the personnel of national (all India) or state government and those of municipalities form part of the same service. Under this system some persons belonging to national and/or state cadres are deputed in municipal services. Its distinctive feature is vertical as well as horizontal transferability of personnel. This system permits the most extensive area basis for recruitment and provides the widest possible career opportunities in public service. It gives the central/state government a greater stake in the improvement of living conditions in small towns. However, the staff may not be as responsive as they should be to local council. Besides, the danger of excessive centralization of authority and lack of adaptation to local needs would be ever present. There is a danger of authoritarianism in relationship between municipal councilors and staff.[51]

Orissa has adopted integrated system where the senior posts of administration and technical are from state cadre. In Bihar, the executive officers of the municipality are from the state cadres.

In reality, none of the states in the country practices any of these systems exclusively. There is a mix of two or all of these personnel systems. The local government is a state responsibility, so there are variations among states in adopting the type of personnel system the states opt to.

Effective urban management and improved urban planning and development efforts need to converge at the local government level to deal with the problems arising as a result of urban growth trends at the city level. All municipal programmes can be translated into action only through well-recruited and trained personnel at the disposal of urban local authorities. Development and maintenance of adequate and skilled manpower with growth potential depend upon the nature and type of recruitment policies and procedures adopted and the efficiency with which they are administered and executed.[52] The policies, methods and procedures adopted by an organization to build up its personnel are of vital significance. However, municipal institutions since their inception seem to have overlooked this important aspect of personnel administration.

Municipal personnel management appears different from personnel management in central/state government on a number of points.[53] Firstly, municipal functions are mostly labour-intensive; secondly, some crucial civic services like water supply, sewerage and drainage, garbage collection and disposal, street lighting and so on are dependent on proper functioning; thirdly, municipal administration is closest to the citizens and the public image of administration depends largely on the functional efficiency of municipal personnel; and fourthly, municipal personnel have to function under the closest public scrutiny by the locally elected councillors as well as the general public. In a nutshell, municipal administration is a complex system where policy makers, implementers and consumers live together. Municipal personnel are to work in the full gaze of public criticism at the local level by the local consumers of municipal services. At this level, almost a face-to-face relationship exists between municipal personnel, local political leadership and citizens.

The State Government normally appoints the Municipal Commissioner in Municipal Corporation on a three-year term basis. Usually he belongs to the Indian Administrative Service or has the seniority in State Civil Service. He is the Chief Executive of the city government in big cities. Apart from the post of municipal commissioner, there is a special provision in the Act for the appointment on the posts of city engineer, medical officer of health, municipal chief auditor, municipal secretary, deputy municipal commissioner and assistant municipal commissioner. Accordingly, as per provision of the municipal acts certain statutory post in the municipalities such as: the Chief Officer, Executive Officer, the Municipal Engineer and the Health Officer are created.

A growing imbalance can be seen in India between the civic needs of citizens and the actual performance of municipal administration. One of the main weaknesses has been the absence of a well-organized and effective system of personnel administration. Sharma (1960) points out that three principal aspects, viz. recruitment by merit, scope for promotion and political neutrality are absent in municipal personnel administration.[54] James (1966) feels that the municipal personnel system is neither well organized nor properly developed owing to the scant attention of the government and the urban local bodies itself.[55] The Rural-Urban Relationship Committee (1966) reveals that the essentials of an effective municipal service viz. integrity, competence, impartiality, contentment and devotion to duty were absent in the municipal personnel.[56] Argal (1967) opines that the municipal services are beset with a number of short comings—spoils system and party affiliations of employees.[57] Murti (1967) expresses that because of the absence of a progressive and an enlightened approach, the municipal services seem to be the Cindrella of the Public Services in India.[58] Venkataraman (1968) expresses the view that ill-paid and unqualified staff will not only fail to raise resources but also cannot exploit well whatever has been raised.[59]

Bhattacharya (1970) justifies the continuation of subordinate appointments to be made by the municipal authorities themselves. He highlights three main problems of municipal personnel viz. absence of proper recruitment rules, unfavourable pay and service conditions and large scale involvement of municipal employees in municipal politics.[60] According to Rao (1985), the problems may be classified as policy issues involved in recruitment, defective provisions in various Municipal Acts specially in relation to recruitment, absence of rules and the State government's in-attention in relation to municipalities in general and personnel process in particular.[61] Venkat Rao (1972) feels that the municipal service is a neglected field, where important aspects like classification of services, recruitment, promotion and training are not based on sound principles.[62]

Surprisingly, no state in India has adopted a single type of personnel system. But the municipal corporations in the country have gone for integrated services from the very beginning of the system. Municipal Commissioners are appointed from all India or state administrative cadres. The state government has a regulatory role in appointment on senior posts. But the municipal government is empowered to recruit its staff. In Tamil Nadu municipal health officers and municipal engineers are from state cadre on integrated manner. In Andhra Pradesh also public health officers and municipal engineers in municipalities belong to state service. Uttar Pradesh also has public health officers from state cadre.

Hoshiar Singh (1972) points out that the dispersal of the recruiting powers among many agencies leads to a great heterogeneity in the control and discipline of municipal personnel.[63] Mathur (1974) opines that the deliberative wing often has the tendency of by-passing officials of the unified cadre and utilizing those of separate cadres. This results in the growing indiscipline and tensions between the two cadres.[64]

The National Commission on Urbanization (1988) recommends that "to make local government service more attractive it is recommended that there should be state-wise cadres of local government employees, at least at supervisory level. These cadres should be controlled overall by the state government so that there is a high degree of protection to the staff".[65]

As regards training to municipal personnel, the Government of India has created four Regional Centres for Urban and Environmental Studies at Lucknow, Hyderabad, Delhi and Mumbai. These pioneer institutions of training, research and, consultancy have been entrusted their exclusive jurisdiction. The centres at Lucknow and Hyderabad have been working as a regular faculty of the University of Lucknow and the Osmania University respectively. The other two centres are the part of the Indian Institute of Public Administration, New Delhi and the All India Institute of Local Self-Government, Mumbai. The Lucknow centre undertakes academic programme as well as to produce urban managers.

In addition, there are a number of regional and state training institutions engaged in the process. But these arrangements are not adequate to cover all the urban actors.

Central-State-Local Relations

The Central Government controls the overall development initiatives in urban areas through the Ministry of Urban Development. Obviously, except in the union territories, the centre has no direct role to play either in the management of cities or in the planning of individual settlements or regions. This is a purely municipal function. However, there are a number of organizations of the Government of India which deal with the subject of urban planning and development, provide a forum for discussion and consensus, and also ensure the flow of funds to the states in the generic area of urban development. The Ministry of Urban Development is the nodal ministry in the field. Its basic function is to oversee, in totality, the process of urbanization and governmental reaction to the process. It is also the ministry which is supposed to evolve urban policy and to try and ensure that suitable plan priorities are assigned to urban development, together with adequate funds.[66] The Government of India has created a new Ministry of Housing and Urban Poverty Alleviation for guiding housing activities and monitoring centrally sponsored schemes for urban poverty alleviation.

Urban planning, development and management being a state subject, it is in the states that the governmental and organizational structure is relatively more elaborate. State governments have a significant control on the staffing, finances and administration of the municipalities. The state governments exercise control through their urban development departments. The directorate of municipal administration functions as an intermediary between urban local bodies and the State Government. The town planning (and valuation) department exercises control on the physical planning of the urban areas as this department prepares the development plans for the cities and towns in their respective states.

Although local government falls under the jurisdiction of the states, the Union Government is to take a leading role in the field of local governance. The Central Government has initiated a number of schemes on sanitation, sewerage, water supply, employment, poverty alleviation, infrastructure development, regional planning etc. but it does not come in direct contact of local government whereas the Federal Government in USA can have access directly to any local body.

Local government is a creature of the state government. State government enacts statutes for local government, urban and rural. Besides, many other departments of the government are also entrusted with local functions. A number of parastatal agencies have been created by the state government for the optimum performance of many municipal functions. The rules for local governance are framed by the state government.

Administratively, the state government exercises administrative authority in development plans. Many local acts seek approval by their respective state governments on any development scheme. The state governments are empowered to dissolve a faulty municipality at least for six months.[67] The chairpersons and other councillors act under the scanner of the state government.

Financially, local government has no fiscal power of its own. The supreme law of the land has not vested any strong extractive power upon the local government; rather the powers of extraction are clearcut under the jurisdiction of centre and state. The local government succumbs to its narrow tax base. It has to sustain only on marginal shares and grants from state government. The properties of central and state governments within the jurisdiction of the local government are immune to local taxation. When the central and state governments enjoy elastic sources of income, relatively inelastic sources are left for the local government.

The Constitution has not assigned any separate list for local taxation. The state governments are always in habit of encroaching upon local taxes.[68] The periodic revision of taxes is done only with the approval by the state government, which is not easy for local government.

The supreme law of the land provides for appointment of State Finance Commission every five years, but the recommendations are purely advisory and under the final approval of the state government. The State Finance Commission is empowered only to make recommendations relating to principles which should govern the distribution of the net proceeds of the taxes, duties, tools and fees leviable by the state between state and Panchayati Raj Institutions and the municipalities; the grant-in-aid from the Consolidated Fund of the State; and recommend measures needed to improve the financial position of local government units-urban and rural.[69]

Thus the object of state supervision and control is to increase the efficiency of local government. While supervision and control must secure the proper performance of the duties entrusted to local authorities, it must at the same time concern itself with the educational and technical support and training services to their staff. In other words, it should not acquire a negative content so as to restrict the initiative, discretion or assumption of responsibility on the part of local government but should be given a positive content helping the local authorities to avoid pitfalls and mistakes, strengthening their self-confidence and enabling them to assume growing responsibility.[70]

Ward Committees

Our system of democratic government bestows on the people the ultimate power and our socialistic society professes the goal of equal opportunities and freedom of expression to all, making people the subject and also the instrument of development. There are other compelling reasons, which make people's participation an important component of city governance and development action. In the circumstances to conserve and augment government's financial and institutional resources, to mobilize and put to productive use the people's untapped creativity, resources and energy, to bring into play new agencies and organizational forms to augment and supplement the efforts of formal systems and institutions, and to offer opportunities to people to invent new, affordable and appropriate responses to their unmet needs in local situations and challenges of development with limited resources, it is necessary to decentralize local governance, to take the grassroot administration amidst the people.[71]

The Indian Constitution provides for constituting Wards Committees in the cities having population of three lakhs or more consisting of one or more wards. Where, a Ward Committee consists of one ward, the member representing the ward acts as chairperson of the committee. In case of a Ward Committee consisting of two or more wards, one of the members is elected by the members of the Ward to act as chairperson.[72]

It is the responsibility of the Wards Committee to take all possible measures in control of the municipality. The state governments are authorized to entrust other responsibilities to these committees.

Kerala and Bihar are the states which have gone beyond and have set up ward sabhas in towns having population less than three lakhs as prescribed in the Constitution.

The Government of Indiá through its model Nagar Raj Bill has advised the states to constitute 'ward sabha' in all the towns on ward basis and 'area sabha' in every ward in every town. This would facilitate to bring local governance nearer to people and also to associate the community at large in managing local affairs locally.

District Planning Committee

Planning in our country has emerged as a comprehensive area of governmental functions. The Directive Principles of State Policy lay down that the state shall strive to promote the welfare of the people by securing and protecting a social order in which justice—social, economic and political shall inform all the institutions of national life. The achievement of these goals calls for planned development of the country based on a national consensus in the formulation of policies and shared action. Planning postulates a cooperative and coordinated approach to development.[73]

Systematic planning in India has hitherto been undertaken at the national level and to some extent at the state level. In both the national and the state plans, allocations of public outlays are made to major sectors of the economy in the light of accepted priorities and desired targets of growth. However, the remoteness of planning agencies from areas of implementation and the vastness of geographical coverage hamper the matching of sectoral financial allocations with location specific needs as well as potential for regulating the distribution of the gains of development. Nor can the sectoral allocation be integrated in a manner that optimize returns in terms of production, employment and the incomes of the community in general and of the people below the poverty line in particular.[74]

India being a vast country with diverse geographical conditions has to take up planning at various levels so as to facilitate the process of planning. Since 'planning from above' cannot hold good for every region of the country, the country is divided into several units and each unit is assigned the tasks of planning and implementation separately without breaking the link from the overall national plan. Since a lower unit can take care of its resources and problems, with the imposition of plans from above proves counter productive. Hence in a country like India the multi-level planning approach has been given much importance.[75]

Interestingly, planning in India is limited to economic planning, at the national level and, physical planning, at the local level. The approach to planning is sectoral, with hardly any effective inter-sectoral co-ordination and interaction. There is thus a wide gap between national and local levels; there is no co-ordination between urban planning and rural planning.

In this context, the Constitution provides for the Constitution of a District Planning Committee in every state at the district level to coordinate the plans prepared by the Panchayats and the Municipalities in the district as a whole. Four-fifths of the total number of members of the committee shall be elected by and from amongst the elected members of the Panchayats at the district level and of the municipalities in the district in proportion to the ratio between the population of the rural areas and of the urban areas in the district. While preparing the draft development plan the District Planning Committee shall have regard to matters of common interest between Panchayats and Municipalities including spatial planning, sharing of water and other physical and natural resources, the integrated development of infrastructure and environmental conservation and the extent and type of available resources-financial or otherwise.[76]

The chairman of the committee shall forward the draft development plan to the state government.

Metropolitan Planning Committee

The main casualty of unplanned, imbalanced and ad-hoc approach to urban development has been the city life deterioration in its quality, distortion of its priorities and diffident handling of its operational problems. Cities grow with migration and natural growth and city limits need to be extended to fringe areas. Extension of civic services like water supply and sanitation, housing and health poses problems, both financial and functional.[77]

The supreme law of the land provides for constituting in every metropolitan area (an urban area spread over one or two districts having population over ten lakhs and consisting of two or more panchayats) a Metropolitan Planning Committee to prepare a draft development plan for the metropolitan area as a whole. Two-thirds of the members of this committee are elected by and from amongst the elected members of the Municipalities and chairpersons of the Panchayats in the metropolitan area in proportion to the ratio between the population of the municipalities and of the panchayats in that area.[78] The representatives of the Union and the State Governments and other organizations may also be put as members.

The Committee, while preparing the draft development plan, shall have regard to the plans prepared by the municipalities and the panchayats in the area, matters of common interest between the municipalities and the panchayats including coordinated spatial planning of the area, sharing of water and other physical and natural resources, the integrated development of infrastructure and environmental conservation, the overall objectives and priorities set by the Union Government and the State Government and the extent and nature of investments likely to be made by the Union and State government and other available resources. The chairperson of the committee shall forward the draft development plan to the State Government.[79]

Relationship between Deliberative and Executive Wings

It is seen that urban local bodies are enshrined with dissimilar characteristics. The senior partners in the Indian Federation i.e. Union and States enjoy unlimited legislative powers, while urban local bodies have no power to legislate. They perform under the legislation passed by the state government. The urban local bodies are empowered to frame bye-laws to implement the provisions of the municipal laws of their own. However, whatever the limited legislative powers are enjoyed by urban local bodies in many states, there is a difference in municipal corporations and that of the other class of municipalities. In the Municipal Corporations the authorities enjoying deliberative and executive powers are separated while in municipalities there is no such clear division.[80]

The Municipal Corporations are the most developed of such institutions and systematically provide for a separation of executive and deliberative functions. The separation was introduced with a view to clearly demarcate the jurisdiction of the elected and appointed officials. This experiment was made first time in Bombay (now Mumbai) and was later applied to the other municipal areas particularly municipal corporations. The separation of powers, as characterized in municipal corporations, however, has not been fully applied to other municipalities. The deliberative wing takes decision on administrative matters also. The administrative powers are shared between the elected head and the appointed executive. Their positions differ from one state to another in matters of appointment and accountability to the State Government.[81]

The clear demarcation of deliberative powers from the executive ones in municipal corporations, results into a better harmonious relationship between both the wings than that of the municipalities, where such a separation is not clear. This ambiguity leads to more critical relationship between the Board/Council and the President/Chairman, between Board and the Executive Officer and also between the members and the Executive Officer.[82]

The directly elected Mayor or President presents himself all powerful. Sometimes, harmony in relationship lacks because of political affiliation of the members and the Mayor or President. The lucrative character of the political posts at higher echelons often hinders the deliberative functioning of urban local bodies. The ideological differences of political parties inhibit the people's representatives at local level to deliberate unbiasedly for the development of the city of their abode. The political compulsions hurdle the local development, although everyone cries for development. But development becomes secondary only after the personal benefits under the garb of political ideologies.[83]

The executive wing also sometimes acts wily. The subordinate staff, being locally, many a time plays hand-in-gloves with the elected representatives. The personnel belonging to the centralized (state) cadres also connive sometimes with the elected representatives. Such associations for personal benefits damage the cordial relationship between the deliberative and executive wings. It casts its shadow on development activities. Occasionally officers instigate the members to settle their score with the Mayor or President or otherwise. All these mischievous activities strain the relationship and also hamper the smooth functioning of urban local bodies.[84]

The subordination of the executive wing to the elected ones in local body does not mean that each and every member of the local body or that even a group of it should so interfere with the execution of the policies made by the entire body that the purpose of local government is frustrated or thoroughly distorted. It is the responsibility and function of the local body to ensure that its policies are promptly, efficiently and honestly executed. Here, comes the question of the comparative independence of the executive machinery. Independence does not mean parallel sovereignty but is rather an essential ingredient of impartiality. In short, the executive machinery should have the power and the authority to carry out the wishes of the local government effectively and yet not make a fetch of independence.[85] A good and honest official should not find it difficult to resist undesirable pressures and influences without any untoward consequences on his career.

There have been interminable and inconclusive debates on relationships between these two wings. People have advocated a strong or weak mayor, an independent city manager, a completely statutorily independent executive, an executive, which is wholly subordinate to the deliberative wing. It is difficult to support any of these except the last one. Yet, to facilitate the implementation of these policies determined by the local government, the executive machinery should be given reasonable freedom from day-to-day interference and allowed to function in an atmosphere not surcharged by individual or group prejudices or whims. A certain amount of power of the surveillance over the executive machinery should vest in the statutory committee of the local government or in the Mayor/President of the local body.[86]

The present trend of making the executive authority completely independent under the statute nullifies the whole purpose and significance of the local body. It has, to a great extent, resulted in the failure of the local government and in maintaining an atmosphere of distrust between the deliberative and executive wings, and creates psychological resistance of an extremely undesirable trend. The deliberative wing must also understand that the members of the executive are not their minions and that they have not been employed to serve their personal interest.[87]

It is often argued that the representatives of the people in urban local bodies are neither well-educated nor well-trained in handling the responsibilities of local government. If we create an organization or institution, we must trust it, give it a chance to function within its range of responsibilities, even to make mistakes.

However, in order that local governments may function smoothly and efficiently and in the public interest, the executive machinery must be given due protection and a sense of security. These can be achieved by various means. But the most important factor would be a high degree of impartiality in the matter of disciplinary control over them, which would include recognition, promotion and punishment, security of tenure, and an independent forum for the hearing of appeals.

A brief mention of the manner in which the deliberative wing can function to the best advantage in creating policy and ensuring its implementation is necessary. Matters of basic importance such as the budget should necessarily be settled in the entire body itself. In order to ensure closer scrutiny of proposals and quicker decisions, the local government can create standing committees for various purposes. Some of these committees can be of advisory character where experts can be co-opted. Other standing committees should enjoy delegated authority. Upto a point, the committees should be allowed to free wheel within the bigger body, but major issues should invariably come upto the local government itself. The standing committees may be empowered to sanction projects of minor issues.[88] But one of their main functions should be to watch and oversee the working of the executive machinery in regard to the policies made by the local government. Then alone will local government be in position to ensure good administration.

N.S. Patil (1990) comments that "the elected representatives stand for election and get elected not necessarily for serving citizens of the town and improving quality of living of the citizens but by and large to advance their own interests by exploiting political parties or citizens and after election by use of the resources of local government. His own interest compels him to advance the causes of his kith and kin, his followers or backers and his groups or parties. In set procedures in local bodies and instructions, orders and circulars issued by higher forum of government are anachronism and designed to obstruct him in furthering his causes. The expectations of followers get translated into pressure by elected representatives on municipal officials for disregarding encroachment, ignoring illegal and irregular construction, ignoring tax arrears and taking undue advantages. Often there are pressures on municipal officials to take councillor's nominees into municipal employment."[89]

Interestingly, there are divergent and contrary views of both the wings of urban local bodies. The elected representatives feel that the municipal executives are not sincerely interested in doing good for the town because they come from outside the town. They have no sentimental attachment with the town. The civic services are in bad shape. There is a high percentage of leakage in water distribution system. The municipal taxes and rates are very much in arrears and there is leakage in the revenue. Contrarily, the executive heads in municipal administration tend to look down on elected representatives as ignorant petty politicians. They tend to ignore them if they don't assert. Interestingly, the officials think they are the depository of all knowledge and expertise in all municipal matters. Whenever, councillors approach them with request to take some action, they evade it or dilly dally it. The net result is inaction and deterioration in civic services.[90]

As a consequence of the 74th Constitution Amendment Act, career municipal officials and elected representatives are essential parts of municipal government. One party cannot wish away the other. It is essential that each side should understand and appreciate the compulsion of councillors and circumstances. For renewing their tenure the elected representatives have to keep many people—supporters, followers, constituents etc. in good humour.

In an interaction with a councillor it is important for an official to remember that it is almost to show that he has the ultimate authority to translate wishes of a councillor into action. It may happen sometimes that the official may not be in a position to act according to the bidding. But such a situation may be handled tactfully. The municipal councillors are certainly an essential part of democratic decentralized administrative set up at local level. When they make certain demands on officials, one has first to understand their points of view by giving a patient hearing and appreciate the fact that they find it worthwhile spending time and energy to get them settled. A municipal official must promise and initiate action to solve problems or difficulties.[91] If there are difficulties in doing they should be explained and his attitude must be one of finding a solution and not just explaining why a thing cannot be done and a solution cannot be found.

Patil (1990) further observes that a municipal official has a choice for responding in five ways in an interaction with an elected representative, each having its own output on relationship and on municipal functioning.[92] One of the easiest ways is to avoid or escape the situation. There is a complete withdrawal and absence of decision. In such a case both the parties are losers. The administration fails to do what it is expected to do and the councillor does not get the work done. In another situation an official firmly refuses to act at the bidding of the councillor who in turn tries to use all methods at his disposal to ensure action. He may try to bring influence on the official or as a last resort threaten him of dire consequences. Both parties are in a way competing with each other to have his own way. There is climate of confrontation and in the outcome one party may be the winner and the other definitely a loser, who waits for an opportunity to hit back. In third situation, there is a complete surrender on the part of municipal official and he obliges the councillor by ensuring action as desired by him. In this case the administration is loser and it tries to accommodate wishes of the elected representatives irrespective of their merit. In the fourth case, both the parties may arrive at a compromise, and agree on a decision, which is not in the best interest of municipal administration or the other party to the decision. But it avoids confrontation and bitter feelings. In a still another situation the parties may sit across the table, discuss the matter thoroughly and arrive at a consensus or optimum decision to the satisfaction of both parties. Both the parties cooperate and emerge winner.

Thus, there emerges a challenge before the municipal administration to adopt the attitude of cooperation and collaboration and ensure on the process, observance of rules, regulations and procedures and also retain goodwill of the elected representatives. The pillars of democracy should also realize the situation and raise themselves from petty abode and strengthen the democratic finding at the grassroot level and treat the local government as a nursery for political ethics, and morality and cooperation.

Urban Government in Scheduled Areas[93]

The Municipalities (Extension to the Scheduled Areas) Act 2001 while extending the provisions of the 74th Amendment to the Constitution makes special provisions for urban administration in the Scheduled Areas covered under Article 244.

Constitution of Municipalities

The Governor may in consultation with or in pursuance of the recommendations of the Tribal Advisory Council by public notification declare and classify an area as an urban area of appropriate category having regard to its population, the percentage of employment in non-agricultural activities, the infrastructure, social services, development potential etc.

The tribal habitation in an urban setting shall be treated as a separate unit for the purpose of local self-government. The habitants, whose economy is predominantly rural, shall be included in Gram Sabha (village assembly) and the habitants who have got assimilated in the urban economy shall be included in Tribal Mohalla or Ward Sabha.

Nagar Panchayats (town panchayat) may be constituted in an area identified as transitional area. The composition will be alike the Municipal Committee.

Standing Committee

A Standing Committee for tribal affairs in each Municipality located within the Scheduled Area shall be constituted. It shall comprise tribal members of the Municipality with the Chairman or the Vice-Chairman as its Chairman. Recommendations of this committee shall ordinarily be binding on the Municipality.

In addition, a standing committee for rural development in each municipality responsible for the advancement of those engaged in agriculture and allied activities shall also be constituted.

Reservation of Seats

Seats may be reserved for the Scheduled Tribes in every municipality in the Scheduled Area in proportion to their population in the municipal area or one-third of the total number of seats, which ever is higher. The seats of all the Gram Sabhas (village assemblies), *Tribal Mohallas*, *Ward Sabhas* included in the municipality may be reserved for the Scheduled Tribes. The remaining seats shall be allotted by rotation among other wards. Either the Chairman or the Vice-Chairman of the urban body shall be a member of the Scheduled Tribe.

Not less than half of the members of Nagar Panchayat shall be from Scheduled Tribes.

In all programmes of development like housing colonies, trading centers and in educational institutions or industrial training institutions reservations shall be made in favour of the tribal people in proportion to their population in the concerned district.

Powers and Authority

The legislature of a state shall endow the Municipality in the Scheduled Area with powers and authority necessary to enable it to function as institution of self-government and the law shall contain provisions for the distribution of powers and responsibilities with respect to preparing five year development plans and annual plan with reference to resources available for development of human resource, socio-economic advancement of the community, provision for reinforcement of the infrastructure and augmentation of civic amenities, fostering tribal endogenous institutions, undertaking schemes and adopting measures relating to development of khadi, cottage and small scale industries, cooperative movement, water supply, public health and sanitation and hospitals, communication, primary and secondary education, non-conventional energy sources, women and child development, social welfare, managing of markets, maintaining places for rest and stay, protecting and maintaining all religious places of tribal people, identifying and removing unauthorized occupation of land, acquiring land for the purpose of education, health, railways, communication, defense, electricity generation, water supply, sanitation, laying electricity lines etc.

Taxation

No urban tax shall be leviable on a tribal who continues to live in his traditional style.

Mayor-in-Council System

This system was first introduced in 1980 in Municipal Corporation of Calcutta (now Kolkata). In later years it spread over in whole state of West Bengal. The other states, which followed the system, are Tripura and Madhya Pradesh; recently, Delhi has also proposed to adopt this system. Such a system was introduced in Maharashtra also in 1998 and the Mayor-in-Council system started in Mumbai and Nagpur. With change in state government, however the system was scrapped within a year.

This system clearly envisages separation of powers of the deliberative wing of the corporation from its executive wing. So far as deliberative functions are concerned, the Corporation at a meeting is the repository of supreme powers. But in all executive matters the Mayor-in-Council is the operative municipal authority whose decision is final.[94]

This system is modelled on the strong mayor pattern of the U.S.A. It vests the Mayor with enormous power. Mayor is the key figure of the Mayor-in-Council which is the repository of all executive powers of the Corporation. He nominates the Deputy Mayor and other members of the Mayor-in-Council who can also be removed from office by a written order of the Mayor. On the other hand the Municipal Commissioner, who is the principal executive officer of the corporation, exercises his statutory powers and functions only under the supervision and control of the Mayor. Thus the Mayor is the City Father in the real sense of the term.[95]

Under this system, the Mayor is relieved of his legislative functions. The Mayor and elected councillors of the Corporation elect a speaker from amongst the elected councillors. The speaker declares a panel of two or three elected councilors every year to preside over the meetings of the Corporation during his absence. The term of the speaker is co-terminous with the term of the Corporation.[96]

A motion of no-confidence may be moved against the mayor at a meeting specially convened for the purpose and if the motion is carried by a majority of more than three-fourths of the elected councillors present and voting in the meeting and if much majority is more than two-thirds of the total number of elected councillors constituting the corporation, the copy of such motion is sent by the speaker to the State Government communicating the decision of the motion.[97]

The Mayor divides the municipal functions among the members of the Mayor-in-Council. Every member is the head of particular function under his command. The Mayor presides over the meetings of the Council and in his absence the members may elect someone from amongst themselves to preside over the meeting. The Speaker may constitute advisory committee for every functional department constituting the elected councillors and headed by an elected councillor other than the member of the Council.[98]

Such a system in municipalities other than Municipal Corporations is known as President-in-Council system.[99]

Parastatals

Besides municipalities, there are also a number of parastatal agencies and functional organizations which are quasi-government bodies. These include development authorities, special area development authorities, housing boards, slum clearance/improvement boards, water and sewerage authorities, water boards etc. Many of these parastatals have been created under separate state enactments. They function within city limits and beyond but are not answerable to the local bodies because they stand above them. The mushrooming of these organizations has resulted into a dichotomy in urban management in which the existing, decaying, largely inadequate services become the responsibility of municipalities, whereas almost the entire capital input into city expansion, together with the profit there from, fall to the share of the functional organizations or development authorities.[100]

In addition, in view of more emphasis on eradicating/alleviating poverty and improvement of slums in urban areas, all the states have got State Urban Development Agency with its units at district level in the form of District Urban Development Agency. In a few states these agencies function parallel to municipal bodies creating a state of confusion at the community level.

Cantonment Board

The determination of cantonment areas, their administration, constitution and powers are indicated in Union List of the Seventh Schedule of the Constitution. The composition of cantonment boards is little different from that of the other local bodies. The elected element in the Board is generally in a minority. The size of population in the jurisdiction of Cantonment Boards being too small and the areas being primarily constituted for military use, their economic base is generally weak.[101]

The dictionary meaning of the word 'cantonment' is the temporary quarters of troops when taking part in manoeuvers etc. But the term has been applied to permanent military stations in India. Certain regulations were promulgated in the 19th century, which dealt with local government. Regulation X of 1801 imposed certain duties on Bengal towns and United Provinces. By Regulation III of 1809 support of police and maintenance of peace within limits of the cantonments was vested in the officer commanding the troops. Thus the duty of the officer commanding was to prevent crime and maintain peace. By Bengal Regulation XX of 1810 the cognizance of petty offences in cantonment was transferred to court-martials. Similar regulations were framed in Madras and Bombay Presidencies.

Regulation XIII of 1813 levied Chowkidar Tax for watch and ward in certain towns. Act X of 1842 was the first real legislation for the creation of a modern municipality. It applied only to Bengal Act XXVI of 1850 dealt with special circumstances of towns. Act XXII of 1865 was enacted to make better provision for administration of the military cantonments. Besides this Madras Cantonment Act I of 1866 and Bombay Cantonment Act II of 1867 were enacted for these presidencies. The Consolidated Cantonments Act III of 1880 gave power to local governments to establish small causes courts in cantonments.

The Cantonment Act XIII of 1889 was extended to all cantonments in India and, for the first time accommodated the Municipal Law in the cantonments. It was replaced by Act XV of 1910 which not only touched subjects such as taxation, cantonment fund etc. and other matters were regarded to rules known as Cantonment Code, 1912 but the Constitution of Cantonment Authority remained the same.[102]

It was felt that the governance of cantonments required to be improved. A select committee was appointed in January 1921 to consider what changes were required to be made in order to induce into the administration of cantonments the spirit of reformed scheme of governance. The committee recommended a complete reunion and amalgamation of the Constitution of Cantonment Act XV of 1910 and the Cantonment Code, 1912, in order to bring into conformity with ordinary municipal law the system under which military cantonments were administered. The Cantonments Bill received the assent on 16th February 1924 after being passed by the Central Legislature. It came on statute book as The Cantonments Act, 1924.[103]

The Act of 1924 was modified and re-enacted in 2006 in the context of 74th Constitution Amendment Act to provide for better urban management in cantonments. The Statement of Objects and Reasons of new enactment mentions that in view of the present day aspirations and needs of the people residing in cantonment areas, and in order to bring in modern municipal management procedures and techniques in such areas, the new legislation was enacted to provide for (i) greater democratization, (ii) reservation of seats in Cantonment Boards for women and to Scheduled Castes/Scheduled Tribes, (iii) better financial management, (iv) extension of centrally sponsored development schemes to such areas, (v) management of defence lands and their audit etc.

The Cantonment Boards are guided by the Union Ministry of Defence according to the provisions of the Cantonments Act, 2006.

Constitution and Composition

For every cantonment area a Cantonment Board is constituted. It is a body corporate having perpetual succession and a common seal with power to acquire and hold property both moveable and immovable and to contract. They are divided into four classes:

(i) *Category I cantonments*, in which the civil population exceeds 50,000;
(ii) *Category II cantonments*, in which the civil population is between 10,000 and 50,000;
(iii) *Category III cantonments*, in which the civil population is between 2,500 and 10,000; and
(iv) *Category IV cantonments*, in which the civil population is less than 2,500.

The *Category I Cantonment Board* consists of the Officer Commanding the station or any other military officer nominated in his place by the General Officer Commanding-in-Chief, the Command; the District Magistrate or an Executive Magistrate not below the rank of Additional District Magistrate; the Chief Executive Officer; the Health Officer, *ex-officio*; the Executive Engineer, *ex-officio*; three military officers nominated, by name, by the Officer Commanding the station; and eight elected members.

In *Category II Cantonments*, the Board consists of the Officer Commanding the station or any other military officer nominated in his place by the General Officer Commanding-in-Chief, the Command; the District Magistrate or an Executive Magistrate not below the rank of Additional District Magistrate nominated by the District Magistrate; the Chief Executive Officer; the Health Officer, *ex-officio*; the Executive Engineer, *ex-officio*; two military officers nominated by the Officer Commanding the station; seven members elected.

In *Category III Cantonments*, the Board consists of the Officer Commanding the station or any other officer nominated in his place by the General Officer Commanding-in-Chief, the Command; the District Magistrate or an Executive Magistrate nominated by him; the Chief Executive Officer; the Health Officer, *ex-officio*; the Executive Engineer, *ex-officio*; one military officer nominated by the Officer Commanding the station; and six elected members.

In *Category IV Cantonments*, the Board consists of the Officer Commanding the station or any other officer nominated in his place by the General Officer Commanding-in-Chief, the Command; the Chief Executive Officer; and two elected members.

The Members of Parliament and Members of Legislative Assembly representing constituencies which comprise wholly or partly the cantonment area, shall be special invitees for meetings but without a right to vote.

The Central Government by reasons of military operations or for the administration of cantonment may make the declaration to such effect and in such case the Board consists of the Officer Commanding the station; the Chief Executive Officer; and one member, not being in the service of the Government, nominated by Central Government in consultation with the General Officer Commanding-in-Chief, the Command.

The term of office of a member of Board shall be five years. The term of *ex-officio* members continues so long he holds the office.

Any elected member may give his resignation in writing to the President of the Board who shall forward it for orders to the Central Government under intimation to the Officer Commanding-in-Chief. Any nominated member may resign by sending his resignation in writing through the President of the Board to the Officer Commanding-in-Chief for orders. [104]

President and Vice-President

The Officer Commanding the station, if a member of the Board, shall be the President of the Board. Where the Officer Commanding the station is not the member, the military officer nominated in his place shall be the President.

In every Board except in Category IV Cantonments, there shall be a Vice-President elected by the elected members from amongst themselves. In case of Category IV Cantonments, the Vice-President is elected by draw of lot under the supervision of the President.

The term of a Vice-President shall be five years or residue of his term of office as member. The Vice-President may resign by notice in writing to the President and on the resignation being accepted by the Board, the office becomes vacant. A Vice-President may be removed from his office at a special meeting convened on a requisition by not less than one half of the elected members by a resolution passed by a majority of not less than two-thirds of the total number of elected members holding the office and attending. Only elected members have the right to vote on the resolution. In case of Category IV Cantonments, the Vice-President may be removed if a resolution to this effect is passed by the Board and the other elected member becomes the Vice-President.

The President is responsible for convening and presiding over the meeting of the Board and to regulate the conduct of business, control, direct and supervise the financial and executive administration of the Board, perform all the duties and exercise all the powers imposed or conferred and to exercise executive powers for the purpose of carrying out the provisions of the Act.

The President may empower the Vice-President to exercise all or any of the powers and duties other than any power, duty or function which he is by resolution expressly forbidden to delegate. It is the duty of the Vice-President to preside at meetings of the Board in the absence of the President to perform all other duty and exercise any other power of the President during the incapacity or temporary absence of the President or pending his appointment or succession, and to exercise any power and perform any duty of the president, which may be delegated to him. [105]

Chief Executive Officer

For every cantonment a Chief Executive Officer is appointed by the

Central Government. The Principal Director may designate an officer under his jurisdiction to perform the duties of the Chief Executive Officer in the event of his temporary absence not exceeding ninety days.

Not less than half of the salary of the Chief Executive Officer is paid by the Central Government and the balance from the Cantonment Board.

The Chief Executive Officer is the Member-Secretary of the Board and of every committee of the Board. He is responsible to exercise all the powers and perform all the duties conferred or imposed upon him; to exercise executive power to ensure that the administration of the Board is carried out; to prescribe the duties of and exercise supervision and control over the acts and proceedings of officers and other employees of the Board; be responsible for the custody of all records of the Board; arrange for the performance of duties relating to the proceedings of the Board or any committee or of any Committee of Arbitration, as those bodies may impose on him; and comply with every requisition of the Board on any matter pertaining to the administration of the cantonment.

The Chief Executive Officer may direct the execution of any work in public interest, and incur such expenditure as may be necessary in executing such work, subject to the financial limits determined by the Board subject to general guidelines issued by the Director General, Defence Estates with the approval of the Central Government. In case of emergency he may direct the execution of any work or doing of any act, which would ordinarily require the sanction of the Board. This power he can exercise with the previous sanction of the President, and shall report the action taken to the Board.[106]

Conduct of Business

Every Board shall ordinarily meet at least once in every month. The President may whenever he thinks fit and shall upon a requisition in writing by not less than one-fourth of the members of the Board convene a special meeting.

The quorum necessary for the transaction of business at a meeting shall be one half of members of the Board holding the office.[107]

Minutes of the proceedings of each meeting are recorded in a book and signed by the person presiding over the meeting and the Chief Executive Officer before the close of the meeting. It shall be open to inspection free of charge by any inhabitant of the cantonment. Copies of the minutes are forwarded for information to every member, the General Officer Commanding-in-Chief, the District Magistrate and the Defence Estates Officer and Command Headquarters of Navy and Air Force, if they are located therein.

Committee for Civil Areas

Every Board in cantonments shall appoint a committee consisting of the elected members of the Board, the Health Officer and the Executive Engineer for the administration of the civil areas and may delegate its powers and duties to such committee. The Vice-President shall be the Chairman of the Committee. The powers, duties and functions of the Board are exercised or discharged in respect of a civil area by this committee. If the Health Officer dissents from any decision on grounds related to health, the matter may be referred to the Board by the President for decision.[108]

Taxation[109]

The Board can, with the prior sanction of Central Government, impose

(i) Property tax; and
(ii) Tax on trades, professions, callings and employments.

In addition, the Board may impose any tax, which under any enactment for the time being is in force may be imposed in any Municipality in the state, where in such cantonment is situated.

The Board shall revise every five years the rates of taxes imposed. It can not abolish any tax without the prior sanction of the Central Government.

The Board can charge the following fees:

(a) license fee on vehicles and animals;
(b) license fee on advertisements other than advertisements in newspapers;
(c) fee relating to maintenance of property records;
(d) processing fee on buildings, payable along with application for sanction of the building plan;

(e) license fee on entry of vehicles;
(f) betterment fee on the increase in land value caused by the execution of any development work; and
(g) any other fee.

The fee charged should not be less than the cost incurred by the Board.

Property Tax

It is levied on lands and buildings in the cantonment. It is not less than ten and not more than thirty per cent of the annual rateable value of lands and buildings. The rate of property tax on lands and buildings used for trade or business purposes is more by one-half of the rates fixed. The tax may be levied on graduated scale.

Obligatory Duties[110]

The Cantonment Boards have to perform following functions:

(a) lighting streets and other public places,
(b) watering streets and other public places,
(c) cleansing streets, public places and drains, abating nuisance and removing noxious vegetation,
(d) regulating offensive, dangerous or obnoxious trades, callings and practices,
(e) removing on the ground of public safety, health or convenience, undesirable obstruction and projection in streets and other public places,
(f) securing or removing dangerous buildings and places,
(g) acquiring, maintaining, changing and regulating places for the disposal of the dead,
(h) constructing, altering and maintaining streets, culverts, markets, slaughter houses, latrines, urinals, drains, drainage works and sewage works and regulating their use,
(i) planting and maintaining trees on road sides and other public places,
(j) providing or arranging for a sufficient supply of pure and wholesome water, guarding from pollution water used for

human consumption and preventing polluted water from being so used,

(k) registering births and deaths,

(l) preventing and checking spread of dangerous diseases; establishing and maintaining a system of public vacation and inoculation,

(m) establishing and maintaining or supporting public hospitals and dispensaries and providing public medical relief,

(n) establishing and maintaining or assisting primary schools,

(o) rendering assistance in extinguishing fires and protecting life and property when fires occur,

(p) maintaining and developing the value of property vested in, or entrusted to the management of the board,

(q) establishing and maintaining civil defence services,

(r) preparing and implementing town planning schemes,

(s) preparing and implementing plans for economic development and social justice,

(t) naming and numbering of streets and premises,

(u) according or refusing permission to erect or re-erect building

(v) organizing, promoting or supporting cultural and sports activities,

(w) celebrating Independence Day and Republic Day and incurring expenditure thereon, and

(x) fulfilling any other obligation imposed upon it.

Discretionary Functions

The Board may perform following functions:[111]

(a) laying streets,

(b) constructing, establishing or maintaining public parks, gardens, offices, dairies, bathing or washing places, drinking fountains, tanks, wells and other works of public utility,

(c) reclaiming unhealthy localities,

(d) furthering educational objects by measures other than the establishment and maintenance of primary schools,

(e) setting up or supporting higher schools, colleges and vocational, professional and special education,

(f) constructing and maintaining works and structures, including rain water harvesting, for providing supply of water for public and private purposes,
(g) constituting, maintaining and managing supply and distribution of electricity, including by exploiting non-conventional energy sources, to public and private premises,
(h) taking a census and granting rewards for information which may tend to secure the correct registration of vital statistics,
(i) making a survey,
(j) giving relief on the occurrence of local epidemics, floods, famines,
(k) securing suitable plans for carrying many offensive, dangerous or obnoxious trades, callings or occupation,
(l) establishing and maintaining a farm for the disposal of sewage,
(m) constructing, subsidizing or guaranteeing tramways and other measures of locomotion and electric lighting,
(n) establishing and maintaining cattle pounds,
(o) arranging for civic reception,
(p) providing housing accommodation for inhabitants,
(q) conservation and maintenance of ancient and historical monuments, archaeological sites and remains or places of public importance in the cantonment,
(r) developing land resources under the management of the Board,
(s) preparing and implementing group housing schemes,
(t) establishing and undertaking remunerative projects,
(u) developing small scale and cottage industries,
(v) developing expertise in different areas of urban governance and local government to be able to provide consultancy to other municipal and development authorities,
(w) adopting measures to promote the safety, health or convenience of the inhabitants of the cantonment,
(x) establishing and maintaining or supporting stadia, gymnasia, *akharas*, and places for sports and games,
(y) establishing and maintaining or supporting libraries, museums, art galleries, botanical or zoological collections,

(z) establishing theatres and cinemas,
(aa) organizing and managing fairs and exhibitions,
(ab) constructing and maintaining rest houses, poor houses, infirmaries, children's home, houses for deaf and dumb and for disabled and handicapped children, shelters for destitute and disabled persons, asylums for persons of unsound mind, old age homes, working women's hostels,
(ac) establishing and maintaining chemical or bacteriological laboratories for the examination or analysis of water, food and drugs for the detection of diseases or research connected with the public health or medical relief,
(ad) providing relief to destitute and disabled persons,
(ae) establishing and maintaining veterinary hospitals,
(af) constructing and maintaining warehouses and godowns,
(ag) constructing and managing garages, sheds, and stands for vehicles and cattle sheds,
(ah) constructing and managing community halls and convention halls, and
(ai) holding seminars, workshops, public debates and similar activities particularly on issues and rules and regulations of civic importance.

Town Planning

The Chief Executive Officer with the approval of the Board causes to be prepared a spatial plan for land use which include earmarking of zones for residential, institutional, commercial and other activities, and improvement schemes for areas considered sub-standard on account of narrowness of streets, poor lighting, poor ventilation or irregular line of buildings in a street.

No person can erect a building on any land in an area, other than the civil area, except with the previous sanction of the Board; and in civil area, except with the previous sanction of the Chief Executive Officer.

Control and Supervision

The Central Government may require a Board to produce any record, correspondence, plan or document in its possession or under its control; to furnish any return, plan, estimate, statement, account or statistics relating to its proceedings, duties or works; to furnish or obtain and furnish any report.

The Central Government may review any decision or order of the Board or the General Officer Commanding-in-Chief, the Command, and pass suitable order.

The Central Government or the General Officer Commanding-in-Chief, the Command, or the Director General or the Principal Director may depute any person in the service of the Government to inspect or examine any department, or any service or work undertaken, or thing belonging to a Board and to report thereon.

The General Officer Commanding-in-Chief or the Principal Director may by order in writing call for any book or document in the possession or under the control of the Board; and require the Board to furnish such statements, accounts, reports and copies of documents relating to its proceedings, duties or works.

If the President dissents from any decision of the Board which he considers prejudicial to the health, welfare, discipline or security of the Forces in the cantonment, he may by order in writing direct the suspension of action thereon for a period not exceeding one month, and report the matter to the General Officer Commanding-in-Chief.

If the District Magistrate considers any decision prejudicial to the public health, safety or convenience, he may after giving notice in writing refer the matter to the Central Government, and pending the disposal no action is taken.

If any Magistrate who is a member of the Board, being present at a meeting, dissents from any decision after giving notice in writing to the President, report the matter to the District Magistrate. On receipt of such notice the President directs the suspension of action on such decision.

If the Chief Executive Officer considers any decision to be in contravention of the Act, rules, regulations or bye-laws and the general guidelines issued by the Central Government, he may after informing the President, refer the matter to the Principal Director who directs the suspension of action for a period not exceeding one month.

The Principal Director refers the matter to the General Officer Commanding-in-Chief along with recommendations and informs the matter to Director General, Defence Estates.

The Central Government, or the General Officer Commanding-in-Chief or the Director General or the Principal Director is of the opinion that any duty imposed on a Board has not been performed or has been performed in an imperfect, inefficient or unsuitable manner; or that adequate financial provision has not been made for the performance of such duty, he may direct the Board to make arrangements to its satisfaction for the proper performance of the duty.

Supersession of Board

If any Board is not competent to perform or persistently makes default in the performance of the duties, or exceeds or abuses its powers, the Central Government may by an order published together with the reasons in the Official Gazette declare the Board to be incompetent or in default or to have exceeded or abused its powers, and supersede it. No Board can be superseded without giving a reasonable opportunity to be heard. All members vacate their offices. During supersession all powers and duties are exercised and performed by the Officer Commanding the station.

Thus, Cantonment Boards, although having jurisdiction over the area under defence forces, make provision for civic services to the inhabitants of civil areas falling under the defence area.

REFERENCES

1. Husain, A. (1989). *Whither Local Bodies in India*, Criterion Publications, New Delhi.
2. Maheshwari, S. R. (1997). *Local Government in India*, Educational Publishers, Agra.
3. Government of India: Memorandum on the Development and Working of Representative Institutions in the sphere of Local Self-Government, Vol. V., p. 1056.
4. Stoker, G. (1991). *The Politics of Local Government*, Macmillan, Londres
5. Husain, *op cit.*
6. Govenment of India, Taxation Enquiry Commission, 1953.
7. Tinker, Hugh (1967). *Foundation of Local Self-Government in India, Pakistan and Burma*, Lalvani Pub. House, New Delhi.
8. Golandaz, H. M. and B. Mohanty (eds.) (1993). Empowerment of Urban Local Government in India (with Special Reference to the Seventy-Third Constitutional Amendment Bill of 1992), in *Urbanization in Developing Countries: Basic Services and Community Participation*, Indian Institute of Social Sciences and Concept Publishing Company, New Delhi.

9. Mohanty, B. (1999). *Glimpses of Local Government*, Gyanjuga, Bhubaneswar.
10. Jha, Gangadhar and B. Mohanty (eds.) (1993). Strengthening of Municipal Government in India: Options for Reform, in *Urbanization in Developing Countries, Basic Services and Community Participation*, Indian Institute of Social Sciences and Concept Publishing Company, New Delhi.
11. Golandaz, H. M. (1994). *Empowerment of Urban Local Government in India, with Special Reference to the Seventy-Fourth Constitutional Amendment Act of 1992,* paper presented at the National Symposium on the Constitutional Seventy-Fourth Amendment Act, organized by the Regional Centre for Urban and Environmental Studies (RCUES), Lucknow, 24-25 June (unpublished).
12. As quoted in Golandaz and Mohanty (eds.), *op cit.*
13. Govenment of India, 1963, Committee for Augmentation of Financial Resources of Urban Local Bodies.
14. Constitution of India, 2005, 27th Ed., EBC, Lucknow.
15. Golandaz, H. M. (1995). Seventy-Fourth Constitutional Amendment Act and Conformity Municipal Legislation in Gujarat and Maharashtra, *Urban India*, Vol. XV, 151-159.
16. Jha, Gangadhar (1993). The Seventy-Fourth Constitution Amendment and the Empowerment of Municipal Government; A Critique, *Urban India*, Vol. XIII, 68-78, July.
17. Government of India, *The Seventy-Fourth Constitution Amendment Act, 1992.*
18. Golandaz, *op cit.*
19. deSouza, Peter; R. (2002). Decentralisation and Local Government: The Second Wind of Democracy in India, in Hasan, Z., Sridharan, E., & Sudarshan, R. (eds.), *India's Constitution: Ideas, Practices, Controversies*, Permanent Black, New Delhi.
20. Bhattacharya, M., *Municipal Government*, Research Publications, New Delhi.
21. Report of the Committee of Ministers (Zakaria Committee), constituted by the Central Council of Local Self-Government, 1963, Augmentation of Financial Resources of Urban Local Bodies.
22. Mohanty, B. (1999). *Glimpses of Local Government*, Gyanjuga, Bhubaneswar.
23. *Ibid.*
24. U.P. Municipal Corporation Act, 1959 prescribes direct election of Mayor for five years.
25. Golandaz and Mohanty, *op cit.*
26. U.P. Municipalities Act, 1916 provides direct election to President.
27. U.P. Municipalities Act, 1916 vests in President financial and administrative powers.
28. Jha and Mohanty, *op cit.*

29. Golandaz, *op cit.*
30. Jain, L.C. (2005). *Decentralisation and Local Governance*, Orient Longman.
31. Husain, *op cit.*
32. Jha and Mohanty, *op cit.*
33. Constitution of India (Article 243).
34. 74th Constitution Amendment Act, *op cit.*
35. Thavraj, M.J.K. (1984). Financing of Local Governments in India, in T.N. Chatkurvedi (ed.), *Local Government*, IIPA, New Delhi.
36. Husain, *op cit.*
37. Constitution of India, 2005, Twenty-Seventh Edition, Eastern Book Company, Lucknow.
38. Sukthankar, D.M. (1995). The Seventy-Fourth Amendment of the Constitution: Initiating a Process of Urban Government Reform in Maharashtra, *Urban India*, Vol. No. XV, 13-26.
39. As quoted in *Ibid.*
40. Bhattacharya, M. (1976). *Management of Urban Local Government in India*, Uppal, New Delhi.
41. Zakaria Committee, *op cit.*
42. *Ibid*; Mishra, S. (2000). *Grassroot Politics in India*, Mittal, New Delhi.
43. *Nagarpalika Network* (2003). 6(4), July-Aug; Lamb, R., and Rappaport, Stephen, P., 1980, *Municipal Bonds: The Comprehensive Review of Tax-Exempt Securities and Municipal Finance*, McGraw Hill.
44. 74th Constitution Amendment Act, *op cit.*
45. Mohanty, *op cit.*; Mathur, O.P. (1999). *India, the Challenge of Urban Governance*, NIPFP, New Delhi.
46. Rao, V. (1972). Municipal Administration in Assam, in Avasthi, A. (ed), *Municipal Administration in India*, Laxmi Narain Agarwal, Agra.
47. United Nations (1966). Local Government Personnel System, New York as quoted in Mukhopadhyay, *op cit.*
48. Mukhopadhyay, *op cit.*
49. Mohanty, *op cit.*
50. Narayan, Rajeev (2006). *Municipal Personnel Management in India*, Serials, New Delhi.
51. United Nations, *op cit.*
52. Mohanty, *op cit.*
53. Mukhopadhyay, Asok (1985). *Municipal Personnel Administration*, IIPA, New Delhi.
54. Sharma, M.P. (1960). *Local Self-Government in India*, Kitab Mahal, Allahabad.
55. James, P.A. (1966). Municipal Administration in Andhra Pradesh, a Ph.D. Thesis (unpublished).
56. Report of the Rural Urban Relationship Committee, Vol. I, Govenment of India, 1966.

57. Argal, R. (1967). *Municipal Government in India*, Agarwal Press, Allahabad.
58. Murti, V.S. (1967). Municipal Services, a paper submitted at a training course, Osmania University, Hyderabad.
59. Venkatraman, K. (1968). Creation of a Cadre of Local Civil Service *Personnel, IJPA*, XIV(3).
60. Bhattacharya, M. (1970). *Essays on Urban Government*, World Press Pvt. Ltd., Kolkata.
61. Rao, A.A. (1985). *Personnel Management and Municipal Administration in India*, Ashish, New Delhi.
62. Rao (1972). *op cit.*
63. Singh, Hoshiar (1972). Municipal Personnel System in Rajasthan: Need for Reform, *Qly. Journal of LSGI*, XIII(4).
64. Mathur, N.S. (1974). Management Problem in Unified Municipal Cadres, *Nagarlok*, VI(4).
65. Report of the National Commission on Urbanisation (1988). Government of India.
66. *Ibid*; Stone, C.N., Whelan, R. K., Murni, W.J. (1979). *Urban Policy and Politics in a Bureaucratic Age*, Prentice Hall.
67. 74th Constitution Amendment Act, 1992.
68. U.P. Government abolished octroi all of a sudden on fictitious ground. Many other states have gone the same way.
69. 74th Constitution Amendment Act, 1992; Rao, M.G. and Sen, T., 1996, *Fiscal Federalism in India: Theory and Practice*, MacMillan India Ltd.
70. Chopra, J.K. (ed.) (2004). *Local Self-Government and Municipal Administration*, Common Wealth, New Delhi.
71. Jha, *op cit.*; Drummond, J.M., 1962, *The Finance of Local Government*, Allen & Unwin.
72. 74th Constitution Amendment Act, 1992; Bland, R.L. (2005). *A Revenue Guide to Local Government*, ICMA.
73. Government of India, Commission on Centre-State Relations (Part I), 1988, 361.
74. Government of India, Planning Commission, 1978, Report of the Working Group on Block Level Planning, 2.
75. Mudgal, R. (1998). *Local Self-Government in India*, Book Enclave, Jaipur
76. 74th Constitution Amendment Act, 1992.
77. Nandedkar, V.G (1992). Metropolitan Planning in India, in S. Bhatnagar and S.L. Goel, (eds.), *Development Planning and Administration*, Deep, New Delhi.
78. 74th Constitution Amendment Act, 1992.
79. *Ibid*; Ross Stephens, G., Wikstrom, Nelson (1999). Metropolitan Government. and Governance: Theoretical Perspectives, Empirical Analysis and the Future, OUP.
80. Das, R.B. and Singh, D.P., (eds) (1968). *Deliberative and Executive Wings in Local Government*, OUP, New Delhi.

81. Humes, S. and Martine, E.N. (1961). *The Structure of Local Government Throughout the World*, IULA, The Hague.
82. Jha, C. (1953). *Indian Local Self-Government*, Novelty, Patna.
83. Sharma, M.P. (1965). *Local Government in India*, Kitab Mahal, Allahabad.
84. Das & Singh, *op cit.*
85. Singh, U.B. (1997). Democratic Leadership in Urban Local Bodies—A study of Uttar Pradesh, *Nagarlok*, XXIX (3), July-Sept., 18-25.
86. Mukerji, R.K. (1958). *Local Government in Ancient India*, Motilal, Delhi.
87. Singh, U.B. (1997). *Urban Local Government*, Rawat, New Delhi.
88. Singh (1997). *op cit.*
89. Patil, N.S. (1990). Relationship between Elected Representatives and Officials in Municipal Bodies, *Qly. Journal of AIILSG*, LXI, Jan-March 11-15.
90. Patil, *op cit.*
91. Bora, P.M., Citizens—Administration Relationships: The Urban Local Government Perspectives, *Qly. Journal of AIILSG*, LXI (I-2), 74-78.
92. Patil, *op cit.*; Singh, Hoshiar (1979). *State Supervision over Municipal Administration*, Associated Publishing House, New Delhi.
93. Municipalities Extension to the Scheduled Areas Act, 2001.
94. A treatise on the Calcutta Municipal Corporation Act, 1980.
95. *Ibid.*
96. M.P. Municipal Corporation Act, 1956.
97. The Tripura Municipality Act, 1994.
98. A treaties on the Calcutta Municipal Corporation Act, 1980.
99. M.P Municipal Corporation Act, 1956 and the Tripura Municipality Act, 1994.
100. National Commission on Urbanization, 1988, Vol. II, Government of India.
101. Zakaria Committee, *op cit.*
102. Preface of the Cantonments Act, 1924.
103. *Ibid.*
104. The Cantonments Act, 2006.
105. *Ibid.*
106. *Ibid.*
107. *Ibid.*
108. *Ibid.*
109. *Ibid.*
110. *Ibid.*
111. *Ibid.*

Chapter 9

Rural Local Government in India

Historical Overview

Village in India has been the pivot of administration since time immemorial. Ancient India was built upon the basis of decentralisation in principle and the government from the sovereign at the top extended through all grades and strata of society down to the lowest classes in the villages. It is a well accepted fact that self-governing village communities characterized by agrarian economics had existed in India from the earliest times. Every village was self-governing unit and there was union of villages and self-governing federations. Rural politics was, to a great extent, independent of state politics. The country owes the preservation of her culture to her self-governing villages.[1]

In the old Sanskrit scriptures, there is a word 'Panchayatan' which means a group of five persons. In the *Rigveda* there is a mention of 'Sabha', 'Samiti' and 'Vidath' as local self-units. The concept of 'Panch Parmeshwar' existed in the ancient days. The study of *Ramayana* indicates that administration was divided into two parts 'Pur' and 'Janpad'. Self-government of a village finds ample expression in *Mahabharata* and *Manusmiriti*. 'Sabha Parva' of the *Mahabharata* mentions Gram Panchayats but it is not clear whether the Panchas were elected by the people or nominated by the kings. *Manusmiriti* stresses on organized system of local self-government. Manu has mentioned 'Village' as the smallest unit of governance.[2] In course of time these village bodies took the form of 'panchayats' (assembly of five persons), which looked after the affairs of the village.

They had both police and judicial powers; custom and religion elevated them to a sacred position of authority. In addition, there were also caste panchayats to ensure that persons belonging to a particular caste adhered to its code of social conduct and ethics. Unlike such a system in north, in the southern part of the country, village panchayats generally had a village assembly consisted of representatives of various groups and castes. Generally these villages both, in north and south India, had been the pivot of administration, the centre of social life and above all, a focus of social solidarity.[3]

During the Classical Age the village assembly was variably known as 'Sabha' or 'Mahasabha'. Its members were called '*Perumakkal*' or great men. According to Meenakshi (1994)[4], the 'Sabha' was placed in charge of several kinds of works. They were in charge of temple endowments and irrigation works, looked after the agricultural lands in the village and also administered local justice. In the Chola Empire it was the village assemblies that exhibited the greatest and the most comprehensive group activity. The village and town assemblies were primary assemblies. The lowest unit of the local administration, the self-governing villages, was of two principal types. The first type had an assembly called the 'Ur' and an executive body the 'Alunganam' or 'Ganam'. The second type, which was specially represented by villages of Brahmanas, had an assembly called the 'Sabha' and various committees of the same to carry out its executive works.

In the Maratha Administration, the self-contained villages remained the primary unit of administration. Each village had a headman, 'Patel', who came from peasant stock and who combined the functions of revenue officer, magistrate, judge and acted as intermediary between the village and the government officials. The Mughals divided the whole country into villages for administrative purposes. Each member of the brotherhood held separate possession of the land which he cultivated and enjoyed the fruits of his labour. In managing the affairs of the village, the members acted as a body, their agents being the 'headman' chosen from among themselves according to the custom of the locality. The villages were grouped into larger units known as 'Paraganas'. There was headman (*Chaudhri*) in each paragana, who received orders from the administration and exercised some sort of local jurisdiction but their judicial powers were curtailed.[6]

With the advent of the British, the self contained village communities and their panchayats ceased to get sustenance, and the British masters, perhaps under the stress of changing circumstances, did not realize the indigenous institutions of the country and built up gradually a new system of their own. The traditional panchayat system, which was rooted in the community and based on customs, did not receive statutory recognition. The government created the modern local bodies for the administration of local funds, raised executively in the beginning but made statutory later, to meet a number of local requirements, the most important of which was initially the construction and maintenance of roads.[7] It is historical fact that local government in India, in the sense of an accountable representative institution, was the creation of the British.

Whatever had been the shape and function of village panchayats in the earlier period, the institution had become completely dormant during the British regime. The British keeping in view their limitations in terms of number and having no interest in the development of the countryside built up a highly centralized imperial structure, where there was little scope for decentralized administration.[8] It may be emphasized here that village panchayats were not the first priority of the British rulers. Concentrated as they were mainly around the trading centres, their interest was limited to the creation of local bodies of nominated members in the major towns.[9]

In the years after 1857, rural self-government received some importance. District funds were set up in a few states and were given powers to levy access on land revenue, education and road accesses. Moreover, the funds available were so small that no proper public services were possible, and the village was hardly touched by the new arrangements.[10] From the year 1870 India saw dawn of representative local institutions. A significant impetus to the development of local governments was given by Mayo's Resolution of 1870. It afforded opportunities for the development of self-government to harness social interest, supervision, and care for the management of funds devoted to education, sanitation, health services and local public works.[11] It was out of a fiscal compulsion that Lord Mayo's resolution on local self government came to be adopted. It was in the wake of this resolution that the first significant step to revive the traditional village panchayat system in Bengal was taken in 1870 through the Bengal Chowkidari Act. This enactment empowered the district magistrates to set up panchayats of nominated members in the villages. These nominated panchayats could levy and collect taxes to pay for the chowkidars or watchmen engaged by them.[12]

It was as late as 1882 when Lord Ripon, the then Viceroy of India, took the initiative in the establishment of popularly elected institutions at local levels to look after specified functions in their areas. The institution of local self-government was not to bring improvement in administration but meant to act as an instrument of political and popular education.[13] The resolution proposed the establishment of rural local boards, two-thirds of whose membership was composed of elected representatives. Although the progress of local self-government on the lines of Ripon's resolution was tardy, the term 'self-government' had began to gain currency. In 1906 the Congress accepted the 'self government' as the political goal for the country. In 1907 the government constituted the Royal Commission on Decentralization which elaborated further the principles enunciated in the Ripon's resolution and recognized the importance of self-government in the Indian context.

The first ever reference of village panchayats as local self-government institutions was made in the report of the Royal Commission on Decentralisation in 1909. The Commission recommended that "it is most desirable, alike in the interests of decentralization and in order to associate the people with the local tasks of administration, that an attempt should be made to constitute and develop village panchayats for the administration of local village affairs".[14] The report of the Commission resulted into the Morley-Minto Reforms of 1909, which led to the enlargement of the elective process in the local self-government structure of India. The Commission viewed that the local self-government should start from the village level instead of from the district level. It stated "*We consider, as the local self-government should commence in the village with the establishment of village panchayats, so the next step be the constitution of boards of areas of smaller size than a district. We desire therefore to see sub-district boards, universally established, as the principal agencies of rural administration*".[15] The recommendations of the Commission recognized the importance of the village panchayats. The Indian National Congress at its session at Lahore in 1909 passed a resolution and urged the Government of India to take early steps to make all local bodies from village panchayats upwards elective with elected non-official chairman and to support them with adequate financial aid.[16]

The years that followed after the First World War saw the advent of national leaders like Tilak and Gandhi. Tilak was conscious that the local government in the real sense of the term was not possible till '*Swaraj*' was obtained, while Gandhiji declared that "*the village panchayats should be now a living force in a special way and India would almost be enjoying self-government suited to its requirements*".[17]

Under the Government of India Act 1919, the local self-government institution was made one of the provincial transferred subjects placed under the jurisdiction of elected Indian Ministries. To make local self-government fully representative and responsible, the Montague-Chelmsford Reforms had suggested that there should be complete popular control in local bodies and the largest possible independence for them of outside control.[18] Accordingly during the Dyarchy regime, several enactments for the establishment of Village Panchayats were passed in major states like Bengal (1919), Bihar (1920), Bombay (1920), Central Province and Berar (1920), Madras (1920), UP (1920), Punjab (1922), and Assam (1925). But these statutory panchayats covered only limited number of villages and had generally limited number of functions.

In 1927, Indian Statutory Commission under the chairmanship of Simon was appointed to go into the details of the working of local self-government. The major drawbacks in the working of the local bodies were traced to the factors such as the inability to realize the importance of having a competent and well-paid official, failure to realize the need for control by the provincial governments over local self-government authorities, inadequacy of financial resources, and lack of public spirit among many voters. To rejuvenate the system, D.P. Mishra, the then Minister of Local Self-Government proposed a scheme in which decentralisation of administration was the main approach. In this scheme, the district was made the principal unit of administration followed by municipalities in urban area and circle boards and village panchayats in the rural area.[19]

The Government of India Act 1935 marked another important stage in the evolution of panchayats in the country. The popularly elected provincial governments felt duty bound to enact legislations for further democratization of local self-institutions.

In spite of adverse development in the arena of local government, the idea of panchayats remained as a vital factor and also as a strategy for the struggle for independence. The main architect behind this was none other than Mahatma Gandhi who fought relentlessly for the cause of *Swaraj*. However, there was no unanimity among the top leaders regarding the status and role to be assigned to the institution of rural local self-government. There were divergent views on the subject. On one extreme Gandhiji was in favour of Village Swaraj and strengthening the Village Panchayats to the fullest extent and on the other extreme, Dr. B.R. Ambedkar was totally opposed to this idea.

Mahatma Gandhi had expressed his will to build the entire Indian polity on the foundation of Village Swaraj. His concept is documented in '*Harijan*' as: "*My idea of village swaraj is that it is a complete republic independent of its neighbour for its own vital wants and yet interdependent for many others in which dependence is a necessity. Thus every village's first concern will be to grow its own food crops and cotton for its cloth. It should have a reserve for its cattle, recreation and playground for its adult and children. Then if there is more land available it will grow useful money crops. The village will maintain a village theatre, school and public well. It will have its own water works ensuring water supply. Education will be compulsory up to the final basic course. As far as possible every activity will be conducted on the cooperative basis. There will be a compulsory service of village guards who will be selected by rotation from the register maintained by the village. The government of the village will be conducted by the panchayat of five persons, elected annually by the adult villagers, male and female both possessing minimum prescribed qualifications. These will have all the authorities and jurisdiction required. This panchayat will be legislature, judiciary and executive combined, to operate for its year of office.*" [20]

Gandhiji further states (1947) that "*Independence must begin at the bottom. Thus every village will be a republic or panchayat having full powers. It follows, therefore, that every village has to be self sustained and capable of managing its affairs ...... If there ever is to be a republic of every village in India then I claim verify for my picture in which the last is equal to the first, or in other words, none is to be the first and none the last.*"[21]

Mathur (1994) has well described the status and role of rural local self-government as: "*Free India forgets Gandhi not to mention Ripon. India thus achieved its cherished objective of self-government in 'all India' terms and its Constituent Assembly proceeded to frame a constitution, which embodied the Westminster style democratic ideology of parliamentary democracy at the centre and state levels. But the long chapter of evolution of rural and urban local self-governments which started in 1882 (and even earlier in several respects) had almost no impact on the public and political life by free India either in the Riponian or Gandhian sense. As far as the rural and urban local government institutions were concerned 15th August 1947 was just like any other day."*[22]

It is an irony that despite commitment to democratic decentralization and to panchayats and Gandhiji's unequivocal propagation of the ideal, the first draft of India's Constitution did not include a provision for panchayats. The primacy of Village Panchayats in Indian polity as propounded by Mahatma Gandhi was however rejected by the founding fathers of the Constitution. On Gandhiji's insistence and support of a few members, a provision was included in Part IV of the Constitution, which is not mandatory. Under Article 40 (in the Directive Principles of State Policy) it was stated that "*the State shall take steps to organize village panchayats and endow them with such powers and authority as may be necessary to enable them to function as units of self-government.*"[23] However, no worthwhile legislation was immediately enacted either at the national or state level to implement it.

In addition, the Constitution in its Seventh Schedule under Article 246 lists local government (Entry 51) legislation as being reserved to the States. The entry is very wide and empowers the State legislature to legislate with respect to local government—rural and urban. The state legislature can also confer such powers including the power of taxation to a local authority as it itself possesses. The only provision of the Constitution that can be invoked by the Union Government is the Presidential veto over State legislation which has been referred by the State Governor.[24]

In decades that followed, *Gram Swaraj* was the sheet anchor of the Sarvodaya Movement inspired by Vinoba Bhave and Jayaprakash Narayan. Under the influence of USA, a very ambitious programme known as Community Development Programme (CDP) was launched on 2nd October 1952. It was the first attempt to tackle the problem of rural India in a comprehensive and organized manner in free India. This programme, which was first introduced in fifty-five blocks spread all over the country, was by stages extended to cover larger areas.[25] The programme professed to be far modern and comprehensive in nature. It also promised economic prosperity by including the desire for development and by securing common participation. The country was divided into over five thousand Community Development Blocks. At the block level the team of subject matter specialists headed by a generalist known as Block Development Officer (BDO) was appointed and during the initial stages of the programme substantial financial assistance was made available for various development activities. After a few years Block Advisory Committee was constituted to associate the community. The committee consisted of block level officials, progressive farmers, representatives of co-operative societies, heads of educational institutions, MLAs and MPs of the area. The main purpose of the committee was to advise the Block Development Officer and his team on planning and implementation of development programmes. This experiment did not achieve the desired results as it had no statutory backing and also there was no organic link between the Village Panchayats, Block Advisory Committees and the District Boards.[26]

The Community Development Projects, inaugurated in 1952 and modelled after the experiments at Marthandam, Shantiniketan, Baroda, Etawah and Nilokheri, soon found themselves in a blind alley in the absence of effective instruments of people's participation.

Balwantray Mehta Committee

After Independence the first landmark in the history of Panchayati Raj Institutions in the country was the appointment of Balwantray Mehta Committee. On 16th January 1957, the Committee on Plan Projects, a body established by the National Development Council set up a team for the study of Community Development Projects. Among other areas the terms of reference of the team included the study of the problems connected to the organic linking of Village Panchayats with popular organization at higher levels and the reorganization of district administration so that the democratic bodies should take over the entire administration.[27]

The Study Team while making its recommendations observed that "*one of the least successful aspects of the Community Projects and National Extension Service work is its attempt to evoke popular initiative.*"[28] The team felt that "*so long as we do not discover or create a representative and democratic institution which will supply the local interest supervision and care necessary to ensure the proper utilization of funds on the felt needs of the people and the area and also provide these bodies adequate powers and assign to them appropriate finances, we will never be able to evoke local interest and initiative in the field of development."* [29] The Study Team recommended a three-tier system for local self-government at the grassroot levels.

The Team proposed to setup an elective self-governing institution known as Panchayat Samiti at the block level. It should be constituted by indirect election from the Village Panchayats, besides some co-opted members. The block level institution should also act as an agent of the State Government in the execution of special schemes of development entrusted to it. The Team recommended that all the Central and State funds to be spent in the block area should be assigned direct to the Panchayat Samiti. Below the Panchayat Samiti would be the Village Panchayats, which should be directly elected by the villagers. It would act as an agent of the Panchayat Samiti in executing any of its schemes. The functions of the Village Panchayats would include: provision of water supply, sanitation, lighting, maintenance of roads, land management, collection and maintenance of records and the welfare of the backward classes. [30]

As regards the district level, the Team suggested three types of arrangements, depending upon the roles, powers and functions assigned to the lower level tiers. The Team proposed that in case a state assigns the Panchayat Samitis and the Village Panchayats the role as suggested, there would be very little left for any higher executive body and the functions of Zila Parishad may include co-ordination and general supervision of Panchayat Samitis, distribution of state funds and the approval of their budgets. In order to achieve these objectives an indirectly elected Zila Parishad consisting of presidents of Panchayat Samitis, MPs, MLAs and district officers would be preferred. A second type was suggested for those State Governments who thought it convenient to have a large local body for the district. Such a body would consist of members of the Panchayats within each Panchayat Samiti area, who would be elected by the Panchayat members from amongst themselves. It would be an executive body and would undertake district level and inter-block activities. The third type of Zila Parishad would be a culmination of process of devolution of powers and functions from the state government to local government. The Team envisaged that the Zila Parishad would supervise the activities of the Panchayat Samitis, which in turn would supervise the working of the Village Panchayats.

The Study Team submitted its report on 24th November 1957. The report was quite exhaustive, with 18 sections. The most dynamic component, however, among all recommendations was the democratic decentralisation. The National Development Council approved these recommendations and communicated to states in January 1958. Consequently, the states and union territories enacted laws for establishment of Panchayati Raj Institutions with the exception of three states e.g. Meghalaya, Mizoram, Nagaland and Union Territory of Lakshadweep. There was acceptance of the Panchayat tiers differently. Three-tier structure was adopted in 12 States and one Union Territory, two-tier structure was adopted in four States and two Union Territories and one-tier structure was adopted in four States and four Union Territories.[32]

Rajasthan was the first state in the country to adopt the Panchayati Raj System (at Nagaur) on the 2nd October 1959, followed by Andhra Pradesh (at Shadnagar). By 1959, all states had passed panchayat acts and by mid-1960's, panchayats had reached all parts of the country. There was enthusiasm in rural India and the people felt that they had a say in affairs affecting their daily lives. As on 31st March 1973, Kerala and Jammu & Kashmir had accepted only one-tier system—the Village Panchayat. Karnataka, Himachal Pradesh, and Orissa had two-tier system—Village Panchayat and Panchayat Samiti. West Bengal had adopted a four-tier system—Zila Parishad, Anchalik Parishad, Anchal Panchayat and Gram Panchayat. The other states had adopted three-tier system.[33] Due to the interest generated by the panchayati raj institutions several states set-up committees to assess their working and to recommend measures for improvement. The critical problem, however, was the domination of these institutions by the economically and socially privileged classes. This was essentially a socio-political problem and could have been tackled to a great extent by holding elections at regular intervals.[34]

To evaluate the achievements of the recommendations, it was observed that the democratic decentralisation concept of the Study Team did not succeed in face of inhibitory determinants from political, financial, functional and administrative ways. The process of decline started after the mid-sixties and, continued for almost two decades. During this period the flow of funds for the development of blocks was reduced considerably. In fact, the non-devolution of the sources of revenues proved to be the greatest stumbling block in the performance of these grassroots level institutions. The elections were indefinitely postponed in many states. For planning and implementation of various rural development and poverty alleviation programmes, parallel bodies were set up at the district level. In early 1960's, the flow of funds under the community development scheme started declining and later era of centrally sponsored schemes was started, thus the very idea of self-governance lost its meaning and scope.

Asoka Mehta Committee

During Janata Rule at the Centre in 1977, a serious view was taken of the weaknesses of the functioning of Panchayati Raj System and a committee under the chairmanship of Asoka Mehta was appointed to examine the whole issue and make suitable recommendations. The Cabinet Secretariat in its resolution dated 12th December 1977 emphasized that "*the Government accords the highest priority to rural development, so as to increase agricultural production, create employment, eradicate poverty and bring about all around improvement in the rural economy. The Government considers that the maximum degree of decentralisation both in planning and in implementation is necessary for the attainment of these objectives. It has accordingly been decided, in consultation with the State Governments and Union Territories, to set up a committee to enquire into the working of the Panchayati Raj Institutions and to suggest measures to strengthen them, so as to enable a decentralized system of planning and development to be effective*".[35]

The committee in its Report remarked that the case of Panchayati Raj has been a story of ups and downs. According to the Report, the period 1959-64 had been a phase of ascendancy, 1965-69 a phase of stagnation and 1969-79 a phase of decline. Pointing out the weaknesses of the system, the Committee observed that except in Maharashtra and Gujarat the Panchayati Raj Institutions have been rarely given any opportunity to take up planning or implementation work on a sizeable scale. The Report states that these grassroot level institutions have not been assigned adequate functions. The development programmes were not channeled through them. Their resource base was very weak and the overall attention given to them niggardly. In the over all analysis there was lack of political and administrative will which led to the decline of the Panchayati Raj Institutions.

The Committee had reviewed the situation in 1978 to recommend an institutional design for Panchayati Raj in the light of the development thrust and technical expertise required for planning and implementation of rural development programmes. The Committee made a number of recommendations and some of the important recommendations are as under:[36]

1. There is a need of constitutional sanction in order to provide continuity and requisite status.
2. The states may adopt a two-tier system—Zila Parishad (at district) and a Mandal Panchayat, each covering a population of 15 to 20 thousand. The block level Panchayat Samiti may be converted into non-statutory executive committee of Zila Parishad.
3. The scheduled castes and the scheduled tribes should be given representation on the basis of their population.
4. The elections to all these bodies should be held simultaneously and the term should be four years.
5. The chairman of the Mandal Panchayat may be elected directly or indirectly but the chairman of Zila Parishad should be elected indirectly.
6. The Zila Parishad should function through committees on various subjects. The composition of all the committees should be on the basis of proportional representation so as to ensure representation of all sections and shades of opinion. A committee of the chairman of subjects committees may function as standing committee of the Zila Parishad.
7. The State Government should not supersede the Panchayati Raj Institutions on partisan grounds. If supersession becomes necessary elections should be held within six months.
8. All the development functions should be placed under Zila Parishad and in no case the Panchayati Raj Institutions should be bypassed in the implementation of district sector schemes. Zila Parishad should handle all the decentralized functions meant for the district.
9. Zila Parishad should be made responsible for planning at the district level and it should take care of rural-urban continuum.

10. The Panchayati Raj Institutions should have compulsory powers of taxation. In fact a select list of taxation should be provided with some taxes being made compulsory.
11. Approval of budget by higher authority seems to be a desirable practice.
12. A sufficiently high-ranking Finance Officer should be placed at the district level as the entire plan and non-plan funds would be under his supervision.
13. Such regulatory functions, which may be helpful in implementation of various development programmes in the field, should be assigned to the appropriate tier of Panchayati Raj.
14. Participation of political parties in elections would ensure clearer orientation towards development programmes and facilitate healthier linkages with higher level political process.

The recommendations of the Asoka Mehta Committee could not be acted upon by the short-lived Janta Party government. However substantiation of democratic decentralisation in the form of Panchayati Raj Institutions was pursued in the states of West Bengal, Karnataka and Andhra Pradesh.

CAARD Report (G.V.K. Rao Committee)

A Committee on Administrative Arrangements for Rural Development (CAARD) was constituted on 31st March 1985 with G.V.K. Rao as its chairman to look into the role of the Panchayati Raj bodies and their relationship with the proposed administrative set-up. The Committee had commented that after the initial enthusiasm following the creation of the Panchayati Raj Institutions, there had been stagnation and later a decline in the functioning of these institutions in many parts of the country. Apart from inadequate resources, elections of these bodies have not been held regularly. The committee had felt that whenever these institutions had been actively involved the implementation of the rural development programmes had been decidedly better and the selection of the beneficiaries and designing of the schemes had been more satisfactory.[37]

The Committee in its report pointed out that the decline of Panchayati Raj Institutions may be attributed to the reluctance of political leadership at the state level to share powers with district leadership. The Committee suggested that the work relating to planning, plan implementation and monitoring of rural development programmes should be entrusted to these local government units at the district level. The Zila Parishad should be the apex body for overall planning at the district level and the plan should be prepared by the District Planning Board and sent to the Zila Parishad for review and authentication.[38]

L.M. Singhvi Committee

The Government of India set up a committee in June 1986 headed by L.M. Singhvi to prepare a concept paper on the revitalization of Panchayati Raj Institutions. The Committee felt that initially democracy and development had marched hand in hand. But within a few years of inauguration of the new era, Panchayati Raj Institutions began to sag, stagnate and decline. Their potential as centres of people's power aroused apprehensions and a jealous hostility all around. The elected representatives in parliament and legislature were not quite willing to share power. There was public apathy and indifference. There was chronic insufficiency of resources at the disposal of these institutions. Programmes after programmes were launched without involving Panchayati Raj Institutions. These programmes have become close preservers of bureaucracy undermining and frustrating the Panchayati Raj Institutions as units of local self-government.[39]

The Committee recommended to protect the Panchayati Raj Institutions by Constitution as third tier of government; regular elections; setting up of Panchayati Raj Judicial Tribunal to adjudicate in respect of elections, suspension, supersession, dissolution etc.; earmarking of adequate financial resources by the Central Finance Commission; setting up of Nyaya Panchayats; model legislation for appropriate local adoptions; evolving the correct role of political parties through consensus etc.[40]

Sarkaria Commission

The Commission on Centre-State Relations, popularly known as Sarkaria Commission, set-up by the Ministry of Home Affairs on 9th June 1983 under the Chairmanship of R.S. Sarkaria also touched the subject of decentralisation at lowest levels. The Committee paid considerable attention to the working of the Panchayati Raj System on the issue of decentralisation of power and the planning process, financial and functional strengthening of the local institutions with regular elections.

The Commission observed: "*While there is considerable reluctance to decentralize powers to the Districts, there has been even greater reluctance in most States to decentralize powers to the lower levels like Municipalities, Panchayat Samitis and Panchayats, in spite of explicit directive in Article 40 of the Constitution……… The objectives of the decentralized planning cannot be achieved unless the Panchayati Raj and other local bodies are allowed full scope to play their role… It is necessary that elections are held regularly and adequate finances are devolved on these institutions*".[41]

A Finance Commission was recommended at state level to enable the State Government to devolve its resources to district level.

Thungan Committee

A sub-committee of the parliamentary consultative committee was set-up in 1988 under the chairmanship of P.K. Thungan to consider the '*type of political and administrative structure in the district for district planning*'. The Thungan Committee examined the subject in greater detail and suggested a three-tier structure with constitutional status, reservation of seats for the scheduled castes, scheduled tribes and women, and setting up of finance commission in every state. The Committee also suggested that a model Panchayati Raj Act should be enacted by the Central Government to maintain uniformity. It also suggested the setting up of a planning and coordination committee at the state level under the chairmanship of the Planning Minister. Presidents of Zilla Parishad should be a member of the committee. The village panchayats were empowered to sort out simple disputes at the village level itself. The term of the Panchayati Raj bodies should be for a period of five years.[42]

C.H. Hanumantha Rao Team

With a view to obtain effective people's participation through the Panchayati Raj Institutions, the Planning Commission experts under the leadership of Dr. C.H. Hanumantha Rao were deputed in 1982 to study as to how to prepare plans at the district level. The Team suggested that decentralisation of planning should take place. Development plans have remained centralized, hence participation of local people has been lacking. People should be associated right from the plan formulation stage.[43]

Congress Party Committee on Policy Programmes

The ruling Congress Party constituted a Committee on Policy Programmes under the chairmanship of V.N. Gadgil. The Committee looked into the matter and recommended three-tier system of Panchayati Raj Institutions at the village, block and district levels. It was felt that the Panchayati Raj Institutions should have a term of five years and in case of dissolution, elections must take place within six months. It strongly recommended the grant of constitutional status to these institutions. There should be reservation for the Scheduled Castes and Scheduled Tribes and women. Elections by Central Election Commission and provision of State Finance Commission were the other main recommendations.[44]

Committees in Various States

Panchayati Raj being the state subject has been the main responsibility of the State Governments. Many states have constituted their own state level committees for studying the organizational pattern, financial resources, administrative powers, personnel system and other facets. The details are as under: [45]

Andhra Pradesh	Purshottam Pai Committee	1964
	Ramchandra Reddy Committee	1965
	Narsimhan Committee	1972
Rajasthan	Mathur Committee	1963
	Sadiq Ali Committee	1963
	G. L. Vyas Committee	1973
	Kharva Committee	1990
	Cabinet Sub-Committee	1992
Karnataka	Basappa Committee	1963
Maharashtra	Naik Committee	1961
	Bongiwar Committee	1963
Uttar Pradesh	Govind Sahai Committee	1959
	Murthi Committee	1965

Constitution (73rd Amendment) Act, 1992

The foregone discussion reflects that the need for granting constitutional status to Panchayati Raj Institutions was felt since the recommendations of the Asoka Mehta Committee Report in 1978. It was however during the Prime Ministership of Rajiv Gandhi when a practical shape was given in the form of introducing 64th Bill to amend the Constitution. The Bill was drafted keeping in view the shortcomings identified in the working of the Panchayati Raj Institutions during the four decades after Independence. Although it was a welcome step, there was serious opposition to it on two basic grounds: (i) the Bill overlooked the states and was seen as instrument of the centre to deal directly with the Panchayati Raj Institutions, and (ii) that it was imposing a uniform pattern throughout the country instead of permitting individual states to legislate the details, keeping in mind the local circumstances. There was an outcry against the Bill. Although the Bill got a two-thirds majority in Lok Sabha, in Rajya Sabha on 15th October 1989 it failed to meet the mandatory requirements. As such the Bill could not be executed and lapsed due to dissolution of the Lok Sabha.

Subsequently under the National Front regime also a revised Bill (combined for urban and rural) known as 72nd Constitution Amendment Bill was drafted and was brought up before a conference of Chief Ministers held in June 1990. The conference endorsed the proposal and the Bill was introduced in the Lok Sabha on 7th September 1990. This Bill never came to discussion and lapsed because of the dissolution of the Lok Sabha. Fresh elections were held in June 1991 and the Congress Party again came to power. The government started the exercise and introduced the 72nd Amendment Bill in the Lok Sabha on 16th September 1991. The Bill was referred to a Joint Parliamentary Committee, which presented its report to the Parliament in July 1992. The Lok Sabha unanimously passed the Bill on 22nd December 1992 and the same was passed by the Rajya Sabha the following day. After ratification by 17 States, the Bill was assented by the President on 20th April 1993. The number was changed and the Constitution (Seventy Third Amendment) Act, 1992 came into effect from 24th April 1993. The Amendment brought about a fundamental change not only in the realm of local self-government but also in the country's federal character.[46]

New Panchayati Raj

The Seventy Third Amendment to the Constitution enshrines in the supreme law of the land certain basic and essential features of Panchayati Raj Institutions. It imparts certainty, continuity and strength to them. A new Part IX with the heading 'Panchayat' has been added to the Constitution, thus the Panchayati Raj Institutions have been made an integral part of the Constitution. Gram Sabha, as an assembly of adult people is a direct democratic body of self-government at primary level.[47] As such, the administration has been brought nearer to the people, democratic decentralisation has been ensured, fiscal devolution has been planned, functional domain has been demarcated, and accountability to the community has been established.

As the provisions of the Constitution (Seventy Third Amendment) Act did not apply to the Scheduled Areas located in ten states[48]—Andhra Pradesh, Madhya Pradesh, Chhattisgarh, Rajasthan, Gujarat, Maharashtra, Himachal Pradesh, Orissa, Bihar and Jharkhand—vide Article 244(i) Parliament extended the coverage of the Act to these areas on 24th December 1996 by enacting the Panchayats (Extension to the Scheduled Areas) Act, 1996. The provisions are however not applicable in the states of Nagaland, Meghalaya and Mizoram and in the hill areas in the Manipur in the part for which District Councils exist.[49]

The provisions of the 73rd Constitution Amendment Act can be classified as mandatory and discretionary. Mandatory provisions are compulsorily to be included in the state legislations, where as certain provisions have been left for the state legislature to take decisions in view of socio-economic conditions of the state.

Mandatory Provisions[50]

Constitution of Panchayats

The 73rd Constitution Amendment Act prescribes a three-tier system of Panchayats at the village, intermediary and district levels. However, the states having population less than 20 lakhs may prefer not to create Panchayat at intermediary level.

Composition of Panchayats

The legislature of the state may make law with respect to the composition of panchayats. All the seats in a Panchayat are filled by persons chosen by direct election. For this purpose each panchayat area is divided in territorial constituencies with almost equal population. The law enacted by state may provide for representation of the chairpersons of the village panchayats in the panchayat at intermediary level or in case a state not having panchayat at intermediary level in the District Panchayat. The members of the Lok Sabha and the Legislative Assembly of the state representing constituencies which comprise wholly or partly a panchayat area may be given representation in panchayats at intermediate and district levels. The members of the Rajya Sabha and the Legislative Council registered as electors within a panchayat area at the intermediate level may represent the panchayat at the intermediate level and a panchayat area at the district level in District Panchayat. The chairperson of a panchayat and other members have the right to vote in the meetings of the panchayats.

The Chairperson of Village Panchayats may be elected in such a manner as the Legislature of a State may provide. The chairpersons of Intermediate Panchayats or District Panchayats are elected by and from amongst the elected members.

Reservation of Seats

Seats are reserved for the Scheduled Castes and the Scheduled Tribes in every Panchayat in proportion to their population in the total population of the area. At least one-third of the seats reserved for the Scheduled Castes and Scheduled Tribes are reserved for women belonging to that section. Not less than one-third of the total number of seats are reserved for women. Such seats may be allotted by rotation to different constituencies in a panchayat. The offices of chairpersons are also reserved for the Scheduled Castes, Scheduled Tribes and women in the same manner. The Legislature of a State may make provisions for reservation of seats for backward classes as well.

Duration

A Panchayat has a fixed term of five years from the date of its first meeting. The state government may dissolve a Panchayat but elections shall be held within six months. Where the remainder of the period of a dissolved Panchayat is less than six months, it is not necessary to hold elections for a dissolved Panchayat. A Panchayat constituted upon the dissolution can continue only for the remainder period for which the dissolved panchayat would have continued, if not dissolved.

Powers, Authority and Responsibilities

The legislature of a state may endow the Panchayats with such powers and authority as may be necessary to enable them to function as institutions of self-government. The law may contain provisions for the dissolution of powers and responsibilities upon panchayats with respect to the preparation of plans for economic development and social justice and the implementation of schemes for economic development and social justice including those in relation to the matters listed in the Eleventh Schedule.

Functions given in the Eleventh Schedule:

1. Agriculture, including agricultural extension.
2. Land improvement, implementation of land reforms, land consolidation and soil conservation.
3. Minor irrigation, water management and watershed development.
4. Animal husbandry, dairy and poultry.
5. Fisheries.
6. Social forestry and farm forestry.
7. Minor forest produce.
8. Small scale industries, including the food processing industries.
9. Khadi, village and cottage industries.
10. Rural Housing.
11. Drinking water.
12. Fuel and fodder.
13. Roads, culverts, bridges, ferries, waterways and other means of communication.
14. Rural electrification, including distribution of electricity.
15. Non-conventional energy sources.
16. Poverty alleviation programmes.
17. Education, including primary and secondary schools.
18. Technical training and vocational education.

19. Adult and non-formal education.
20. Libraries.
21. Cultural activities.
22. Markets and fairs.
23. Health and sanitation, including hospitals, primary health centres and dispensaries.
24. Family welfare.
25. Women and child development.
26. Social welfare, including welfare of handicapped and mentally retarded.
27. Welfare of weaker sections and in particular of the Scheduled Castes and the Scheduled Tribes.
28. Public distribution system.
29. Maintenance of community assets.

Taxation Powers

The legislature of a state may authorize a Panchayat to levy, collect and appropriate taxes, duties, tolls and fees; assign such taxes, duties, tolls and fees levied and collected by the State Government.

Constitution of Finance Commission

The Governor of the State shall constitute every five years a Finance Commission to review the financial position of the Panchayats and make recommendations to the Governor as to the principles which should govern the distribution between the state and the panchayats of the net proceeds of taxes, duties, tolls and fees leviable by the state which may be divided between them and the allocation between the panchayats at all levels of their respective share of such proceeds. The Finance Commission constituted at state level is common for both, the Municipalities and Panchayats.

Elections to the Panchayats

The superintendence, direction and control of the preparation of electoral rolls, conduct of all elections to the panchayats shall be vested in a State Election Commission consisting of a State Election Commissioner appointed by the Governor.

Discretionary Provisions

The Central Act has given adequate discretionary powers on the nomenclature of Panchayats at different levels; composition, powers and functions, devolution of powers, the modes of election of chairpersons of Village Panchayats, the manner of reservation of seats, taxes, duties, fees etc.

Personnel Administration

Except certain minor variations, rural personnel administration across the country is uniform.

A senior officer of state civil service or of the IAS cadre is appointed as Chief Executive Officer of Zilla Panchayat. In many states he is known as District Development Officer or Chief Development Officer, District Education Officer, Accounts Officer, Project/Assistant Project Officer, Taxation Officer, Agriculture Officer, Irrigation Officer, Animal Husbandry Officer, Panchayat Officers are the other officers manning the District Panchayat.

At intermediary level, Block Development Officer is the chief executive. In many states he is appointed by State Public Service Commission, while in others he comes on deputation from other departments. Deputy/Assistant Block Development Officer, Block Education Officer, Extension Officer, Junior Engineers are the other officials.

At Village Panchayat level two functionaries exist: Gram Sevak or Village Development Officer and Panchayat Secretary. Village Development Officer is responsible for undertaking development activities under the guidance and supervision of Block Development Officer at Block Level and Chief Development Officer at the District level. The Panchayat Secretary works as Secretary to Village Panchayat under the direct control of District Panchayat Officer through Assistant District Officer (Panchayats) at Block level. This dual arrangement keeps village panchayat away from implementation of development programmes at village level.

Thus, the rural bureaucracy in the country is very weak and unstable. The officers from various government departments with no development orientation are deputed in Panchayats at different levels. They are governed by the rules of their respective parent departments.

Almost all the states have understood the importance of training for elected representatives and the staff of the Panchayati Raj Institutions. Training institutes have been established at the state level. State Institute of Rural Development (under the National Institute of Rural Development as apex body) exists in almost all the state headquarters. Regional Training Centres and District Training Centres also impart training at regional and district levels.

Financial Administration

Generally Panchayati Raj Institutions in the country have no fixed tax base. They are empowered to levy taxes on persons, property and business. They include general property taxes, service taxes, taxes on land revenue, rent of land, taxes on trades, professions and callings, taxes on animals and vehicles, octroi, pilgrim tax, taxes on fairs etc. Besides the panchayats collect fees for services rendered, license fees and fees in the nature of fines and penalties. Ponds and tanks as well as fairs and markets yield some income to the panchayats.[51] However, in many states, land revenue is the major tax source in rural areas. This source comes under the Revenue Department. In many states collection of land revenue has been transferred to Panchayati Raj Institutions. The Panchayats at different levels earn some income from toll, fees on ponds, markets etc.

In reality, the Panchayati Raj System in the country is running basically on grants-in-aid.[52] Generally, the grants are specific and tied to the head of expenditure and very little amount is untied. Panchayati Raj Institutions at all the levels implement various development and poverty alleviation programmes under the financial assistance from the government. The absence of income from own resources makes these grassroot institutions lethargic, uncommitted and interested in spending grant.[53]

Realizing the sense of lacking responsibility at the local level, K.R. Narayanan (former President of India) in his address to the nation on the eve of Independence Day, 2000 advocated fiscal federation, saying "*for Panchayats to grow as genuine units of self-government, it is essential that they have a financial base of their own.*"[54] Unfortunately, many State Finance Commissions have also failed to appreciate the fiscal weakness of Panchayati Raj Institutions in the country.

The Panchayats (Extension to the Scheduled Areas) Act, 1996[55]

This Act extends the provision of Part IX to the Scheduled Areas subject to a state not authorized to make any law inconsistent with the customary law, social and religious practices of community resources. The affairs of a village are managed in accordance with the traditions and customs. Every village shall have a Gram Sabha consisting of persons whose names are included in the electoral rolls for the panchayats at the village level. Every Gram Sabha shall be competent to safeguard and preserve the traditions and customs of the people, their cultural identity, community resources and the customary mode of dispute resolution.

Every Gram Sabha shall approve plans, programmes and projects for social and economic development before such plans, programmes and projects are taken up for implementation by the Panchayats at the village level. It will be responsible for the identification or selection of persons as beneficiaries under the poverty alleviation and other programmes. Panchayats shall be required to obtain from Gram Sabha a certification of utilization of funds for the plans, programmes and projects.

The reservation of seats at every Panchayat shall be in proportion to the population of the communities in that panchayat for whom reservation is sought to be given. The reservation for the Scheduled Tribes shall not be less than one-half of the total number of seats and all seats of Chairpersons at all levels shall be reserved for the Scheduled Tribes. The State Government may nominate persons belonging to Scheduled Tribes as have no representation in the Panchayat at the intermediate level or the Panchayat at the district level. Such nominations shall not be become one-tenth of the total number to be elected in that Panchayat. Panchayats at the appropriate level shall be consulted before making the acquisition of the land in the Scheduled Areas for development projects and before setting or rehabilitating persons affected by such projects.

The actual planning and implementation of the projects shall be coordinated at the state level. Planning and management of minor water bodies shall be entrusted to Panchayats at the appropriate level. The recommendations of the Gram Sabha or Panchayat at the appropriate level shall be mandatory prior to grant of prospecting license or mining lease for minor minerals and for grant of concession for the exploitation of minor minerals by auction.

While endowing Panchayats in the Scheduled Areas with such powers and authority as may be necessary to enable them to function as institutions of self-government, state legislature shall ensure that the Panchayats at the appropriate level and the Gram Sabha are endowed specifically with:

(i) The power to enforce prohibition or to regulate or restrict the sale and consumption of any intoxicant.
(ii) The ownership of any forest produce.
(iii) The power to prevent alienation of land in the Scheduled Areas and to take appropriate action to restore any lawfully alienated land of a Scheduled Tribe.
(iv) The power to manage village markets.
(v) The power to exercise control over money lending to Scheduled Tribes.
(vi) The power to exercise control over institutions and functionaries in all social sectors.
(vii) The powers to control local plans and resources for such plans including tribal sub-plans.

The State Legislature shall endow to follow the pattern of Sixth Schedule while designing the administrative arrangements in the Panchayats at district level.

REFERENCES

1. Singh, U.B. (1998). *Administrative System in India*, APH, New Delhi.
2. Joshi, R.P. and Narwani, G.S. (2002). *Panchayati Raj in India*, Rawat, Jaipur
3. Mathew, George (2000). *Panchayati Raj in India—An Overview*, in Status of Panchayati Raj in the States and Union Territories of India, Institute of Social Science, Concept, New Delhi.
4. Meenakshi, S.S.S. (1994). *Decentralization in Developing Countries*, Concept, New Delhi.
5. Singh, U.B. (1998). *Administrative System in India*, APH Publications, New Delhi.
6. Ghosal, U.N. (1988). Political Theory and Administrative Organization in the Classical Age, in R.C. Majumdar (ed.) *The History and Culture of Indian People*, Vol. III, Bhartiya Vidya Bhawan, Bombay.
7. *Ibid*; Hussain, A. (1962). *Community Development in India*, AMU Press, Aligarh.

8. Bajpai, Ashok and Verma, M.S. (1995). *Panchayati Raj in India* (A New Thrust), Sahitya Prakashan, Delhi.
9. Mathew, George (ed.), 1995, *Status of Panchayati Raj in the States of India*, Institute of Social Sciences, Concept, New Delhi.
10. Drummond, J.H. (1937). *Panchayati Raj in India*, OUP, London.
11. Venketarangaiah, M. and Pattabhiram, M. (1969). *Local Government in India: Selected Readings*, Allied Publishers, New Delhi.
12. Mathew, (2000), *op cit.*; Behera, M.C. (2006). *Globalising Rural Development: Competing Paradigms and Emerging Relations*, Sage, New Delhi.
13. Government of India (1994). Reviewing Local self Government in India, Ministry of Rural Development, Occasional Paper-6.
14. Malviya, H.D. (1956). *Village Panchayats in India*, AICC, New Delhi.
15. Jathar, R.V. (1964). Evolution of Panchayati Raj in India, JSS Institute of Economic Research, Dharwar and also Shiviah *et al.*, 1976, *Panchayati Raj: An Analytical Survey*, NIRD, Hyderabad.
16. *Ibid*; Dunham, A. (1967). Currents in Community Development in Newly Developing Countries, *Community Development*, 15th issue, January, Manchester, England.
17. Gandhi, as quoted in Shiviah *et al.* (1976). *Panchayati Raj: An Analytical Survey*, NIRD, Hyderabad.
18. Khanna, B. (1994). *Panchayati Raj in India; Rural Local Self-Government*, Deep & Deep, New Delhi.
19. Venkatarangaiya & Pattabhiram, *op cit.*
20. Mahatma Gandhi, *Harijan*, 26th July 1942.
21. Harijan, June 1, 1947 and also Gandhi, M.K., *Panchayati Raj*, Navjivan Publishing House, Ahmedabad, 1959, compiled by R.K. Prabhu.
22. Mathur P.C., 1994, Rural Local Self-Government in India, in Government of India, *op cit.*
23. Constitution of India, 2005, 27th ed., EBC, Lucknow.
24. Maddick, H. (1970). *Panchayati Raj: A Study of Rural Local Government in India*, Longman, New Delhi.
25. Mohanty, B. (1999). *Glimpses of Local Government*, Gyanajuga Pub., Bhubaneswar.
26. Bajpai & Verma., *op cit.*; Gurumurthy, G. (1987). *Panchayati Raj and the Weaker Sections*, Ashish Publishing House, New Delhi.
27. Maddick, *op cit.*; Varshney, A. (1998). *Democracy, Development, and the Countryside: Urban-Rural Struggles in India*, Cambridge University Press.
28. Report of the Team of Study of Community Projects and National Extension Service, Committee on Plan Projects, 1957, Government of India, New Delhi.
29. *Ibid*; Jain, L.C. (2005). *Decentralisation and Local Governance*, Orient Longman.
30. Bajpai & Verma, *op cit.*

31. Maddick, *op cit.*; George, M. (1995). *Panchayati Raj: From Legislation to Movement*, Concept Publication, New Delhi.
32. Mohanty, *op cit.*
33. Reddy, G Ram (ed.) (1977). *Patterns of Panchayati Raj in India*, McMillan, New Delhi.
34. Report of the Committee to Review the Existing Administrative Arrangements for Rural Development and Poverty Alleviation, 1985, Department of Rural Development, Ministry of Agriculture, New Delhi.
35. Report of the Committee on Panchayati Raj Institutions, Government of India, August 1978.
36. *Ibid*, as quoted in Bajpai & Verma, *op cit.*
37. Recommendations of the G.V.K. Rao Committee, *Kurukshetra*, XXXVII (5), February 1989, A Journal of the Department of Rural Development, Government of India.
38. Bajpai & Verma., *op cit.*
39. Mohanty, *op cit.*; Dreze, J., and Sen, A. (2002). *India: Development and Participation*, OUP, Delhi.
40. Recommendation of L.M. Singhvi Committee, *Kurukshetra*, XXXVII (5), February 1989, *op cit.*
41. Report of the Commission on Centre-State Relations, Government of India, 1988, Part I.
42. Government of India, Report of the Thungan Committee, 1988, Ministry of Personnel, Public Grievances and Pension.
43. Joshi & Narwani, *op cit.*
44. Bajpai & Verma., *op cit.*; Mukherjee, A. (1994). *Decentralisation: Panchayats in the Nineties*, Vikas Pub. House, New Delhi.
45. Joshi & Narwani, *op cit.*; Bird, R.M. (2001). *Intergovernmental Fiscal Transfers: Some Lessions from International Experience*, University of Toranto.
46. Mathew (1995). *op cit.*; Mishra, S. N., Mishra, S., and Pal, C. (2000). *Decentralised Planning and Panchayati Raj Institutions*, Mittal Pub., New Delhi.
47. Ambedkar, S.N. (2000). *New Panchayati Raj at Work*, ABD Publishers, Jaipur
48. Constitution (73rd Amendment) Act, 1992.
49. Panchayats (Extension to the Scheduled Areas) Act, 1996.
50. Constitution (Seventy-Third Amendment), Act, 1992.
51. Thavraj, M.J.K. (1984). Financing of Local Governments in India, in T.N. Chaturvedi (ed.), *Local Government*, IIPA, New Delhi.
52. Evaluation of Panchayati Raj Institutions (1994-1999), 2000, UNNATTI, NGO, Institute for Development Education.
53. Jain, L.C., *et al.* (1985). *Grass without Roots*, Sage, New Delhi.
54. Panchayati Raj Update, New Delhi, August, 2000.
55. The Provisions of the Panchayats (Extension to the Scheduled Areas) Act, 1996.

Chapter 10

Local Government in New Millennium

Introduction

Local Government has been under intense pressure over the past several decades to do more with less. Citizens resent at proposals to pay increased taxes but they consistently require more, efficient services from their local governments. Elected representatives, officials and professional public administrators on the local level feel the pressure to improve the quality and efficiency of their governments. Because of the demands placed and fiscal restriction they face, local and the state governments have turned to numerous new approaches to improve service delivery, cut cost and prepare for the future.

Population is an important source of development; yet it is a major source of environmental degradation when it exceeds the threshold limits of the support systems. Unless the relationships between the multiplying population and the life support can be stabilized, development programmes however innovative are not likely to yield desired results. Population impacts on the environment primarily through the use of natural resources and production of wastes and is associated with environmental stresses like loss of bio-diversity, air and water pollution and increased pressure on available land, mushrooming of slums and shanties, etc.

Urbanization, Development and Poverty

Urbanization is a truly 20th century phenomenon. In 1800, only 2 per cent of the world's population was urbanized. By the year1900, only 15 per cent of the world's population lived and worked in urban areas. This number was lower than the total urban population of India alone in 2001. By the year 1950, the proportion of urban to total global population had risen to 30 per cent. By the year 2000, 1.8 billion people lived in urban areas, equally approximately 49 per cent of the world's population. So the pace of urbanization witnessed in the 20th century was truly unprecedented.[1]

The world's cities are growing in total by more than 60 million each year. Between 2000 and 2025, according to UN projections, as the world's urban population doubles from 2.4 billion (in 1995) to 5 billion, the proportion that is urban is expected to rise from 47 per cent to over 61 per cent. But this growth will be unequally distributed; the explosive growth is occurring and will occur, in the cities of the developing world.[2] Three great forces have forged the explosive growth of cities in the century just passed:[3] first, industrialization and its concomitant de-industrialization, which transformed the now developed world before 1950 and has transformed the developing world since then; second, the transportation revolution, mass transit and private automobiles; and third the parallel telecommunication revolution. The great transforming force of the twenty first century is the informational revolution. Thus the twentieth century brought the urban transformation; the twenty first century will transform the urban experience. The 20th century industrial and transportation revolution freed millions of people from their life long bondage to the land- though too often, its first impact was to move them into equally degrading and exhausting forms of self exploiting labour in the city.[4] In the beginning of the new millennium the overwhelming problem is not urban growth in itself, but the fact that city administration lacks the will and competence or the resources to manage that growth, and concentration of population in few larger urban centers.

Moving to the city level urbanization trends, the growth of urban agglomerations in developing countries is found tremendous. In 1950, there was only one city with a population of over 10 million people, New York City. In 2000, there were 17 cities with a population above 10 million, 22 cities with population between 5 and 10 million, 402 with a population of 1 to 5 million, and 433 in the 0.5 to1 million category. An important characteristic of urbanization in Asia has been the emergence of mega cities. There were no such agglomerations in Asia in 1950, two in 1975 and by 2000, 10 of the 17 global mega cities were in Asia. It is expected that 12 out of the 21 mega cities in the year 2015 will be in Asia.[5]

The urban phenomenon of the 21st century will be mega cities, high density metropolises of more than 10 million inhabitants. As hubs of trade, culture, information and industry, they will be vested with such power that at many levels they will act as city states that are independent of national and regional mediation. Today mega cities are home to less than 10 per cent of the global urban population. And their pace of growth has in the past been slower than that of smaller cities of 5-10 million people. However, the developing world, where mega cities will be the hallmark of future urbanization, is experiencing extra ordinary spurts of growth in its largest cities.[6]

One of the stark realities of a rapidly urbanizing world is that the locus of poverty is shifting to towns and cities. The economic growth models used by governments and local authorities have widened not only disparities between rural and urban populations, but also inequalities between high and low income populations within cities. Poverty is already becoming a severe, pervasive and largely unacknowledged feature of urban life. Poverty is shifting to urban areas and growing in magnitude. Thus poverty is a by-product of increase in population and growth in development. Developing countries need manpower to increase the pace of development. The additional manpower is attracted from rural areas or smaller towns towards big cities. This trend is leading to growing urbanization and concentration of population in larger urban areas. Bigger the city, more the economic activities, more the manpower, less the space and basic facilities and services, and larger the number of poor. In real sense, developmental activities in urban areas are causing transfer of poverty from rural to urban areas.

Urbanization is increasing in both the developed and developing countries. However, rapid urbanization, particularly the growth of large cities, and the associated problems of unemployment, poverty, inadequate health, poor sanitation, urban slums, and environmental degradation pose formidable challenge in many developing countries. Available statistics show that more than half of the world's population live in urban areas, crowded into 3 per cent of the earth's land area.[7] All these have let deteriorated the urban life in developing countries. Thus the greatest challenge before the governments in new millennium is to make their cities, the engines of their growth, livable.

The 21st century is loaded with multiple complexities arisen due to increase in population, concentration of population in urban centres especially in developing world, local and demanding but apathetic community. The technological advancement has led and squeezed the whole world. This all has made the new millennium as the century of cities. The difference between the rural and urban is reducing. The community requirements are similar. The change in community coupled with changing technological advancement requires local governments to adapt to new situation and apply the modern management tools for better delivery of services in an entrepreneurial way.

Local Government to Local Governance

The move from local government to local governance implies that traditional institutions have become less important in local politics. Such a breakdown of certain types of formalized and routinised patterns of behaviour and organization follow from the influence of globalization, economic competition, and the impact of new public management and the fragmentation of organization. Old pattern of party politics and traditional forms of bureaucracy which were central features of local governing systems, are more suited to managing the institutions of the traditional welfare state and accessing the state government for resources and favourable treatment than for responding to current conditions. The changes mean that local decision-makers adapt to new challenges and institutional frame works. Economic development policies and governing in public-private partnership create long-term networks between organizations which municipalities copy across and within nation states. In a similar fashion, reformers become tempted by new public management reform to fragment and de-centre formerly hierarchical public bureaucracies. The debureaucratization and democratisation of the local government is the hub of local governance. More diffuse networks, the lack of predictability, complex policy challenges, gridlock and multi-level decision-making characterize the most local government systems.[8]

Governance is more than a synonym for government. "Governance signifies a change in the meaning of government, referring a new process of governing, or a changed condition of ordered rule or the new method by which society is governed".[9] Thus a baseline definition of governance is that it refers to the action manner of system of governing in which the boundary between organizations and public and private sectors has become permeable. Governance recognizes the interdependence of organizations. The essence of the governance is the interactive relationship between and within governmental and non-governmental forces. Beyond it is helpful to distinguish two perspectives on governance: the administrative and the systemic. The former presents a less radical and profound challenge. Its prime focus is on the emerging new processes of governing. The systemic view, in contrast, suggests that the focus should be less on the changing tools of government and more on the emergence of a system of self-governing networks. Government is not just changing its tools; it is changing its meaning.[10]

Within contemporary social science, the term 'governance' is used in at least four disciplines of study: Political Theory, Development Studies, International Relations and Public Administration. For political theorist, 'governance' is used most often in the context of democratic theory and state-citizen relations. New forms of social and economic governance are offered as a supplement to representative democracy and market economies.[11] Within the debate of development studies Leftwitch presents three positions, as governance for him means efficient and accountable public service. He comments: "From a systemic point of view the concept of governance is wider than that of government which conventionally refers to the formal institutional structure and location of authoritative decision-making in the modern state. Governance on the other hand, refers to a looser and wider distribution of both internal and external political and economic power. In this broad sense, governance denotes the structure of political and crucially economic relationship and rules by which the productive and distributive life of a society is governed."[12]

The concept of governance in international relations is used to capture the attempts of nation states to cooperate in order to enhance their national interests.[13] Governance is seen in terms of "rule systems that function without clear cut loci of sovereign authority." Another related definition describes governance as "managing a no body-in-charge world."[14] Within public administration, governance can be associated with the rise of New Public Management.[15] The traditional systems of public bureaucracy are seen as having failed and government needs to be re-tooled with a range of approaches that emphasize a commitment to separating policy decisions from service delivery. Governance captures the steering role (policy decisions) that government needs to develop.[16] New Public Management encourages new processes of governing as entrepreneurial governments develop a concern with competition, markets, customers and outcomes.[17]

The World Bank has identified three distinct aspects of governance:[18]

(a) the form of political regime,
(b) the process by which the authority is exercised in the management of country's economic and social resources for development, and
(c) the capacity of governments to design, formulate and implement policies and discharge functions,

The OECD further expanded the World Bank's definition and included the...[19]

(d) degree of democratization for legitimacy of the State,
(e) media freedom,
(f) transparency in decision-making for accountability of government,
(g) individual and group rights,
(h) competence of governments to formulate policies and deliver services,
(i) respect for human rights and rule of law,
(j) security framework for socio-economic activity, and
(k) people's participation.

Accordingly, the concept of governance denotes the use of political exercise and control in a society in relation to the management of its resources for social and economic development. This broad definition encompasses the role of public authorities in establishing the environment in which economic operators function and in determining the distribution of benefits as well as the nature of the relationship between the ruler and the ruled.

The United Nations Development Programme (UNDP) views it as the exercise of political, economic and administrative authority in the management of a country's affairs at all levels.[20] It comprises mechanism, processes and institutions through which citizens and groups articulate their interests, exercise their legal rights, meet their obligations and mediate their differences.[21]

The Commission on Global Governance feels that governance is sum of many ways individuals and institutions, public and private, manage their common affairs. It is a continuous process through which conflicting or diverse interests may be accommodated and cooperative action may be taken.[22] It includes formal institutions and regimes empowered to enforce compliance as well as informal arrangements that people and institutions either have agreed or perceive to be their interest.[23]

Kettle observes that government is an institutional superstructure that society uses to translate politics into policies and legislation, whereas, governance is the outcome of the interaction of government, the public services, and citizens throughout the political process, policy development, programme design, and service delivery. Governments are specialized institutions that contribute to governance. Representative governments seek and receive citizen support, but they also need the active cooperation of their public servants. Governance is the outcome of politics, policies, and programmes. The institution of government involves a narrower range of considerations than the wider functions of governance.[24] The main characteristics of government are: Superstructure,[25] Decisions[26], Rules[27], Roles[28], Implementation[29], and Outputs[30]. The governance, on the other hand, is characterized by: Functionality[31], Processes[32], Goals[33], Performance[34], Coordination[35], and Outcomes[36].

Hoshiar Singh (2000) observes that to undermine local government, state governments have created parallel local organizations to perform various functions. Some functions at local levels are being performed by state departments such as medical and health, electricity, and so on, and for some special purpose authorities have been created such as school boards, housing boards, water supply boards, and development authorities etc. to deprive local government their rightful functions. The new magistracy created in the form of nominated bodies for development functions at people's level such as District Rural Development Agencies, District Urban Development Agencies, neighbourhood committees, community development societies etc. have replaced local authorities for performance of various development functions. The enabling role of state, by providing finances to various organizations at local level, made them strong vis-à-vis local government. Thus a vicious circle has been created to chain local government bodies to create the impression in people's mind that these bodies are ineffective and unable to solve the problems of the people at the local level. This kind of state activities forced the local people to look for the institutional means to fulfil their needs; hence idea of local governance emerged on the local government unit. Local authorities are now working along with other public, private and voluntary organizations in providing services for a locality. Thus local government has been replaced by local governance in which decision-making authority and service provision is shared by different agencies.[37]

One tool for improving the effectiveness of local governments is goal setting or management by objectives. Total quality management as another tool has been introduced in local government after its success in private sector has been established.

Productivity Measurement in Local Government

The increased importance of service industries and current concern over productivity growth has stimulated interest in productivity measures for this expanding sector of economy. The service sector encompasses the major industry groupings of trade, finance, insurance, communications, public utilities, transportation, and government, as well as business and personal services. It accounts for about three-fourths of the Nation's employment and provides the greatest potential as well as some of the greatest difficulties, for developing productivity measures.[38]

Productivity is the average output produced by input—a combination of human and capital resource. Productivity measures relate real physical output to real input. They range from single factor measures, such as output per unit of labour input or output per unit of capital input. Such measures also reflect changes in technology, scale of production, educational levels of workers, managerial techniques, and many other factors in addition to the contributions, the particular inputs.[39] Productivity measurement essentially means relating the amount of inputs of a service or product to the amount of outputs. Traditionally, this has been expressed as a ratio such as number of units produced per man-hour. Productivity management is not as easily accomplished for the local government sector because its products primarily fall into the classification of services, hard to measure quality of service, then becomes an essential ingredient of output along with physical output measurements such as number of cases processed or tons of solid waste collected.[40]

Thus a principal difficulty in productivity management for local government services is in defining and measuring output, a familiar problem to public administrators. Some government services such as utilities do have physical outputs but here too, quality is an important aspect. For example, treating so many million gallons of water or sewage is important but the quality of the treated water or effluent is an equally important dimension.

Solid waste collection offers a more typical and subtle example. Suppose that tonnes of solid waste collected is used as the measure of output. However, the quality in the service to the public will has been diminished, that's part of the collection activity transporting the garbage from door to bins has been shifted to the customer. Furthermore, obtaining the tonnes of garbage collected fails to indicate whether the streets are clean. A city could show an increase in total tonnage collected while the streets were actually getting dirtier.

Thus simplistic notions of productivity measurement should be treated with great caution. Rather, it seems advisable to consider a multiple set of measurements and other local condition factors. The major enablers of productivity are: having staffed with appropriate skill sets; having a good training and personnel development programme; having a clear management structure; and good resource planning. Interestingly, while employees recognize the benefits of training and development in increasing personal productivity, employment of their job is the most important enabler of employee productivity—"a happy worker is a productive one."[41]

Total Quality Management in Local Government

Total Quality Management (TQM) is a management strategy aimed at embedding awareness of quality in all organizational processes. It has become increasingly important in government in recent years. It provides an umbrella under which everyone in the organization can strive and create community (consumer/customer) satisfaction. TQM is a set of principles, tools and processes for managing and improving the quality of government services.[42] As defined by ISO, "Total Quality Management is a management approach for an organization centred on quality, based on the participation of all its members and aiming at long-term success through satisfaction, and benefits to all members of the organization and to society." Local governments may find TQM attractive because it helps departments better understand the needs of their communities. Public agencies can thereby avoid designing their services exclusively around the customer, who are most vocal in their complaints. TQM also allows administration to contain costs and improve services.[43] This is important to local governments that face increased responsibilities, decreased revenues and public cynicism about their capabilities.

TQM is relatively modern productivity improvement strategy that is characterized by a commitment to meeting the needs of customers and constituents. Citizens are currently demanding more custom tailored, timely and cost-effective services, and the objective of the TQM are consistent with these goals.[44] The efficacy of TQM depends not on the use of esoteric tools but rather on organizational change, empowerment and systematic analysis. Empowerment gives public officials the latitude to identify and respond to the needs of individual customers without seeking time consuming approvals. Systematic analysis involves both system-wide perspective of agency outputs and a logical ordering of problems, approaches and priorities. Milakovich (1991) notes that TQM could challenge traditional administrative systems that are designed to control rather than empower and to provide uniform services rather than adaptability.[45]

In TQM agencies and individuals are called upon to identify all of their stakeholders and to design services to ensure that the objectives meet the needs of all stakeholders. Consumer satisfaction should be periodically assessed and managers should continuously strive to improve upon customer satisfaction and service delivery processes. Improvements should be based on measures that are SMART: specific, measurable, accountable, realistic and team based. This is because specific, measurable and realistic indices make it easier to detect improvements, and because accountability is needed to ensure that such improvements are carried out.[46] Employee empowerment is an important strategy for ensuring that customer needs are met. Empowerment is a general approach that allows individuals and teams to make important decisions about their work and work environment. In TQM employees and teams are given widespread responsibility to satisfy and delight their customers. Empowerment allows employees to be more flexible and timely in responding to diverse needs of customers. Empowerment involves the delayering of middle management as well as the adoption of supportive and coaching styles of supervisory management.[47]

TQM uses a variety of logical and statistical tools to assess the performance of delivery processes. None of these tools is very complicated to use, most TQM applications use only one or two at a time.[48] The tools are:[49] work flow and system analysis, cause and effect or fishbone diagrams (trace errors in delivery processes), Pareto charts (to identify the frequency of problems and complaints), scatter diagrams (to show the relationship between variables), control charts (to monitor the performance) and histograms (to display the spread of data). The applicability of such tools to local government has been demonstrated.

Productivity improvement is a by-product of quality improvement that happens through[50] (i) getting things right the first time, (ii) re-engineering services to ensure cost effectiveness, and (iii) eliminating unnecessary layers of management through empowerment. TQM implementation in local government is well underway and current trends suggest that quality initiatives will increase in future years. TQM is consistent with up-to-date professional notions of public administration of providing responsive and cost effective services.

Illustrative Set of Workload Measures

Selected Services	*Illustrative workload measures*	*Illustrative quality factors that should be considered in interpreting productivity*	*Illustrative local factors that should be considered in interpreting productivity*
1. Solid Waste Collection	Tonnes of solid waste collected	• Visual appearance of streets • Backdoor collection • Fire/health hazard conditions from solid waste accumulation • Service delays	• Frequency of collection • Private *vs.* Public collection • Local weather conditions • Composition of the solid waste
2. Liquid Waste (sewage) Treatment	Gallons of sewage treated	• Quality level of effluents • Water quality level resulting where dumped	• Initial quality of water ways into which sewage effluent is released • Community liquid waste generation characteristics
3. Health and Hospital	Number of patient days	• Reduces numbers and severity of illness • Condition of patients after treatment • Duration of treatment and pleasantness of care, accessibility of low income groups to care	• Availability and price of health care • Basic community health conditions

(*Contd.*)

Selected Services	Illustrative workload measures	Illustrative quality factors that should be considered in interpreting productivity	Illustrative local factors that should be considered in interpreting productivity
4. Water treatment	Gallons of water treated	• Water quality indices such as hardness and taste • Amount of impurities removed	• Basic quality of water supply source
5. Street maintenance	Square yards of repairs made	• Smoothness/bumpiness of streets • Safety • Travel time • Community disruption • Dust and noise during repairs	• Density of traffic • Density of population along roadway • Location of residences, houses, shopping areas, recreational opportunities etc.
6. Primary and secondary education	Pupil days Number of pupils	• Achievement test scores and grade levels • Continuation/dropout rates	• Socio-economic characteristics of pupils and neighbourhoods • Basic intelligence of pupils • Number of pupils

Source: Hatry and Fish,[51] 1971.

New Public Management in Local Governance

While earlier paradigms of Public Administration reflected a dominant role of the Government (bureaucracy) in providing services, the New Public Management seeks to offer more efficient mechanism for delivering goods and services and for raising governmental performance levels.[52] Many ideas behind the New Public Management are stated by the World Bank and IMF to countries seeking their assistance. Since 1980s New Public Management has emerged as an important idea. Accordingly New Public Management has in response to a number of environmental forces[53], which governments everywhere have faced in the last two decades or so. First, expensive public sector puts pressure to cut programmes and for increase in efficiency. Second, there have been massive technological innovations over the years, particularly the development of Information Technology. Third, the globalization of economy sector following heavy burden being imposed upon the national exchequer as a result of mismanagement, corruption, inefficiency in resource management, bureaucratic bungling etc. Fifth, in the competitive world the people are demanding quality goods and services.

Adoption of New Public Management will imply not only administrative changes and reforms but also a paradigm shift from the role of Government, the relationship between politicians and administrators, the abilities and qualities, the accountability and so on.[54]

Globalization is ushering far reaching changes in the political, economic, social, cultural and environmental spheres. It is resulting in a formidable global spread of goods, services, technology, processes and practice. The new public management has certain postulates which include focusing on achieving results rather than conforming with processes, introducing competition and contracting out in the provision of goods and services, making administration customer-driven to enhance service ethics and efficiency, assigning the role steering to the government rather than rowing, relying on non-governmental sector for better and efficient service, associating the consumers with the delivery and cost recovery of services etc.[55]

Kelly (1998) points out certain concerns that the New Public Management initiatives address. These include:[56]

1. *Productivity*—more service with less tax.
2. *Marketisation*—using market principles.
3. *Service orientation*—programmes more responsive to the needs of the citizen.
4. *Decentralization*—shifting responsibility to lower levels of government.
5. *Accountability for results*—improving government's ability to deliver services.

Osborne and Gaebler (1992) have listed ten principles of Reinventing Government, which later on became the sound base of New Public Management. These principles are:[57]Catalytic Government (steering, rather than rowing), Community-owned Government (empowering, rather than serving), Competitive Government (injecting competition into service delivery), Mission-driven Government (transforming rule-driven organizations), Results-oriented Government (funding outcomes, not outputs), Customer-driven Government (meeting the needs of the customer, not the bureaucracy), Enterprising Government (earning, rather than spending), Anticipatory Government (prevention rather than cure), Decentralized Government (from hierarchy to participation and teamwork), and Market-oriented Government (leveraging change through the market).

Thus New Public Management provides foundations to the concept of good governance and has aimed at entrepreneurial role of public organizations with a market based public administration resulting in effectiveness and economy in the functioning of public organizations.[58] For operationalising the New Public Management structural adjustments and new type of state intervention to seek co-operation and help from community organizations and citizens have to be made. This needs to be supplemented by effective accountability through operating system.[59] The administration is apparently moving from rule to result orientation, from systems to enterprise, obedience to reward, inaction to action, centralization to decentralization and from the duties of administration to the rights of citizens.[60]

Good Governance

Good governance means openness, listening, motivating, integrating or convincing people to participate according to their own goals: goals which are a part of wider democratic will, self-regulating.[61] Good governance is a necessity for development and poverty reduction, not a luxury. It is a major contributor to development while people living in ineffective or venal states suffer from a lack of economic and social development.[62]

Good governance is such a move that simply regulates the behaviour of the government. It is cooperative effort for sustainable development, undertaken in concern by local government, civil society groups and the private business sector. It is entrepreneurship to achieve public goals. It is a creative answer to local needs, using local resources, creating organizations and institutions, which coordinate a multitude of efforts integrating community organizations, private companies and governmental actors.[63]

Good governance will not be possible if public administration is corrupt or inefficient. It will not be possible if neighbourhood groups act in isolation without assistance from NGOs or public agencies. It will not be possible if the private sector acts as an isolated profit maximiser neglecting the burden imposed on private households who have to live with the pollution or squalor created by unfettered production activities. Good governance needs a climate of tolerance and cooperation.[64] It has to survive with a permanent tension that will always occur between stable organizations and spontaneous activities which arise as answers to urgent needs of urban crises.

At the beginning of 21st century, accumulated knowledge and experience of the last century has brought a consensus that sustainable development should be the guiding principle for policy and governance. This means that searching for a policy that will successfully achieve rapid growth and also redistribute incomes, a struggle to reduce social inequalities, to promote social and political integration and achieve the protection of the environment. The efficiency and effectiveness of the grassroots institutions in turn, depends on its adopted delivery mechanism and the supportive framework of rules and procedures.[65]

The task thus becomes compounded by the fact that there are interrelationships between different strategies. For the purpose, we need to integrate environmental concerns into our economic decision-making and develop suitable capacity at the grassroots level governance. It is in tune that grassroots institutions are at the cutting edge of administration and they are the real face of our whole system in view of their constant interface with the community.[66]

Rules for Good Governance[67]

Subsidiarity and Solidarity

Subsidiarity means that decision-making should be made at the lowest possible level, and that services should be provided at the lowest level, which is technically able to provide cost effective services without creating too many overspill effects. Solidarity is important because without it, local autonomy can all too easily lead to intolerable inequality.

Government and Civil Society

Good governance demands that government limits itself to the most urgent and most productive tasks and that outside energies and resources are mobilized. This means close cooperation with civil society in all shapes and forms: with neighbourhood groups, with NGOs, with religious groups, and self-help activities and also with individuals willing to improve the supply of collective goods, or to build up networks among people needing help and other people willing to provide assistance.

Integrated Action of the Various Levels of Government

Governments have to fulfil various economic functions. In abstract terms, three tasks have to be resolved;

- Stabilisation,
- Distribution, and
- Allocation.

Best practice normally reserves the stabilization and distribution functions to the central/federal level of government, while allocation dominates the local level. Fundamental equity issues must be handled essentially at the central government level. At local level the basic principle should be that people pay for publicly provided local services according to cost. In this case development should bring decentralization.

The Need to Prioritise

This principle is one of the fundamentals of economics and indeed of the rational life. It is impossible to do everything at once. One top priority must be to respect human life. That means first priority for health. The second should be to education as economic progress depends on human capital. General priority rules however are no substitute for careful assessment of the individual situation.

Delivering Local Services Locally: Decentralization

People want to exercise control on their own affairs, and should have that control. Autonomy demands decentralization. Decentralization however must not be seen, as the result of generous central/state government giving away powers it owns. Decentralization is optimization of powers and responsibility which belong to people, the people have to decide how best it suits them to express and organize their political will. Therefore, all decentralization systems have to be given priority to communication, exchange of experiences or imitation of best practices.

Separating Policy from Delivery

The basic general principles are fiscal autonomy, internal checks and balances and a public sector, which provides basic goods for the development of the city.

Community Based Planning: Integrated Participatory Development

Planning for development should be based on the needs of the community. The community should be empowered to identify their development needs, prioritize them and plan for their accomplishment. The planning should be integrated, participatory and holistic rather than sectoral and centralized in the name of decentralized planning.

Matching the Functional Responsibilities with Fiscal Resources

The functional domain of government should match the financial resources at its command. There should be an inter-linkage between functions assigned and finances available. Decentralization and devolution must go simultaneously.

Objectives of Good Governance

Good governance is an integrated effort on the part of local government, civil society and the private sector and it sets sustainable development as its central objective. The effort should involve people groups, individual companies and a multitude of public, state and local agencies, as demonstrated in Fig. 10.1.

Good governance thus acts as the motor and political driving force, keeping the different elements of sustainable development in balance, integrating them in policies and ensuring that all the different agencies in the city share the responsibilities and the benefits. Sustainability as the principle, good governance as the practice, thus becomes the twin aspects of development in real sense.

Good governance is among other things, participatory, transparent and accountable. It is also effective and equitable and promotes the rules of law fairly. Good governance ensures that the voices of the poorest and the most vulnerable are heard in decision-making over the allocation of development resources and that political, social and economic priorities are based on broad consensus among the three stakeholders—the state, private sector and civil society.[68]

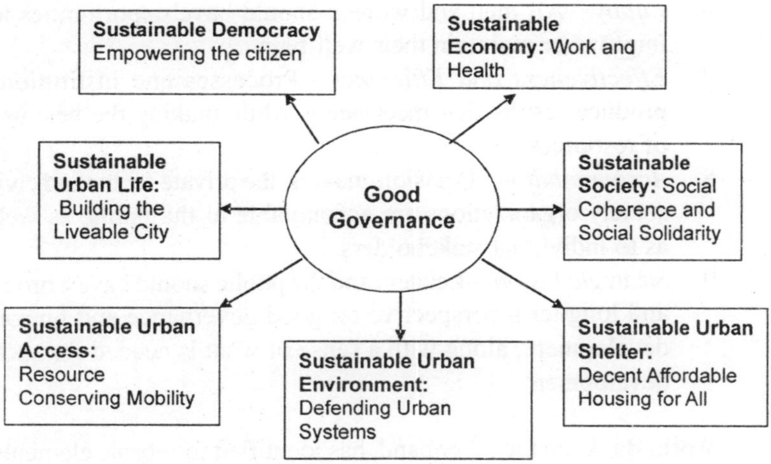

Fig. 10.1: Objectives of Good Governance

Source: Peter Hall and Ulrich Pfeiffer, *Urban Future 21.*[69]

Elements of Good Governance

In its publication entitled Governance for Sustainable Human Development, UNDP identifies nine core characteristics covering selected key issues, which measure good governance. These core characteristics are:[70]

1. *Participation*—All sections of the society should have a voice in decision-making. Such broad participation is built on freedom of association and capacities to participate constructively.
2. *Rule of Law*—Legal framework should be fair and enforced impartially.
3. *Transparency*—Processes, instructions and information are directly accessible to those concerned with them, and enough information is provided to understand and monitor them.
4. *Responsiveness*—Institutions and processes try to serve all stakeholders.
5. *Consensus Orientation*—Good governance mediates differing interests to reach a broad consensus on what is in the best interest of the group, and where possible, on policies and procedures.

6. *Equity*—All men and women should have opportunities to improve or maintain their well-being.
7. *Effectiveness and Efficiency*—Processes and institutions produce results that meet needs while making the best use of resources.
8. *Accountability*—Decision-makers, the private sector and civil society organizations are accountable to the public as well as to individual stakeholders.
9. *Strategic Vision*—Leaders and the public should have a broad and long-term perspective on good governance and human development, along with a sense of what is needed for such development.

World Bank, on the other hand, has identified four basic elements of good governance. These are: [71]

(i) *Accountability*—Accountability is imperative to make public officials answerable for government behaviour and responsive to the entity from which they derive authority. It also means establishing criteria to measure the performance of public officials, as well as oversight mechanism to ensure that the standards are met.

(ii) *Participation*—The principle of participation derives from an acceptance that people are at the heart of development. They are not only the ultimate beneficiaries of development, but are also the agents of development. At the grassroots level, participation implies that government structures are flexible enough to offer beneficiaries, and those affected, the opportunity to improve the design and implementation of public programmes and projects. This increases ownership and enhances results.

(iii) *Predictability*—Predictability refers to the existence of laws, regulations and policies to regulate society and their fair and consistent application.

(iv) *Transparency*—Transparency refers to the availability of information to the general public and clarity about government rules, regulations and decisions. Thus it both complements and reinforces predictability.

For good governance administration should be nearer to the people to serve their needs that arise in the locality differ from place to place and must be managed differently in each community, because of local variation, wealth, topography, occupations, resources and sentiments. Therefore, administration should be near to the doorstep of the people to solve their day-to-day problems. Problem solving and development need people's participation, which can be best ensured by local government inistitutions.[72]

Decentralization

Decentralisation and community-driven management acquire special importance in the context of the on-going process of globalization and associated economic reforms. While the process of globalization acts in ways in which the market acquires supremacy to the detriment of people who lose control over their livelihood patterns as well as other choices, the process of decentralization could act as a countervailing force enabling people to acquire control over decisions that influence their lives in critical areas. As market integration and technological innovation renders the national frontiers more permeable, it is crucial to put in place and strengthen systems of negotiation, regulation and decentralized governance. These can ensure that the voices and concerns of the poorest of the poor are centre-stage in policy dialogue at the global, regional, national, and local levels.[73]

Decentralization is a twin process of decentralization and devolution.[74] In decentralization a superior officer in order to make his department function effectively and efficiently delegates it to his subordinates the power to act in his name without transferring to them the authority he enjoys. Devolution, which also implies dispersal of authority, is a process wherein power is transferred from one organ of government to another by means of legislation or constitution. Deconcentration is another form of decentralization that involves only a minimum power transfer. It involves shifting of workload from a central government ministry to its field staff without transferring corresponding authority to make decisions on the spot. Devolution, on the other hand, is regarded by the administrative theorists as the most advanced form of decentralization. Devolution implies a legal deposit of power to discharge specified functions within formally constituted state and local authorities. Under devolution, authority for making final decision on certain issues is vested in sub-national units of government. Decentralization cannot be classified into watertight compartments, because, in practice, public administration system reveals a mixture of elements, devolution and decentralization.[75]

The literary meaning of decentralization is the process of transferring the functions from a higher level government to the local units. Such distribution of authority and power is horizontal rather than hierarchical.[76] Decentralization does not merely denote division of the functions of the State between the state government and the local government, but it means and includes devolution of the state's functions on local bodies. The local government units are fully free to decide the priorities between the various activities and the suitability of the areas in which the functions should be undertaken. The fundamental purpose of such efforts is to train local leadership to assume higher responsibilities and to serve the people with maximum efficiency and economy.[77]

Although decentralization is a common theme the concept is difficult to define and is often used in different ways. In general, decentralization is a process in which decisional powers are transferred from the centre to operational units. Thus decentralization affects the author (the central, state) as well as the subjects of the decisions (the regions). There are at least three meanings of term:[78]

1. First, in public and private organizations decentralization gives more autonomy to operational units. They still accomplish the mission of the global organization but they can freely adapt to the local demand.
2. Second, in regional planning decentralization is relocating enterprises and public agencies across the national territory.
3. Third, in governmental reforms, decentralization can be functional or territorial, the transferring decision powers to local governments resulting in a greater emphasis on the special dimensions of public policies. In other cases decentralization can be the shifting of responsibilities between the public and the private spheres.

Thus decentralization is a process through which a national government modifies the hierarchical chain of command by conferring more authority to local governments and by giving more weight to the territorial specificities.

According to Appleby, "Democratic decentralization appears to suggest that decentralization automatically enhances democracy."[79] In fact very little developmental activity can be visualized until effective decentralization has taken place. Proponents of decentralization point out three basic virtues[80] i.e. Participation, Responsiveness and Efficiency.

Decentralization embraces both the process of devolution and decentralization.[81] The motivation for decentralization does not lie upon coercion but upon its ability to enable the people to have a feel of power i.e. sharing of power in matters relating to the multifaceted development of their own area.[82] The importance of decentralization lies in the fact that centralization breeds bureaucratization which in turn, stultifies the initiative of the people, curbs people's participation and slows down the rapid pace of economic growth.[83]

Advantages of Decentralisation

While discussing the advantages of decentralization Henry Maddick (1966) has rightly said that development would result through decentralisation. To quote him "local authorities will provide opportunity to local people to participate in local decisions and local systems within general national policies and to act above all as local centres of initiative and activity conducive to development".[84] Goel (2005) classifies advantages of decentralization as under:[85]

(a) Decentralization lightens the work of the upper echelon in administration.
(b) Decentralization promotes quick disposal of work.
(c) Decentralization generates interest among employees.
(d) Decentralization develops leadership.
(e) Decentralization promotes effective supervision and control.

Kanesalingam (1971) points out three advantages of decentralization of power and functions and popular participation at local level:[86]

(i) The people will have a better understanding of what the government proposes,

(ii) The Central Government's development activities can be made more realistic by involving the people locally in important decisions, and

(iii) Popular participation increases the likelihood that services and amenities which are established will be maintained and even expanded.

Disadvantages of Decentralisation

Despite having these advantages, decentralization has a number of disadvantages as well. These include difficult co-ordination, expensive services, not suited in emergency, encouraging divisiveness, creating local interests etc. Thus extensive decentralization is not to be blindly applied. Decentralization is not without cost. No enterprise can decentralize to the extent that its existence is threatened and the achievement of its goals is frustrated. If organizational disintegration is to be avoided, decentralization must be tempered by selective centralization of certain areas of vital major policy.[87]

Objectives

Hambleton[88] and Hambleton, Hoggett and Burns[89] have identified objectives for decentralizing as under:

- Improving service,
- Strengthening local accountability,
- Achieving distributional aims,
- Encouraging political awareness,
- Developing staff, and
- Controlling cost.

Moises (2000) classifies objectives according to the two basic dimensions of local government the administrative and the political:[90]

- *Administrative dimension*: Improving services, strengthening local accountability, encouraging local awareness, developing staff, controlling costs, localization, delegation of management authority, changing the organization culture.

- *Political dimension*: Strengthening local authority, accountability, achieving distributional aims, encouraging political awareness, delegation, democratisation.

For improving services, local government units increase services, provide information effectively; for strengthening local accountability, they introduce new technology and rationalize municipal administration, set-up effective complaints mechanisms, promote effective citizen participation, regenerate neighbourhood. With the purpose of encouraging local awareness they promote citizen participation, promote and introduce a new breed of local government staff. For developing staff and controlling costs, they bring the management closer to its citizens, creation of one-stop-shops. For achieving distributional aims, they fight imbalance and inequalities among different groups and areas in the city, give a greater say to local communities.[91]

The three objectives (improve and increase services, introduce new technology and rationalize municipal administration and bring management closer to the citizens) aim at managerial improvements and the quality of the services delivered by the local body, and consequently the major focus for change is the internal organization and working procedures of the staff. [92]

Localization means the physical relocation of service in a neighbourhood level so that services would be delivered closer to the public. Integration of services refers to integrating the different services by breaking up the specialisms and differences among the diverse departments, so that a more general view of needs and problems is envisaged.[93] Decentralizing local government implies the extension of representative democracy into new areas. Delegation of management authority means to transfer the responsibilities for service delivery to more peripheral managers or councillors. Changing the organizational culture means the activities of the staff-putting the notion of public as a key issue in local government service delivery. Since local government is comprised of two kinds of elements-elected and appointed. When changing the values of them it would be necessary to identify whose assumptions are intended to be modified in the councillors' assumption about their role as representatives of the local authority, or the officers' convictions about their expertise in delivery of services.

All the objectives, which are considered achieved as a result of decentralization point to a flatter, open and flexible organization in order to be more sensible in responding to the demands from outside. In other words, the city governments appear to pursue a breaking of the bureaucratic model of organization. A movement away from the bureaucratic way would mean a possibility for establishing citizen partnership as consultative service. In a bureaucratic model partnership from members outside cannot be allowed because bureaucrats are experts in defining problems and providing solutions, they are professionals. The idea of ladder of participation of Sherry Arnstein sheds light on this point.[94]

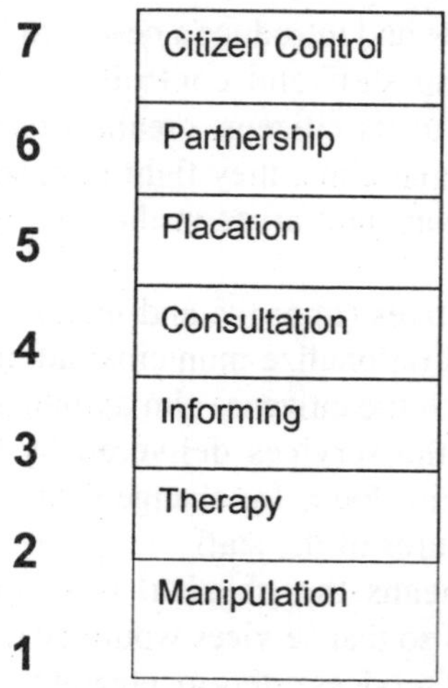

This device was invented during seventies based on experiences of sixties. At that time model of provision of services was mainly bureaucratic under a system of representative democracy. Now in India we have a political alternative as a result of 73rd and 74th Amendments to the Constitution, to that system which reinforced bureaucracy. The bureaucratic model of organization is being dismantled (decentralizing for managerial concerns), new opportunities for citizen participation have been created. A challenge to the bureaucratic and monopolistic provision of services is not inherent in the concept of citizen participation.

Local governments are infra-sovereign geographical sub-division of a sovereign national or quasi-sovereign state. They give institutional legitimacy to local interests and they provide an area based component for a pluralistic society.[95] Local authorities are involved in projects that have distinctively political goals of promoting popular participation in public affairs.[96] This is the strongest argument for local government as democratic institution on the grounds of participation.

Public Participation

In the democratic set-up of governance the administration—citizen relations are significant because the support and the consent of the governed is a prerequisite for the sustenance of representative government. The citizens who are voters and beneficiaries of services are keener to get services supplied than the subtle aspects of how to get them.[97] The government is more democratic when citizens participate in its day-to-day work.[98] The impact of popular participation in government affairs is the greatest at the local level. It is here that the public services are more meaningful to the citizen. Fuller benefits of participation are more likely with a political commitment and strategy for participatory development, ensuring greater involvement of local community in their own development.[99] Community involvement and collective efforts for solving neighbourhood problems are the first step towards realization of lager goals of democracy and development.[100] Thus popular participation through local government serves, three-fold purpose of development:[101] developing administrative capability, determining programme priorities, and bringing reforms in administration.

Participatory function is training for diffusing power among the populace. It is a potent self-education and means of breeding harmonious local commitment.[102] Such political education has a central place in democratic reasoning.[103] Thus Thornhill (1978) points out that local government's vital contribution is that it is a political institution by which the people share in government and resolve their differences.[104] Brick (1953) argues that participation is vital to democracy since people appreciate and tolerate each other's views and learn the art of politics.[105]

Purposes of Public Participation

A number of purposes have been advanced for public participation in planning and policy decision-making. One is simply for decision makers to acquire information about the public's preferences so they can play a part in the decisions about projects, policies or plans. A stronger way to put it is that public participation is designed to help assure that the people's will is done. A second and closely related purpose is to improve the decisions that are made by incorporating the knowledge of the public or members of the public into the calculus of the decision. Thus, it may be that the people in a local community know about the traffic or crime problems on a particular street, and the planners and decision makers can learn about this through public involvement. Both these purposes are increasingly important as government gets larger and more impersonal and more distant from its constituencies. Public participation is ostensibly also about fairness and justice. There are systematic reasons why the least advantaged groups' needs and preferences are likely to be unrecognized through the normal analytic procedures and information sources of bureaucrats, legislative officials and planners. These needs may only come onto their radar screen when an open public participation process occurs. So public participation gives at least the opportunity for people, who were overlooked or misunderstood in the early stages, to be heard. A fourth purpose follows from these others. That is, public participation is about getting legitimacy for public decisions. If a planner can say, "We held a dozen public hearings and reviewed hundreds of comments and everyone who wanted to had a chance to say his piece", then whatever they decide to do is, at least in theory, democratic and therefore legitimate. Public participation may be done to build support for plans among the public as well. Last, but not least, public participation is something planners and public officials do because the law requires them to.[106]

Collaborative Planning and Public Participation

Public participation means many different things for practicing planners. The confusion over public participaton, what it is and what it should be can be traced to four competing tacit models.[107] These include the technical/bureaucratic model, the political influence model, the social movement model and the collaborative model.[108]

The fourth model of planning incorporates very different notions from the first three about what participation is and how it works. In the collaborative model, the essential idea is that planning should be done through face-to-face dialogue among those who have interests in the outcomes, or stakeholders. For this dialogue to work most effectively and produce feasible and well informed choices, innovations, and joint action, various conditions must hold: (i) the full range of interests must be involved; (ii) the dialogue must be authentic in the sense that people must be able to speak sincerely and comprehensibly to each other; that what they say must be accurate and that they must speak as legitimate representatives of a stakeholder interest; (iii) there must be both diversity and interdependence among the collaborators [109]; (iv) all issues must be on the table for discussion with nothing off limits—the *status quo* cannot be sacred; (v) everyone in the discussion must be equally informed, equally listened to and thus empowered as members of the collaborative discussion; and (vi) agreements are only reached when consensus is achieved among the vast majority of participants and only after substantial serious effort has been made to satisfy the interests of all players. In this model, participants jointly develop a mission and purpose, lay out their interests (avoiding taking positions) for all to understand, develop a shared understanding of a problem and agreement on what they need to do, and then work through a series of tasks which lead to action or agreements that all, or most, believe will improve their ability to meet their own interests and, in the process, improve the collective welfare. They reach these results, not by argument, but by cooperative scenario building, role playing and bricolage—piecing together the ideas, information and experiences all members have to create new strategies that often can get the group out of some impasse that would otherwise have prevented action.[110]

This model of planning is particularly well suited to conditions where diverse interests have a stake in an issue, and where these interests are too interdependent to be able to accomplish their goals working alone or with only a few of the ideal conditions, they nonetheless often accomplish a good deal. They can get agreement or buy-in from a wider range of stakeholders than other methods on a strategy; they can satisfy participants and observers that a process was open and fair; they can generate substantial learning among the participants that pays off in the longer run; they can help a variety of participants to develop shared understandings and agendas as well as common heuristics to guide their actions, even when full-fledged agreements and implementation remain elusive.[111] These methods, however, are far from becoming the norm in policy making or planning practice. Indeed institutions, practices, laws and regulations, not only do not typically provide the opportunity for such dialogue, they often make it very difficult or even illegal. Most often these dialogues are outside of formal government, though sometimes they include participants from public agencies. Other times they are instigated by public agencies but include a full range of stakeholders.[112]

With the proliferation of collaborative planning methods and more individuals learning how to communicate constructively and develop the skills and norms for collaboration, they will provide a growing core of a civic community in city after city. They will develop the capacity for authentic deliberative democracy. [113] They will develop a sense that they can have an influence through their collaboration and conversation, and they will become less alienated as they see results from their dialogues.

A New Paradigm for Citizen Participation

The existing primary paradigm for citizen participation in planning is based on the idea of direct communication between government and the individual citizen[114] through activities like public hearings, public "education", elections, polls and written comments on proposals. The government communicates information or questions to the citizens and the citizen may communicate preferences, information. While information can flow in both directions, the process is not interactive. The government may be rather passive waiting to hear views so that inevitably some interests and values are not heard or perhaps not even developed in the first place because some citizens do not have the opportunity to become knowledgeable enough to express them. More ominously, government may manipulate public opinion towards its own ends. Social movements develop when important values are sufficiently ignored and when leadership mobilizes grass roots support for them so they can be heard. But these movements remain either oppositional or outside government or may be incorporated into government and at least partially co-opted. The issue of sustaining informed citizen engagement is still not resolved.[115]

Local Agenda 21 may be a tool about civil society and deliberative democracy. It "asks for more than participation for legitimacy purposes. It aspires to 'shared responsibility' which means a redefinition of the role of government and societal actors. The Local Agenda 21 represents at least an attempt to extend the civil society at the expenses of the role of the state. The role of local authorities changes from director to facilitator".[116]

E-Governance

Public managers world wide aspiring to improve the quality of government services are increasingly deploying E-government strategies that apply the capabilities of information and communication technologies to redesign government services. Through these E-government strategies, both governments expect to satisfy citizen demand for effective service provision and democratic policy processes that allows them to reduce transaction costs and facilitate greater citizen participation.[117] E-government applications converged rapidly in the developing world in last decades of the 20th century. Many countries use e-government as an enabling tool to increase efficiency, enhance transparency, collect more revenue and facilitate public sector reform. While e-government is not a panacea that can improve the performance of the public sector, it is a powerful enabling tool that has aided governments achieved some of their development and administrative reform goals. Although e-government can be a catalyst for change, it is not a complete solution and it must be part of a broader commitment to reform the public sector.[118]

The term e-government is of recent origin and there is no commonly accepted definition. The term was perhaps coined about a decade ago after the success of electronic commerce to represent a public sector equivalent to e-commerce. The term is used in a loose manner to describe the legacy of any kind of use of information and communication technology within the public sector. Analogous to the concept of e-commerce, which brings customers closer to business and enables businesses to transact with each other more efficiently, e-government aims to make the interaction between government and citizens, government and business enterprises and inter-agency dealing friendly, convenient, transparent and less expensive. E-government is understood as the use of ICT to promote more efficient and cost effective government, facilitate more convenient government services allow greater public access to information, and make government more accountable to citizens.[119]

In simple terms, E-Governance can be defined as giving citizens the choice of when and where they access government information and services. Putting the citizen at the centre of government means taking a delivery channel view. This would mean using more and more of Electronics and Information Technology in many of the government functions. In fact, Information Technology and

Information Highways are going to dominate the 21st century. Government therefore has to take this fact into account and create SMART governance (simple, moral, accountable, responsive, and transparent government).[120]

The term E-government is some times confused with e-governance and the two terms are often used interchangeably. E-governance has been defined as the process of enabling transactions between concerned groups and the government through multiple channels by linking all transaction points, decision points, enforcing implementation points and repositories of data using information and communication technologies to improve the efficiency, transparency, accountability and effectiveness of a government.[121] E-governance is the use of ICT by the government, civil society and political institutions to engage citizens through dialogue and feedback to promote their greater participation in the process of governance of these institutions. E-governance consists of two distinct but intimately intertwined dimensions:[122] one political and the other technical, relating to issues of efficiency and public management. E-government is about a process of reform in the way governments work, share informations and deliver services to external and internal clients. Specifically, e-government harnesses information technologies to transform relations with citizens, businesses and other arms of government. These technologies can serve a variety of ends:[123] better delivery of government services to citizens, improved transactions with business and industry, citizen empowerment through access to information, or more efficient government management. The characteristics of E-Government include: Electronic Service Delivery,[124] Electronic Workflow,[125] Electronic Voting,[126] and Electronic Productivity.[127]

E-governance is not about technology and investment in Information Technology alone. It basically leads to re-engineering of the processes behind the screen that actually deliver the services. Thus e-governance is not synonymous to the good governance but is a tool for the latter.[128] While finalizing an e-governance project, one has to keep in mind as what kind of good governance will be achieved through it. The characteristics of E-Governance are: Electronic Engagement,[129] Electronic Consultation,[130] Electronic Controlling,[131] and Networked Societal Guidance.[132]

E-government applications normally evolve through a four stage process.[133] The first stage includes the publication of information on a website for citizens to seek knowledge about procedures governing the delivery of different services. The second stage allows for interactivity online. Clients can download applications for receiving services. The third stage involves electronic delivery of documents. The fourth stage results in electronic delivery of services where more than one department may be involved in processing a request or service.

Governments around the world are embracing e-government. But e-government is not a short cut to economic development, budget savings or clean, efficient government. If not well conceived and implemented, e-government initiatives can waste resources, fail in their promise to deliver useful services and thus increase public frustration with the government. Information and communication technologies have a potential to help meet good governance goals in developing countries. E-government can advance the agenda of governance and fiscal reform, transparency, anti-corruption, empowerment and poverty reduction.[134]

As government organizations make subsequent investments to reposition their services around an E-government agenda, executives and managers of public organizations are experiencing great challenges in managing E-government systems successfully. E-government systems consist of complex process innovations and reengineering strategies that rely heavily on the systematic integration of old and new information and communication technology components with critical functions of the service delivery system. E-government system also involves some level of coordination and communication with almost every functional unit of the organization where working relationships among employees are constrained by new and old business processes, and layers of complex institutional and organizational policies, practices, and norms. Consequently, the likelihood of a government organization finding success in its E-government strategy depends on how well its managers can leverage its technology, organizational, and human resources.[135]

Public administration has transformed into more business type structures and management practices in the last century. One may coin these transformations as more managerial factors embedded into government, and the rise of new management paradigm. Snellen once succinctly pointed out two of the most important developments in modern public administration: the emergence of horizontal network relationships and the introduction of ICTs where the latter development has reinforced the latter. These two developments have undoubtedly impacted structures and management in government.[136] ICTs have an impact on traditional Weberian bureaucratic organizations; private sector process management practices may become more customer friendly enterprises when managed more like a business, ideally as one-stop shop structures.[137]

E-Governance thus involves new styles of leadership, new ways of debating and deciding policies and investment, new ways of accessing education, new ways of listening to citizens and new ways of organizing and delivering information and services. The purpose of implementing E-governance is to enhance good governance.[138]

Thus the local government has to be developed as a full-fledge government at the lowest level equipped with all the managerial approaches, technological advancement and efficient communication skills. The local government in the new millennium has to have infused a new life in its working style, structural framework and behavior to meet the challenges of the new millennium.

Citizen's Charter

Citizen's Charter is a British political initiative launched by John Major in July, 1991. It aimed to improve public services by: making administration accountable and citizen friendly; ensuring transparency and right to information; taking measures to cleanse and motivate civil service; adopting a stakeholder approach.[139]

Citizen's Charter is a document which represents effort to focus on the commitment of the organization towards its citizens in respect of standard of services, information choice and consultation, non-discrimination and accessibility, grievance redressal, courtesy and value for money. This also includes expectations of the organization from the citizens for fulfilling the commitment of the organization.

It is a tool for facilitating the delivery of services to citizens with specified standards quality and time frame etc. with commitments from the organization and its clients.[140]

The citizen's charters give clear guarantees on service quality and availability; provide for redress if things go wrong, which adequately compensates the user and gives the organization an incentive to live up to the performance promise; are well publicized, and are shaped and improved by the voice of users; are not necessarily legal rights, but are capable of being enforced.

The main components of a good Citizen's Charter should be; Vision and Mission Statement of the Organisation; Details of Services provided by the Organisation; Details of Clients, Consumers, Users; Statements of services including standards, quality, time frame etc. provided to each user group separately and how/where to get the services; Details of Grievance Redress Mechanism and how to access it; Expectations from the citizens/users; and Additional commitments such as compensation in the event of failure of service delivery.[141]

Local Agenda 21

Local Agenda 21 is an international sustainability planning process that provides an opportunity for local governments to work with their communities to create a sustainable future. It recognizes that local governments and the wider communities they represent are ideally positioned to take the lead in achieving ecologically sustainable development through integrating environmental, social and economic goals on a local level. Through it local councils across the globe are to implement strategies with their communities to meet the environmental, social and economic needs of the present generations, without comprising the ability of future generations.

Local Agenda 21 is the mandate to local governments to translate the United Nations Action Plan for the 21st century at the local level. In 1987, the Brundtland Commission produced a report entitled Our Common Future. The Rio-de Janeiro Conference on Environment and Development in 1992 focussed world attention on critical issues of sustainability and natural resources, and mapped out a plan of action for future global partnership to achieve concrete goals. Agenda 21 was one of five documents produced.[142]

Agenda 21 is the plan to implement the agreements of Rio. It guides business and government policies into the 21st century. It identifies population, consumption and technology as the primary driving forces of environmental change and proposes what needs to be done to reduce wasteful and inefficient consumption patterns in some parts of the world while carefully managing natural resources. It provides options for combating degradation of the land, air and water, conserving forests and the diversity of species of life. It deals with poverty and excessive consumption, health and education, cities and farmers. It says that sustainable development is the way to reverse both poverty and environmental destruction.

Agenda 21 calls on governments to adopt national strategies for sustainable development. These should be developed with wide participation, including NGOs and the public. It puts most of the responsibility for leading change on national governments. Agenda 21 recognises that local councils, "the level of governance closest to the people", are a major group that can implement a global planning process for sustainability through their own programmes and initiatives. Chapter 28 of Agenda 21 notes the pivotal role of local government in fulfilling the objectives of sustainable development: "local authorities construct, operate and maintain economic, social and environmental infrastructure, oversee planning processes, establish local environmental policies and regulations, and assist in implementing national and sub-national environmental policies. As the level of governance closest to the people, they play a pivotal role in educating, mobilizing and responding to the public to promote sustainable development."[143]

Key Elements

The key elements are full community participation, assessment of current conditions, target setting for achieving specific goals, monitoring and reporting. The major key elements are: Managing and improving the local authority's own environmental performance; Integrating sustainability development aims into the local authority's policies and activities; Awareness raising and education; Consulting and involving the general public; Partnerships; and Measuring monitoring and reporting on progress towards sustainability.

Guiding Principles

The guiding principles of Local Agenda 21are: a continuing process; integration; local solutions to global problems; a community partnership; a process to achieve the principles of environmentally sustainable development.

Local Agenda 21 is a local government led, community wide, and participatory effort to establish a comprehensive action strategy for environmental protection, economic prosperity and community well being in the local jurisdiction or area. This requires the integration of planning and action across economic, social and environmental spheres.

REFERENCES

1. Angotti, T. (1993). *Metropolis 2000: Planning, Poverty, and Politics*, Routledge, London.
2. UNCHS (Habitat) (1996). *An Urbanizing World: Global Report on Human Settlements*, OUP, New York; UN (2002). *World Urbanization Prospects: The 2001 Revision, Data Tables and Highlights*, UN Secretatiat, Population Division, New York.
3. Hall, P. and Pfeiffer, U. (2000). *Urban Future 21*, The Federal Ministry of Transport Building and Housing of the Republic of Germany, E& FN Spon, London.
4. *Ibid*; Caulfield, J., Larsen, H.O. (2002). *Local Government at the Millennium*, Leske Budrich.
5. Bocquier, Philippe (2004). *World Urbanisation Prospects: An Alternative to the UN Model of Projection Compatible with Urban Transition Theory*, DIAL, Paris.
6. Cohen, B. (2004). Urban Growth in Developing Countries: A Review of Current Trends and a Caution Regarding Existing Forecasts, *World Development*, 32(1), 23-51; Hugo, G. Champion (2003). *New Forms of Urbanisation*, Ashgate, Aldershot.
7. UNFPA, 1993, The State of the World; United Nations Population Fund; UN Habitat, 2003, Slums of the World: The Face of Urban Poverty in the New Millennium? Monitoring the Millennium Development Goal, Target 11- World-Wide Habitat, Nairobi.
8. John, Peter (2001). *Local Governance in Western Europe*, Sage, London.
9. Rhodes, R. (1995). *The New Governance: Governing without Government*, the State of British Seminar, 11, Swindon: ESRC, 1-2.
10. Stroker, G. (1997). Local Governance: A Conceptual Challenge, in Hoshiar Singh (ed.) *Local Governance*. Concepts and Networks, Jaipur, RBSA, 14.
11. King, D. and Stoker, G. (1996). (eds.), *Rethinking Local Democracy*, London: Macmillan.
12. Leftwich, A. (1994). Governance, the State and the Politics of Development, *Development and Change*, vol 25, 363-386.
13. Halliday, F. (1994). *Rethinking International Relations*, London: Macmillan.
14. Tang, P. (1994). Institutional Instability, Governance and Telematics, IPSA Paper, Berlin, August, 21-25.
15. Hord, C. (1990). De-Sir Hemphreyfing, The Westminster Model of Governance, *Governance*, Vol. 33, 205-14.
16. Osborne, D. and Gaebler, T. (1992). *Rethinking Government, Reading MA*: Addison-Wesley.
17. Hord, C. (1991). A Public Management for all seasons, *Public Administration*, Vol. 69 (spring), 3-19; Prior, D. (1993). Review Article: In Search of the New Public Management, *Local Government Studies*, 19 (3), Autumn, 447-460.

18. World Bank (1994). Governance: The World Bank's Experience, Washington D.C., World Bank Publication.
19. OECD, (2003). Engaging Citizen's on Line for Better Policy Making; Does e-Government Imperative: Main Findings, *OECD Observer*, March.
20. UNDP (1997). *Reconceptualising Governance*, UNDP Publication.
21. UNDP (unpublished mimeo), 2002, Document on Good Governance by Report Card.
22. AIT, Bangkok (unpublished material of training programme), 2002, Planning and Administering Good Governance.
23. Government of India (2001). *Proceedings of Good Urban Governance Campaign*, India Launch.
24. Kettle, Donald F. (2002). *The Transformation of Governance*, John Hopkins University Press.
25. Breton, Albert (1998). *Competitive Governments*, Cambridge University Press, Cambridge.
26. Salamon, Lester M. (ed.) (2002). *The Tools of Government*, Oxford University Press.
27. Weber, Max (1997). *The Theory of Social and Economic Organisation*, The Free Press (Reprint), New York.
28. Coakes, E. (2002). *Knowledge Management in the Socio-Technical World*, Springer.
29. Argeron, C. and Cornford, T. (1993). *Developing Information Systems*, Macmillan, London.
30. Taylor, R. S. (1986). *Value-Added Processes in Information Systems*, Ablex.
31. Rhodes, R. A. W. (1997). *Understanding Governance*, Open University Press.
32. Behu, Robert (2001). *Rethinking Democratic Accountability*, Brookings Institution.
33. Graham, K. A., and Phillips, S. D. (1996). *Citizen Engagement*, Institute of Public Administration.
34. Brostek, Michael (2000). *Federal Rulemaking*, US General Accounting Office.
35. Klapp, Orvin E. (1964). *Symbolic Leaders*, Aldine Publishing.
36. Strassmann, Paul (1999). *Information Productivity*, Information Economics Press.
37. Singh, Hoshiar (ed.) (2000). *Local Governance: Concepts and Networks*, RBSA, Jaipur.
38. Mark, Jerome A. (1982). Measuring Productivity in Service Industries, *Bureau of Labour Ststistics*, Monthly Labour Review, June.
39. NOP World (2001). People and Productivity (Executive Summary), Investors in People UK, October; Hamilton, B.C., 2000, Performance Measurement: A Managerial Approach to Organisation-Wide Improvement Accountability, A.F. Cowan, Thompson Financial.
40. Hatry, H.P. (2003). Issues in Productivity Measurement for Local Government, in Douglas J. Waston and Wendy L. Hassett (eds.), *Local*

Government Management: Current Issues and Best Practices, New York: M.E Sharpe.

41. NOP World, *op cit.*; ICMA (2001). What Works: Management Application of Performance Measurement in Local Government.
42. Keehley, P. (1992). TQM for Local Government, Public Management, August 10-16; Compton, Dennis (ed.) (2002). *Performance Measures and Benchmarks in Local Government*, CMA.
43. Sensenbrenner, J. (1991). Quality Comes to City Hall, *Harvard Business Review*, March-April, 64-75.
44. Denhardt, R.B. (1993). *The Pursuit of Significance*, Belmon, C.A, Wadsworth.
45. Milakovich, M. (1991). Total Quality Management in the Public Sector, *National Productivity Review*, 10(2), 195-204.
46. Logothetis, N. (1992). *Managing for Total Quality*, Prentice Hall, New York.
47. Berman, E.M. and West, J.P. (1997). Total Quality Management in Local Government, in J.J. Gargan (ed.) *Handbook of Local Government Administration*, Marcel Dekker, Inc., New York.
48. Cohen and Eimicke (1994). as quoted in Petroni, Giorgia (ed.), *New Technology in Public Administration*, IOS Press, Amazon.
49. Kline, J.J. (1995). Quality tools are Applicable to Local Government, in J.P. West (ed.), *Quality Management Today*, ICMA, Washington D.C.
50. Leferve, H. (1992). *Government Quality and Productivity Success Stories*, ASQC Quality Press, Milwaukee, WI.
51. Hatry, H.P and Fish, D.M. (1971). *Improving Productivity and Productivity Measurement in Local Governments*, Washington D.C., National Commission on Productivity.
52. Kelly (1998). as quoted in Christopher, William F. and Thor, Carl G. (2004). *Handbook for Productivity Measurement and Improvement*, Terre Haute.
53. Borins (1995). Minocue (1998) and Hughes (1998). as quoted in Christopher and Thor, *op cit.*; Andrisani, P. J., Hakim, S., Savas, E. S. (eds.) (2002). *The New Public Management: Lessons from Innovating Governors and Mayors*, Kluwer Academic Pub.
54. Verma, S.P. (2005). New Public Administration *vs.* New Public Management, Keynote Address delivered at the Seventh Conference of NEPASI, held at Mizoram University, Aizawl on May 5-7 (unpublished).
55. Medury, U. (2004). Reinventing Public Administration: The New Public Management Perspective, in Ramesh K. Arora (ed.) *Public Administration (Fresh Perspectives)*, Aalekh Publishers, Jaipur.
56. Kelly (1998). *op cit.*; Sumonth, David J., *Total Productivity Management*, CRC Press.
57. Osborne, D. and Gaebler, T. (1992). *Reinventing Government: How Entrepreneurial Spirit is Transforming the Public Sector*? Reading- Addison Wesley.

58. Hord (1991). as quoted in Christopher and Thor, *op cit.*
59. Sharma, Ashok (2005). Application of New Public Management in Local Government, presented at Mizoram University, Aizawl, May 5-7 (unpublished).
60. Lane, J.E., *The Public Sector: Concept, Models and Approaches*, New Delhi.
61. *Encyclopedia of Social Sciences*, 2001, Fitzroy Dearborn Publishers, London.
62. World Bank (2002). *Poverty in India (The Challenge of Uttar Pradesh).*
63. Document of the Earth Summit, Johannesburg, 2002.
64. UNDP (1994). *Governance for Sustainable Human Development.*
65. World Bank (2002). India: Reducing Poverty, Accelerating Development.
66. Singh, U.B. (2003). Good Urban Governance in India (A Conceptual Overview), *National Seminar at IIPA*, New Delhi.
67. Hall, Peter and Pfeiffer, U. (2000). *Urban Future* 21, Federal Ministry of Transport, Building and Housing of the Republic of Germany, 164-313.
68. Phatak, J.M. (unpublished), *Key Issues in Good Municipal Governance*, Mumbai.
69. Hall, Pete and Pfeifter, U. (2000). *Urban Future 21,* Federal Ministry of Transport, Building and Housing of the Republic of Germany.
70. UNDP (1994). *op cit.*
71. World Bank (1994). *op cit.*
72. Singh, Hoshiar (ed.) (2000). *Local Government: Concepts and Networks*, Jaipur, RBSA.
73. UNDP (2000). *Decentralisation in India, Challenges and Opportunities*, Human Development Rresource Centre, New Delhi.
74. White, L.D. (ed.) (1951). *Encyclopedia of Social Sciences*, The Macmillan Company, Vol. 5.
75. Asibuo, S.K. (1992). Decentralization in Ghana—Myth or Reality, *IJPA*, XXXVII, April-June.
76. Young, U. (1979). *Compliance and Public Authority*, Baltimore: John Hopkins, 29.
77. Sharma, S.K. (1977). Democratic Decentralization & Development of Backward Areas, *IJPA*, XXIII (3), 76.
78. Bennett, R. J. (1993). Sons La Direction De, Local Government in the New Europe, Belhaven Press, Londres.
79. Appleby, *op cit.*
80. Ashford, D.E. (1967). *National Development and Local Reform*, Princeton: University Press, 10.
81. Uphorg, N.T. (1982). *Rural Development and Local Organization in Asia*, Delhi: Macmillan India, 227.
82. Maddick, H. (1975). *Democratic Decentralisation and Development*, New York: Asia Publication House, 23.
83. Prasad, N. (1972). *Decentralisation in Yugoslavia and India*, Uarauasia: Navchetna Prakashan, XII.

84. Maddick, Henry (1966). *Democracy, Decentralisation and Development*, Bombay, Asia Publication House.
85. Goel, S.L. (2005). *Advanced Public Administration*, Deep & Deep, New Delhi.
86. Kaneshalingam, V. (1971). *A Hundred Years of Local Government in Ceylon (1865-1965)*, Modern Plastic Works, Colombo.
87. Koontz, *et al.* (1984). *Management*, Seventh Edition, McGraw, NJ.
88. Hambleton, R. (1992). Decentralization and Democracy in the local government, *Public Money and Management*, July-Sept.
89. Hambleton, R., Hogge, H.P. and Burns, D. (1994). A Framework of Understanding area based Decentralization, *Local Government Policy Making*, 20(4).
90. Amoros, Moises (2000). Decentralization and New Governance: A Comparison between Barcelona and Birmingham, in Hoshiar Singh (ed.), *Local Governance: Concept and Network*, RBSA Pub, 137-177.
91. *Ibid*, 144; Frederickson, H.G. (ed.) (2002). *The Future of Local Government Administration*: The Hausell Symposium, ICMA.
92. Amoros, *op cit.*, 145.
93. Hambleton (1992). *op cit.*
94. Arnsetein, S. (1969). A Ladder of Citizen Partnership, *Journal of the American Institute of Planners*, 214-224.
95. Davenport, T., Short, J. (1990). The New Industrial Engineering: Information Technology and Business Process Redesign, *Sloan Management Review*, 31(4), 11-26.
96. National Research Council (2002). Computer Science and Telecommunications, Board of Information Technology Research, Innovation and E-Government, National Academy of Sciences, Washington DC.
97. Jagannadhan, V. (1971). Administration and the Citizen, *IJPA*, XVII (4), 601-2.
98. Appleby, Paul (1962). Some thoughts on Decentralisation in Democracy, *IJPA*, VIII (14), 453.
99. United Nations (1971). Public Administration in the Second United Nations Development Decade: Report of the Second Meeting of Experts.
100. Biddle, W. W. and Biddle, L.J. (1965). *The Community Development Process*, Halt: Richard & Winston, 1-2.
101. Mohanty, B. (1999). *Glimpses of Local Government*, Gyanjuga, Bhubaneaswar.
102. Report of the Committee of Enquiry into Local Government Finance (The Layfield Committee), HMSO, London, 203-20, as Quoted in Johnston, R.J., 1999, Political Electorate and Spatial Systems—An Essay on Political Geography, Oxford: Clarendan Press, 27.
103. Wibon, C.H. (1948). *Essay on Local Government*, Basic Blackwell, 11-24.
104. Thornhill, W. (1978). *The Growth & Reform of English Local Government*, London: Wiedenfield and Hicholsm, 29-30.

105. Brick, K.P. (1953). Local Government & Democracy—A Rejoinder, *Public Administration*, Vol. 31, 344-7, Vol. 32, 1954, 438-40.
106. Glass, James J. (1979). Citizen Participation in Planning: The Relationship between Objectives and Techniques, *Journal of the American Planning Association*, 45(2), 180-189.
107. Innes, Judith E. and Booher, David E. (2000). Public Participation in Planning: New Strategies for the 21st Century, Working Paper 2000-07, Institute of Urban and Regional Development, University of California, Berkeley.
108. Innes, Judith E. and Booher, David E. (eds.) Planning Institutions in the Network Society: Theory for Collaborative Planning, Revival of Strategic Spatial Planning, William Salet and Andreas Faludi, Royal Netherlands Academy of Sciences, Amsterdam.
109. Booher, David E. and Innes Judith E., Network Power in Collaborative Planning, *Journal of Planning Education and Research*.
110. Innes, J. E. and Booher, D. E. (1999). Consesus Building as Role Playing and Bricolage: Toward a Theory of Collaborative Planning, *Journal of the American Planning Association*, 65(1), 9-26.
111. Sanoff, Henry (1999). *Community Participation in Design and Planning*, John Wiley, New York.
112. Ostrom, Elinor (1990). *Governing the Commons: The Evolution of Institutions for Collective Action*, Cambridge University Press, Cambridge, MA.
113. Dryzek, John (2000). *Deliberative Democracy and Beyond: Liberals, Critics, Contestations*, Oxford University Press, Oxford.
114. Day, Diane (1997). Citizen Participation in the Planning Process: An Essentially Contested Concept, *Journal of Planning Literature*, 11(3), 421-32.
115. Bohman, James (1996). *Public Deliberation: Pluralism, Complexity and Democracy*, MIT Press, Cambridge, MA.
116. Coenen, F. H. J. M., Dave, H. and Lawrence, J. O'Toole, Jr., (eds.) (1998). *Participation and the Quality of Governmental Decision-Making*, Kluwar Academic Publications, Boston.
117. Gant, John P., Nam, Won-joon, Bretschneider, S. and Choi, H. The Transformation of E-governance in Local Government: Comparison of Critical Success Factors, Gangnam-Gu, Seoul, South Korea, and Washington DC, USA, MaxwellSchool.
118. Bhatnagar, S. (2004). *E-Government*, Sage, New Delhi.
119. World Bank, *E-Government*, http://www1,worldbank.org/publicsector/egov/india.htm
120. Budhiraja, Renu, *Electronic Governance—A key issue in the 21st century*, Ministry of Information Technology, Government of India.
121. Srivastava, A. (2002). *E-Governance or Development What Comes First: Issues and Correlations*, The Maxwell School of Citizenship and Public Affairs, Syracuse University, Syracuse.
122. Bhatnagar, *op cit.*; Electronic Government: Third International Conference,

EGOV 2004, Zaragoza Spain, Roland (EDT), Traunmuller, Springer, Amazon.com
123. http://searchnetworking.techtarget.com/s Definition/D, sid7_gci214117, 00.html
124. Dawes, S. and Prefontaina, L. (2003). Understanding New Models of Collaboration for Delivering Government Services, *Communications of the ACM*, 46(1), January.
125. Golubchik, L., *et al.* (2003). Bistro: A Scalable and Secure Data Transfer Service for Digital Government Applications, *Communications of the ACM*, 46(1), January.
126. PUMA (2002). Government Relations with Citizens & Civil Society, *OECD Observer*, February.
127. OECD (2003). The e-government imperative: main findings, *OECD Observer*, March.
128. Baweja, Y. (2005). Does E-Governance Mean Good Governance?, *Yojana*, 49 (Guest).
129. OECD (2003). Engaging Citizens Online for Better Policy- making, *OECD Observer*, March.
130. Fountain, Jane (2003). Prospects for Improving the Regulatory Process Using E- Rulemaking, *Communications of the ACM*, 46(1), January.
131. Pearlson, Keri E. (2001). *Managing and Using Information Systems*, Wiley.
132. Cullen, R. and Cushman, D. (2000). *Transitions to Competitive Government*, SUNY.
133. Bhatnagar, *op cit.*; Rao, T. P. Rama, Rao, V. Venkata, Bhatnagar, S. C., and Satyanarayana, J. (2004). E-Governance Assessment Frameworks (EAF Version 2.0), Department of Information Technology, Government of India, New Delhi.
134. Heeks, R.B., Understanding E-Governance for Development in Government, Paper No. 11, IDPM, University of Manchester, http://www.man.ac.uk/idpm_dp.htm
135. Kling, R. (2000). Learning from Social Informatics: Information and Communication Technologies in Human Contexts, Centre for Social Informatics, Indiana University.
136. Snellen, Ignace (2002). Electronic Governance: Implications for Citizens, Politicians, and Public Servants, *International Review of Administrative Sciences*, 68(2), 183-9.
137. Furukawa, Shunichi (2004). *E-governance: Changes in administrative structures and processes*, IIAS-IISA.
138. UNESCO-CI (2005). *Defining E-Governance*, Francais.
139. The Rio-de Janeiro Conference on Environment and Development, 1992
140. Hall & Pfeiffer (2000). *op cit.*
141. Frederickson (2002). *op cit.*
142. McSwite, O.C. (2002) *Invitation to Public Administration*, M.E. Sharpe.
143. Johannesburg Summit on Sustainable Development, 2002.

Chapter 11

Government of Major Cities

CITY OF NEW YORK

Introduction

New York City (officially the City of New York) is the largest city in the United States and one of the world's major global cities. The city is situated on the three major islands of Manhattan, Staten Island, and western Long Islands. The Bronx is the only borough that is part of the mainland United States.[1]

Located in the State of New York, the City has a population of over 8.1 million within an area of 830 km^2, making it the most densely populated major city in the North America. According to 2004 U. S. Census Bureau estimates, there were 8,143,197people (up from 7.3 million in 1990) residing in the city. This amounts to about 40 per cent of New York State's population and a similar percentage of the metropolitan regional population.[2] Demographers estimate that New York's population will reach 9.4 million by 2025. With a population of 18.7 million, the New York Metropolitan Area is one of the largest urban areas in the world.[3]

The two key demographic features of the city are its density and diversity. The city has an extremely high population density of 10194 per km. New York City is exceptionally diverse. Throughout its history the city has been a major point of entry for immigrants. In 2000, 36 per cent of the city's population was foreign born.[4]

Popularly known as the Big Apple or the City That Never Sleeps, the New York City attracts people from all over the world.[5]

New York City became the first capital of the newly formed United States on September13, 1788 under the U. S. Constitutional Convention. It remained the capital until 1790 when the honour was transferred to Philadelphia. New York grew as an economic centre. By 1835, New York City had surpassed Philadelphia as the largest city in the United States. After the American Civil War (1861-1865), the rate of immigration from Europe grew steeply, and New York became the first stop for millions seeking a new and better life in the United States, a role acknowledged by the dedication of the Statue of Liberty in 1886.[6]

Throughout the first half of the 20th century, the city became a world centre for industry, commerce and communication. New York City became the most populous city in the world in 1925, overtaking London. Like many U. S. cities, New York suffered population decline, an erosion of its industrial base gained a reputation for being a crime ridden relic of history. In 1975, the city government was on the brink of financial collapse and had to restructure its debt. The 1980s saw a rebirth of Wall Street, and the city reclaimed its role as the centre of the world wide financial industry. In the 1990s, crime rates dropped drastically and the outflow of population turned around, as the city once again became the destination not only of immigrants from around the world, but of many U.S. citizens seeking to live a cosmopolitan lifestyle that only New York can offer.[7]

New York City was a site of the September 11, 2001 attacks by a terrorist strike at World Trade Center. The Freedom Tower, exactly 1776 feet tall is built on the site.

City Government

The government of New York City is organized under the City Charter and provides for a strong mayor-in-council system. The government of New York is more centralized than that of most of other U. S. cities.[8] In New York City, the central government is responsible for public education, correctional institutions, libraries, public safety, recreational facilities, sanitation, water supply and welfare services.

The New York City's political geography is unusual. It is made up of five counties, each co-terminous with the five boroughs. When New York City was consolidated into its present form in 1898, all previous local governments were abolished and replaced with the current unified, centralized city government.[9] However, there are separate criminal court systems and district attorneys in the five counties.

Executive Branch

Executive branch of New York City consists of mayor, and his deputies. The heads of about 50 city departments are appointed by the mayor.[10] The mayor also appoints several Deputy Mayors to head major offices within the executive branch of the city government. Deputy Mayors report directly to the Mayor.

The executive branch is responsible for all city services, police and fire protection, enforcement of all city and state laws property and all public agencies.

In addition to the Mayor, residents elect the Comptroller and Public Advocate by city-wide vote every four years.

The five boroughs are co-terminous with their respective counties, but the counties do not have actual county governments. Each borough elects Borough President by direct popular vote. Under the current city charter, the borough President's powers are limited. Borough presidents advise the Mayor on issues relating to each borough, comment on all land use items in their borough, advocate borough needs in the annual municipal budget process, administer a small discretionary budget for projects within each borough, appoint Community Boards, and chair the borough Boards.[11]

The Comptroller is the city's chief financial officer. In addition to managing the city's pension fund, the Comptroller advises the mayor and the city council on all financial matters, fiscal policy and financial transactions. The Office of the Comptroller is empowered with limited investigational power over all city expenditures and finance and is responsible for auditing the finances of all city agencies. The Comptroller is a member of the Board of all city pension funds, and is responsible for managing the assets of the pension funds. The Comptroller also has responsibilities for issuing and marketing all city funds.[12]

The Public Advocate is directly elected executive official and heads the Office of the Public advocate. The Public Advocate's primary responsibility is to ease public relations with the government, investigate complaints regarding city agencies, mediate disputes between city agencies and citizens, serve as the city's ombudsman and advise the Mayor on community relations. The Public Advocate serves as the presiding officer of the New York City Council and is an *ex-officio* member of all Council committees.[13] The Public Advocate is permitted to introduce legislation in the Council.

Additionally, all city council members whose council districts cover part of a community district are non-voting, *ex-officio* Board members. Borough Presidents appoint the voting Council Board members, with half of the appointees nominated by council members representing the district.

Legislative Branch[14]

Legislative power in New York City is vested in the New York City Council. The Council is a unicameral body consisting of 51 council members, whose districts are defined by geographic population boundaries that each contains approximately 1,57,000 people. Council members are elected for four years, except for two consecutive two year terms every twenty years.

Bills passed by a simple majority are sent to the mayor, who may sign them into law. If the mayor vetoes a bill, the Council has 30 days to override the veto by a two-thirds majority vote.

The Council serves as balance of power against the mayor in a strong mayor-council government model. The council monitors performance of city agencies and makes land use decisions as well as legislating on a variety of other issues. The City Council also has sole responsibility for approving the city budget. The head of the City Council is called the Speaker.

The Council has several committees with oversight of various functions of the city government. Each council member sits on at least three standing, select or sub-committees. The standing committees meet at least once per month. The Speaker of the Council, the Majority Leader, and the Minority Leader are all *ex-officio* members of every committee.

Judicial Branch

New York City has civil, criminal, and family court systems. All have a presence in each borough and have city wide jurisdiction. The Civil Court handles all small cases (up to $ 5000) and all civil cases in the city with a monetary value up to $ 25,000, as well as residential and commercial landlord-tenant disputes. Judges of this court are elected to 10 year terms in either borough-wide or district elections.[15]

The Criminal Court is the beginning level trial court of criminal cases in the city. The court handles arraignments, misdemeanors and minor felony cases. Criminal motions are also handled in this court, along with some jury trials. Major felony cases are referred to the New York State Supreme Court. Judges of this court are appointed by the Mayor to 10 year terms.[16]

The Family Court hears matters involving children and families. Its jurisdiction includes custody and visitation, support, family offence, persons in need of supervision, delinquency, child protective proceedings, foster care approval and review, termination of parental rights, adoption and guardianship. Judges are appointed by the Mayor to 10 year terms.

The New York City Supreme Court is the trial court of unlimited original jurisdictions, but it generally only hears cases that are outside the jurisdiction of other trial courts of more limited jurisdiction. It exercises civil jurisdiction and jurisdiction over felony cases.

Community Boards

New York City is divided into 59 administrative districts, each served by a Community Board. Community Boards are local representative bodies that serve as advocates for New York City residents and communities. Each Board has up to 50 voting members, with one-half of the membership appointed each year for two year terms; there are no term limits. Additionally, all city council members whose council districts cover part of a community district are non-voting *ex-officio* Board members. Borough Presidents appoint the voting Community Board members, with half of the appointees nominated by council members representing the district. Broadly assigned by the city charter to "consider the needs of the district which it serves", the Boards have been limited in their ability by ineffective local communication channels, small budgets and old technology. This has led to loss of public confidence in some Community Boards.[17]

Mayor

The Mayor of the New York City is the chief executive of the city government, as stipulated by the Charter of the City of New York. The office entails being the head of the government and chief administrator for the five boroughs of Manhattan, Brooklyn, the Bronx, Staten Island and Queens that make up the City of New York.

In 1665, Governor appointed the first mayor of New York. For the next 156 years the mayor would be appointed and have limited power. In 1821, the Common Council, which included elected members, gained the authority to choose the mayor. An amendment to the New York State Constitution in 1834 provided for the direct popular election of the mayor.[18]

Municipal Reforms

Three paramount themes have recurred over the institutional history of New York City.[19] The first concerns local autonomy. Throughout New York's history the city has sought to rule itself, while the state government seated in Albany has consistently imposed serious compromises to municipal self-governance.

The second issue concerns the devolution of authority from the central institutions of the city government to those at the borough and community levels. The borough asserted them almost immediately after the consolidated city was created and then saw their roles diminished over time. A community role was preserved in early charters. But the movement towards community government really became prominent in the 1960s and was the focal point of the Goodman Charter Commission reforms in 1975. The efficacy of community based institutions remains a seriously debated policy issue today with regard to both charter reform and educational governance.

The third issue of concern is the distribution of authority among the major city wide actors and institutions—the mayor, the comptroller, the council president, the borough presidents, the City Council, and the Board of Estimates.

REFERENCES

1. Encyclopedia Britannica: Character of the City.
2. U.S. Census Bureau, Residential Population and Components of Change, New York State and Counties, April 1, 2000 to July 1, 2005, retrieved on 19-07-2006.
3. Roberts, Sam (2006) By (2025). Planners see a Million New Stories in the Crowded City, *New York Times,* Feburary 13, 2006.
4. U.S. Census Bureau, Annual Estimates of the Population of the Metropolitan and Micropolitan Statistical Areas: April 1, 2000 to July 1, 2004.

5. *New York Times,* January 1, 2004.
6. U.S. Census Bureau, *op cit.*
7. U.S. Census Bureau, Census 2000 Data for the State of New York, Retrieved on 19-07-2006.
8. Swift, N. (2003). *Mayors Play the Central Role in U.S. Municipal Government, City Mayors Government*, http.//city mayors.com/government/us_locgov.html.
9. Burrows, Edwin G. and Wallace, Mike (1998). Gotham: A history of New York City to 1898, Oxford University Press.
10. Berman, D.R. (1984). State and Local Politics, Allyn and Bacon, Inc., Boston.
11. Jackson, Kenneth T. (ed.). *The Encyclopedia of New York City*, Yale University Press.
12. Retrieved from http://en.wikipedia.org.
13. Watson, D.J. and Hassett, W.C. (eds) (2003). *Local Government Management* (*Current Issues and Best Practices*), M.E. Sharpe, Armonk, New York.
14. Retrieved from http://en.wikipedia.org.
15. Benjamin, Gerald, Mauro, Frank J. (1989). *Restructuring the New York City Government, the Reemergence of Municipal Reform*, Academy of Political Science.
16. Burns, Ric (2003). Transcript: The Centre of the World—New York: A Documentary Film, PBS, Retrieved on 20-07-2006.
17. Benjamin, *op cit.*
18. Binghan, R.D. (ed.) (1991). *Managing, Local Government: Public Administration in Practice*, Sage, New York.
19. Benjamin, *op cit.*

CITY OF BEIJING

Introduction

Beijing (Chinese pronunciation Pinyin), a city in northern China, is capital of the People's Republic of China. The recorded history of Beijing as a city can date back to more than 3000 years ago. It was formerly known in English as Peking or Peiking. Beijing is also one of the four municipalities of the China, which are equivalent to provinces in China's administrative structure.[1]

Beijing literally means "northern capital". In China the city has many names. In 1928, the Nanjing-based nationalist government of the Republic of China designated Beijing as the Beiping Special Municipality. In 1930, the municipality was re-named as Beiping City. Between 1928 and 1949, it was known as Beiping, literally 'northern peace'. The name was changed to reflect the fact that with the Kuomintang government having established its capital in Nanking, Peking was no longer the capital of China. The Communist Party of China reverted to Beijing (Peking) in 1949 again in part to emphasise that Beijing had returned to its role as China's capital. Yanjing is and has been another popular informal name for Beijing, a reference to the ancient State of Yan that existed during the Zhou Dynasty. During the Yuan Dynasty, Beijing was known as Khanbaliq which is the Cambuluc described in Marco Polo's accounts.[2]

Beijing is China's second largest city in terms of population (2004—14,930,000), after Shanghai. It is a major transportation hub. It is recognized as the political, educational and cultural centre of the People's Republic of China, while Shanghai and Hong Kong predominate in economic fields. The population of Beijing Municipality, defined as the total number of people who reside in Beijing for 6 months or more per year, was 15.38 million in 2005. Of these, 11.87 million people had permanent residence and the remainder was on temporary residence permits. In addition, there are a large number of migrant workers who live illegally in Beijing without any official residence permit or unregistered people. The population of the city proper is around 7.5 million. The current registered population of Beijing is 13 million.[3]

At the time of the founding of the People's Republic, Beijing Municipality consisted of just its urban area and the immediate suburbs. The urban area was divided into many small districts inside what is now the 2nd Ring Road. Since then several surrounding counties have been incorporated into the Municipality, enlarging the limits of Beijing Municipality by many times and giving in its present shape. The Beijing city wall was torn down between 1965 and 1969 to make way for the construction of the 2nd Ring Road. Following the economic reforms of Deng Xiaoping, the urban area confines of the 2nd Ring Road and the 3rd Ring Road, the urban area of Beijing is now pushing at the limits of the recently—constructed 5th Ring Road and 6th Ring Road.[4]

The area of Beijing is 16,808 km^2 with a density of 888 per km^2. The expansion of Beijing has also brought to the forefront problems of heavy traffic, poor air quality, the loss of historic neighbourhoods, and significant influx of migrants from poorer regions of the country, especially rural areas. Early 2005 saw the approval by government of a plan to finally stop the sprawling development of Beijing in all directions. Development of the Chinese capital would now proceed in two semi-circular bands just outside the city centre instead of being on concentric rings.[5]

City Layout

Major neighbourhoods in urban Beijing include 15 neighbourhoods which may overlap across multiple districts. There are seven towns within Beijing Municipality but outside the urban area. Beijing Municipality currently comprises 18 administrative sub-divisions, county level units governed directly by the municipality. Of these 16 are districts and 2 are counties. The urban and suburban areas of the city are divided into eight districts. Beijing's 18 districts and counties are further subdivided into 273 lower (third) level administrative units at the township level: 119 towns, 24 townships, 5 ethnic townships and 125 sub-districts.[6]

The development of Beijing continues to proceed at a rapid pace and the vast expansion of Beijing has created a multitude of problems for the city. Beijing is known for its smog as well as the frequent 'power-saving' programmes instituted by the government. Citizens of Beijing as well as tourists frequently complain about the quality of water and the cost of the basic services such as electricity and natural gas.

City Management

The Beijing Municipal People's Congress is the organ that exercises state power in the area under Beijing Municipality's jurisdiction. Deputies to the district and county people's congresses are chosen through direct election. Deputies to the Beijing Municipal People's Congress are elected by the people's congresses of the districts and counties. The Municipal People's Congress elects a standing committee to serve as its permanent body. The mayor and deputy mayors are chosen at Congress sessions through election. The Congress serves a term of five years.

The People's Government of Beijing Municipality is the executive body of the Beijing Municipal People's Congress and the administrative body exercising state power in the area under jurisdiction of the municipality. It works under the leadership of the State Council, China's Central Government.

The People's Government of Beijing Municipality exercises the following powers:[7]

- Implementing decisions of the Beijing Municipal People's Congress and its Standing Committee;
- Implementing decisions and orders of the State Council;
- Adopting administrative measures and promulgating decisions and orders; and
- Exercising leadership over the work of its own working departments and people's governments at district and county levels.

Executing municipal plans and budgets for economic and social development, and administering undertakings of economy, education, science, culture, public health and urban and rural construction, as well as administrative work related to finance, civil affairs, public security, ethnic groups, law-enforcement, supervision and family planning in the area under its jurisdiction.

The Municipal Government consists of the mayor, deputy mayors, a secretary-general, and directors of different municipal commissions, offices and bureaus. The People's Government of Beijing Municipality is elected for a term of five years.

The Beijing Municipal Committee of the Chinese People's Political Consultative Conference is the municipal organization of patriotic united front work. Led by the Beijing Municipal Committee of the Communist Party of China, it comprises representatives from the Communist Party of China's Beijing Municipal Committee, the various democratic parties, non-party democrats, non-governmental organizations and ethnic minorities as well as overseas Chinese and compatriots from Taiwan, Hong Kong and Macao and guest members. All local organizations of China's eight democratic parties are represented in the Beijing Municipal Committee, and so are local people's organizations. The Committee serves a term of five years.[8]

REFERENCES

1. *Encyclopedia of Social Sciences*; Peking, Today and Yesterday, 1956 and Peking: A Tourist Guide (1960). Official Press in Peking.
2. History of China: *Encyclopedia, Britannica*; Asia Research Center, 1968, The Great Cultural Revolution in China, Rutland, Vermont.

3. *Ibid*; Boorman, H.L. and Howard, R.C. (eds) (1967). *Biographical Dictionary of Republican China*, 5 vols, Columbia, UP.
4. Kwangchih Chang (1968). The Archaeology of Ancient China; Buchnan, K.M., 1970, The Transformation of the Chinese Earth; Ch'en, Population Growth and Urbanisation in China, 1953-1970, *Geog.*, *Rev.*, 1, 1973.
5. Buchnan, K.M. (1970). The Transformation of the Chinese Earth; Ch'en, Population Growth and Urbanisation in China, 1953-1970, *Geog.*, *Rev.*, 1, 1973; http://english.people.com.cu.
6. *Ibid*; http://www.China.org.cu/english/features/beijing/ 30785.html Chang, SeuDon (1965). Peking: The Growing Metropolis of Communist China, *Geogr. l.Rev.* 55:313-327.
7. http://en.wikipedia.org/wiki/Bejing.
8. *Encyclopedia Bri[illegible]nica*; Fairbank, J.K. (1971). *The United States and China*, 3rd ed.

CITY OF TOKYO

Introduction

Tokyo (literally Eastern capital) is the capital of Japan. It is the seat of the Japanese government and the Imperial Palace, the home of the Japanese Imperial Family. It is the most populous city in the country and most populous metropolitan area in the world. With a population of over 35 million people in the Greater Tokyo Area, Tokyo is one of the largest cities in the world with over 8 million people living in the city alone.[1]

Prior to 1943, Tokyo was the name of both one of the 47 prefectures of Japan, Tokyo-fu, and the populous city of Tokyo in the eastern half of the prefecture. In 1943 the city and the prefecture were merged into a unique prefecture level government entity, known as Tokyo-to or 'Tokyo Metropolis'. This administrative region includes the 23 special wards of the former city, many suburban cities in the western half of the prefecture, and two chains of islands. Within Tokyo are 23 municipalities (special wards) which *de facto* form the "city of Tokyo", though no such city exists *de jure*. About 12 million people (10 per cent of Japan's population) live in Tokyo. It is the centre region of the world's most populous metropolitan area. It is considered one of the world's major global cities and a mega city.[2]

As one of the major cities of the world, Tokyo has over eight million people living within its 23 wards, and during the day time, the population swells by over 2.5 million as workers and students commute from adjacent areas. This effect is even more pronounced in the three central wards, whose collective population is less than 3,00,000 at night, but over two million during the day. The population of Tokyo Prefecture is 12.36 million, Special Wards 8.34 million, Tama Area 4 million and Islands 27,000. The day time population is 14.667 million but in night it is 12.017million.[3]

Tokyo's rise to importance can be largely attributed to two men: Tokugawa Ieyasu and Emperor Meiji. In 1603, after unifying the warring states of Japan, Shogun Tokugawa Ieyasu made Edo (now Tokyo) his base. As a result, the city developed rapidly and grew to become one of the largest cities in the world with a population topping one million by the 18th century. It became the *de facto* capital of Japan even while the emperor lived in Kyoto, the imperial capital. After 263 years, the shogunate was overthrown under the banner of restoring imperial rule. In 1819, the figurehead 17 year old Emperor Meiji moved to Edo, which was renamed Tokyo the year before. Tokyo was already the nation's political, economic, and cultural centre, and the emperor's residence made it a *de facto* imperial capital as well with the former Edo Castle becoming the Imperial Palace. The city of Tokyo was established, and continued to be the capital until it was abolished as a municipality in 1943 and merged with the Metropolitan Prefecture of Tokyo. After the Second World War, Tokyo was completely rebuilt. It became the largest city in the world in 1965 (taking the lead from New York).[4]

Tokyo Prefecture consists of three major parts: the twenty three special wards (constituting the former Tokyo City), Tama and the Islands. Tokyo Prefecture also includes two island chains in the Pacific Ocean: the Igu Islands and the Ogasawara Islands.

Administrative Structure

In 1868, the medieval city Edo was renamed Tokyo. Then the offices of Tokyo Prefecture (-fu) were opened. The extent of Tokyo Prefecture was initially limited to the former Edo city (15 wards). In 1878, 15 wards and 6 districts were placed under Tokyo Prefecture. In 1889, Tokyo City (-shi) was formed with these 15 wards. In 1932, Tokyo City was augmented with 20 wards from surrounding districts. In 1943, Tokyo City and Tokyo Prefecture were united into Tokyo Metropolis (-to). The previous wards became directly administered by the Metropolis. Tokyo ceased to be the name of a city at that time.[5]

Under Japanese law, Tokyo is designated as a 'to' (often translated metropolis). Its administrative structure is similar to that of Japan's other prefectures. Within Tokyo lie dozens of smaller entities, most of them conveniently referred to as cities. It includes twenty-three special wards (ku), which until 1943 comprised the city of Tokyo but are now separate, self-governing municipalities, each with a mayor, and a council, and having the status of a city. In addition, Tokyo also encompasses 26 more cities (shi), five towns (cho or machi), and eight villages (son or mura), each of which has a local government. The Tokyo Metropolitan Government is headed by a publicly elected governor and metropolitan assembly.[6] They govern all of Tokyo, including lakes, rivers, dams, farms, remote islands, and national parks in addition to its famous neon jungle, skyscrapers and crowded sub-ways.

Special Wards

Each special ward of Tokyo is a municipality with its own elected mayor and assembly, differing from an ordinary city in that certain governmental function is handled by the Tokyo Metropolitan Government, and for most, also differing in having no particular centre and little cultural or similar distinctiveness from the immediate surroundings.

The term "central Tokyo" may refer to the special wards, area within the Yamanote Line loop, or to the three 'central wards' of Chiyoda, Chuo and Minato. While the generally accepted centre of Tokyo is the Imperial Palace, there are a number of major urban centres where business, shopping, and entertainment are concentrated around major train stations.

As of September 1, 2003, the official total population of the special wards combined was about 8.34 million, with a population density of 13,416 per km^2.[6]

To the west of the special wards, Tokyo Prefecture consists of cities, towns, and villages that enjoy the same legal status as that elsewhere in Japan. Collectively, those are often known as Tama Area or Western Tokyo. Twenty-six cities lie within the western part of Tokyo Prefecture.

The special ward system has undergone a number of reforms. Through a reform undertaken in 1974, the 23 special wards were given the authority to elect their mayors by popular vote and handle affairs similar cities.[7] However, since the wards continued to be viewed as internal organizations of Tokyo Metropolis, various issues arose. These included a lack of clarity in the allocation and sharing of roles and administrative responsibilities of the wards and the metropolitan government; interference with the autonomy of the wards; and the inability of the metropolitan government to implement thorough urban administration from a comprehensive view point.

In order to resolve these issues, the metropolitan government and the 23 special wards requested the national government to revise the related laws. As a result, it was decided that jurisdiction over administrative operations that touch closely on residents' lives, such as waste management, should be transferred to the wards. The Local Autonomy Law was partially revised in1998. By increasing the independence and autonomy of the wards through the strengthening of their fiscal autonomy, this law established the wards as basic local public entities. The new ward system came into operation on April 1, 2000.

Tokyo Metropolis and the 23 Special Wards

Tokyo is a regional government encompassing 23 special wards, 26 cities, 5 towns and 8 villages, but its certain characteristics distinguish it from the other prefectures. In the ward area, the metropolitan government takes on part of the work usually assigned to the municipalities including water works, to keep their unity and cohesion as a single city. A special administrative system therefore exists between the government and the special wards, which is not seen elsewhere in the country. This system is called the special ward system.[9]

The metropolitan government manages services such as water works, sewerage and fire fighting for the whole 23 special ward area as a single body. These services are managed by the metropolitan government to ensure uniform, efficient services across the whole of the densely—populated ward area. In other parts of the country, by law these services are under the jurisdiction of the municipal governments of ordinary cities.

Since the metropolitan government takes on some of the administrative work which elsewhere in the country would be handled by the city authorities, it levies and collects municipal taxes which would be collected by the cities elsewhere. These taxes include the corporate portion of residents' taxes, and the fixed assets tax.

The metropolitan government makes financial adjustments both between itself and the special wards and among the special wards themselves. In the ward area, the government and the special wards are responsible for the administrative affairs usually covered by cities, and they share the tax revenue sources required for the costs incurred. The financial adjustment system is designed to ensure a balanced distribution of these financial resources. At present, a certain proportion of the tax revenue from the three metropolitan taxes (corporate portion of the residents' tax, fixed assets tax and special land ownership tax) is allocated to the ward governments. The financial adjustment among the 23 special wards is also designed to redress imbalances in an individual ward's fiscal revenues due to uneven distribution of financial resources. When a ward's basic fiscal needs exceeds its basic fiscal revenues, the difference is made up in the form of allocations from the metropolitan government.[10]

Tokyo Metropolitan Government and the Municipalities

Tokyo Metropolis in addition to the special wards also contains 39 municipalities—26 cities (shi), 5 towns (cho) and 8 villages (son)—that are ordinary local public entities. The administrative and financial systems for the metropolitan government and its municipalities are the same as those for other prefectures.[11] The metropolitan government handles the broader administrative work and the municipalities oversee services closer to the every day lives of local residents.

Fire fighting services and waterworks are sectors that are generally designated as municipal services by law. In Tokyo Metropolis, however, the prevailing view is that these services can be handled more efficiently on a broader scale and that such an approach also serves to lessen the financial burden. Therefore, with the exception of certain municipalities, the metropolitan government oversees all of these services.

For services that can be handled with greater effectiveness and efficiency on a broad basis, the related municipalities establish cooperatives serving as special local public entities, based on the stipulations of the Local Autonomy Law. The number of such cooperatives in the municipalities is 30 and they handle a broad range of services, which include the establishment and management of waste disposal sites and incineration plants, the operation of public hospitals and profit-making projects.

The metropolitan government promotes measures aimed at tackling the challenges faced by the Tama area, the outlying islands and other regions, and also furnishes assistance customized for the administrative requirements of each individual municipality. The metropolitan government takes an active stance to promote regional administration through various supportive measures such as financial assistance in the form of Tokyo Metropolitan Government-disbursed funding, and technical advice to upgrade regional sewerage systems.[12]

Organisational Structure of Tokyo Metropolis

Legislative Organs

The Tokyo Metropolis has a Tokyo Metropolitan Assembly consisting of 127 members directly elected by Tokyo citizens to serve a term of four years. The members from amongst themselves elect a President, who presides over its sessions and supervises its affairs. He expresses the opinions of Assembly externally. As a support organization for the Assembly, a Secretariat is provided and the President is empowered to appoint and dismiss its staff employees.[13]

The workings of the metropolitan administration have become increasingly varied and complex and the metropolitan government have become large and unwieldy. The Assembly establishes standing committees and special committees to consider special subjects.

The Tokyo Metropolitan Assembly is the main decision-making body having authority to enact, amend and repeal metropolitan ordinances, certify settlement of the budget, and elect members of the Election Administration Commission. In addition, the appointments of the Vice-Governor and the Comptroller General are made by the Governor in consultation with the Assembly. It has the powers to investigate and inspect all aspects of administrative affairs.[14]

Executive Organs

The Governor is directly elected by the citizens and represents the Metropolis of Tokyo for a term of four years. He has overall control of metropolitan affairs, and the authority and responsibility for maintaining the collective integrity of the metropolitan administration.[15] In the 23 special-ward area, the Governor may take on the nature of mayor.

To assist the Governor, Vice-Governors, a Comptroller General and other staff are provided.

Financial System

There are several items that are taxed directly by the metropolitan government in the 23 special wards, which in other prefectures would not be levied by the prefectural authority but will come under municipal taxes. 52 per cent of tax revenues obtained from the three taxes—Municipal Residents Tax paid by corporations, the Fixed Assets Tax, and the Special Land Ownership Tax—is allocated to each of the wards to provide them with their own financial resources. Since October 1, 2002, the metropolitan government has been levying an Accommodation Tax on stays in hotels.[16]

The metropolitan government levies taxes on 16 items the largest proportion of the total metropolitan tax revenue is from the two corporation taxes (Corporate Business Tax and Corporate Residents Tax), which together account for approximately 38 per cent. This is followed by the Fixed Assets Tax and the City Planning Tax at around 26 per cent of total metropolitan tax revenue.[17]

Metropolitan taxes provide for 67.2 per cent of the total metropolitan revenue, whereas local taxes accounted for just 34.4 per cent of the total combined revenue of all local public entities in fiscal 2003.[18]

National treasury disbursements hold a smaller share in the overall metropolitan revenue than that of other local governments. In fiscal 2003, national treasury disbursements accounted for 13.8 per cent of total local government finances, while it accounted for only 7.0 per cent of the metropolitan finances in fiscal 2004.[19]

The expenditure of the metropolitan government has significant differences from the expenditure of other local authorities. First, as well as being responsible for the administration at a prefectural level, the government is also responsible for part of the administration in the ward area that elsewhere would be carried out at the municipal level. Another important difference is the special ward financial adjustment allocations, an expenditure item only found in Tokyo.[20]

REFERENCES

1. Statistics Bureau, Ministry of Public Management, Home Affairs, Posts and Telecommunications, "Population Census".
2. Tokyo Metropolitan Government, Nishi-Shinjuku 2-chome, Shinjuku, Tokyo Ministry of Economy, Trade and Industry, "Census of Commerce".

3. Statistics Division, Bureau of General Affairs, TMG, "Households and Population in Tokyo in Accordance with the Basic Register of Residents".
4. Statistics Bureau, *op cit.*
5. http://www.metro.tokyo.jp. Wikipedia.
6. Local Administration Division, TMG Bureau of General Affairs, "Reports on Land Area of Tokyo Municipalities".
7. Abbes, H., Shindo, M. and Sadefurm, K., 1994, *The Government and Politics of Japan*, Tokyo University Press, Tokyo.
8. Stevens, A. (2004). *Local Government in Japan*, Council of Local Authorities for International Relations, Tokyo.
9. Kubbota, J. (2004). *Local Government Innovations in Japan*, Council of Local Authorities for International Relations, Tokyo.
10. Statistics Division, TMG Bureau of General Affairs, "Tokyo's Economic Calculation".
11. Rowat, D.C. (ed.) (1980). *International Handbook on Local Government Reorganisation*, Greenwood Press, Westport.
12. Shindo, M. (1982). *Relations between National Government and Local Government in Public Administration in Japan*, Senshu University.
13. Stevens, *op cit.*
14. Rowat, *op cit.*
15. Kubbota, *op cit.*
16. TMG Bureau of General Affairs, Statistical Division, *op.cit.*
17. Hyoe, M. and Johannes, H. (eds.) (1979). *Politics and Economics in Contemporary Japan*, Japan Cultural Institute, Tokyo.
18. TMG Bureau of General Affairs, *op cit.*
19. *Ibid.*
20. Inoguchi, T. and Ukimoto, D. (eds.), *The Political Economy of Japan*, Vol. II, Stanford University Press, Palo, Alto, CA.

CITY OF DELHI

Introduction

Delhi is a metropolis in northern India. It also refers to the National Capital Territory of Delhi, which is a special union territory jointly administered by the Central Government. The 69th Amendment to the Constitution of India, in 1991 granted Delhi the status of a special union territory and officially changed its name to the National Capital Territory of Delhi.[1] The National Capital Territory of Delhi comprises of nine districts, 27 tehsils, three statutory towns viz. Municipal Corporation of Delhi, New Delhi Municipal Council and Delhi Cantonment Board, 59 census towns and 165 villages.[2] It is spread over an area of 1483 km^2. Out of the total area, 783 km^2 is rural and

700 km^2 is urban. The Municipal Corporation of Delhi covers 1397.3 km^2 areas and the extent of the New Delhi Municipal Council is only 42.7 km^2 and that of the Delhi Cantonment Board is 43 km^2.[3]

The metropolis of Delhi and the National Capital Territory of Delhi are coextensive and for most practical purposes they are considered to be the same entity. New Delhi is an urban area within the metropolis of Delhi, and is the seat of the Government of India.

Delhi is the sixth most populous metropolis in the world with a population of 15.3 million (2005). Delhi's metropolitan area, informally known as the National Capital territory, has an estimated population of 19.7 million. In 2003, the National Capital Territory of Delhi had a population of 14.1 million, making it the second largest metropolitan area in India after Mumbai. According to the Economic Survey of Delhi held in 2001, 2.6 million people were living in slum designated areas across Delhi while 1.7 million and 3.3 million were living in regularized and planned colonies respectively.[4]

The Delhi metropolitan area has three urban local bodies: Municipal Corporation of Delhi, New Delhi Municipal Council (population of 2,95,000, in 2003) and Delhi Cantonment Board (population in 2003 was 1,25,000). The Delhi Municipal Corporation is one of the largest municipal corporations in the world providing civic amenities to an estimated 13.78 million people.[5] Delhi's relatively high per capita income, better living standards and high economic growth rate has attracted a lot of people from rural areas in neighbouring states. Due to high migration rate, Delhi registers as one of the fastest growing cities in the world. According to a United Nations report, Delhi will be the third largest agglomeration in the world after Tokyo and Mumbai by 2025.[6]

The capital of India, New Delhi, falls under the administration of New Delhi Municipal Council, whose chairperson (Chief Executive Officer) is appointed by the Government of India in consultation with the Chief Minister of Delhi.

The National Capital Territory of Delhi is divided into nine districts. Each district is headed by a Deputy Commissioner and has three sub-divisions. A sub-division Magistrate heads each sub-division. All Deputy Commissioners report to the Divisional Commissioner. The District Administration of Delhi is the enforcement department for all kinds of State and Central Government policies and exercises supervisory powers over numerous other functionaries of the Government.

Government and Politics

As a special Union Territory, the National Capital Territory of Delhi has its own Legislative Assembly, Lt. Governor, Council of Ministers and Chief Minister. The Legislative Assembly seats are filled by direct elections from territorial constituencies. However, the Union Government of India and the Government of National Capital Territory of Delhi jointly administer New Delhi. The legislative assembly was re-established in 1993 for the first time since 1956, with direct federal rule in the span.[7]

Managing New Delhi[8]

New Delhi, an urban area in Delhi, is the seat of both the State Government of Delhi and the Government of India. Managing this area is the responsibility of the New Delhi Municipal Council. The New Delhi Municipal Council includes a chairperson, two members nominated by the Chief Minister of National Capital Territory of Delhi and five members nominated by the central government. The Chairperson is appointed by the Central Government for a term of five years.

The region is governed under the provisions of the New Delhi Municipal Council Act, 1994.

Delhi Municipal Corporation[9]

Other urban areas of the metropolis of Delhi are administered by the Municipal Corporation of Delhi under the provisions of the Panchayati Raj Act, and hence are not considered a part of the capital city.

The Municipal Corporation of Delhi consists of direct elected councillors, ten persons who have special knowledge or experience in municipal administration, members of the House of the People representing constituencies and one-fifth of the members of the Legislative Assembly of the National Capital Territory of Delhi representing constituencies in the region. The number of councillors in no case be more than 134 and less than 80.

The Corporation at its first meeting every year elects one of its members as Mayor and another member to be Deputy Mayor.

The corporation is administered under the Delhi Municipal Corporation Act, 1957.

The water supply in Delhi is managed by the Delhi Water Board, consisting of a Chairperson (Minister In-charge of the Government), a Vice-Chairperson (nominated by the Speaker), Chief Executive Officer (nominated by the Government), three members of the Legislative Assembly of the National Capital Territory of Delhi (nominated by the Speaker), two members of the Municipal Corporation of Delhi (nominated by the Mayor), the Commissioner of the Municipal Corporation of Delhi, the Chairperson of the New Delhi Municipal Council, a member of water supply, drainage, finance, administration each, secretary in-charge of the Government, a representative of the Ministry of Urban Development, Delhi Cantonment Board and Central Ground Water Authority each.[10]

The Board functions under the provisions of the Delhi Water Board Act, 1998.

REFERENCES

1. The Constitution (Sixty-Ninth Amendment) Act, 1991.
2. Rowe, P. and Coster, P. (2004). Delhi (Great Cities of the World), World Almanac Library; http://delhiplanning.nic.in/Economic %.
3. http://www.citypopulation.de/World.htmi; http://www.censusindia.net/profiles/del.html; http://www.indiatourism.com/delhi-history/index.html.
4. http://wikipedia.org.
5. http://isc.nic.in/delhi.html.
6. Economic Survey of Delhi (2005-06), Planning Department, Government of National Capital Territory of Delhi.
7. First City? a Symposium on Remembering Delhi (http://www.india-seminar.com/2002/515.html).
8. The New Delhi Municipal Council Act, 1994. http://www.ndmc.gov.in.
9. The Delhi Municipal Corporation Act, 1957. http://www.medonline.gov.in/
10. The Delhi Water Board Act, 1998.

CITY OF MOSCOW

Introduction

Moscow, the Federal City, is known as Federal City of Moscow (Federalny Gorod Moskva) and consists of one Federal City Municipality, 10 Administrative Districts (rayon), and 128 Urban Regions. It constitutes a maximum level federal entity (subyekty) within the Russian Federation. According to the U. N.'s Urban Agglomerations 2003, the population of the Federal City of Moscow was 10,382,754 within an area of 1092 km^2. The density was 9516 hab/km^2. The federal city constitutes about 7.15 per cent of total population of the Russian Federation.[1]

City Management

The city is made up of 10 regions and 128 districts. The districts formally have the status of municipalities and have their own institutions, heads of district and district assemblies, with members elected every four years. Their function is to administer the local economy and services. Each of the 10 administrative regions has a Prefect, who is appointed and responds before the Mayor and the government.[2] The Prefect is in charge of administering, coordinating and controlling the functions of the city government in his respective region.

The federal city does not have a down town area; the urban core is scattered across the city. Its government and administration are independent of the government of Moscow Province.

The main function of the federal city is to provide services to the public. It develops its activity in the following areas of authority: housing, (it is the owner or administrator of a high percentage of the city's housing stock and builds new public housing); owning and managing the water and sewerage systems; managing and executing urban rubbish collection; facilitating health care services within the framework of the state public service; providing and managing the highway infrastructure; operating the mass public transport system and managing security and emergencies in conjunction with the state.[3]

City Council

State statutes provide for the two forms of municipal government within the State of Idaho, the Council-Mayor form and the Council-Manager form. The City of Moscow has the Council-Mayor form of government within which there are six council members and a Mayor which are elected separately and serve a four year term. There are six council members, all elected at large. Council member elections are held every two years.[4] Terms are staggered so that three of the six seats are open at each election.

Moscow City Duma represents the legislative power of the city and is able to issue city laws and approve the budget act. It also exercises political control over activities of the Mayor, approves the city's development plan and sectoral development plans. It is responsible for the administrative organization and budgetary assignment of districts and administrative regions. The Duma is made up of 58 members directly elected in single-member districts every four years.[5]

The council serves as the legislative and judicial arm of the city government and enacts ordinances (local laws), passes resolutions (statements of policy), confirms the Mayor's appointments of city officials and citizen advisory commission members, approves the city's annual budget, and serves as the quasi-judicial hearing body for public hearings and appeals of other city boards and commissions.

The council elects a President from amongst its members at its first meeting in January every year. The Council President serves as Mayor in his absence and has such other duties and responsibilities as the council may from time-to-time direct by vote or resolution. The council also elects a Vice-President at the first January meeting each year. The Council Vice-President serves as Mayor when Mayor and the council President are both either absent from the city or are incapacitated, and as Council President when the President is absent from the city or incapacitated. The Council Vice-President also has such other duties and responsibilities as the council may from time-to-time direct by vote or by resolution.[6]

Mayor

The Mayor is the superintending and administrative officer of the city. He enjoys executive power in the city and is responsible for the administration and management of the city. The Mayor signs officially for and behalf of the city on all contracts, including all deeds, bonds, bills, notes, obligations and other agreements to which the city is a party, and may borrow money on the credit of the city when authorized by the council.[7]

The Mayor has the power to veto or sign any ordinance or resolution passed by the council, provided that any ordinance or resolution vetoed by the Mayor may be passed over the veto by a vote of one-half plus one of the members of the full council. He has the support of an administrative political structure, the City

Government, organized around primary spheres of activity: economy, and infrastructure, building, land management and development and social policies.

The Mayor has the power to require a report from any city officer, and to report to the council on any subject pertaining to the Office of the Mayor.

The Mayor has the jurisdiction over all places within five miles of the corporate limits of the city for the enforcement of any health or quarantine ordinance, and has jurisdiction in all matters except taxation within one mile of the corporate limits.

The Mayor is elected by direct popular vote every four years and may currently only exercise two mandates consecutively.[8]

REFERENCES

1. Chew, A.F. (1970). *An Atlas of Russian History: Eleven Centuries Changing Borders*, Yale University Press, New Haven.
2. Walker, E.W. (1995). *Federalism Russian Style: The Federation Provisions in Russia's New Constitution, Problems of Post-Communism*, July-August.
3. *Russian Regions Today: Atlas of the New Federation*, 1994. International Centre, Washington.
4. Goskomstat (2000). *Forming Local Self-Governance in the Russian Federation.*
5. http://www.moscowcity.ru/; http://www.citynext.ru.
6. http://en.wikipedia.org/wiki/Moscow-City.
7. Russian Classification of Objects of Administrative Division (OKATO); http://www.incube3d.ru/portfolio/ vis/ani/mmde/
8. Lipman, M. and Lapteva, L. (1994). *Russia*, Institute for Local Government and Public Service, Moscow.

CITY OF PARIS

Introduction

Paris is the capital city of France and a French 'department'. Situated on the banks of the river Seine in north-central France, it is also the capital of the Ile-de-France region (also known as Paris Region), which encompasses Paris and its suburbs. The Paris Region is France's most dynamic centre of economic activity. It produces more than a quarter of France's wealth.[1] Paris is a leading global cultural, business and political centre and has a major international influence in fashion, gastronomy and the arts. It is widely regarded as one of the world's major global cities, with the headquarters of international organizations such as UNESCO, the OECD, the ICC, or the informal Paris Club. Dubbed "the City of Light"(la Ville Lumiere) since the 19th century owing to its early adoption of street-lighting, Paris is regarded by some as one of the most romantic cities in the world. It is also the most visited city in the world, with more than 30 million visitors per year.[2]

The city derives its name from the Gallic Parisii tribe. The city known as Lutetia during the Roman Empire began to adopt its present-day name towards the end of the Roman era. Since the 20th century, Paris has been known in French slang as Paname.[3]

Modern Paris is the result of a vast mid-19th century urban remodeling. For centuries it had been a labyrinth of narrow streets and half-timber houses, but beginning in 1852, the BaronHaussmann's vast urbanization leveled entire quarters to make way for wide avenues lined with neo-classical stone buildings.[4] Save for a few examples, Paris seems an essentially flat city when compared to some of the world's other metropolises.

The population of the city of Paris was 2,125,246 at the 1999 census, lower than the historical peak of 2.9 million in 1921. This decline was because of the relocation of people to the suburbs caused by deindustrialization, high rent, the gentrification of many inner quarters and the transformation of living space into offices, although not on the scale seen in some Western cities. Paris had an estimated mid-2004 population of 2,144,700. The Paris urban area, extending well beyond the city boundaries, has today an estimated population of 9.93 million. The Paris metropolitan area, including satellite towns, stood at 11.5 million in 1999, and is one of the most populated metropolitan areas in Europe.[5]

The City of Paris is much smaller than its urban growth. The city's urban area fills a ring of Paris' three neighbouring departments—also known as 'petite couronne'(small ring) and extends into an 'outer ring' of four 'grande couronne departments' beyond. These eight departments together complete the Ile-de-France region. The Paris agglomeration or urban area covers 2723 km^2, or about 26 times larger than the city of Paris. Beyond this, the couronne peri-urbaine commuter belt region reaches well beyond the limits of the Ile-de-France region, and combined with the Paris agglomeration, completes a metropolitan area covering 14, 518 km^2, or an area about 138 times that of Paris itself.[6]

City Government

Paris has been a commune (municipality) since 1834. At the 1790 division of France into communes in the beginning of the French Revolution, and again in 1834, Paris was a city only half its modern size, but in 1860 it annexed bordering communes, some entirely, to create the new administrative map of twenty municipal *arrondissements* the city still has today.[7]

Paris as a commune from 1790 became the prefecture (capital) of the Seine department that encompassed Paris and a number of neighbouring communes, but this department was split in 1968 into four smaller ones: the city of Paris became a department distinct from suburban communes in retaining the Seine department. The result of this division is that today Paris's limits as a department are exactly those of its limits as a commune, a situation unique in France.[8]

The city of Paris, distinct from the surrounding Ile-de-France region, is itself both a department and a county for administrative purposes. The city is subdivided into 20 smaller governmental units, the *arrondissements*, which themselves are further divided into 80 quartiers, or quarters—four per *arrondissement*. Each of these 20 *arrondissements* has a directly elected council, which in turn elects an *arrondissement* mayor. A selection of members from each *arrondisement* council forms the Council of Paris, which in turn elects the mayor of Paris.[9]

In medieval period Paris was governed by a merchant-elected municipality whose head was the provost of the merchants. In addition to regulating city commerce, the provost of the merchants was responsible for some civic duties, such as the guarding of city walls and the cleanliness of city streets. This role was seconded from the 13th century by the provost of Paris, a direct representative of the king responsible for law and order in the city and its surroundings.[10]

Although the municipal council was recreated in 1834, Paris spent most of the 19th and 20th centuries, along with the larger Seine department of which it was a centre, under the direct control of the State—appointed prefect of the Seine, in charge of general affairs there. The State appointed Prefect of Police was in charge of police in the same jurisdiction. Paris, save for a few brief occasions, would have no mayor until 1977, and the Paris Prefecture of Police is still under State control today.[10] Despite its double existence as commune and department, Paris has a unique council to governing both; the

Council of Paris, presided by the mayor of Paris, meets either as a municipal council or as a departmental council depending on the issue to be debated.[11]

REFERENCES

1. Encyclopedia Britannica: Character of the City, http://www.britannica.com/eb/article 59646.
2. INSEE, Government of France (2005). http://www. recensement.insee.fr/fr/ffc/docs_reg.xls.
3. Nigam, S.R. (1982). *Local Government* (*England, France, USA, USSR & India*), S.Chand & Company, New Delhi.
4. Laxmikant, M. (2001). *Public Administration,* New Delhi, Tata McGraw Hill.
5. Inventory of World Cities, Ga W C, Loughborough University; http://www.Iboro.ac.uk/gawe/citylist.html; Government (from Paris)-Britannica Student Encyclopedia, 2006; http://www.britannica.com/ebi/article-206161.
6. Paris-Ile-de-France, Regional Chamber of Commerce and Industry, IAURIF, INSEE Ilw-de-France (226); Paris Region: Key Figures, 2006 (http://www.paris-iledefrance.cci.fr/pdf/eco_regionale/chiffres_cles/2006/anglais/cc_2006_en_15-21.pdf; http://siteresources.worldbank.org/DATASTATISTICS/Resources/GDP.pdf.
7. Sharma, A . (2005). *Local Government in France: Recent Reforms*, Nagarlok, XXXVII(2).
8. Goldsmith, M. (1992). *Local Government*, Urban Studies, 29 (3/4).
9. Cochrane, A., 1993, *Whatever happened to local government*? O.U.P. Buckingham; INSEE, Government of France; http://www.recensement.insee.fr/RP99/rp99wr_page.affiche? p_id_ nivgeo=M &p_id_loca=001&p_id_prince=POPI&p_theme=ALL&p_typeprod=ALL &p_langue=FR; http://www.insee.fr/fr/insee_regions/idf/zoom/chif_cles/uu99/fuu99008 51.html.
10. Ronald, D.V. (ed.) (1988). Public Administration in Developed Democracies (A Comparative Study), Marcel Dekkar Inc, New York & Basel.
11. Lorrain, D., (1992), *The French Model of Urban Services*, West European Politics, No. 2.

CITY OF GREATER LONDON

Introduction

The restructuring of the British economy in the depression years between the two world wars was accompanied by a movement of population into the south east of the country. As a result, Greater London extended into the surrounding counties and contained in total 117 separate organs, of which all but 4 were directly elected.[1] The Royal Commission on Local Government in Greater London was established in 1957 to examine the present system and working of local government in the Greater London area; to recommend whether any changes in the local government structure and the distribution of local authority functions in the area would better secure effective and convenient local government.[2]

The Royal Commission recommended the creation of a Greater London Authority extending over an area with a population of some 8.5 million—roughly double the population of the London County Council area. Within this area they recommended 52 London boroughs with populations ranging from 1 to 2.5 lakhs. The exception was the City of London with a population of less than 5,000.[3] The Bill was enacted in 1963 and came into effect in April 1965.

The Greater London was established in 1965 as an aministrative unit covering the London metropolis. It was not defined as a county but had a two-tier structure, with the lower tier being the London boroughs. The Greater London Council started operations in 1965 following sweeping changes in the structure of local government in London and had overall responsibility for planning and managing London at a regional or strategic level.[4] The Greater London Council worked closely with the 32 London Boroughs and the City of London Corporation which are in effect separate entities within Greater London and are the primary units of Local Government. The 1963 London Government Act which created the Greater London Council also created the Inner London Education Authority which controlled education in 12 Inner London Boroughs and the City of London and was an autonomous executive committee of the Greater London Council.[5]

The Greater London Council's policy was determined by a Council comprising 92 Councillors, each elected for single member electoral areas and elections took place every four years. The Chairman of the Council was the ceremonial head and was elected annually by the Council. The Leader of the Council was elected by the Majority Party and was the political head of the Council.[6]

Council policy is implemented by officers of the Council's permanent staff. Although organized in Departments reflecting their professional and other disciplines, the Council operates a corporate management structure comprising six programme areas—planning, transportation, housing, public health and safety, arts and recreation, general services. The head of the permanent staff is the Director-General who is assisted by eight principal chief officers (Controllers) each responsible for a core area.[7]

The Greater London Council's major strategic role is in planning, and applications for permission for specific development, for example, airports, railway, large shopping centres, and high buildings must be referred by Borough Councils to the Greater London Council before a decision is taken. The Greater London Council's role in relation to transport and traffic is one of coordination. It has financial and policy control over London Transport and is the overall traffic authority for Greater London. The Borough Councils are agents of the Greater London Council for the construction and maintenance of local roads and the Greater London Council is directly responsible for metropolitan roads. Trunk roads are the responsibility of the Government.[8]

The reorganization done in 1980s was found ineffective in the case of Greater London and the six metropolitan counties.[9] Hence the conservatives abolished both the metropolitan counties and the Greater London County. Following the abolition of the Greater London Council (GLC) in 1986 services were allocated to the London boroughs which became single-tier authorities, but Greater London was still widely recognized, especially for statistical and mapping purposes. In 2000 however a two-tier structure was re-established when the new Greater London Authority adopted responsibility for a range of citywide policy areas.[10]

The Greater London Authority (GLA) administers the 1579 sq. km. of Greater London, covering the 32 London boroughs and the City of London. Entering on its functions on July 3, 2000, the Authority consists of an elected Mayor and 25 member Assembly. This current organization to some extent replaces the Greater London Council (1965-1986), which was abolished by Conservative prime minister Margaret Thatcher on grounds of alleged inefficiency, but also because elected Labour Party members were commonly in the majority, and in particular because of Livingstone's then radical populist policies and spending on social programmes.[11]

The Greater London Authority was created to improve the coordination of the various London boroughs, and the Mayor of London's role is to give London a single person to represent it. The Mayor proposes policy and the budget, and makes appointments to the capital's strategic transport and development bodies. One of the primary purposes of the London Assembly is to hold the Mayor of London to account, and to scrutinize their actions and decisions.[12] The Assembly must also accept or amend the budget and may make proposals.

Although weaker than the Greater London Council, the Greater London Authority has some powers that the Greater London Council never had, such as the right to appoint members of the Police Authority for the Metropolitan Police Service. The Greater London Authority should be distinguished from the Corporation and Lord Mayor of the City of London, which only control the square mile of the city, London's chief financial centre. While the Greater London Authority has a modern constitution, the organization of the City of London has barely changed since the middle ages, and is mainly controlled by city business interests.[13]

There are 32 actual boroughs, with a status similar to metropolitan districts, and also the City of London, which is a City Corporation and has a number of additional roles. Seventy-three Boroughs are subdivided into electoral wards.

Corporation of London

The City of London covers a square mile in the heart of London. It comprises principally the area of the ancient city. It became an important trading centre dating back to Roman times. The city is a unique international financial and commercial centre. It has within its boundaries the principal banking, insurance and financial institutions. Its problems have arisen from a number of causes, the damage caused by bombing during the Second World War, the change in the pattern of commercial activity and the need to improve the standards of the city's working environment.[14]

This gave the Corporation the opportunity of undertaking an extensive programme of comprehensive redevelopment. The city has thus been able to meet the demands of British and foreign firms operating therein who require modern offices. When the reconstruction of the city was planned it was decided that residential accommodation should be provided for more people to live in the city and an imaginative concept emerged which is known as Barbican Redevelopment, providing flats for some 5000 people, a school each for girls, Music and Drama and an Arts Centre. The whole complex is situated near to the remains of the Roman Wall inside the city's northern boundary. Thus the well being of the working population in the city has been greatly enhanced in the quality of their working conditions and the general environment.[15]

The 1888 Act created the London County Council as administrative county comprising parts of Middlesex, Surrey and Kent. The picture was completed in 1899 by the creation of 28 London boroughs within the area.[16] The City of London itself retained its ancient privileges and independence.

It is governed by the Corporation of London, which has a unique structure. The Corporation has been broadly untouched by local government reforms and democratization. The business vote was abolished for other parts of the country in 1969, but due to the low resident population of the city this was thought impractical.[17]

The elected Mayor of London sets out plans and policies for the capital covering transport, planning and development, economic development and regeneration, culture as well as a variety of environmental issues including ambient noise, wastes disposal and air quality.

The elected Mayor, with the separately elected London Assembly, together makes up the Greater London Authority. Around 600 paid staff helps the Mayor and the 25 members Assembly in their duties. The Mayor is London's spokesman. He sets budgets for the Greater London Authority, Transport for London, the London Development Agency, the Metropolitan Police and London's fire services. As Mayor, he chairs Transport for London. The Assembly scrutinizes the Mayor's activities and is able to question his decisions. The Assembly also has authority to investigate other issues of importance to Londoners, publish its findings and recommendations, and make proposals to the Mayor.[18]

London voters elect both the Mayor and the London Assembly every four years. The electoral system used to elect Assembly members is complex. It is designed to produce a distribution of seats that will always be proportional to the total votes cast across London. Assembly Members elect a Chair and Deputy Chair in May each year. The Assembly provides a check and a balance on the Mayor in a number of ways.[19]

REFERENCES

1. Robson, W.A. (1948). *The Government and Misgovernment of London*, Allen and Unwin, London.

2. Herbert, Sir, E. (Chairman) (1960). Report of the Royal Commission on Local Government in London, 1957-60, Cmnd 1164, HMSO, London.
3. *Ibid.*
4. www.oxfordjournals.org
5. Ponsonby, Lord of Shalbrede (1979). The Greater London Council and the Government of London, in Golden Jubilee Commemoration Volume, *AIILSG*, Mumbai.
6. www.infor4local.gov.uk
7. Ponsonby (1979). *op cit.*
8. Hampton, *op cit.*
9. Department of Environment, *op cit.*
10. Wikipedia article "Greater London Authority", Answers.com
11. *Ibid*; http://en.wikipedia.org/wiki/Greater_London
12. Hampton, *op cit.*
13. *Ibid.*
14. Answer.com
15. Ponsonby, 1979, *op cit.*
16. Clayton, S.J. (1979). City of London, in *AIILSG* (ed), Golden Jubilee Commemoration Volume, Mumbai.
17. *Ibid.*
18. Hampton, *op cit.*
19. Moore, *op cit.*; Saint, A. (1989). Politics and the People of London; The London County Council (1889-1965).

Bibliography

Books

Abes, H., Shindo, M. and Sadefumi, K. (1994). *The Government and Politics of Japan*, Tokyo: Tokyo University Press.

Agarawal, V. S. (1953). *India as known to Panini*, Lucknow.

Alexander, A. (1982). *Local Government in Britain since Reorganization*, London: George Allen and Unwin.

Alford, R.R. and Scooble, M. (1965). Political and Socio-Economic Characteristics of American Cities, *Municipal Year Book.*

Allen, G. (1993). *Independent Local Government*, London: European Policy Forum.

Allinson, G.D. (1975). *Japanese Urbanism; Industry and Politics in Kariya, 1872-1972*, Berkeley: University of California Press.

Amies, F.A., *et al.* (1965). *Law of Rating*, Rating Publishers.

Angotti, T. (1993). *Metropolis 2000: Planning Poverty and Politics*, London: Routledge.

Apter, D. E. and Nagayo, S. (1984). *Against the State: Politics and Social Protest in Japan*, Cambridge, MA: Harvard University Press.

Argal, R. (1954). *Municipal Government in India*, Allahabad.

Argeron, C. and Cornforld, T. (1993). *Developing Information Systems*, London: Macmillan.

Arora, Ramesh K. (ed.) (2004). *Public Administration (Fresh Perspectives)*, Jaipur: Aalekh Publishers.

Ashford, D.E. (1982). *British Dogmatism and French Pragmatism*, London: George Allen and Unwin.

Ashford, D. E. (1967). *National Development and Land Reform*, Princeton: University Press.

Aslund, A. (ed.) (1994). *Economic Transformation in Russia*, London: Pinter.

Austin, L. (ed.) (1976). *Japan: The Paradox of Progress*, New Havel, CT: Yale University Press.

Auty, Robert and Dmitry, O. (eds.) (1976). *An Introduction to Russian History, 1:-Companion to Russian Studies*, Cambridge: Cambridge University Press.

Avasthi, A. (ed.) (1972). *Municipal Administration in India*, Agra: Laxmi Narain Agarwal.

Bajpai, Ashok, Verma, M.S. (1995). *Panchayati Raj in India (A New Thrust)*, Delhi: Sahitya Prakashan.

Banerji, P. N. (1961). *Public Administration in Ancient India*, Calcutta.

Bebey, G.L. (1938). Personnel Administration, ICMA, The Municipal Year Book.

Behu, Robert (2001). *Rethinking Democratic Accountability*, Brookings Institution.

Benjamin, G. and Michael, J.M. (eds.) (1992). *Limiting Legislative Terms*, Washington, DC: Congressional Quarterly Press.

Bennett, R. J. (1982). *Central Grants to Local Governments*, London: Cambridge University Press.

Bennett, R.J. (ed.) (1990). *Decentralization, Local Governments and Markets Towards a Post-welfare Agenda*, Oxford: Clarendon Press.

Bennett, R. J. (ed.) (1994). *Local Government and Market Decentralization*, Paris: NU Press.

Bentwich, H. (1962). *Our Councils: The Story of Local Government*, London: Routledge & Kegan Paul.

Berman, David R. (1984). *State and Local Politics*, Boston: Allen and Bacon.

Bhargava, B. S. and Ramarao, S. (1978). *Indian Local Government—A Study*, New Delhi: Minerva.

Bhatnagar, S. (2004). *E-Government*, New Delhi: Sage.

Bhatnagar, S. and Goel, S.C. (eds.) (1992). *Development Planning and Administration*, New Delhi: Deep & Deep.

Bhattacharya, M. (1970). *Essays on Urban Government*, Calcutta: World Press Pvt. Ltd.

Bhattacharya, M., *Municipal Government*, New Delhi: Research Publications.

Biddle, W.W. and Biddle, L. J. (1965). *The Community Development Process*. Halt: Richard & Winston.

Bohman, James (1996). *Public Deliberation: Pluralism, Complexity and Democracy*, Cambridge, MA: MIT Press.

Bocquier, Phillippe (2004). *World Urbanization Prospects: An Alternative to the UN Model of Projection Compatible with Urban Transition Theory*, Paris: DIAL.

Bollens, J.C. (1952). *Appointed Executive Local Government: The California Experience*, Los Angles: The Haynes Foundation.

Bowman, M. and Hampton, W. (eds.) (1983). *Local Democracies: A Study in Comparative Local Government*, Cheshire, Melbourne: Longman.

Bromage, A.W. (1970). *Urban Policy Making: The Council Manager Partnership*, Chicago: Public Administration Service.

Bryce, J. (1991). *Modern Democracies*, New York: Macmillan.

Bretton, Albert (1998). *Competitive Governments*, Cambridge: Cambridge University Press.

Burns, N.E. (1994). *The Formation of American Local Governments: Private Values in Public Institutions*, New York: OCIP.

Burrows, Edwin G. and Wallace, Mike (1998). *Gotham: A history of New York City*, Oxford University Press.

Byrne, Tony (1990). *Local Government in Britain*, London: Penguin Books.

Byrne, T. (1994). *Local Government in Britain*, Harmondsworth: Penguin.

Chapman, B. (1953). *Introduction to French Local Government*, London: Allen & Unwin.

Chandar, A. (1958). *Indian Administration*, London.

Chandler, J. A. (ed.) (1993). *Local Government in Liberal Democracies*, London: Routledge.

Charlot, S. and Paty, S. (2005). The French Local Tax Setting: Do Interactions and Agglomerations Force Matters? INTRA-ENESAD, UMR CESAER, Bd Dr Petitjean DIJON Cedex.

Chaturvedi, T.N. (ed.) (1984). *Local Government*, New Delhi: IIPA.

Chew, A.F. (1970). *An Atlas of Russian History: Eleven Centuries of Changing Borders*, New Haven: Yale University Press.

Chopra, J. K. (ed.) (2004). *Local Self-Government and Municipal Administration*, New Delhi: Commonwealth.

Christopher, R.C. (1985). *The Japanese Mind: The Goliath Explained*, Fawcett Columbine.

Christopher, W. F. and Thor, C. G. (2004). *Handbook for Productivity Measurement and Improvement*, Terre Hante.

Clarke, John J. (1948). *Local Government of the United Kingdom*, London.

Clarke, John J. (1955). *A History of Local Government of the United Kingdom*, Jenkins.

Clarke, John J. (1956). *Local Government of the United Kingdom*, Pitman.

Clarke, John J., (1992). *Outlines of Local Government of the United Kingdom*, Pitman.

Clayton, S.J. (1979). City of London, in *AIILSG* (ed.), *Golden Jubilee Commemoration Volume*, Mumbai.

Clyde, F. Suyder (1965). *American State and Local Government*, New York: Appleton-Century-Crofts.

Coakes, E. (2002). *Knowledge Management in the Socio-Technical World*, Spinger.

Coenen, F.H.J.M., Dave, H. and Lawrence, J.O. Toole, Jr. (eds.) (1998). *Participation and the Quality of Governmental Decision-Making*, Boston: Kluwar Academic Publications.

Cohen, S.F. (1985). *Rethinking the Soviet Experience: Politics and History since 1917*, New York: OUP.

Cole, Alistair and Peter, John (2001). *Local Governance in England and France*, London: Routledge.

Conlan, Timothy (1980). *New Federalism: Intergovernmental Reform from Nixon to Reagan*, Washington DC: Bookings.

Connor, Karen'O and Sabato, Larry J. (1997). *American Government (Continuity and Change)*, Boston: Allyn and Bacon.

Crenson, M. A. (1993). *A Neighbourhood Politics*, Cambridge: Harvard University Press.

Curzon, Lord (1925). *British Government in India*, Vol. II, London.

Cullen, R. and Cushman, D. (2000). *Transitions to Competitive Government*, SUNY.

Dahl, R.A. (1996). *Who Governs? Democracy and Power in an American City*, New Haven: Yale University Press.

Das, R.B. and Singh, D.P. (eds.) (1968). *Deliberative and Executive Wings in Local Government*, New Delhi: OUP.

Datta, K.K. (1960). *An Advanced History of India*, Part III, New Delhi: MacMillan.

Denhardt, R. B. (1993). *The Pursuit of Significance*, Belomon: CA, Wadsworth.

Dillon, J.F., 1911, *Commentaries on the Law of Municipal Corporation*, Boston: Little Brown & Co.

Dmytrystyn, B. (1977). *A History of Russia, Englewood Cliffs*, NJ: Prentice Hall.

Donald, C. Rowat, (ed.) (1988). *Public Administration in Developed Democracies (A Comparative Study)*, New York and Basel: Marcel Dekker Inc.

Douglas, J. Watson and Wendy, L. Hassett (eds.) (2003). *Local Government Management: Current Issues and Best Practices*, New York: M. E. Sharpe.

Dowdy, E. (1973). *Japanese Bureaucracy: Its Development and Modernisation*, Melbourne: Cheshire.

Drain, G. (1966). *The Organisation and Practice of Local Government*, Heinemann.

Dryzek, John (2000). *Deliberative Democracy and Beyond: Liberals, Critics, Contestations*, Oxford: OUP.

Dunleavy, P. (1981). *The Politics of Mass Housing in Britain, 1945-75*, London: Clarendon Press.

Dye, Thomas R. (1990). *American Federation: Competition among Government*, Lexington, MA: D.C. Health.

East, John P. (1965). Council Manager Government: The Political Thought of its Founder, R.S. Childs, Chapel Hill: University of North Carolina Press.

Elkins, S. and Eric, McKionick (1993). *The Age of Federalism*, New York: Oxford.

Elocock, H. (1991). *Local Government*, London: Methuen.

Erie, S. P. (1998). *Rainbow's End: Irish American and the Dilemmas of Urban Machine Politics*, Berkeley: University of California Press.

Fiorina, Morris P. (1992). *Divided Government*, New York: Macmillan.

Fiorina, M.P. and Peterson, Paul P. (1997). *The New American Democracy*, Boston: Allyn and Bacon.

Foster, C.D., Jackman, R. and Perlman, M. (1980). *Local Government Finance in a Unitary State*, London: Allen and Unwin.

Fraser, D. (1976). *Urban Politics in Victorian England: The Structure of Politics in Victorian Cities*, Leicester University Press.

Gandhi, M.K. (1959). *Panchayati Raj*, Ahmedabad: Navjivan Publishing House, compiled by R.K. Prabhu.

Gardiner, Vince and Mathews, Hugh (eds.) (2000). *The Changing Geography of the United Kingdom*, London: Routledge.

Gargan, John J. (ed.) (1997). *Handbook of Local Government Administration*, New York: Marcel Dekker, Inc.

George, S. Blair (1964). *American Local Government*, New York: Harper & Row.

Goel, S.L. (2005). *Advanced Public Administration*, New Delhi: Deep & Deep.

Golding, L. (1975). *Local Government*, London: Cox Wayman Ltd.

Goskomstat (2000). Forming Local Self-governance in the Russian Federation.

Graham, K.A. and Phillips, S.D. (1996). *Citizen Engagement*, Institute of Public Administration.

Grant, John P., Nam, Won-joon, Bretschneider, S. and Choi, H., The Transformation of E-governance in Local Government: Comparison of Critical Success Factors, Gangnam-Gu, Seoul, South Korea, and Washington DC: Maxwell School.

Green, D. G. (1981). *Power and Party in a English City*, London: Allen & Unwin.

Greenwood, R., Walsh, K., Hinngs C.R. and Ranson, S. (1980). *Patterns of Management in Local Government*, Oxord: Martin Robertson.

Grrenwood, R., Stewart, J.P. (1974). *Corporate Planning in English Local Government*, Charles Knight & Co.

Gremion, P. (1976). *Le Pouvior Peripherique*, Paris: Du Secuit.

Griffith, J.A.G. (1966). *Central Departments and Local Authorities*, London: Allen & Unwin.

Gupta, B.B. (1968). *Local Government in India*, Allahabad: Central Book Depot.

Gyosei (2001). *The Origins and System of Local Government*, Tokyo.

Hall, P. and Pfeiffer, U. (2000). *Urban Future 21*, London: The Federal Ministry of Transport Building and Housing of the Republic of Germany, E&FN Spon.

Halliday, F. (1994). *Rethinking International Relations*, London: Macmillan.

Hampton, W. (1970). *Democracy and Community*, London: OUP.

Hampton, W. (1987). *Local Government and Urban Politics*, London: Longman.

Hampton, W. (1991). *Local Government and Urban Politics*, London: Longman.

Harris, G. M. (1948). *Comparative Local Government*, London.

Hatry, H.P. and Fish, D.M. (1971). *Improving Productivity and Productivity Measurement in Local Government*, Washington DC: National Commission on Productivity.

Hewett, E.A. (1988). *Reforming the Soviet Economy*, Washington: Brookings Institution.

Hicks, U.K. (1961). *Development from Below*, Oxford.

Hill, D.M. (1974). *Democratic Theory and Local Government*, London: George Allen & Unwin.

Hirashima, A. (2004). *Economic Development and Human Security*, Tokyo: Ministry for Public Management, Home Affairs & Posts & Telecommunications.

Hittle, J.M. (1979). *The Service City: State and Townsmen in Russia, 1600-1800*, Cambridge: Harvard University Press.

Hogan, J.B. (1976). *The Chief Administrative Officers: An Alternative to council-Manager Government*, Tueson: The University of Arizone.

Hoogenboom, A. (1961). *Outflowing the Spoils: A History of the Civil Service Reform Movement, 1865-1883*, Urbane, IL: University of Illinois Press.

Horton, P. (2002). *Lonely Planet Delhi*, Lonely Planet Publications.

Hugo, G. Champion (2003). *New Forms of Urbanisation*, Aldershot: Ashgate.

Humes, S. and Martin, E. (1961). *The Structure of Local Government*, The Hague.

Humes, S. and Martin, E. (1961). *The Structure of Local Government Throughout the World*, The Hague, IULA: Martinus Nijhoff.

Husain, A. (1989). *Whither Local Bodies in India*, New Delhi: Criterion Publications.

Hyoe, M. and Johannes, H. (eds.) (1979). *Politics and Economics in Contemporary Japan*, Tokyo: Japan Cultural Institute.

Hyung-ki Kim, Michio Muramastu, T.J. Pempel and Kozo Yamumura (eds.) (1995). *The Japanese Civil Service and Economic Development: Catalysts of Change*, Oxford: OUP.

Indian Institute of Social Sciences (ed.) (1993). *Urbanization in Developing Countries: Basic Services and Community Participation*, New Delhi: Concept Publishing House.

Innes, J. E. and Booher, D. E. (eds.), Planning Institutions in the Network Society: Theory for Collaborative Planning, Revival of Strategic Spatial Planning, Amsterdom; Royal Netherlands Academy of Sciences.

Inoguchi, T. and Okimoto, D. (eds.) (1984). *The Political Economy of Japan*, Palo Alto, CA: Stanford University Press.

INTRA-INSEE (1988). Les campagnes et leuss villes, serie Contours et caracteres, Paris: INSEE.

Jackson, Kenneth T. (ed.) (1995). *The Encyclopedia of New York City*, Yale University Press.

Jain, L.C., *et al.* (1985). *Grass without Roots*, New Delhi: Sage.

Jathar, R.V. (1964). *Evolution of Panchayati Raj in India*, Dharwar: JSS Institute of Economic Research.

Jenks, E. (1925). *An Outline of English Local Government*, London: Metheu & Co.

Jennings, I. (1947). *Principles of Local Government*, London.

Jewell, N.E., and Marcia, Lynn Whicker (1994). *Legislative Leadership in the American States*, Ann Arbor: University of Michigan Press.

Jha, C. (1953). *Indian Local Government*, Patna: Novelty.

Jocqueville, Alexis de (1953). *Democracy in America, New York*: Alfred A. Knoft.

John, Peter (2001). *Local Governance in Western Europe*, London: Sage.

Johnson, R. J. (1999). *Political, Electorate and Spatial Systems—An Essay in Political Geography*, Oxford: Clarandon Press.

Jones, G. and Stewart, J. (1985). *The Case of Local Government*, London: Allen & Unwin.

Jones, G.W. and Travers, T. (1994). *Attitudes to Local Government in Westminster and Whitehall*, London: Commission for Local Democracy.

Jones, G.W. and Norton, A. (1978). *Political Leadership in Local Authorities*, London: Institute of Local Government Studies.

Joshi, R.P. and Narwani, G.S. (2002). *Panchayati Raj in India*, Jaipur: Rawat Publications.

Kammerer, G.M., *et al.* (1962). City *Managers in Politics: An Analysis of Manage Tenure and Termination*, Gainesville, Flo: University of Florida Press.

Kaneshalingam, V. (1971). *A Hundred Years of Local Government in Ceylon (1865-1965)*, Colombo: Modern Plastic Works.

Kaye, J. W. (1953). *The Administration of the East India Company*, London: Longman.

Keith Lucas, B. (1958). *The History of Local Government in England*, Macmillan, London.

Keith Lucas, B. (1977). *English Local Government in the Ninteenth and Twentieth Centuries*, London: Historical Association.

Keith Lucas, B. (1980). *The Unreformed Local Government System*, Croom Helm.

Keating, M., Midwinter, A. (1983). *The Government of Scotland*, Mainstream Publishing.

Kettle, Donald F. (2002). *The Transformation of Governance*, John Hopkins University Press.

Khanna, B. (1994). *Panchayati Raj in India*, New Delhi: Deep & Deep.

Khera, S.S. (1960). *District Administration in India*, New Delhi.

King, D. and Stoker, G. (eds.) (1996). *Rethinking Local Democracy*, London: Macmillan.

Kitayama, T. (2001). *Local Government Policy Initiatives in Japan*, Washington, DC: The World Bank.

Kling, R. (2000). *Learning from Social Informatics: Information and Communication Technologies in Human Contexts*, Centre for Social Informatics, Indiana University.

Klinger, D. E. and Nalbandian, J. (1993). *Public Personnel Management: Context and Strategies*, Englewood Cliffs, NJ: Prentice Hall.

Klapp, Orvin E. (1964). *Symbolic Leaders*, Alding Publishing.

Koontz, *et al.*, (1984). *Management*, Seventh Edition, NJ: McGraw.

Kumar, U. (1990). *Kautilya's Thought on Public Administration*, New Delhi: National Book Organ.

Lane, J. E. (1994). *The Public Sector: Concept, Models and Approaches*, New Delhi.

Lankina, T. (2000). Municipal Government in Russia's Regions, Stanford, CA: Centre for International Security and Cooperation, Stanford University.

Lapidus, G.W. (ed.) (1995). *The New Russia: Troubled Transformation*, Boulder, Colorado: Westview Press.

Laski, H.J. (1960). *Grammar of Politics*, London.

Laxmikant, M. (2001). *Public Administration*, New Delhi: Tata McGraw Hill.

Layfield, F. (1976). *Local Government Finance*, London: HMSO.

Leach, S., Davis, H., Game, C. and Sketcher, C. (1992). *After Abolition: The Operation of the Post-1986 Metropolitan Government System in Britain*, Birmingham: INLOGOV.

Leferve, H. (1992). Government Quality and Productivity Success Stories, Milwankee, W.I.: ASQC Quality Press.

Lipman, M. and Lapteva, L. (1994). *Russia*, Moscow: Institute for Local Government and Public Service.

Lipman, V.D. (1949). *Local Government Areas, 1834-1945*, Basil Blackwell.

Logothetis, N. (1992). *Managing for Total Quality*, New York: Prentice Hall.

Loi, Theodore J. (1969). *The End of Liberation*, New York: W.W. Norton Co.

Loughlin, M. (1986). *Local Government in the Modern State*, London: Sweet & Maxwell.

Maas, Arthur (1959). *Division of Powers: An Areal Analysis*, Glence, IL: Free Press.

Machin, Howard (1977). *The Prefect in French Public Administration*, London: Crown.

Mac Dougall, T.E. (1975). *Political Opposition and Local Government in Japan*, New Haven, CT: Yale University.

Maddick, H. (1966). *Democracy, Decentralization and Development*, Bombay: Asia Publication House.

Maddick, H. (1970). *Panchayati Raj: A Study of Rural Local Government in India*, New Delhi: Longman.

Maddick, H. (1975). *Democratic Decentralisation and Development*, New York: Asia Publication House.

Maddox, R. W. and Fuquay, R.F. (1975). *State and Local Government*, New York: D. Vaw Nostrand Co.

Mahajan, V.D. (1972). *British Rule in India and After*, Delhi; S. Chand & Co.

Maheshwari, S. R. (1994). *Local Government in India*, Agra: L.N. Aggarwal.

Maiviya, H.D. (1956). *Village Panchayats in India*, New Delhi: AICC.

Majumdar, R.C. (ed.) (1988). *The History and Culture of Indian People*, Vol. III, Mumbai: Bhartiya Vidya Bhawan.

Margnerite, J. Fisher and Donald, G. Bishop (1950). *Municipal and Other Local Governments*, New York: Prentice Hall.

Mary and Stevens, A. (ed.) (2001). *Local Government in France*, Paris: Institut International d' administration publique.

Mathew, George, (ed.) (1995). *Status of Panchayati Raj in the States of India*, New Delhi: Institute of Social Sciences and Concept.

Mathew, George, (ed.) (2000). *Status of Panchayati Raj in the States and Union Territories of India*, New Delhi: Institute of Social Sciences and Concept.

Meenakshi, S.S.S. (1994). *Decentralization in Developing Countries*, New Delhi: Concept.

Mckean, M.A. (1981). *Environmental Protest and Citizen Politics in Japan*, Berkeley and Los Angeles: University of California Press.

Mishra, B.B. (1955). *The Central Administration of the East India Company (1773-1834)*, Manchester.

Mitrokhin, S. (1999). *Implementation of the Municipal Project in Russia: Some Aspects of Federal Policy.*

Mill, J. S. (1954). *Representative Government*, London: Every Man's Library Edition.

Mills, W. and Davis, H.R. (1962). *Small City Government*, New York: Random House.

Mohanty, B. (1999). *Glimpses of Local Government*, Bhubaneswar: Gyanjuga.

Mosher, F.C. (1982). *Democracy and Public Service*, New York: OUP.

Mukherji, P. (1915). *Indian Constitutional Documents*, Calcutta.

Mukherji, R.K. (1958). *Local Government in Ancient India*, Delhi: Motilal.

Mukhopadhyay, Ashok (1985). *Municipal Personnel Administration*, New Delhi: IIPA.

Muttalib, M.A. and Khan, M.A.A. (1993). *Theory of Local Government*, New Delhi: Sterling Publishers.

Narayan, R. (2006). *Municipal Personnel Management*, New Delhi: Serials.

Nigam, S.R. (1982). *Local Government (England, France, USA, USSR and India)*, New Delhi: S. Chand & Co.

Nolting, O. F. (1969). *Process and Impact of the Council-Manager Plan*, Chicago: Public Administration Service.

Nove, A. (1990). *The Soviet Economic System*, London: George Allen & Unwin.

Orlovsky, D.T. (1981). *The Limits of Reforms: The Ministry of Internal Affairs in Imperial Russia*, 1807-1881, Cambridge: Harvard University Press.

Osborne, D. and Gaebler, T. (1992). Rethinking Government, *Reading MA: Addison-Wesley.*

Osborne, D. and Gaebler, T. (1992). Reinventing Government: How Entrepreneurial Spirit is Transforming the Public Sector?, *Reading MA: Addison-Wesley.*

Ostrom, Elinor (1990). *Governing the Commons: The Evolution of Institutions for Collective Action*, Cambridge, MA: Cambridge University Press.

Ozawa, I. (1994). *Blueprint for a New Japan: The Rethinking of a Nation, Tokyo*: Kodansha.

Panikkar, K.M. (1929). *The Evolution of British Policy towards Indian States (1774-1858).*

Pearlson, Kevi E. (2001). *Managing and Using Information Systems*, John Wiley.

Perupel, T.J. (1982). *Policy and Politics in Japan: Creative Conservatism*, Philadelphia: Temple University Press.

Peter, G. Richards (1970). *The New Government System*, London: George Allen & Unwin.

Peterson, Paul E. (1995). *The Price of Federalism*, Washington, DC: Brookings.

Petroni, Giorgia (ed.) (1994). *New Technology in Public Administration*, Amazon: IOS Press.

Ponsonby, Lord of Shalbréde (1979). The Greater London Council and the Government of London, in Golden Jubilee Commemoration Volume, *AIILSG*, Mumbai.

Prasad, N. (1972). *Decentralisation in Yugoslavia and India*, Urasia: Navchetna Prakashan.

Ranney, Austin (1958). *Governing the Man*, New York.

Rao, A. A. (1985). *Personnel Management and Municipal Administration in India*, New Delhi: Ashish.

Rao, V. and Hazarika, N. (1980). *Local Self-Government in India*, New Delhi: S. Chand & Co.

Reddy, G., Ram, (ed.) (1977). *Patterns of Panchayati Raj in India*, New Delhi: McMillan.

Reed, S. (1986). *Japanese Prefectures and Policy-making*, Pittsburg: University of Pittsburg Press.

Rhodes, R.A.W. (1997). *Understanding Governance*, Open University Press.

Richards, P.G. (1973). *The Reformed Local Government System*, London: George Allen & Unwin Ltd.

Riker, W.H. (1964). *Federalism; Origin, Operation, Significance*, Boston: Little Brown.

Riper, Van (1958). *History of the United States Civil Service*, Evanston, IL: Row Peterson.

Robin, J. and Dodd, D. (eds.), *State and Local Government*, New York and Basel: Marcel Dekker Inc.

Robson, W.A. (1963). *Encyclopedia of Social Sciences*, The Macmillan & Co.

Robson, W.A. (1948). *The Government and Misgovernment of London*, 2nd ed., London: Allen and Unwin.

Roche, D. (1982). *Local Government in Ireland*, Dublin: Institute of Public Administration.

Rogger, H. (1987). *Russia in the Age of Modernization and Reform, 1881-1917*, London: Longman.

Rowat, D. C. (ed.) (1980). *International Handbook on Local Government Reorganisation*, Aldwych Press.

Rowat, D.C. (ed.) (1988). *Public Administration in Developed Democracies: A Comparative Study*, New York and Basel: Marcel Dekker Inc.

Rowe, P. and Coster, P., *Delhi (Great Cities of the World)*, World Almanac Library.

Ruxton, Ian (ed.) (2006). *The Diaries of Sir Ernest Satow, British Envoy in Peking (1900-06)*, Lulu Press Inc.

Ryan M. (1993). *Social Trends in Contemporary Russia: A Statistical Source Book*, New York: St. Martin's Press.

Saikal, Amin and William, Maley (1995). *Russia in Search of Its Future*, Cambridge: Cambridge University Press.

Samuels, R. J. (1983). *The Politics of Regional Policy Japan*, Princeton, NJ: Princeton University Press.

Samuels, R. J. (1987). *The Business of the Japanese State*, Cornell, NY: Cornell University Press.

Sanoff, Henry (1999). *Community Participation in Design and Planning*, New York: John Wiley.

Sarkar, J.N. (1952). *Mughal Administration*, IV Edition, Calcutta: Sarkar & Sons.

Sastri, K.A.N. (ed.), *A Comprehensive History of India, Historical Series No.13*, Madras: University of Madras.

Sayre, W. S. (1962). *American Local Government*, College Outline Series, New York: Barnes & Noble, Inc.

Semeis, G., Population Statistics and Administrative Services, Tokyo: Government of Japan.

Sharma, M.P. (1965). *Local Self-Government in India*, Allahabad: Kitab Mahal.

Shindo, M. (1982). *Relations between National Government and Local Government in Public Administration in Japan*, Senshu University.

Shiviah, *et al.* (1976). *Panchayati Raj: An Analytical Survey*, Hyderabad: NIRD.

Srivastava, A., 2002, *E-Governance or Development, What Comes First: Issues and Correlations*, Syracuse: The Maxwell School of Citizenship and Public Affairs, Syracuse University.

Srivastava, O.P. (1980). *Municipal Government and Administration in India*, Allahabad: Chugh.

Stanyer, J. (1967). *County Government in England and Wales*, London: Routledge.

Stewart, J. (1974). *The Responsive Local Authority*, Charles Knight & Co.

Stewart, J. (2000). *Nature of British Local Government*, Palgrave: Macmillan.

Stewart, J. (2003). *Modernising British Local Government*, Palgrave: Macmillan.

Stewart, J. and Stoker, G. (1995). *Local Government in the 1990's*, Basingstoke: Macmillan.

Stones, P. (1963). *Local Government for Students*, London: MacDonald and Evons Ltd.

Singh, Hoshiar (1997). *Local Government*, Allahabad: Kitab Mahal.

Singh, Hoshiar (ed.) (2000). *Local Governance: Concepts and Networks*, Jaipur: RBSA.

Singh, U.B. (1997). *Urban Local Government*, Delhi and Jaipur: Rawat.

———(1998). *Administrative System in India*, New Delhi: APH.

———(2003). *Fiscal Federalism in Indian Union*, New Delhi: Concept.

Sreeram, K. (1979). *Committee System in English Government*, Lucknow: RCRTMA.

Swift, N. and Karvelle, G. (2003). *A Complex System Aims to Bring French Local Government to the People*, European Editor, Paris: Association of French Mayors.

Taylor, R.S. (1986). *Value-Added Processes in Information System*, Ablex.

Thomas, D. (1964). *Local Government: An Introduction to the British System*, Peramion Press.

Thornhill, W. (1978). *The Growth and Reform of English Local Government*, London: Wiedenfield and Hicholsm.

Tinker, Hugh (1967). *Foundation of Local Self-Government in India, Pakistan and Burma*, New Delhi: Lalwani Pub. House.

Travers, T. (1995). *Local Government in the 1990's*, London: Basingstoke.

Treadgold, D.W. (1987). *Twentieth Century Russia, Boulder*, Colorado: Westview Press.

Tsuji, K. (ed.) (1984). *Public Administration in Japan*, Tokyo: Institute of Administrative Management and University of Tokyo Press.

Uphorg, N.T. (1982). *Rural Development and Local Organisation in Asia*, Delhi: Macmillan India.

Venkat Rao V. (1960). *A Hundred Years of Local Self-Government in the Andhra and Madras States (1850-1959)*, Mumbai: AIILSG.

Venkatraman, K. (1964). *Local Finance in Perspective*, Mumbai: Asia publishing House.

Venkatrangiya, M. J. and Pattabhiram, M. (eds.) (1969). *Local Government in India (Selected Readings)*, Mumbai: Allied.

Vincent, Ostram, Robert Bish, Elinor Ostram (1988). *Local Government in the United States*, Sanfransisco: ICS Press.

Vogel, E. (1979). *Japan as Number One*, Cambridge, MA: Harvard University Press.

Wager, P.W. (ed.) (1950). *County Government Across the Nation*, Chapel Hill: University of Carolina Press.

Wallich, C. (1992). *Fiscal Decentralisation, International Relations in Russia*, Washington: World Bank.

Wallich, C. (ed.) (1994). *Russia and the Challenge of Fiscal Federation*, Washington: World Bank.

Ward, R.E. (1978). *Japan's Political System*, Englewood Cliffs, NJ: Prentice Hall.

Ward, R.E. and Ruston, D. (eds.) (1964). *Political Modernization in Japan and Turkey*, Princeton, NJ: Princeton University Press.

Watson, Douglas J. and Hassett, Wendy L. (eds.) (2003). *Local Government Management: Current Issues and Best Practices*, New York: M.E. Sharpe.

Webb, S. and Beatrice (1960). *English Local Government from the Revolution to the Municipal Corporation: The Parish and the County*, London: Longmans Greene & Co.

Webb, S. and Webb, B. (1963). *The Development of English Local Government (1689-1835)*, London: OUP.

Weber, Max (1997). *The Theory of Social and Economic Organisation*, New York: The Free Press (Reprint).

Welsh, L. (1967). *Royal Commission on Local Government*, Knight.

Welsh, O. (1991). *Local Government Structure in Wales*, London: HMSO.

West, J.P. (ed.) (1995). *Quality Management Today*, Washington: ICMA.

Wilson, C. H. (1948). *Essays on Local Government*, Basic Blackwell.

Wilson, D. and Game, C. (1994). *Local Government in the United Kingdom*, Basingstoke: Macmillan.

Wiseman, H.V. (1967). *Local Government at Work*, London: Routledge & Kegan Paul.

Wiseman, H.V., (ed.) (1970). *Local Government in England (1958-69)*, London: Routledge & Kegan Paul.

Yanaga, C., *1968*, *Big Business in Japanese Politics*, New Haven: Yale University Press.

Young, U., *1979*, *Compliance and Public Authority*, Baltimore: John Hopkins.

Journals

Alford, R. and Eugene, C. Lee, Voting Turnout in American Cities, *American Political Science Review,* 1968, September.

Appleby, Paul (1962). Some thoughts on Decentralisation in Democracy, *IJPA*, 1962, XVII (4).

Arnsetein, S., A Ladder of Citizen Partnership, *Journal of the Institute of Planners,* 1969.

Asibno, S.K., Decentralisation in Ghana-Myth or Reality, *IJPA*, 1992, XXXVII (April-June).

Baweja, Y., Does E-Governance Mean Good Governance? *Yojana*, 2005, 49.

Bayton, R.P. and Wright, D.S., Mayor-Manager Relations in larger Council-Manager Cities: A Reinterpretation, *Public Administration Review*, 1971, 31.

Booher, David E. and Innes, J. E., Network Power in Collaborative Planning, *Journal of Planning Education and Research.*

Bora, P. M., Citizens-Administration Relationships: The Urban Local Government Perspectives, *Qly. Journal of AIILSG*, LXI (1-2).

Bose, Richard C., Searching for the Best Structure for American Local Government, *International Journal of Public Administration,* 18(4).

Brick, K.P., Local Government and Democracy—A Rejoinder, *Public Administration*, 1953, 31 & 32.

Cohan, B., Urban Growth in Developing Countries: A Review of Current Trends and a Caution regarding Existing Forecasts, *World Development*, 2004, 32(1).

Cole, M. and Boyne, G., So You Think You Know What Local Government is?, *Local Government Studies*, 1995, 21(2).

Dawes, S. and Prefontaina, L., Understanding New Models of Collaboration for Delivering Government Services, *Communications of the ACM*, 2003, 46(1).

Davenport, T., Short, J., The New Industrial Engineering: Information Technology and Business Process Redesign, *Sloan Management Review*, 1990, 31(4).

Day, Diane, Citizen Participation in the Planning Process: An Essentially Contested Concept, *Journal of the Planning Literature*, 1997, 11(3).

Fountain, Jane, Prospects for Improving the Regulatory Process Using E-Rulemaking, *Communications of the ACM*, 2003, 46(1), January.

Gales, P.L., John, Peter, Is the Grass Greener on the Other Side? What went wrong with the French Regions and the Implications for England, *Journal of Policy and Politics,* 25(1).

Glass, J.J., Citizen Participation in Planning: The Relationship between Objectives and Techniques, *Journal of the American Planning Association,* 1979, 45(2).

Golandaz, H.M., Seventy-Fourth Constitutional Amendment Act and Conformity Municipal Legislation in Gujarat and Maharashtra, *Urban India,* 1995, XV.

Goldman, M.I., Economic Problems in the Soviet Union, *Current History,* 1983, 82, October.

Golesbchik, L. *et al.*, Bistro: A Scalable and Secure Data Transfer Service for Digital Government Applications, *Communications of the ACM*, 2003, 46 (1), January.

Hambleton, R., Decentralisation and Democracy in Local Government, *Public Management*, 1992, July-September.

Hambleton, R., Hogga, H.P. and Burns, D., A Framework of Understanding area based Decentralization, *Local Government Policy Making*, 1994, 20(4).

Hanson, Philip, Structural Change in the Russian Economy, *Transition*, 1996, 2(2), January, 26.

Hord, C., De-Sir Hemphreyfing, The Westminster Model of Governance, *Governance*, 1990, 33.

Hord, C.; A Public Management for all seasons, *Public Administration*, 1991, 69 (Spring).

Innes, J. E. and Booher, D. E., Consensus Building as Role Playing and Bricologe: Towards a Theory of Collaborative Planning, *Journal of the American Planning Association*, 1999, 65(1).

International Review of Administrative Sciences, 1982, 48(2).

Jackson, W.E., Local Government in England, *Civic Affairs*, 1965, 12(11).

Jagannadhan, V., Administration and the Citizen, *IJPA*, 1971, XVII(4).

Jha, Gangadhar, The Seventy-Fourth Constitution Amendment and the Empowerment of Municipal Government: A Critique, *Urban India*, 1993, XIII (July).

Keehley, P., TQM for Local Government, *Public Management*, 1992, August.

Kurukshetra, 1989, XXXVII (5), February.

Lampard, E. E., History of Cities in the Economically Advanced Areas, *Economic Development and Cultural Change*, 1954, Vol. II.

Leftwich, A., Governance, the State and Politics of Development, *Development and Change*, 1994, 25.

Mark, Jerome A., Measuring Productivity in Service Industries, Bureau of Labour Statistics, *Monthly Labour Review*, 1982, June.

Mathur, N. S., Management Problem in Unified Municipal Cadres, *Nagarlok*, 1974, VI(4).

Milakovich, M., Total Quality Management in the Public Sector, *National Productivity Review*, 1991, 10(2).

Mintricher, Nicoledge, The Prefect and State Reform, *Public Administration*, 2000, 78(3).

Mizuno, K., Leading by example: Local Government in Japan, *ISO Management System*, 2002, May-June.

Myriad Leaves, The Newsletter of the Japan Local Government Centre, London, 2006, June.

Nagarpalika Network, 2003, 6 (4), July-August.

OECD, The e-government imperative: main findings, *OECD Observer*, 2003, March.

OECD, Engaging Citizens Online for Better Policy-making, *OECD Observer*, 2003, March.

Panchayati Raj Update, 2000, August.

Patil, N. S., Relationship between Elected Representatives and Officials in Municipal Bodies, *Qly. Journal of AIILSG*, 1990, XXI (January-March).

Prior, D., In Search of the New Public Management, *Local Government Studies*, 1993, 19(3), Autumn.

PUMA, Government Relations with Citizens and Civil Society, *OECD Observer*, February.

Rhodes, R., The New Governance: Governing without Government, Swindon: *ESRC*.

Rowland, R. H., Declining Towns in the Former USSR, *Post-Soviet Geography*, 1994, 35 (6), June.

Sayre, W. S., The general manager idea for larger cities, *Public Administration Review*, 1954, 14.

Seusenbrenner, J., Quality Comes to City Hall, *Harvard Business Review*, 1991, March-April.

Sharma, A., Local Government in France: Recent Reforms, *Nagarlok*, 2005, XXXVII(2).

Sharma, S. K., Democratic Decentralisation & Development of Backward Areas, *IJPA*, 1971, XXIII(3).

Singh, Hoshiar, Municipal Personnel System in Rajasthan: Need for Reform, *Qly. Journal of LSGI*, 1972, XIII(4).

Singh, U. B., Democratic Leadership in Urban Local Bodies—A Study of Uttar Pradesh, *Nagarlok*, 1997, XXIX(3).

Snellen, Ignace, Electronic Governance: Implications for Citizens, Politicians and Public Servants, *International Review of Administrative Sciences*, 2002, 68(2).

Somanathan, E., Empowering Local Government, Lessons from Europe, *Economic and Political Weekly*, 2001, October, 13.

Sukhtankar, D. M., The Seventy-Fourth Amendment of the Constitution: Initiating a Process of Urban Government Reform in Maharashtra, *Urban India*, 1995, XV.

Tolz, V., Problems of Building Democratic Institutions in Russia, *RFE/RL Research Report*, 1994, 3 (10), March, 4.

Venkatraman, K., Creation of a Cadre of Local Civil Service Personnel, *IJPA*, 1968, XIV(3).

Reports/Documents/Papers

Administrative Management Agency (1982). *Administrative Management in Japan*, Tokyo.

Association of Municipal Corporations (1954). *Re-organisation of Local Government*, U. K.

Bains, M., (Chairman) (1972). *The New Local Authorities, Management and Structure,* London: HMSO.

Brostek, Michael (2000). *Federal Rulemaking, U.S. General Accounting Office.*

Budhiraja, Renu, *Electronic Governance—A key issue in the 21st century,* Government of India, Ministry of Information Technology.

Calcutta Municipal Corporation Act, 1980.

Census Bureau, US, *Residential Population and components of Change, New York State and Counties,* April, 2000 to July, 2005.

Commonwealth Secretariat, 2003, *The U.K. Experience of Public Administration Reform,* Stylus Publications, Inc.

Constitution of India, 27th Edition, EBC, Lucknow.

Constitution of Republic of France, 1958.

Constitution of Russian Federation, 1993.

Council of Local Authorities for International Relations (CLAIR), 1990, *An Introduction to Local Administration in Japan,* Tokyo.

CLAIR, 2004, *Local Government in Japan,* Tokyo.

Department of Environment (1972). *The New Local Authorities: Management and Structure,* London: HMSO.

Department of Environment (1983). *Streamlining the Cities*, London: HMSO.

Department of Environment (1983). *Rates*, London: HMSO.

Department of Environment, U.K. (1986). *Paying for Local Government*, London: HMSO.

Department of Environment, U.K. (1992). *Policy Guidance to the Local Government Commission for England,* London.

Economy of the Russian Federation in1990, Statistical Reference Book, Republican Information Publishing Centre, Moscow, 1991.

Electronic Government: Third International Conference, EGOV-2004, Zaragoza Spain, Roland (EDT).

Encyclopedia Britannica, London.

Encyclopedia of Social Sciences, 1967, New York: Macmillan.

Encyclopedia of Social Sciences, London: Fitzroy Dearborn Publishers.

Evaluation of Panchayati Raj Institutions (1994-1999), 2000, UNNATI, Institute for Development Education.

Government of India (1953). *Taxation Enquiry Commission.*

Government of India (1957). *Report of the Team for Study of Community Projects and National Extension Service*, Committee on Plan Projects.

Government of India (1963). *Report of the* Committee of Ministers (Zakaria·Committee) on *Augmentation of Financial Resources of Urban Local Bodies.*

Government of India (1966). *Report of the Rural—Urban Relationship Committee.*

Government of India (1978). *Report of the Working Group on Block Level Planning,* Planning Commission.

Government of India (1978). *Report of the Committee on Panchayati Raj Institutions.*

Government of India (1985). *Report of the Committee to Review the Existing Administrative Arrangements for Rural Development and Poverty Alleviation,* Ministry of Agriculture, Department of Rural Development.

Government of India (1988). *Report of the National Commission on Urbanisation.*

Government of India (1988). *Report of the Commission on Centre-State Relations.*

Government of India (1988). *Report of the Thungan Committee,* Ministry of Personnel, Public Grievances and Pension.

Government of India (1994). *Reviewing Local Self-Government in India,* Ministry of Rural Development, Occasional Paper 6.

Government of India (2001). *Proceedings of Good Urban Governance Campaign,* India Launch.

Government of India, *Memorandum on the Development and Working of Representative Institutions in the sphere of Local Self-Government,* Vol. V.

Government of Russia (1991). *Law on Local Self-Government in Russian Federation,* Moscow.

Government of USSR (1990). *General Principles of Local Self Government and Local Economy in USSR,* Moscow.

Heeks, R. B., *Understanding E-Governance for Development in Government,* Paper No. 11, IDPM, University of Manchester.

Herbert Sir, E. (Chairman) (1960). *Report of the Royal Commission on Local Government in London, 1957-60,* London: HMSO.

ICMA (1960). *Municipal Personnel Administration.*

Innes, Judith E. and Booher, David E. (2000). *Public Administration in Planning: New Strategies for the 21st Century,* Working Paper 2000-07, Berkeley: Institute of Urban and Regional Development, University of California.

Institute of Local Government (Japan) (1994). *Outline of Japanese Local Autonomy System.*

Law on Local Self-Government (Russia), 1991.

Law on Local Government Finance (Russia), 1997.

Law on Foundations of Municipal Service in the Russian Federation, 1998.

Layfield, F. (Chairman) (1976). *Local Government Finance,* Report of the Committee of Inquiry, London: HMSO.

Local Government Commission (1993). *Renewing Local Government in the English Shires,* London: HMSO.

Local Government Cronicle, 1967.

LGBC (1972). *Local Government Boundary Commission for England*, Report No.1, London: Cmnd 5148, HMSO.

Lord Ripon's Resolution of 1882on Local Self-Government.

Mackenjie, W. J. H. (1961). *Theories of Local Government,* Greater London Paper, London: LSE.

Madhya Pradesh Municipal Corporation Act, 1956.

Mallaby, G. (Chairman) (1967). *Staffing of Local Government*, Report of the Committee on the Staffing of Local Government, London: HMSO.

Ministry of Internal Affairs and Communications, Administrative Division, Japan, 2004, *Overview of the Nation's Cities, Towns and Villages.*

Ministry of Internal Affairs and Communications (2002). *Local Finances* (White Paper).

Ministry of Housing and Local Government, Committee on the Management of Local Government, 1967, *Management of Local Government,* London: HMSO.

Municipalities (Extension to the Scheduled Areas) Act, 2001.

National Research Council (2002). *Computer Science and Telecommunications, Board of Information Technology Research, Innovation and E-Government*, Washington: National Academy of Sciences.

Panchayats (Extension to the Scheduled Areas) Act, 1996.

Radcliff Maud, Lord (Chairman), 1969, Royal Commission on Local Government in England (1966-1969), Report, London: HMSO.

Rao, T.P. Rama, Rao, V. Venkata, Bhatnagar, S.C. and Satyanarayana, J., 2004, E-*Governance Assessment Frameworks*, New Delhi: Government of India, Department of Information Technology.

Report of the *Committee of Enquiry into Local Government Finance* (The Layfield Committee), London: HMSO.

Russian Regions Today: Atlas of the New Federation, 1994, Washington: International Center.

Tang, P. (1994). *Institutional Instability, Governance and Telematics*, IPSA Paper, Berlin, August.

Teague, E. (1994). *Russia's Local Elections Begin*, REF/RL, Research Report, 3(7), February.

The Cantonments Act, 1924.

The Cantonments Act, 2006.

Tripura Municipality Act, 1994.

United Nations (1971). *Public Administration in the Second United Nations Development Decade*, Report of the Second Meeting of Experts.

United Nations (2000). *World Urbanization Prospects: The 2001 Revision, Data Tables and Highlights.*

UNCHS (Habitat) (1996). *An Urbanizing World; Global Report on Human Settlements.*

UNDP (1994). *Governance for Sustainable Human Settlements.*

UNDP (1997). *Reconceptualising Governance.*

UNDP (2000). *Decentralisation in India: Challenges and Opportunities*, New Delhi: Human Resource Development Centre.

UNDP (2002). *Document on Good Governance by Report Card.*

UNFPA (1993). *The State of the World.*

United Nations Population Fund (2003). *Slums of the World: The Face of Urban Poverty in the New Millennium*? Monitoring the Millennium Development Goals, Target 11- World wide Habitat, Nairobi.

White, L. D. (ed) (1951). *Encyclopedia of Social Sciences*, The Macmillan Co..

Widdicombe, D. (1996). The Conduct of Local Authority Business Report, London: HMSO.

World Bank (1994). *Governance: The World Bank's Experience*, Washington, DC.

World Bank (2002). *Poverty in India (The Challenge of Uttar Pradesh).*

World Bank (2002). *India Reducing Poverty, Accelerating Development.*

Web Sites

www.ComadreCoaching.com
http://web.japan.org

http://web.mofa.go.jp
http://web.japan.org
http://web.jiia.or.jp
http://web.nira.go.jp
www.clair.or.jp/e/
http://www.petrozavodsk.ru
http://citymayors.com/government/us-locgov.html
www.keele.ac.uk
www.british-history.ac.uk
www.palgrave-usa.com
www.westminsterbookshop.co.uk
http://citymayors.com/government/uk_loccccgov.html
www.uk-governmentdirectory.co.uk
www.british-towns.net
www.udbs.dur.ac.uk
www.algebra.com
www.sylviamlne.btinternet.co.uk
www.citymayors.com
www.abcounties.co.uk
http://en.wikipedia.org
http://www.recensement.insee.fr/fr/ffc/docs_reg.xls
http://www.britannica.com/eb/article59646
http://www.lboro.ac.uk/gawc/citylist.html
http://www.prnewswire.com/egibin/stories
http://Encarta.msn.com/encyclopedia
http//www.paris.culture.fr/en/ow_chrono.html
www.paris.culture.fr.Paris
http://www.paris.culture.fr/en/html
http://www.paris-iledefrance.cci.fr
http://siteresources.worldbank.org
www.oxfordjournals.org
www.infor4local.gov.uk
http://www1.worldbank.org/publicsector/egov/india.htm
http://searchnetworking.techtarget.com
http://www.man.ac.uk/idpm_dp.htm
www.nyc.gov
http://www.nyccouncil.info/
http://www.cosmopolis.ch
http://users.skynet.be
www.british-history.ac.uk

http://www.ebeijing.gov.cn/
http://en.wikipedia.org/wiki/Beijing
http://www.china.org.cn/english/features/beijing/30785.htm
http://english.people.com.cn
http://www.metro.tokyo.jp
wikipedia.org
http://isc.nic.in/delhi.htm
http://www.censusindia.net/profiles/del.html
http://www.citypopulation.de/World.html
http://www.indiatourism.com/delhi-history/index.html
http://www.ndmc.gov.in
http://www.mcdonline.gov.in/
http://delhiplanning.nic.in/Economic%
http://dfs.delhigovt.nic.in
http://www.un.org/esa/population/publications/wup
http://www.india-seminar.com/2002/515.htm
http://in.ourcity.yahoo.com/delhi
http://wikimapia.org
http://www.moscowcity.ru/
http://www.citynext.ru
http://www.a-s-r.ru/tabid/247/Default.aspx
http://www.icube3d.ru/portfolio/vis/ani/mmdc/
http://en.wikipedia.org/wiki/Moscow-City
http://www.mos.ru/index.shtml
http://www.constitution.ru/en/10003000-01.htm
http://encarta.msn.com

Index